Solution Manual for Student Text

UCSMP
SCOTTFORESMAN

THE UNIVERSITY OF CHICAGO SCHOOL MATHEMATICS PROJECT

ALGEBRA

SCOTTFORESMAN INTEGRATED MATHEMATICS

INTRODUCTION

This Solution Manual contains answers for all exercises in the lessons, Progress Self-Tests, and Chapter Reviews of the ScottForesman UCSMP Algebra student's text.

Most answers include only one method of solving that particular exercise. Remember, however, there is often more than one way to find an answer. Answers that involve measures are often approximations, as are computations with decimals. In some cases, even though the equal sign is used, the answer is an approximation.

ScottForesman

A Division of HarperCollins*Publishers*

ScottForesman
Editorial Offices: Glenview, Illinois
Regional Offices: Sunnyvale, California • Tucker, Georgia
Glenview, Illinois • Oakland, New Jersey • Dallas, Texas

ISBN: 0-673-45775-3

2 3 4 5 6 — MH — 9 9 9 8 9 7 9 6 9 5

CHAPTER 1
USES OF VARIABLES

LESSON 1-1 pp. 6–10

1. The lightning is about $\frac{8}{5}$ or 1.6 miles away.

2. A variable is a letter or other symbol that can be replaced by any number (or other object) from some set.

3. sentence, open sentence, and an inequality

4. none of these

5. sentence, open sentence, and an equation

6. sentence and an inequality

7. $\approx$ **8.** $>$

9. a. $\frac{5}{8} > \frac{4}{7}$

    b. Sample: Change each to a fraction with a denominator of 56.
$\frac{5}{8} = \frac{35}{56}$ and $\frac{4}{7} = \frac{32}{56}$

    Since $\frac{35}{56} > \frac{32}{56}$,

    then $\frac{5}{8} > \frac{4}{7}$ or

         $\frac{4}{7} < \frac{5}{8}$.

10. a. $\frac{5}{6} < \frac{17}{20}$

    b. Sample: Change each to a decimal.
$\frac{5}{6} \approx .833$ and $\frac{17}{20} = .850$

    Since $.833 < .850$,

      then $\frac{5}{6} < \frac{17}{20}$.

11. (c) $100 \le z$

12. 6 is a solution.

    (Try 5. Does $2 \cdot 5 + 3 = 4 \cdot 5 - 9$?
        Does $10 + 3 = 20 - 9$?
        No, $13 \ne 11$.
    Try 6. Does $2 \cdot 6 + 3 = 4 \cdot 6 - 9$?
        Does $12 + 3 = 24 - 9$?
        Yes, $15 = 15$.
    Try 7. Does $2 \cdot 7 + 3 = 4 \cdot 7 - 9$?
        Does $14 + 3 = 28 - 9$?
        No, $17 \ne 19$.)

13. a. 12 is a solution since $12^2 = 144$.

    b. The solution not mentioned in part a is -12; $(-12)^2 = 144$.

14. The solutions to $n^2 = 100$ are 10 and -10; $10^2 = 100$ and $(-10)^2 = 100$.

15. Samples: 2, 3, and 10

16. Samples: -3, 0, and $\frac{1}{3}$

17. a. $t > 10°$

    b. Samples: 11°, 15°, and 18°

18. $\ne$, $\approx$, $<$, $\le$

19. $\frac{2}{3} < \frac{7}{10} < \frac{3}{4}$ $\left(\frac{2}{3} = \frac{40}{60}, \frac{7}{10} = \frac{42}{60}, \frac{3}{4} = \frac{45}{60} \right)$

20. a. 15.3125 in.

    b. No, $15\frac{1}{4} = 15.25$ which is less than 15.3125.

21. 2 and 4 are solutions.
    ($5 \cdot 2 = 10$ which is less than 40,
    $5 \cdot 4 = 20$ which is less than 40,
    $5 \cdot 8 = 40$ which is not less than 40,
    $5 \cdot 16 = 80$ which is greater than 40)

22. (b) $20 < m$

23. a. $y < 1990$

    b. $p > 2.1$

24. $-2 + -3 = -5$

25. $-4 + 7 = 3$

26. $-7 + -5 = -12$

27. $-11 + 7 = -4$

28. $8 + -20 + 17 = 25 + -20 = 5$

29. Sample: 0.3333

30. $10 \cdot 3.7 = 37$ (Move decimal one position to the right.)

31. $1\frac{1}{2} \cdot 2 = 3$

32. $4 \cdot \$2.25 = \$9.00$

33. a. Sample: $\frac{111}{200}$; $\frac{11}{20} = 0.55$ and $\frac{14}{25} = 0.56$, and 0.555 is between 0.55 and 0.56.
$0.555 = \frac{555}{1000}$ which can be written as $\frac{111}{200}$.

    b. Samples: $\frac{222}{450}$, $\frac{223}{400}$

    c. infinitely many; Sample: You can always find the average of any two fractions. This gives you a fraction between the two.

34. From Greek: *hier* means sacred or holy; *glyphen* means to carve.

1. The objects in a set are called elements or members.

2. Samples: brother, father

3. 2 or -6

4. Samples: $\sqrt{6}$, $\frac{3}{4}$, -1.34

5. A and B (They contain the same elements.)

6. **a.** no (It's negative.)
   b. yes
   c. yes

7. **a.** yes $\left(\frac{6}{2}=3\right)$ **b.** yes **c.** yes

8. **a.** no **b.** no **c.** yes

9. **a.** yes **b.** yes **c.** yes

10. **a.** yes **b.** yes **c.** yes

11. **a.** no **b.** no **c.** yes

12. **a.** The set of whole numbers less than 3

   b. the set of integers less than 3

   c. the set of real numbers less than 3

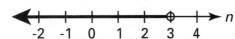

13. **a.** the set of whole numbers greater than or equal to 3

   b. the set of integers greater than or equal to 3

   c. the set of real numbers greater than or equal to 3

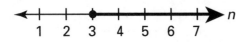

14. **a.** the set of whole numbers greater than 5

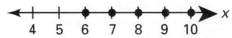

   b. the set of integers greater than 5

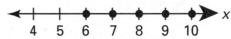

   c. the set of real numbers greater than 5

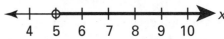

15. (a) (The number of people cannot be negative or fractional.)

16. (d) (Time should be positive and may be fractional.)

17. **a.** The domain could be the set of positive real numbers. (It is not reasonable for length to be negative or zero.)
   b. $23 \le \ell \le 46$
   c.

18. **a.** $2 < x < 9$, where x is a real number

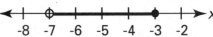

   b. The interval is open.

19. **a.** $-7 < x \le -3$, where x is a real number

   b. The interval is neither.

20. **a.** $-8 < y < 8$, where y is a whole number

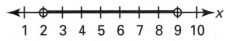

   b. $-8 < y < 8$, where y is an integer

21. **a.** closed
   b. x is greater than or equal to zero and less than or equal to ten.
   c. $0 \le x \le 10$

22. **a.** open
   b. y is greater than negative three and less than four.
   c. $-3 < y < 4$

23. a. neither

   b. z is greater than or equal to negative ten and less than negative four.

   c. $-10 \leq z \leq -4$

24. a. all real numbers

   b. $-86 \leq E \leq 6194$

   c.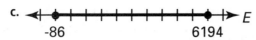
     -86   6194

25. $\{6, 9\}$

   ($5 \cdot 3 + 2 = 17$ which is not greater than 23, $5 \cdot 4 + 2 = 22$ which is not greater than 23, $5 \cdot 6 + 2 = 32$ which is greater than 23, and $5 \cdot 9 + 2 = 47$ which is greater than 23.)

26. $t > 100$

27. $y > -15$

28. $x = 4$ or $x = -4$ ($4^2 = 16$ and $(-4)^2 = 16$)

29. 256 ($16^2 = 256$)

30. a. $-5 + -9 = -14$

   b. $-5 + 9 = 4$

   c. $5 + -9 = -4$

31. $3 \cdot (-5) = -15$

32. $4 \cdot (-10) = -40$

33. $5 \cdot (-70) = -350$

34. $-8 \cdot -25 = 200$

35. \$350.00 ($5 \cdot \$70.00 = \$350.00$)

36.
cloud of gnats	nest of crows
colony of ants	pride of lions
exaltation of larks	school of fish
gaggle of geese	skulk of foxes
hive of bees	watch of nightingales
leap of leopards	yoke of oxen
mob of kangaroos	

37. Samples: society, citizen; club, member; faculty, teacher

---

LESSON 1-3   pp. 17–22

1. The intersection of sets A and B is the set of elements that are in both A and B.

2. The union of two sets A and B is the set of elements in either A or B or both.

3. $A \cap B = \{6\}$

4. $A \cup B = \{2, 3, 4, 6, 8, 9, 10, 12, 15\}$

5. $R \cap S = \{5, 6\}$

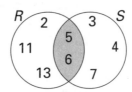

6. $R \cup S = \{2, 3, 4, 5, 6, 7, 11, 13\}$

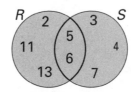

7. a. the empty set or null set (a set which has no elements in it)

   b. Sample: whole numbers less than zero

8. a. $W = \{0, 1, 2, 3, 4\}$

   b. $X = \{6, 7, 8, 9\}$

   c. $W \cup X = \{0, 1, 2, 3, 4, 6, 7, 8, 9\}$

   d. $W \cap X = \{ \}$ or $\varnothing$

9. a. $x \geq -3$, where x is a real number

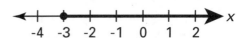

   b. $x \leq 7$, where x is a real number

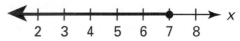

   c. $x \geq -3$ and $x \leq 7$, where x is a real number

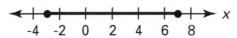

   d. $x \geq -3$ or $x \leq 7$, where x is a real number

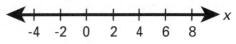

10. a. I   **b.** III   **c.** II

11. $z < -2$ or $z \leq 4$, where z is a real number

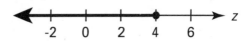

12. a. Mrs. King: $68 \leq t \leq 75$
Mr. King: $65 \leq t \leq 70$

  b. temperatures comfortable for Mrs. King and Mr. King is the set $68 \leq t \leq 70$, where t is a real number

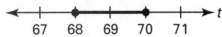

  c. the set $68 \leq t \leq 70$, where t is a real number, is the intersection of the two sets in **part a.**

13. $F = \{1, 3, 5, 7, 9\}$, $F = \{3, 6, 9\}$

  a. $E \cap F = \{3, 9\}$

  b. $E \cup F = \{1, 3, 5, 6, 7, 9\}$

14. $S = \{4, -4\}$, $T = \{14\}$

  a. $S \cup T = \{-4, 4, 14\}$

  b. $S \cap T = \{ \ \}$ or $\varnothing$

15. $a < 5$ or $a > 62$ where a is a real number

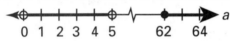

16. a. $20 < k < 25$, where k is a real number

  b. The graph in **part a** is the intersection of the three graphed sets given.

17. a. $Z < \frac{8}{3}$, where Z is a whole number

  b. $Z < \frac{8}{3}$, where Z is a real number

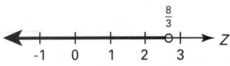

18. a. Sample: 1 (any integer greater than or equal to 0)

  b. Sample: -1 (any integer less than 0)

19. true $(13.23 \times 10^5 = 1{,}323{,}000)$

20. true
$(-0.1 = -0.100$ and $-0.200 < -0.125 < -0.100)$

21. true

22. a. -5   **b.** -10   **c.** -15
Sample pattern: $5 \cdot (-n) = -(5 \cdot n)$

23. a. 4   **b.** 8   **c.** 12
Sample pattern: $-4 \cdot (n) = -(4 \cdot n)$

24. No; the intersection of sets A and B contains only those elements common to both sets, while the union of the sets contains all the elements in either set or both.

LESSON 1-4   pp. 23–26

1. numerical

2. algebraic

3. algebraic

4. $12 - 2 \cdot 4 = 12 - 8 = 4$

5. $5^2 + 2^2 = 25 + 4 = 29$

6. $(5 + 2)^2 = 7^2 = 49$

7. $3(10 - 6)^3 + 15$
  $= 3 \cdot 4^3 + 15$
  $= 3 \cdot 64 + 15$
  $= 192 + 15$
  $= 207$

8. $5 - \frac{4}{8} = 4\frac{4}{8} = 4\frac{1}{2} = 4.5$

9. $15 + \frac{9}{3} - 6 = 15 + 3 - 6$
  $= 18 - 6$
  $= 12$

10. $5 \cdot 3^2$
  $= 5 \cdot 9$
  $= 45$

11. $(5 \cdot 3)^2$
  $= 15^2$
  $= 225$

12. $(-1 + 3)^3$
  $= 2^3$
  $= 8$

13. $(11.6 + 2 \cdot 9.2) \div 5$
  $= (11.6 + 18.4) \div 5$
  $= 30 \div 5$
  $= 6$

14. a. $0.5 * 32 * (0.7 + 32)$

  b. $0.5 * 32 * (32.7) = 16 * 32.7 = 523.2$

15. $((7 * X + Y) \div (X - 6 * Y))$ ^ 4

16. $4 \cdot 10 + 2 \cdot 35 = 40 + 70 = 110$ mm

4

17. $3 \cdot 10^2 - 9 \cdot 10 + 6 - 3(10-1)(10-2)$
$= 3 \cdot 100 - 90 + 6 - 3 \cdot 9 \cdot 8$
$= 300 - 90 + 6 - 216$
$= 0$

18. $6 + (5 - (4 + (3 - 2)))$
$= 6 + (5 - (4 + 1))$
$= 6 + (5 - 5)$
$= 6 + 0$
$= 6$

19. $(2 \cdot 12 \cdot 10) \div (12 + 10) = 240 \div 22 \approx 10.9$ mph

20. $(2 \cdot 800 \cdot 700) \div (800 + 700) \approx 746.67$ km/h

21. $P \cap E = \{2\}$; 2 is the number which is both even and prime.

22. a. closed
   b. The interval is the intersection of $-4 \le y$ and $y \le 6$.

23. a. $d > 1800$
   b.
   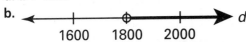

24. a. -56   **b.** -56   **c.** 56

25. $\frac{1}{2} \cdot 3\frac{3}{8} = \frac{1}{2} \cdot \frac{27}{8} = \frac{27}{16} = 1\frac{11}{16}$ yd

26. a. 9 square units
   b. Sample: three rows multiplied by three columns

27. a. 8 square units
   b. Count the number of whole squares and add it to the number of half squares.
   $4 + 8\left(\frac{1}{2}\right) = 4 + 4 = 8$

28. a. $1 = 1$
   $2 - 1 = 1$
   $3 - (2 - 1) = 3 - 1 = 2$
   $4 - (3 - (2 - 1)) = 4 - (3 - 1) = 4 - 2 = 2$
   $5 - (4 - (3 - (2 - 1)))$
   $= 5 - (4 - (3 - 1))$
   $= 5 - (4 - 2) = 5 - 2 = 3$
   $6 - (5 - (4 - (3 - (2 - 1))))$
   $= 6 - (5 - (4 - (3 - 1)))$
   $= 6 - (5 - (4 - 2))$
   $= 6 - (5 - 2) = 6 - 3 = 3$
   b. The pattern of answers is 1, 1, 2, 2, 3, 3, 4, 4, 5, 5.
   c. Prediction is 5; it follows the pattern in **part b**; it is correct.

1. $A = \ell w$

2. 64; $(.8(200 - 120) = .8 \cdot 80 = 64)$

3. (d) 205 (The average is over 200.)

4. 0; $(.8(200 - 200) = .8 \cdot 0 = 0$; the handicap of a 200 bowler is zero.)

5. L, d, and s

6. about 204 cars;
$$\frac{20 \cdot 3 \cdot 10560}{600 + 50^2}$$
$$= \frac{633600}{3100}$$
$$= 204.3871 \text{ or about } 204$$

7. about 633 cars;
$$\frac{20 \cdot 4 \cdot 7920}{600 + 20^2}$$
$$= \frac{633600}{1000}$$
$$= 633.6$$
Round down to 633 because $1\frac{1}{2}$ miles is not long enough for the 634th car to travel at a safe distance.

8. 1.2×10^{16} km^3
$$\left(\frac{4}{3}\pi (142,000)^3\right.$$
$$= \frac{4}{3}\pi (2.8633 \times 10^{15})$$
$$= 1.1994 \times 10^{16}$$
$$\left.\approx 1.2 \times 10^{16}\right)$$

9. 23 cm $(C = \pi \cdot 7.3 = 22.933626)$

10. the set of whole numbers

11. 87°F
$\left(\frac{1}{4} \cdot 200 + 37 = 50 + 37 = 87\right)$

12. 74.5°F
$\left(\frac{1}{4} \cdot 150 + 37 = 37.5 + 37 = 74.5\right)$

13. a. L * W; 2 * L + 2 * W
   b. area $= 52.5 \cdot 38 = 1995$
   perimeter $= 2 \cdot 52.5 + 2 \cdot 38$
   $= 105 + 76$
   $= 181$

14. 382 $(77 \cdot 8 - (29 \cdot 8 + 2)$
   $= 616 - (232 + 2)$
   $= 616 - 234$
   $= 382)$

15. a. + **b.** / **c.** * **d.** ^

16. (3/(Y + 2)) ^ 10

17. $q < -36$, $q > 12$

18. a. (The domain is the set of real numbers.)

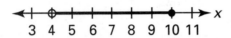

b. (The domain is the set of whole numbers.)

19. a. 0

b. Sample: -1 (any negative integer)

c. Sample: $\frac{1}{2}$

20. 3.14159 (3.141592654 rounded to 5 places to right of the decimal)

21. $1\frac{3}{4}$ cups $\left(3\frac{1}{2} \cdot \frac{1}{2} = \frac{7}{2} \cdot \frac{1}{2} = \frac{7}{4} = 1\frac{3}{4}\right)$

22. a. E represents energy, m represents mass of an object, and c represents speed of light.

b. This formula describes the relationship between the mass of an object and the energy it contains.

LESSON 1-6   pp. 31–36

1. square root

2. 8.5 is a square root of 72.25.

3. $17m$ is the length of a side since 17 is the square root of 289.

4. $\sqrt{A}$

5. 10

6. -9

7. 90

8. 5 $\left(\sqrt{3^2 + 4^2} = \sqrt{9 + 16} = \sqrt{25} = 5\right)$

9. 12 $\left(\sqrt{3^2 \cdot 4^2} = \sqrt{9 \cdot 16} = \sqrt{144} = 12\right)$

10. 8 $\left(\sqrt{17^2 - 15^2} = \sqrt{289 - 225} = \sqrt{64} = 8\right)$

11. a.

$\sqrt{n}$	n	n^2
1	1	1
1.414	2	4
1.732	3	9
2	4	16
2.236	5	25
2.449	6	36
2.646	7	49
2.828	8	64
3	9	81
3.162	10	100
3.317	11	121
3.464	12	144
3.606	13	169
3.742	14	196
3.873	15	225
4	16	256
4.123	17	289
4.243	18	324
4.359	19	361
4.472	20	400

b. Sample: In the n^2 column, the units digits seem to follow a pattern of repeating 1, 4, 9, 6, 5, 6, 9, 4, 1, 0.

12. a. 20.17

b. 20.17^2
= 20.17 · 20.17
= 406.8289 ≈ 407; it checks.

13. a. 8

b. 8

c. 24

14. 2

15. 4 and -4

16. a. $x = \sqrt{121}$ or $x = -\sqrt{121}$

b. $x = 11$ or $x = -11$

17. a. $b = \sqrt{301}$ or $b = -\sqrt{301}$

b. $b = 17.35$ or $b = -17.35$

18. a. $\sqrt{18}$ units

b. 4.24 units

19. $\sqrt{32}$ is between $\sqrt{25}$ and $\sqrt{36}$, so $\sqrt{32}$ is between 5 and 6.

20. $m = 6$ or $m = -6$
$$m^2 + 64 = 100$$
$$m^2 = 36$$
$$m = 6 \text{ or } -6$$

21. **a.** $9\sqrt{4} = 9 \cdot 2 = 18$
b. $\sqrt{4 \cdot 9} = \sqrt{36} = 6$
c. $4\sqrt{9} = 4 \cdot 3 = 12$

22. **a.** 3.5
b. The sides of the square are 3.5 cm.
c. The square root of a number is the length of a side of a square whose area is the number.

23. 2.5 seconds
$$\left(\sqrt{\frac{100}{16}} = \frac{10}{4} = 2.5 \right)$$

24. $T \approx 2\pi \sqrt{\frac{.85}{9.8}} \approx 6.283 \cdot \sqrt{0.087}$
$6.283 \cdot .2945 \approx 1.8503$ sec

25. **a.** $A = 1000 + 1000 \cdot 3\%$
$= 1000 + 1000 \cdot .03$
$= 1000 + 30$
$= \$1030$
b. $A = 1000 + 1000 \cdot 4.5\%$
$= 1000 + 1000 \cdot .045$
$= 1000 + 45$
$= \$1045$

26. $5^2 \cdot 5^3 = 25 \cdot 125 = 3125$
27. $57 - 3 \cdot 18 = 57 - 54 = 3$
28. $(11 - 7)^3 = 4^3 = 64$
29.

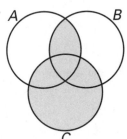

30. **a.** the set of whole numbers
b. $1 \le n \le 6$ where n is a whole number
c.

31. **a.** the set of positive real numbers
b. $2 \le w \le 6$ where w is a real number
c.

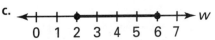

32. 2 and 6 make the sentence true:
$(15 + -4 + -11 = 0$ which is not > 0,
$15 + 2 + -11 = 6$ which is greater than 0,
$15 + 6 + -11 = 10$ which is greater than 0)

33. **a.** $\frac{2}{3} + \frac{4}{3} = \frac{6}{3} = 2$
b. $\frac{2}{3} + \frac{4}{9} = \frac{6}{9} + \frac{4}{9} = \frac{10}{9}$
c. $\frac{2}{3} + \frac{4}{13} = \frac{26}{39} + \frac{12}{39} = \frac{38}{39}$

34. **a.** Samples: 4 $\boxed{+/-}$ $\boxed{\sqrt{\ }}$ or $\boxed{\sqrt{\ }}$ $\boxed{-}$ 4
$\boxed{\text{ENTER}}$
b. Error
c. In the domain of real numbers, a negative number has no square root.

35. 1806
$(42^2 = 1764; \ 43^2 = 1849;$
$44^2 = 1936.$ So, $x = 43;$
$1849 - 43 = 1806)$

LESSON 1-7 pp. 37–43

1. **a.** Samples:
$\frac{10 \cdot 7}{2} = 5 \cdot 7$ is true, since $\frac{70}{2} = 35$.
$\frac{10 \cdot -3}{2} = 5 \cdot -3$ is true, since $\frac{-30}{2} = -15$.
$\frac{10 \cdot 41.2}{2} = 5 \cdot 41.2$ is true, since $\frac{412}{2} = 206$.
b. $\frac{10 \cdot n}{2} = 5 \cdot n$

2. Samples: $2 \cdot 1 = 2; \ -7 \cdot 1 = -7$
3. Samples: $5 \cdot 9 = 9 \cdot 5; \ 7.2 \cdot 12.9 = 12.9 \cdot 7.2$
4. Samples: 3 dogs have $4 \cdot 3$ legs; 18 dogs have $4 \cdot 18$ legs.
5. **a.** The population will decrease by $250 \cdot 10$ or 2500 people in 10 months.
b. The population will decrease by $250m$ people in m months.
c. Yes, the population will not have decreased in zero months.

6. $(3 + n) + 2 = 5 + n$

7. $n + 2 \cdot n = 3 \cdot n$

8. $6 \cdot a + 6 \cdot b = 6 \cdot (a + b)$

9. $31 (2 \cdot 8 + 3 \cdot 5 = 16 + 15 = 31)$

10. A counterexample is an instance which shows that a pattern is not always true.

11. Sample: If $a = 7$ and $b = 9$, the pattern would say $7 + 9 = 7 \cdot 9$ which is not true because $16 \neq 63$.

12. Sample: If $a = 10$ and $b = 2$, then the pattern would say $(10 - 3) + 2 = 10 - (3 + 2)$ which is not true because $7 + 2 \neq 10 - 5$.

13. **a.** L heads of lettuce and T tomatoes cost $L \cdot 89¢ + T \cdot 24¢$.

   b. Sample: 10 heads of lettuce and 4 tomatoes cost $10 \cdot 89¢ + 4 \cdot 24¢$.

   c. $C = .89L + .24T$

14. **a.** Sample:
   $2 + 2 + 2 = 3 \cdot 2$;
   $5 + 5 + 5 = 3 \cdot 5$;
   $7 + 7 + 7 = 3 \cdot 7$

   b. Yes; the pattern is true for all real numbers. Adding a number to itself three times gives the same result as tripling the number.

15. **a.** Sample:
   $10(11 - 0) = 10 \cdot 11 - 0$ is true because $10(11 - 0) = 10 \cdot 11 = 110$ and $10 \cdot 11 - 0 = 110 - 0 = 110$.
   $10(4 - 4) = 10 \cdot 4 - 4$ is false because $10 \cdot 0 \neq 40 - 4$.
   $10(0 - 10) = 10 \cdot 0 - 10$ is false because $10 \cdot {-10} \neq 0 - 10$.

   b. The pattern is not true for all real numbers. Counterexamples can be found.

16. **a.** Sample:
   $(4^2)4 = 4^3$; true, since $16 \cdot 4 = 64 = 4^3$.
   $(-5)^2(-5) = (-5)^3$; true, since $25 \cdot {-5} = -125 = (-5)^3$.
   $(0.1)^2 \cdot 0.1 = (0.1)^3$; true, since $0.01 \cdot 0.1 = .001 = (0.1)^3$.

   b. Yes, multiplying the square of a number by that number is the same as multiplying the number three times.

17. **a.** $n \cdot n > n$

   b. Sample: $-8 \cdot {-8} > -8$ is another instance of the pattern.

   c. Sample: $0 \cdot 0 > 0$ is an integer counterexample.

   d. Sample: $\frac{1}{2} \cdot \frac{1}{2} < \frac{1}{2}$

18. **a.** 8 pieces are made with 4 cuts

   b. $p = 2c$

   c. 24 pieces $(2 \cdot 12 = 24)$

19. **a.**

   b. Sample: The first design has three pennies, the second design has $3 \cdot 2$ pennies, the third design has $3 \cdot 3$ pennies, and so on.

   c. 60 pennies $(3 \cdot 20 = 60)$

20. 7

21. 20

22. 401

23. **a.** $\sqrt{3000} = 54.77226$ feet

   b. Sample: 60 feet by 50 feet (To the nearest tenth of a foot, 54.7 ft is the maximum length of a square plot that can be seeded with one bag of the grass seed.)

24. **a.** 25 sq units (Count the squares.)

   b. 5 units $\left(\sqrt{25} = 5\right)$

25. 176 pounds (6 ft = 72 in.;
   $w = \frac{11}{2}(72) - 220$
   $= 396 - 220$
   $= 176$)

26. **a.** 0 pounds $\left(\frac{11}{2} \cdot 40 - 220 = 220 - 220 = 0\right)$

   b. 40 inches is outside the domain of most adult heights, so the answer has no meaning.

27. **a.** Sample: $n = 4 \left(\frac{4}{3} > 1\right)$

   b. Sample: $n = 2 \left(\frac{2}{3} < 1\right)$

   c. $n = 3 \left(\frac{3}{3} = 1\right)$

28. a. No

    b. $V \cap W = \{15\}$ so $T \cup (V \cap W) = \{10, 12, 14, 15, 16, 18, 20\}$;
$T \cup V = \{10, 12, 14, 15, 16, 18, 20\}$
so $(T \cup V) \cap W = \{10, 15, 20\}$;
thus $T \cup (V \cap W) \neq (T \cup V) \cap W$.

29. $1.245 \leq d \leq 1.255$ (Add and subtract the tolerance, 0.005, from the diameter, 1.25.)

30. a. The sum is 9 times the middle date; it seems to always work.

    b.

$N - 8$	$N - 7$	$N - 6$
$N - 1$	N	$N + 1$
$N + 6$	$N + 7$	$N + 8$

    c. $N - 8 + N - 7 + N - 6 + N - 1 + N + N + 1 + N + 6 + N + 7 + N + 8 = 9N - 22 + 22 = 9N$;
this explains why the result in **part a** is true.

IN-CLASS ACTIVITY   p. 44

1.

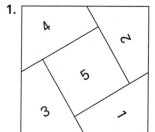

2. Answers will vary.

3. The sum of the areas of the two smaller squares is equal to the area of the largest square.

LESSON 1-8   pp. 45–51

1. The longest side of a right triangle is called the hypotenuse.

2. a. The legs are j and n.

    b. The hypotenuse is k.

3. The area of square I plus the area of square II equals the area of square III.

4. Pythagorean Theorem: In a right triangle with legs of length a and b and hypotenuse of length c, $a^2 + b^2 = c^2$.

5. a. 34 square units $(9 + 25 = 34$; the sum of the areas of squares B and C)

    b. $\sqrt{34}$ units ≈ 5.8 units

6. 25 units $(24^2 + 7^2 = 625; \sqrt{625} = 25)$

7. 17 units $(8^2 + 15^2 = 289; \sqrt{289} = 17)$

8. $\sqrt{157} \approx 12.53$ units $(6^2 + 11^2 = 157)$

9. $\sqrt{325}$ mi ≈ 18 mi $(10^2 + 15^2 = 325)$

10. True, $\angle X$ is a right angle as are all angles in a rectangle.

11. $\sqrt{306}$ m ≈ 17.5 m $(9^2 + 15^2 = 306)$

12. 60 inches $(36^2 + 48^2 = 3600; \sqrt{3600} = 60)$

13. a. 6 km $(4 + 2 = 6)$

    b. 4.5 km $(4^2 + 2^2 = 20; \sqrt{20} \approx 4.5)$

    c. 1.5 km $(6 - 4.5 = 1.5)$

14. a. 8 cm $\left(\sqrt{64} = 8\right)$

    b. $\sqrt{128} \approx 11.3$ cm $(8^2 + 8^2 = 128)$

15. a. $\sqrt{12} \approx 3.5$ cm $(3^2 + \sqrt{3}^2 = 12)$

    b. Check students' drawings. The hypotenuse should be ≈ 3.5 cm.

    c. Sample: Both answers are close to 3.5 cm.

16. a. $\frac{2}{3} \cdot \frac{3}{2} = \frac{6}{6} = 1$

    $\frac{4}{5} \cdot \frac{5}{4} = \frac{20}{20} = 1$

    $\frac{9}{10} \cdot \frac{10}{9} = \frac{90}{90} = 1$

    $\frac{-3}{5} \cdot \frac{5}{-3} = \frac{-15}{-15} = 1$

    b. $\frac{a}{b} \cdot \frac{b}{a} = 1$

    c. Sample: $\frac{-2}{-5} \cdot \frac{-5}{-2} = \frac{10}{10} = 1$

17. $\sqrt{25} + \sqrt{4} > \sqrt{29}$ $(5 + 2 > \sqrt{29}; 7 > 5.4)$

18. $\sqrt{887}^2 = 887$

19. 41.4 meters
$(h = -4.9 \cdot 2^2 + 30 \cdot 2 + 1$
$= -19.6 + 60 + 1$
$= 41.4)$

20. $g = -2$: $10 \cdot (-2)^2 = 10 \cdot 4 = 40$
$g = 0$: $10 \cdot 0^2 = 10 \cdot 0 = 0$
$g = 7$: $10 \cdot 7^2 = 10 \cdot 49 = 490$

21. $3\frac{1}{2}$ $\left(3\frac{1}{2} = 3.5\right)$

22. $\frac{9}{4}$ $\left(\frac{9}{4} = 2.25, \frac{9}{5} = 1.8\right)$

23. $\frac{5}{6}$ $\left(\frac{4}{5} = .8, \frac{5}{6} = .8\overline{3}\right)$

24. $7.2 \cdot 10^{15}$; $6.5 \cdot 10^{14}$; $9.4 \cdot 10^{13}$

25. $\approx \$4.50$ $(\$30 \cdot 15\% = 30 \cdot .15 = 4.5)$

26. **a.** $AC = \sqrt{1^2 + 1^2} = \sqrt{1 + 1} = \sqrt{2}$
$AD = \sqrt{1^2 + \sqrt{2}^2} = \sqrt{1 + 2} = \sqrt{3}$
$AE = \sqrt{1^2 + \sqrt{3}^2} = \sqrt{1 + 3} = \sqrt{4} = 2$
$AF = \sqrt{1^2 + 2^2} = \sqrt{1 + 4} = \sqrt{5}$
$AG = \sqrt{1^2 + \sqrt{5}^2} = \sqrt{1 + 5} = \sqrt{6}$

b.

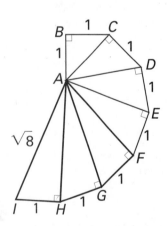

27.

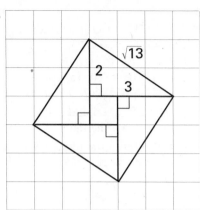

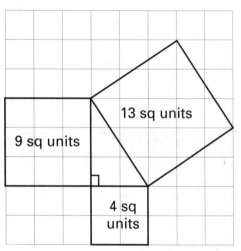

28. Yes. If either or both x and y are 0, then $\sqrt{x^2 + y^2} = x + y$. If x and y are greater than 0, then $\sqrt{x^2 + y^2} < x + y$ is true. This tells us that the length of the hypotenuse is always less than the sum of the lengths of the two legs.

IN-CLASS ACTIVITY p. 52

1.

5th
5th

6th
6th

2. The perimeter of the 3rd design is 12.

3.

n	p
1	4
2	8
3	12
4	16
5	20
6	24

4. a. The perimeter of the 10th design is 40.
   b. The perimeter is 4 times the number of the design.

5. $p = 4n$

LESSON 1-9   pp. 53–59

1. a. 10 units ($P = 8 + 2 = 10$)
   b.

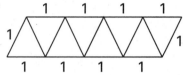

2. 75 blocks ($3 \cdot 25 = 75$)

3. True   **4.** (b) $y = 5x$

5. (c) $y = 5^x$ **6.** (a) $y = x + 5$

7. 4 (2^2)   **8.** 16 ($2^4 = 16$)

9. A represents number of ancestors; n represents number of generations back.

10. Sample: Some ancestors may share ancestors.

11. a.

w	1	2	3	4	5
p	2	4	6	8	10

   b. Sample: The total number of panes in a design is equal to twice the number of panes in one row.
   c. $p = 2w$

12. a.

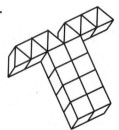

b. 30 blocks will be needed to make the 7th instance; 16 will be triangular and 14 will be square. The number of square blocks is twice the number of the instance. The number of triangular blocks is two more than the number of square blocks.

13. a. 2
   b. 4
   c.

n	1	2	3	4
t	2	4	8	16

   d. $t = 2^n$
   e. 512 ($2^9 = 512$)

14. $y = 3^x$

15. (b) $b = 2w + 2$

16. 3.25 units $\left(\sqrt{1.25^2 + 3^2} = \sqrt{1.5625 + 9} = \sqrt{10.5625} = 3.25\right)$

17. $\sqrt{45}$ units $\left(\sqrt{3^2 + 6^2} = \sqrt{9 + 36} = \sqrt{45}\right)$

18. a. $AC = \sqrt{5}$ cm
   b. $BC = \sqrt{20}$ cm
   c. $AB = \sqrt{20 + 5} = \sqrt{25} = 5$ cm

19. a. \$37.50 ($6 \cdot 5.00 + 5 \cdot 1.50 = 30 + 7.5 = 37.5$)
   b. $5.00a + 1.50c$

20. a. $a = 5, b = 8, c = 3, d = 7$
   b. $S = \frac{5 \cdot 7 + 8 \cdot 3}{8 \cdot 7} = \frac{35 + 24}{56} = \frac{59}{56}$
   c. $S = \frac{-2 \cdot 2 + 3 \cdot 1}{3 \cdot 2} = \frac{-4 + 3}{6} = \frac{-1}{6}$

21. ≈ 5.7 kg
$\left(W = 70 \cdot \left(\frac{6400}{6400 + 16,000}\right)^2 = 70\left(\frac{2}{7}\right)^2 = \frac{40}{7} \approx 5.7\right)$

22. (d) $-2 < x \le 2$

23. a. 0
   b. -6
   c.

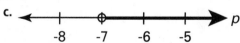

   d. No. Between any two real numbers, there are always an infinite number of real numbers.

24. a. 24 cubes

b. 24 cubic inches $(2 \cdot 3 \cdot 4 = 24)$

25. a. $2^{100} \approx 1.268 \times 10^{30}$

b. Yes. Even a "thick" phone book would only be 1000 or 2000 pages.

c. Sample: If a phone book has 1000 pages, it would take $1.268 \cdot 10^{27}$ phone books to equal the height of the folded paper.

26. Answers will vary.

CHAPTER 1

PROGRESS SELF-TEST   pp. 63–64

1. $2(a + 3b)$ when $a = 3$ and $b = 5$
$2(3 + 3 \cdot 5) = 2 \cdot 18 = 36$

2. $5 \cdot 6^n = 5 \cdot 6^4 = 5 \cdot 1296 = 6480$

3. $\frac{p + t^2}{p - t}$ when $p = 5$, $t = 2$
$\frac{5 + 2^2}{5 - 2} = \frac{9}{3} = 3$

4. $\left(\sqrt{50}\right)^2 = \sqrt{50} \cdot \sqrt{50} = 50$

5. $10 * 3 \wedge 2 + 5 = 10 * 9 + 5 = 95$

6. $3\sqrt{42} \approx 3 \cdot 6.481 \approx 19.4$ rounded to the nearest tenth

7. a. $M \cup N =$
$\{2, 3, 4, 6, 8, 9, 10, 12, 14, 15, 16\}$

b. $M \cap N = \{6, 12\}$

8. $s > 25$

9. (a) set of whole numbers

10. 8 (Does $4 \cdot 8 + 7 = 2 \cdot 8 + 23$?
Does $32 + 7 = 16 + 23$?
Yes, $39 = 39$.)

11. Samples: 6, 7, 7.9

12. 98 cents (Round 3.2 to 4 ounces.
$23(4 - 1) + 29$
$= 69 + 29$
$= 98$

13. $28m^2$ $(\pi(3)^2 = 9\pi \approx 28.274)$

14. False $\left(\sqrt{100} + \sqrt{36} = 10 + 6 = 16\right.$
$$\sqrt{136} \approx 11.662$$
$$\left. 16 \neq 11.662\right)$$

15. 13

16. $\$3.50n$ where n represents the number of tickets

17. Samples:
$$\frac{4}{5} - \frac{1}{5} = \frac{4 - 1}{5}$$
$$\frac{9}{5} - \frac{3}{5} = \frac{9 - 3}{5}$$
$$\frac{8}{5} - \frac{4}{5} = \frac{8 - 4}{5}$$
$$\frac{3}{5} - \frac{2}{5} = \frac{3 - 2}{5}$$
$$\frac{12}{5} - \frac{2}{5} = \frac{12 - 2}{5}$$
$$\frac{1.9}{5} - \frac{6.13}{5} = \frac{1.9 - 6.13}{5}$$

18. $y = 8x$

19.

20. a. $x \geq 10$

b. Answers will vary.

21.

22. ≈ 46.1 $\left(\sqrt{45^2 + 10^2} = \sqrt{2025 + 100} = \sqrt{2125} \approx\right.$
46.0977

23. $\sqrt{193600} = 440$ yd

24. $d = 25$ in.
$\left(\sqrt{15^2 + 20^2} = \sqrt{225 + 400} = \sqrt{625} = 25\right)$

CHAPTER 1

REVIEW   pp. 65–68

1. 4 (Does $2 \cdot 4 + 13 = 3 \cdot 4 + 9$?
Does $8 + 13 = 12 + 9$?
Yes, $21 = 21$.)

2. $\{1\}$ $(7 \cdot 1 - 13 = -6$ which is less than 2)

3. Sample: -5, -4.2, -3

4. Sample: 75, 75.5, 76

5. $x = 3$ or $x = -3$

6. $x = \sqrt{90}$ or $x = -\sqrt{90}$

7. a. $A \cap B = \{15, 25\}$

b. $A \cup B = \{10, 11, 15, 19, 20, 23, 25, 30\}$

8. a. $(C \cup D) \cap E = \{2, 4, 8, 9, 12\} \cap \{6, 8, 9\}$
$= \{8, 9\}$

b. $C \cup (D \cap E) = C \cup \{8\} = \{2, 8, 9\}$

9. **a.** $W \cup X = \{-1, 0, 1, 2, 3, \dots\}$
   b. $W \cap X = \{0, 1, 2\}$
10. **a.** $O \cap P = \{3, 5, 7, 11, 13\}$
    b. $O \cup P = \{1, 2, 3, 5, 7\}$
11. **a.** $3 - \frac{2}{5} + 6 = 8\frac{3}{5}$
    b. $(3 - 2)(5 + 6) = 1 \cdot 11 = 11$
12. $-35 + 5 \cdot 2 = -35 + 10 = -25$
13. $(3 + 4 * 5)^2 = 23 \cdot {}^2 = 529$
14. $-2 \cdot 3.5 = -7$
15. $4 \cdot 12^2 = 4 \cdot 144 = 576$
16. $4(13.8 - 5.4) = 4 \cdot 8.4 = 33.6$
17. $5\left(\frac{2}{5} + \frac{1}{5}\right) = 5 \cdot \frac{3}{5} = 3$
18. $\left(\frac{36}{4}\right)^3 = 9^3 = 729$
19. 9
20. -7
21. $3 \cdot 10 = 30$
22. $6 + 8 = 14$
23. False, $\sqrt{25} + \sqrt{4} = 5 + 2 = 7$
24. $=$, $\sqrt{144} \cdot \sqrt{9} = 12 \cdot 3 = 36$
25. 4 and 5
26. 2 and 3
27. 14.107
28. $\sqrt{200^2 + 300^2} = \sqrt{40000 + 90000} = \sqrt{130000} \approx$ 360.555
29. 50
30. $\{-1, 0, 1, 2, 3\}$
31. **a.** null or empty set
    b. Sample: the set of integers between -3 and -2
32. False
33. 7
34. $8 \cdot 15 = 120$
35. 39
36. 6 square units
37. Samples: $2 + 2 = 2 \cdot 2$; $-3 + -3 = 2 \cdot -3$; $4.9 + 4.9 = 2 \cdot 4.9$
38. Sample: $8(7 + 9) = 8 \cdot 7 + 8 \cdot 9$
    $8(-10 + 4) = 8 \cdot -10 + 8 \cdot 4$
    $8\left(\frac{1}{2} + 2.1\right) = 8 \cdot \frac{1}{2} + 8 \cdot 2.1$

39. Sample:
    $9 = 4.5 \cdot 2$ (2 hammers and 9 wrenches),
    $36 = 4.5 \cdot 8$ (8 hammers and 36 wrenches)
40. Sample: $\frac{17}{74} \neq \frac{1}{4}$
41. n sheep have $n \cdot 4$ legs
42. S shirts and J jeans cost $S \cdot \$19 + J \cdot \$27$
43. **a.** 21000 (A decade is ten years. $2100 \cdot 10 = 21000$)
    b. $2100y$
44. $11x = y$
45. $4^x = y$
46. **a.**

n	1	2	3	4
t	1	4	9	16

   b. $t = n^2$
47. (c) (Distance is positive.)
48. (c) (Weight is positive.)
49. (d) (Altitude can be positive or negative.)
50. (a) (The number of people cannot be fractional nor negative.)
51. 25% $\left(p = 100\left(1 - \frac{15}{20}\right) = 100(1 - .75) = 100(.25) = 25 \right)$
52. 1357.17 cu cm
    $\left(V = \pi \cdot 6^2 \cdot 12 \right.$
    $= 432\pi$
    $\left. \approx 1357.17 \right)$
53. \$399
    $\left(c = 19.95 \cdot \frac{12 \cdot 15}{9} \right.$
    $= 19.95 \cdot \frac{180}{9}$
    $= 19.95 \cdot 20$
    $\left. = 399 \right)$
54. \$239.74
    $\left(c = 8.99 \cdot \frac{8 \cdot 30}{9} \right.$
    $= 8.99 \cdot \frac{240}{9}$
    $\approx 8.99 \cdot 26.67$
    $\left. \approx 239.74 \right)$

55. 10 ft $\left(\sqrt{6^2 + 8^2} = \sqrt{36 + 64} = \sqrt{100} = 10\right)$

56. $\sqrt{500}$ m ≈ 22.4 m $\left(\sqrt{20^2 + 10^2} = \sqrt{400 + 100}\right)$

57. ≈ 1.78 ft or about 2 ft
(Plan A: $\sqrt{8^2 + 20^2} = \sqrt{64 + 400} = \sqrt{464} \approx$
21.54 ft;
Plan B: $\sqrt{20^2 + 12^2} = \sqrt{400 + 144} = \sqrt{544} \approx$
23.32 ft;
difference $\approx 23.32 - 21.54 \approx 1.78$ ft)

58. a. 316 ft $\left(\sqrt{300^2 + 100^2} = \sqrt{90,000 + 10,000}\right.$
$= \sqrt{100,000} \approx 316.23\left.\right)$

b. 84 ft (300 + 100 = 400 ft is the distance
walking along the edges; difference =
400 − 316 = 84 ft)

59.
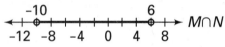

60. a. $45 \le s \le 65$

b.
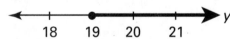

61. a. $M \cap N$

```
        -10              6
   +--○--+--+--+--+--+--○--+--→ M∩N
  -12  -8  -4   0   4   8
```

b. $M \cup N$

```
   ←+--+--+--+--+--+--+--+--→ M∪N
  -12  -8  -4   0   4   8
```

62.
```
 ◄--+--●--+--+--+--+--●--+--►
    3  4  5  6  7  8  9  10 11
```

63. a. domain: set of real numbers
```
   ←--+----●----+----●----+----►  y
      18   19   20   21
```

b. domain: set of integers
```
   ←--+----●----●----●----►  y
      18   19   20   21
```

64. (c)

65. (b)

66. a. $50 < n < 65$, where n is a real number
b. Answers will vary

67. a. $n \ge 18$ where n is a real number

b. Sample: A U.S. citizen may vote when he
or she is at least 18 years old.

CHAPTER 1

1. $4.7 \cdot 3.21 = 15.087$

2. $0.04 \cdot 312 = 12.48$

3. $666 \cdot 0.00001 = 0.00666$

4. $.17 \cdot .02 = 0.0034$

5. $\frac{2}{3} \cdot 30 = 20$

6. $\frac{5}{2} \cdot 11 = \frac{55}{2}$

7. $\frac{2}{9} \cdot \frac{3}{4} = \frac{6}{36} = \frac{1}{6}$

8. $\frac{1}{4} \cdot \frac{1}{3} \cdot \frac{1}{2} = \frac{1}{24}$

9. $1\frac{1}{4} \cdot 2\frac{1}{8} = \frac{5}{4} \cdot \frac{17}{8} = \frac{85}{32} = 2\frac{21}{32}$

10. $30\% \cdot 120 = 36$

11. $3\% \cdot \$6000 = \$180$

12. $5.25\% \cdot 1500 = 78.75$

13. $150 \cdot 180 = 27000$ cartons

14. $\$6.50 \cdot 37.5 = \$243.75$

15. $33.5 \cdot 12 = 402$ miles

16. $625 \cdot 2\frac{1}{2} = 1562.5$ miles

17. $3 \cdot \text{-}2 = \text{-}6$

18. $11 \cdot \text{-}11 = \text{-}121$

19. $\text{-}6 \cdot 4 = \text{-}24$

20. $\text{-}5 \cdot \text{-}5 = 25$

21. $0 \cdot \text{-}1 = 0$

22. $\text{-}14 \cdot 130 = \text{-}1820$

23. $\text{-}60 \cdot \text{-}59 = 3540$

24. $\text{-}3 \cdot \text{-}2 \cdot \text{-}1 \cdot \text{-}1 = 6$

25. $3x = 12$
$x = \frac{12}{4} = 3$

26. $5y = 110$
$y = \frac{110}{5} = 22$

27. $10z = 5$
$z = \frac{5}{10} = \frac{1}{2}$

28. $1 = 9w$

$\frac{1}{9} = w$

29. $6 = 50a$

$\frac{6}{50} = \frac{3}{25} = a$

30. $b \cdot 21 = 14$

$b = \frac{14}{21} = \frac{2}{3}$

31. $8c = 4$

$c = \frac{4}{8} = \frac{1}{2}$

32. $7 = 2d$

$\frac{7}{2} = d$

33. 15 in. $\cdot$ 12 in. = 180 in.^{2}

34. 4.5 cm $\cdot$ 3.2 cm = 14.4 cm^2

35. 2m $\cdot$ 4m = 8m^2

36. 100 ft $\cdot$ 82 ft = 8200 ft^2

37. 8 cm $\cdot$ 4 cm $\cdot$ 3 cm = 96 cm^3

38. 12 in. $\cdot$ 9 in. $\cdot$ $1\frac{1}{2}$ in. = 162 in.^{3}

39. $\frac{1}{2}$ ft $\cdot$ $\frac{1}{2}$ ft $\cdot$ $\frac{1}{2}$ ft = $\frac{1}{8}$ ft^3

40. 60m $\cdot$ 50m $\cdot$ 10m = 30000m^3

CHAPTER 2
MULTIPLICATION IN ALGEBRA

LESSON 2-1   *pp. 72–78*

1. The estimate would be 40 planets with life in our galaxy.
$(100{,}000{,}000{,}000 \cdot .4 \cdot 1 \cdot 1 \cdot 1 \cdot .1 \cdot \frac{1}{100{,}000{,}000} = 40)$.

2. Area Model for Multiplication: the area of a rectangle with length ℓ and width w is ℓw.

3. (b) The area is measured in square inches.

4. 30.96 cm^2 $(7.2 \cdot 4.3 = 30.96)$

5. $8y \text{ in}^2$ $(8 \cdot y = 8y)$

6. Count the number of dots in one column. Then count the number of dots in one row. Multiply to find the total number of dots. $(102 = 6 \cdot 17)$

7. 188 mm^2 (Split the figure into two rectangles, one 6 mm by 14 mm and the other 13 mm by 8 mm. The areas are $6 \cdot 14 = 84 \text{ mm}^2$ and $13 \cdot 8 = 104 \text{ mm}^2$; hence the figure has area $84 + 104 = 188 \text{ mm}^2$; the figure can be split other ways.)

8. $\frac{1}{48} \text{ ft}^3$ $\left(\frac{1}{4} \cdot \frac{2}{3} \cdot \frac{1}{8} = \frac{1}{48}\right)$

9. $21xy$ cubic units $(3 \cdot 7x \cdot y = 21xy)$

10. $108p^3$ cubic units $(9p^2 \cdot 12p = 108p^3)$

11. Commutative Property of Multiplication

12. Sample: The Commutative Property switches the order in which numbers are multiplied. It deals with two numbers. The Associative Property deals with two or more multiplication operations and changes the order in which they are performed.

13. a. No
    b. Yes
    c. No
    d. Sample: Washing your hair followed by drying your hair; it is not commutative.

14. $34100x$ (Change $25 \cdot x \cdot 4 \cdot 341$ to $25 \cdot 4 \cdot 341 \cdot x$ since $25 \cdot 4 = 100$.)

15. $240x^2$ (Change $(2 \cdot 3x)(8x \cdot 5)$ to $(8x \cdot 3x)(2 \cdot 5)$.)

16. a. 2700 ft^2 $(45 \cdot 60 = 2700)$
    b. 210 ft (Find the perimeter. $45 + 45 + 60 + 60 = 210$)

17. a. kn square units
    b. $k + n + k + n$ or $2k + 2n$ units

18. a. $3a$
    b. $2b$
    c. $3a \cdot 2b$
    d. $6ab$

19. 576 m^2 (Split the figure into rectangles of dimensions 12 m by 10 m, 6 m by 56 m, and 12 m by 10 m. Find the area of each and find their sum. $(120 + 336 + 120 = 576 \text{ m}^2)$

20. $12x^3 \text{ cm}^3$ $(x \cdot 2x \cdot 6x)$

21. 180 in^3 (5 in. $\cdot$ 1 ft $\cdot$ 3 in. = 5 in. $\cdot$ 12 in. $\cdot$ 3 in. = 180 in^3)

22. 27 ft^3 (1 yd $\cdot$ 1 yd $\cdot$ 1 yd = 3 ft $\cdot$ 3 ft $\cdot$ 3 ft = 27 ft^3)

23. Sample: Area is the measure of the amount of 2-dimensional surface; volume is a measure of 3-dimensional space. The amount of space in a box is its volume; the size of one of its sides is an area.

24. a. $c > 3$ where c is any real number
    b.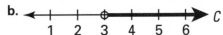

25. $2L$

26. $\frac{1}{3}L$ or $\frac{L}{3}$

27. $\frac{3}{10}$ (The numerator and denominator have a common factor of 12.)

28. 147 $(392 \cdot \frac{3}{8} = 147)$

29. a. 14 books. The length and width of the book are about $10\frac{1}{4}$ in. and $8\frac{1}{16}$ in. So 2 books will fit in each layer. The book is about $1\frac{9}{16}$ in. thick, so 7 layers of 2 books each will fit.
    b. Sample: $\ell = 38$ in., $w = 8.5$ in., $h = 10.5$ in. If you stand each book up on end, 24 books could fit in a box with these dimensions.

1. one and zero
2. one
3. one
4. multiplicative inverse
5. Sample: The product of reciprocals is 1, but 0 times any number is zero.
6. $\frac{1}{10}$ $\left(10 \cdot \frac{1}{10} = 1\right)$
7. 9 $\left(\frac{1}{9} \cdot 9 = 1\right)$
8. $\frac{7}{6}$ $\left(\frac{6}{7} \cdot \frac{7}{6} = 1\right)$
9. $\frac{12}{13}$ $\left(\frac{13}{12} \cdot \frac{12}{13} = 1\right)$
10. 2.5 $(2.5 \cdot 0.4 = 1)$
11. $\frac{1}{y}$ $\left(y \cdot \frac{1}{y} = 1\right)$
12. p square units $(1 \cdot p = p)$
13. 1 square unit $\left(\frac{5}{2} \cdot \frac{2}{5} = 1\right)$
14. **a.** 1 square unit $\left(\frac{1}{3} \cdot 3 = 1\right)$

   b.
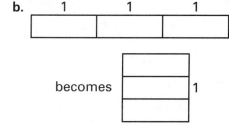

15. The prefix *milli* means $\frac{1}{1000}$, so $1000 \cdot$ $\frac{1}{1000}$ meter = 1 meter. This is an instance of the property of reciprocals.
16. **a.** $(-3 + 1)(-3 + 2)(-3 + 3)(-3 + 4)$
    $= (-2)(-1)(0)(1) = 0$
    b. $(3 + 1)(3 + 2)(3 + 3)(3 + 4) =$
    $(4)(5)(6)(7) = 840$
17. (c) $(4.1 - 4.1 = 0)$
18. (b) $((0 - 2)(0 - 1)(0 + 1)(0 + 2) =$
    $(-2)(-1)(1)(2) = 4)$
19. **a.** reciprocals
    b. $200(0.005) = 1$

20. **a.** not reciprocals
    b. $\frac{1}{4}(0.25) = 0.0625 \neq 1$
21. **a.** reciprocals
    b. $1.5 \cdot \frac{2}{3} = 1$
22. **a.** not reciprocals
    b. $\frac{3}{5} \cdot \frac{-3}{5} = \frac{-9}{25} \neq 1$
23. $\frac{5}{2}$, or $2\frac{1}{2}$, times $\left(\frac{2}{5} \cdot \frac{5}{2} = 1\right)$
24. $-2, 3, -6$
25. 0 $(9875 \cdot (1676 - 1675 - 1) = 9875 \cdot 0 = 0)$
26. $\frac{4}{x}$
27. $\frac{q}{p}$
28. $0¢$ $(0 \cdot b = 0)$
29. **a.** 3080 ft^2 (The area of the auditorium is $40 \cdot 80 = 3200$; the area of the stage is $8 \cdot 15 = 120$; the area of the remaining floor space is $3200 - 120 = 3080$ ft^2.)
    b. 513 people $\left(\frac{3080}{6} \approx 513\right)$
30. 12,000 cm^2 or 1.2 m^2 (Change 80 cm to .8 m or 1.5 m to 150 cm and find the area.
    $.8 \cdot 1.5 = .12$ m^2
    or $80 \times 150 = 12{,}000$ cm^2)
31. **a.** $10s^3$ cubic units $(5s \cdot 2s \cdot s = 10s^3)$
    b. 10
    c. Sample: The rectangle is 2 cubes deep and 5 cubes high for a total of 10 cubes

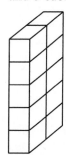

32. **a.** $\frac{3}{8}$ in^3 $\left(\frac{1}{2}\text{ in.} \cdot \frac{1}{4}\text{ in.} \cdot 3\text{ in.} = \frac{3}{8}\text{ in}^3\right)$
    b. $\frac{3}{8}$

33. Sample: In French, one is "un." In Latin, one is "unus." In German, one is "ein." They seem to have a common origin.

34. Sample: $a = 2, b = 5, c = 9$
$(2^5 \cdot 9^2 = 32 \cdot 81 = 2592)$

IN-CLASS ACTIVITY
p. 84

1. a.

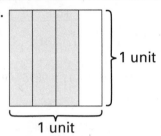

- 1 unit
- 1 unit

b.

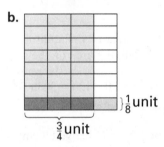

$\}\frac{1}{8}$ unit

$\frac{3}{4}$ unit

c. There are 32 rectangles in the square. There are 3 shaded in both colors, hence $\frac{3}{32}$ of the square is shaded in both colors.

d. $\frac{1}{8} \cdot \frac{3}{4} = \frac{3}{32}$

2. a. The product is $\frac{3}{8} \cdot \frac{3}{4} = \frac{9}{32}$

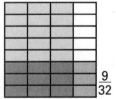

$\frac{9}{32}$

b. The product is $\frac{2}{3} \cdot \frac{5}{6} = \frac{10}{18} = \frac{5}{9}$

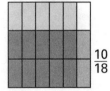

$\frac{10}{18}$

---

3. Sample: Multiply the two numerators. Then multiply the two denominators.

4. $\left(\frac{3}{32}\right)^2 s^2$ square units

LESSON 2-3
pp. 85–90

1. Multiplying Fractions Property: For all real numbers $a, b, c,$ and d, with b and d not 0, $\frac{a}{b} \cdot \frac{c}{d} = \frac{ac}{bd}$.

2. a.

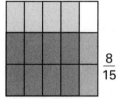

$\frac{8}{15}$

b. The product is $\frac{2}{3} \cdot \frac{4}{5} = \frac{8}{15}$; 8 of the 15 small rectangles are shaded.

3. a. $\frac{1}{2}bh$ units $\left(\frac{3}{4} \cdot \frac{2}{3}bh = \frac{6}{12}bh = \frac{1}{2}bh\right)$

b. $\frac{2}{3}b \cdot \frac{3}{4}h = \frac{1}{2}bh$.

4. $\frac{ab}{14}$
5. $\frac{xy}{3z}$

6. True $\left(\frac{1}{5} \cdot \frac{n}{1} = \frac{n}{5}\right)$

7. $\frac{4}{9}x = \frac{4}{9} \cdot \frac{x}{1} = \frac{4x}{9}$

8. (d) (t is in the denominator and 12 is a factor of the numerator.)

9. $\frac{800}{1900} = \frac{8 \cdot 100}{19 \cdot 100} = \frac{8}{19}$

10. $\frac{20y}{5y} = \frac{4 \cdot 5y}{5y} = 4$

11. $\frac{3mn}{9mt} = \frac{n \cdot 3m}{3t \cdot 3m} = \frac{n}{3t}$

12. $\frac{24gr}{18gr^2} = \frac{6gr \cdot 4}{6gr \cdot 3r} = \frac{4}{3r}$

13. $\frac{3m}{n} \cdot \frac{7m}{9} = \frac{21m^2}{9n} = \frac{3 \cdot 7m^2}{3 \cdot 3n} = \frac{7m^2}{3n}$

14. $\frac{6a}{b} \cdot \frac{b}{6a} = \frac{6ab}{6ab} = 1$

15. $\frac{24c}{5d} \cdot \frac{20d}{21} = \frac{480cd}{105d} = \frac{15d \cdot 32c}{15d \cdot 7} = \frac{32c}{7}$

16. $\frac{50}{9x} \cdot \frac{18x^2}{25y} = \frac{900x^2}{225xy} = \frac{225x \cdot 4x}{225x \cdot y} = \frac{4x}{y}$

17. a. The second rectangle is $\frac{1}{8}$ the size of the first rectangle in area. The first rectangle with width w and length ℓ has area $A = \ell w$. The second rectangle has width $\frac{w}{2}$ and length $\frac{\ell}{4}$ and area $A = \frac{\ell w}{8}$.

b.  $\frac{1}{8}$

18. a. The Marshalls' garden is $\frac{1}{6}$ the area of the Chens' garden.

b. Sample: If the Chens' garden is 6 ft by 4 ft, it has an area 24 ft^2. The Marshalls' garden will be $\frac{2}{3} \cdot 6 = 4$ ft long and $\frac{1}{4} \cdot 4 = 1$ ft wide, so it will have area 4 ft^2. This is $\frac{1}{6}$ the area of the Chens' garden.

19. a. 5   **b.** 9
   c. a **d.** a

20. (c) $\left(\frac{90}{100} = \frac{9}{10}; \text{all other fractions equal } \frac{9}{11}.\right)$

21. (c) $\left(\frac{38}{100} = \frac{19}{50}; \text{all others equal } \frac{5}{13}.\right)$

22. $\frac{ace}{bdf}$

23. 1

24. $6a$ (The numerator and denominator have common factors of $77a^2b$.)

25. $\frac{21xy}{5}$ (The numerator and denominator have common factors of $6xy^2$.)

26. a. $\frac{b^3}{6}$ cubic units $\left(b \cdot \frac{b}{2} \cdot \frac{b}{3} = \frac{b^3}{6}\right)$

b. If $b = 12$, the dimensions of the aquarium would be $12 \times 6 \times 4$, so the volume is 288 cubic units. Using the formula for part **a**, the volume is $\frac{12^3}{6} = 288$.

c. 6 (A cube with sides of length b has volume b^3. The aquarium has volume $\frac{b^3}{6}$. Six aquariums would have volume $6 \cdot \frac{b^3}{6} = b^3$.)

27. Sample: $\frac{12x}{y^2} \cdot \frac{x}{5y}$

28. a. $\frac{1}{4}$
  b. 9
  c. $\frac{9}{4}$

29. 280 $((2 \cdot 5) \cdot (7 \cdot 4))$

30. 180 $((2.5 \cdot 4) \cdot (2 \cdot 9))$

31. The maximum square footage is 3025 ft^2 with width 55 ft $(75 - 10 - 10)$ and length 55 ft $(100 - 25 - 20)$.

32. a. True   **b.** True
  c. False $\left(\frac{4}{5}z = 96 \text{ if } z = 120\right)$
  d. True

33. a. $\frac{1}{3}; \frac{1}{4}; \frac{1}{5}$

b. Sample: The product is the reciprocal of the last denominator.

c. $\frac{1}{1997}; \frac{1}{n+1}$

LESSON 2-4   pp. 91–95

1. a. A secretary types *70 words per minute*
  b. 70 words/min
  c. 70 $\frac{\text{words}}{\text{min}}$

2. a. There are exactly *2.54 centimeters per inch.*
  b. 2.54 cm/in.
  c. 2.54 $\frac{\text{cm}}{\text{in.}}$

3. a. 6 dollars/hour
  b. 6 $\frac{\text{dollars}}{\text{hour}}$

4. a. 1500 beats
$\left(150 \frac{\text{beats}}{\text{minute}} \cdot 10 \text{ minutes} = 1500 \text{ beats}\right)$
  b. 150m beats
$\left(150 \frac{\text{beats}}{\text{minute}} \cdot m \text{ minutes} = 150m \text{ beats}\right)$

5. 2973.36 miles

$\left(123.89\frac{\text{miles}}{\text{hour}} \cdot 24 \text{ hours} = 2973.36 \text{ miles}\right)$

6. 950 miles $\left(380\frac{\text{miles}}{\text{hour}} \cdot 2.5 \text{ hours} = 950 \text{ miles}\right)$

7. $0.0833\frac{\text{km}}{\text{sec}}$

$\left(300\frac{\text{km}}{\text{h}} \cdot \frac{1 \text{ h}}{60 \text{ min}} \cdot \frac{1 \text{ min}}{60 \text{ sec}} = \frac{1 \text{ km}}{12 \text{ sec}} = 0.08\overline{3}\frac{\text{km}}{\text{sec}}\right)$

8. (b)

9. ≈ 2.7 ounces

$\Big($Using the calculation from Example 4:

$\frac{2 \cdot 300}{3500}$ pound $\cdot 16\frac{\text{ounces}}{\text{pound}} \approx 2.7$ ounces.$\Big)$

10. 143,000 people in 10 years

$\left(14300\frac{\text{people}}{\text{year}} \cdot 10 \text{ years} = 143,000 \text{ people}\right)$

11. a. 2880 ounces

$\left(24\frac{\text{bottles}}{\text{case}} \cdot 12\frac{\text{ounces}}{\text{bottle}} \cdot 10 \text{ cases} = \right.$

$\left. 2880 \text{ ounces}\right)$

b. 288c ounces

$\left(24\frac{\text{bottles}}{\text{case}} \cdot 12\frac{\text{ounces}}{\text{bottle}} \cdot c \text{ cases} = \right.$

$\left. 288c \text{ ounces}\right)$

12. about 152.4 cm

$\left(60 \text{ inches} \cdot 2.54\frac{\text{cm}}{\text{in.}} = 152.4 \text{ cm}\right)$

13. size: 32 in. belt $\left(80 \text{ cm} \cdot \frac{1 \text{ in.}}{2.54 \text{ cm}} \approx 3.15 \text{ in.}\right.$

The size closest to 80 cm is 32 in.$\Big)$

14. 0.0155 hours $\approx .932$ minutes ≈ 55.95 seconds

$\left(2.5 \text{ miles} \cdot \frac{1 \text{ hour}}{160.872 \text{ mile}} = 0.0155 \text{ hours}\right)$

15. a. $2k\frac{\text{dish}}{\text{min}}$

b. $\frac{1}{2k}\frac{\text{min}}{\text{dish}}$

16. 5 shrimp $\left(30\frac{\text{shrimp}}{\text{lb}} \cdot \frac{1 \text{ lb}}{6 \text{ \$}} = 5\frac{\text{shrimp}}{\text{dollar}}\right)$

17. 5 days $\left(2400 \text{ meter} \cdot \frac{1 \text{ hour}}{48 \text{ meter}} \cdot \frac{1 \text{ day}}{10 \text{ hours}} = 5 \text{ days}\right)$

18. Sample: If you go 100 mph for 15 minutes, how far do you travel?

19. Sample: If you can read magazines at a rate of 120 minutes per magazine and each magazine has 40 pages, what is your speed in minutes per page?

20. about 4,082,400 babies

21. (d) (x is in the denominator.)

22. $\frac{8b}{7c} \cdot \frac{21a}{2x} \cdot \frac{5c}{1} = \frac{840abc}{14xc} = \frac{60ab}{x}$

23. Sample: $\frac{8}{15} \cdot \frac{x}{y} = \frac{8x}{15y}$

24. a. 1

b. Property of Reciprocals

25. a. 0

b. Multiplication Property of Zero

26. 1

27. a. $x^3\left(2x \cdot x \cdot \frac{x}{2} = x^3\right)$

b. Sample: $3x \cdot x \cdot \frac{x}{3}; 16x \cdot \frac{x}{4} \cdot \frac{x}{4}$

28. a. revolutions per minute; sample: a car engine

b. pounds per square inch; sample: air pressure in bicycle tires

29. a. January 2000; it will take 11.574 days to count to 1 million this way;

$1,000,000 \text{ sec.} \cdot \frac{1 \text{ min}}{60 \text{ sec}} \cdot \frac{1 \text{ h}}{60 \text{ min}} \cdot \frac{1 \text{ day}}{24 \text{ h}} = $

11.574 days

b. September 2031; it will take 11,574.1 days = 11574.1 days $\cdot \frac{1 \text{ year}}{365 \text{ days}} = 31.71$ yr = 31 yr 259.3 days to count to 1 billion.

c. It would take approximately 31,689 years to reach 1 trillion. You would not reach this number in your lifetime.

LESSON 2-5 pp. 96–101

1. a.

Years from present	Change in Brazil's rain forest compared to now
20	-276,000 km²
5	-69,000 km²
1	-13,800 km²
-1	13,800 km²
-5	69,000 km²

b. "-5 years from now" means 5 years ago.

2. a. a loss of 1.2 inches of topsoil or -1.2 in.

   b. 4 years $\cdot$ -0.3 $\frac{\text{in.}}{\text{year}}$

   c. 1.5 inches more

   d. -5 years $\cdot$ -0.3 $\frac{\text{in.}}{\text{year}}$

3. a. -18   **b.** -18xy

4. a. -36   **b.** -36ps

5. a. 35   **b.** 35t^2

6. a. 1   **b.** 1

7. a. 9   **b.** -9

   c. $\frac{-9}{11}$ **d.** $\frac{-9}{11k}$

8. -23 $\left(-3 \cdot (-2)^2 + 6 \cdot -2 + 1 = -12 + -12 + 1 = -23\right)$

9. The product is positive. (The product of two negative numbers is positive.)

10. The product is positive. (The product of an even number of negative numbers is positive.)

11. The product is negative. (The product of an odd number of negative numbers is negative and the product of a negative and a positive number is negative.)

12. 24

13. -1

14. a. i. 729   **ii.** -2187

       iii. 6561   **iv.** -19,683

   b. the even powers

   c. the odd powers

15. a. True $((-5)^3 = -5 \cdot -5 \cdot -5 = -125;$

   $-5^3 = -5 \cdot 5 \cdot 5 = -125;$

   $-125 = -125)$

   b. False $((-5)^4 = -5 \cdot -5 \cdot -5 \cdot -5 = 625;$

   $-5^4 = -5 \cdot 5 \cdot 5 \cdot 5 = -625;$

   $625 \neq -625)$

16. $4a^2$

17. $9x^2$

18. $-1000n^3$

19. $(2a)^2(-2a)^3 = 4a^2 \cdot -8a^3 = -32a^5$

20. a. $\frac{1}{3}$ **b.** $\frac{-1}{4}$

   c. $\frac{1}{5}$ **d.** $\frac{-1}{10}$

21. a. positive   **b.** negative

   c. positive   **d.** positive

   e. zero   **f.** negative

22. Since the exponent is even, the result is positive.

23. not a rate

24. rate (miles per gallon)

25. rate (miles per hour)

26. a. $14,400 (2 years = 24 months; 24 $\cdot$ $600 = $14,400)

   b. $7200y ($y$ years = 12y months; 12y $\cdot$ $600)

27. about 0.14 km

   $\left(\frac{50 \text{ km}}{\text{hour}} \cdot \frac{1 \text{ hour}}{60 \text{ min}} \cdot \frac{1 \text{ min}}{60 \text{ sec}} \cdot 10 \text{ sec} \approx 0.1389 \text{ km}\right)$

28. a. 10 ft = $3\frac{1}{3}$ yd; 36 ft = 12 yd;

   6 in. = $\frac{1}{2}$ ft = $\frac{1}{6}$ yd

   b. 7 cu yd $\left(\frac{10}{3} \cdot 12 \cdot \frac{1}{6} = \frac{120}{18} = 6\frac{2}{3} \text{ cu yd}\right)$

   c. $875 (7 $\cdot$ $125 = $875)

29. $\frac{9a}{7}$

30. $\sqrt{6}$

31. n being odd results in $(-1)^n = -1$; n being even results in $(-1)^n = 1$. Similarly, the number of about-faces being odd results in the soldier facing reverse. And the number of about-faces being even results in the soldier facing forward. We know facing reverse is the opposite of facing forward just as 1 is the opposite of negative 1.

LESSON 2-6   pp. 102–108

1. a. 10w = 16 oz

   b. $w = \frac{8}{5}$ oz

2. a. 6b

   b. Multiplication Property of Equality

3. Sample: It changes the coefficient of the variable to 1.

4. 18 rows (Solve 28r = 500; r = 17.86 or 18 rows.)

5. a. 5   **b.** $\frac{1}{5}$

   c. $\qquad 5n = 61$

$$\tfrac{1}{5} \cdot 5n = \tfrac{1}{5} \cdot 61$$

$$n = \tfrac{61}{5} = 12\tfrac{1}{5}$$

6. a. -32

   b. $-\frac{1}{32}$

   c. $\qquad -32x = 416$

$$-\tfrac{1}{32} \cdot -32x = -\tfrac{1}{32} \cdot 416$$

$$x = -13$$

7. a. $\frac{1}{4}$ **b.** 4

   c. $\qquad -12 = \tfrac{1}{4}p$

$$4 \cdot -12 = 4 \cdot \tfrac{1}{4} \cdot p$$

$$-48 = p$$

8. a. $\frac{3}{32}$ **b.** $\frac{32}{3}$

   c. $\qquad \tfrac{3}{32}A = \tfrac{3}{4}$

$$\tfrac{32}{3} \cdot \tfrac{3}{32}A = \tfrac{32}{3} \cdot \tfrac{3}{4}$$

$$A = 8$$

9. a. -4.2   **b.** $\frac{-1}{4.2}$

   c. $\qquad -210 = -4.2y$

$$\tfrac{-1}{4.2} \cdot -210 = \tfrac{-1}{4.2} \cdot (-4.2)y$$

$$50 = y$$

10. a. -16.5   **b.** $\frac{-1}{16.5}$

   c. $\qquad 36.3 = -16.5r$

$$\tfrac{-1}{16.5} \cdot 36.3 = \tfrac{-1}{16.5} \cdot (-16.5)r$$

$$-2.2 = r$$

11. $\frac{1}{a}$

12. no $\left(\tfrac{1}{3} \cdot \tfrac{1}{4} = \tfrac{1}{12} \right)$

13. .4 hours or 24 minutes $\left(270 \text{ miles} \cdot \dfrac{1 \text{ hr}}{60 \text{ miles}} = \right.$

   $4.5 \text{ hrs}; 4.9 - 4.5 = .4 \text{ hrs}; .4 \text{ hours} \cdot \dfrac{60 \text{ min}}{1 \text{ hour}} =$

   $\left. 24 \text{ min} \right)$

14. 196.6 miles $\left(1966 = r \cdot 10 \right.$

   $\left. r = \tfrac{1966}{10} = 196.6 \right)$

15. $\frac{d}{t} = r$ $\left(\text{Multiply both sides by } \tfrac{1}{t}. \right)$

16. a. $\qquad \tfrac{5x}{3} = 60$

$$\tfrac{3}{5} \cdot \tfrac{5x}{3} = \tfrac{3}{5} \cdot 60$$

$$x = 36$$

   b. $\qquad 60 = \tfrac{-5y}{3}$

$$\tfrac{-3}{5} \cdot 60 = \tfrac{-3}{5} \cdot \tfrac{-5}{3}y$$

$$-36 = y$$

17. a. 30.48

   b. Multiply both sides of the equation by 12 to get $12 \cdot 1$ in. $= 12 \cdot 2.54$ cm.

18. a. $12x$

   b. $\qquad 1.5 \cdot 8x = 300$

$$12x = 300$$

$$\tfrac{1}{12} \cdot 12x = \tfrac{1}{12} \cdot 300$$

$$x = 25$$

   c. $1.5(8 \cdot 25) = 1.5 \cdot 200 = 300$

$$1.5(200) = 300$$

$$300 = 300$$

19. $\qquad 6.5 = 5 \cdot 10x$

$$6.5 = 50x$$

$$\tfrac{1}{50} \cdot 6.5 = \tfrac{1}{50} \cdot 50x$$

$$0.13 = x$$

20. 5.3 hours $\left(\tfrac{3500}{660} = 5.3 \right)$

21. The box must be 8 cm high. $\left(\text{The base} \right.$ covers area $12.5 \cdot 5 = 62.5 \text{ cm}^2$, hence the height should be $\left. \tfrac{500}{62.5} = 8. \right)$

22. **a.** 12.41 cm $\left(\frac{39}{\pi} = 12.41$ rounded to the nearest hundredth$\right)$

b. $\frac{C}{\pi} = d$

23. $\frac{F}{m} = a$

24. .52 mile (cheetah: $d = 70\left(\frac{1}{60}\right) \approx 1.167$;

greyhound: $d = 39\left(\frac{1}{60}\right) = .65$; $1.167 - .65 \approx .52$)

25. **a.** y is positive.

b. y is negative.

c. $y = 0$

26. **a.** 256   **b.** -256

c. 256   **d.** -512

e. -512

27. 4.5 yd $\cdot$ 36 $\frac{\text{in.}}{\text{yd}}$ $\cdot$ 2.54 $\frac{\text{cm}}{\text{in.}}$ = 411.48 cm

28. 2 $\frac{\text{dribbles}}{\text{sec}}$ $\cdot$ $\frac{1}{4.5}$ $\frac{\text{sec}}{\text{ft}}$ $\cdot$ 60 ft = 26.7 dribbles

Round down to 26 for completed dribbles.

29. DP dollars

30. $\frac{-2}{21x}$

31. **a.** 660 ft^2 (Subdivide into rectangles with dimensions: 14 ft by 6 ft, 24 ft by 10 ft, and 14 ft by 24 ft.)

b. Sample: 14 $\cdot$ 6 + 24 $\cdot$ 10 + 14 $\cdot$ 24 = 660; and 32 $\cdot$ 30 $-$ 14.8 $-$ 8 $\cdot$ 10 $-$ 18 $\cdot$ 6 = 660 ft^2

c. 1320 ft^2

d. If a square floor plan, then the dimensions are $\sqrt{660}$ ft by $\sqrt{660}$ ft or about 25.7 ft by 25.7 ft.

32. **a.** Yes $(18 \leq 20)$

b. Yes $(19.5 \leq 20)$

c. No $(21 > 20)$

33. **a.** A is the area of a triangle, b is a side of that triangle, and h is the altitude to that side.

b. C is the circumference of a circle with radius r.

c. I is the simple interest earned on a principal of p dollars at an interest rate r for the time t.

1. Zero does not have a reciprocal.

2. **a.** The solution is 0.

b. {0}

3. **a.** There is no solution.

b. { } or ∅

4. **a.** The solution is all real numbers.

b. Set of real numbers

5. (d)   **6.** -1

7. $x = -40$ **8.** $y = 3$

9. $z = 0$

10. **a.** A = 0; B = 1.8   **b.** 80

c. NO SOLUTION

11. **a.** A = -1; B = 24   **b.** 60

c. SOLUTION IS -24

12. **a.** A = 0; B = 0   **b.** 70

c. ALL REAL NUMBERS

13. If L = 0 then N = 0.

14. **a.** $70 = 0t$

b. 0 times t must be 0, not 70.

15. Sample: You are traveling 13 mph. How long does it take you to go 0 miles?

16. **a.** $x = 18.5$ **b.** $x = -18.5$

17. $x = -15$

Check: $(6 - 7)(-15) = (-1)(-15) = 15$

18. Sample: $x^2 = 36$

19. **a.** $\qquad\qquad -4p = 12$

$$-\tfrac{1}{4} \cdot -4 \cdot p = -\tfrac{1}{4} \cdot 12$$

$$p = -3$$

Check: $-4(-3) = 12$

b. $\qquad\qquad 12p = -4$

$$\tfrac{1}{12} \cdot 12 \cdot p = \tfrac{1}{12} \cdot -4$$

$$p = -\tfrac{1}{3}$$

Check: $12\left(-\tfrac{1}{3}\right) = -\tfrac{12}{3} = -4$

20. $\frac{7}{9}q = 140$

$\frac{9}{7} \cdot \frac{7}{9}q = \frac{9}{7} \cdot 140$

$q = 180$

21. $\frac{3n}{5} = 2$

$\frac{5}{3} \cdot \frac{3n}{5} = \frac{5}{3} \cdot 2$

$n = \frac{10}{3}$

22. $20 = 0.04m$

$\frac{1}{0.04} \cdot 20 = \frac{1}{0.04} \cdot 0.04 \cdot m$

$500 = m$

23. $\frac{1}{3} = 4x$

$\frac{1}{4} \cdot \frac{1}{3} = \frac{1}{4} \cdot 4x$

$\frac{1}{12} = x$

24. 3 crates (There are 50,000 packages in 834 boxes in 35 cases in 3 crates.)

25. Sample: $8x = c$

26. $\frac{3}{4}n = 165$

$\frac{4}{3} \cdot \frac{3}{4}n = \frac{4}{3} \cdot 165$

$n = 220$

220 employees

27. $340h = 5100$

$\frac{1}{340} \cdot 340h = \frac{1}{340} \cdot 5100$

$h = 15$

28. a. 1 (There are an even number of factors.)
b. -1
c. If the exponent of -1 is odd, the result is -1. If the exponent is even, the result is 1.

29. 7608 m^2 (Subdivide the field into rectangles with dimensions 75 m by 40 m, 64 m by 36 m, and 64 m by 36 m.)

30.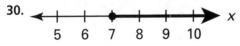

31. a. Yes **b.** Yes
c. Yes
d. No (The solution is all x such that $x > -5$.)

32. a. $\frac{1}{n}x = 10$
b. $x = 10n$
c. $\frac{1}{100}x = 10$
d. $x = 1000$
e. As n gets larger the equation is getting closer to $0x = 10$. The solutions are increasing without bound.

LESSON 2-8 $\hspace{2cm}$ pp. 114–118

1. $120 < 180$
2. $8 < 12$
3. $-80 > -120$
4. a. $8x \le 42$

$\frac{1}{8} \cdot 8x \le \frac{1}{8} \cdot 42$

$x \le 5.25$

b. $\{5.25, 4, 0\}$

c.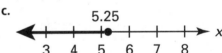

5. a. i. No $\hspace{1.5cm}$ **ii.** No
  iii. Yes $\hspace{1.3cm}$ **iv.** No
  v. No $\hspace{1.4cm}$ **vi.** No

b. $x > 2$

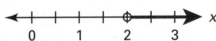

6. Part 2 involves multiplying by a negative number which requires changing the direction of the inequality.

7. $>$ $\hspace{2cm}$ **8.** $\le$

9. $5x \ge 10$

$\frac{1}{5} \cdot 5x \ge \frac{1}{5} \cdot 10$

$x \ge 2$

Check: Does $5 \cdot 2 = 10$? Yes.
$\hspace{1.3cm}$ Try a number that works in $x \ge 2$.
$\hspace{1.3cm}$ We use 4. Is $5 \cdot 4 \ge 10$?
$\hspace{1.3cm}$ Yes, $20 \ge 10$.

10. $-3y < 300$

$-\frac{1}{3} \cdot (-3)y > -\frac{1}{3} \cdot 300$

$y > -100$

Check: Is $-3 \cdot -100 = 300$? Yes.
Try a number that works
in $y > -100$. We use 0.
Is $-3 \cdot 0 < 300$? Yes, $0 < 300$.

11. $-4A < -124$

$-\frac{1}{4}(-4)A > -\frac{1}{4} \cdot -124$

$A > 31$

Check: Is $-4 \cdot 31 = -124$? Yes.
Try a number that works
in $A > 31$. We use 40.
Is $-4 \cdot 40 < -124$?
Yes, $-160 < -124$.

12. $13 > 2z$

$\frac{1}{2} \cdot 13 > \frac{1}{2} \cdot 2z$

$6.5 > z$

Check: Is $2 \cdot 6.5 = 13$? Yes. Try a
number that works in $z < 6.5$. We
use 1. Is $13 > 2 \cdot 1$? Yes, $13 > 2$.

13. $-2 \leq 5a$

$\frac{1}{5} \cdot -2 \leq \frac{1}{5} \cdot 5a$

$-\frac{2}{5} \leq a$

Check: Is $5 \cdot -\frac{2}{5} = -2$? Yes. Try

a number that works in $a \geq -\frac{2}{5}$.

We use 0. Is $-2 \leq 5 \cdot 0$. Yes, $-2 \leq 0$.

14. $0.09 > -9c$

$-\frac{1}{9} \cdot 0.09 < -\frac{1}{9} \cdot -9c$

$-0.01 < c$

Check: Is $-9 \cdot -0.01 = 0.09$? Yes. Try a
number that works in $c > -0.01$.
We use 0. Is $0.09 > -9 \cdot 0$? Yes,
$0.09 > 0$.

15. The width is less than 7.7 cm.
(Solve: $20w < 154; w < 7.7$)

16. The length of the foundation should be less
than or equal to 160 ft.
(Solve: $125l \leq 20000; l < 160$)

17. The auditorium has at least 32 rows.
(Solve: $48r > 1500$, $r > 31.25$ where r is a
whole number.)

18. At most 90 people can attend the dinner.
(Solve: $27.5p < 2500$, $p \leq 90.90$ where p is
a whole number.)

19. $m > -8$

20. $2 \leq n$

21. $\frac{1}{4}x \geq 96$

$4 \cdot \frac{1}{4}x \geq 4 \cdot 96$

$x \geq 384$

22. $\frac{2}{3}p \leq \frac{1}{4}$

$\frac{3}{2} \cdot \frac{2}{3}p \leq \frac{3}{2} \cdot \frac{1}{4}$

$p \leq \frac{3}{8}$

23. $x < 272$ $\left(\text{Solve: } \frac{3}{4}x < 204\right)$

24. $x = 4$ (from Clue 2: $x < 5$; from Clue 3:
$x > 3$; from Clue 1: There is only one integer
between 3 and 5.)

25. **a.** $n = 4$ **b.** no solution
    c. $n = -2$ **d.** $n = -\frac{1}{2}$

26. $d = 30$

27. $x = -10$

28. There are 60 notes in the five measures.
($4 \cdot 3 = 12$ notes per measure, $12 \cdot 5 = 60$
notes in the five measures)

29. $\frac{x^2}{15}$

30. 57 in^3 (The dimensions of the box are 2 by
2.5 by 11.4.)

31. $A = \frac{1}{2}s^2$

32. $3^2x^3y^5$

33. Sample: $x = -0.23$

1. A person can enter through a north gate and leave through gate G in 4 ways.

2.

	E	**F**	**I**
A	(A,E)	(A,F)	(A,I)
B	(B,E)	(B,F)	(B,I)
C	(C,E)	(C,F)	(C,I)

3. **a.** There are 81 ways that a person could enter through any gate and leave through any gate. $(9 \cdot 9 = 81)$

   b. There are 72 ways that a person could enter through any gate and leave through any other gate. $(9 \cdot 8 = 72)$

4. Multiplication and Counting Principle: If one choice can be made in m ways and a second choice can be made in n ways, then there are mn ways of making the first choice followed by the second choice.

5. In mathematics, a procedure is said to be *elegant* if it is clever and simple at the same time.

6. **a.** There are $4 \cdot 2 \cdot 2 = 16$ choices.

   b.

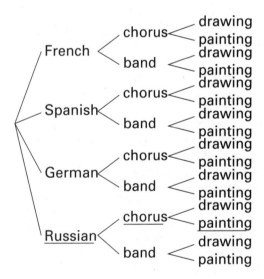

   c. See underlined portions in part **b**.

7. **a.** There are $2^{20} = 1,048,576$ ways to answer the test.

   b. The chances of getting all the right answers is $\frac{1}{1,048,576} \approx .000001$.

8. **a.** There are $x \cdot x \cdot 2 \cdot 2 \cdot 2$ ways to answer the test.

   b. There are $2^3 x^2$ ways to answer the test.

9. There are $2^5 q^5 = 32q^5$ ways to answer the test.

10. **a.** 2 choices for the first letter

    b. 26 choices for the second letter

    c. There are 35,152 different 4-letter station names possible. $(2 \cdot 26 \cdot 26 \cdot 26)$

11.

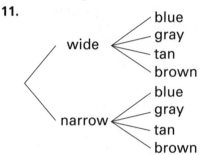

12. **a.**

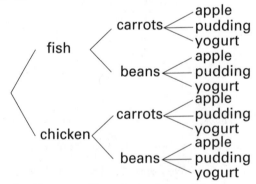

    b. There are 12 such meals possible.

13. **a.** Possible "Royal Couples" are:
    AJ, AK, AL, BJ, BK, BL, CJ, CK, CL, DJ, DK, and DL.

    b. The probability that the Royal Couple is Aram and Kara is $\frac{1}{12}$.

14. a. There were 144 possible area codes before 1989. $(8 \cdot 2 \cdot 9 = 144)$

b. There were 200 possible area codes after 1989. $(10 \cdot 2 \cdot 10 = 200)$

c. There were 56 possibilities added by the policy change.

15. Sample: A girl can choose from 2 jackets, 3 skirts, and 5 blouses. How many 3-piece outfits are possible?

16. a. 64 (There are 6 pits to toss and each can land one of two ways or $2^6 = 64$)

b. $\frac{2}{64} = \frac{1}{32}$ (There are 2 out of 64 possible ways to score 5 points.)

17. a. 2 sets of answers

b. $2 \cdot 2 = 4$ sets of answers

c. $2 \cdot 2 \cdot 2 = 8$ sets of answers

d. $2^{10} = 1024$ sets of answers

e. 2^n sets of answers

18. $j < \frac{13}{4}$

19. $k = -\frac{1}{25}$

20. $m > -\frac{1}{18}$

21. $n = 1200$

22. a. $\frac{1}{3}I < 12750$

b. $I < 38250$

23. a. no solution

b. $x = 0$

c. $x < 0$

d. $x > 0$

24. a. $8x$

b. $x = 50$

c. Sample: Part **a** asks for the answer to a multiplication question. Part **b** asks for the solution to an equation.

25. $x = -102$ $(x = 17 \cdot -6 = -102)$

26. 5.6 acres would produce a harvest of 224 bales of hay. $\left(\frac{1}{40} \cdot 224 = 5.6\right)$

27. $2x + 48$ (separate into rectangles $4 \cdot 12$ and $2 \cdot x$)

28. $6\left(3 \cdot -\frac{7}{3} \cdot -\frac{32}{5}\right) = \frac{1344}{5}$

29. a. $\left(-\frac{1}{2}\right)^3 = -\frac{1}{8}$

b. $3 \cdot -\frac{1}{2} + 4 = -\frac{3}{2} + 4 = \frac{5}{2}$

c. $-8\left(-\frac{1}{2}\right)^4 = -8 \cdot \frac{1}{16} = -\frac{1}{2}$

30. $\frac{3}{32}$

31. a. National Aeronautics & Space Administration

b. United Nations International Children's Fund

c. Central Intelligence Agency

d. International Business Machines

e. intercontinental ballistic missile

f. American Federation of Labor-Congress of Industrial Organizations

g. National Football League

h. North Atlantic Treaty Organization

i. United Nations Educational, Scientific and Cultural Organization

32. No, there are $26 \cdot 26 \cdot 26 \cdot 26 = 456,976$ ways, which is less than a half million.

LESSON 2-10 pp. 125–130

1.

1st place	2nd place	3rd place
Washington	Jefferson	Lincoln
Washington	Lincoln	Jefferson
Jefferson	Washington	Lincoln
Jefferson	Lincoln	Washington
Lincoln	Washington	Jefferson
Lincoln	Jefferson	Washington

2. There are 23 other orders possible.

3. 6!

4. the product of the integers from n down to 1

5. a. $1! = 1$ **b.** $2! = 2$
   c. $3! = 6$ **d.** $4! = 24$
   e. $5! = 120$ **f.** $6! = 720$

6. $15! \approx 1.3077 \cdot 10^{12}$

7. $30! \approx 2.6525 \cdot 10^{32}$

8. A permutation is an arrangement of objects in order.

9. There are five singers who could be asked to sing first. There are only four singers left who could be asked to sing second. Then there are only three singers left who could be asked to sing third. Then there are two singers left who could be asked to sing second, and the remaining person will be last.

10. 18! ways or about $6.402 \cdot 10^{15}$

11. $n!$

12. **a.** $\frac{11!}{9!} = \frac{11 \cdot 10 \cdot 9!}{9!} = 11 \cdot 10 = 110$

    b. Sample: key in 11 $\boxed{x!}$ $\boxed{\div}$ 9 $\boxed{x!}$ $\boxed{=}$

13. 120 $(6 \cdot 5 \cdot 4 = 120)$

14. 25

15. 20! or about $2.4 \cdot 10^{18}$

16. **a.** $8 \cdot 7 = 56$

    b. $8! = 40,320$

17. **a.** True

    b. True

    c. $n! = n(n-1)!$

18. **a.** $\frac{10!}{9!} = 10$

    b. Sample: $\frac{11!}{10!} = 11$

    c. $\frac{n!}{(n-1)!} = n$

19. Sample: $100^{100} = 100 \cdot 100 \cdot 100 \cdot \ldots \cdot 100$ whereas $100! = 100 \cdot 99 \cdot 98 \cdot \ldots \cdot 1$, so you get a bigger product from 100^{100}.

20. **a.** $3 \cdot 2 \cdot 5 = 30$ choices

    b. You would have 6 more choices.

21. $\frac{1}{1600}$ (There are $4 \cdot 4 \cdot 4 \cdot 5 \cdot 5 = 1600$ possible ways to answer the test.)

22. **a.** $a = -\frac{7}{2}$ **b.** $a = -\frac{2}{7}$

    c. $a \geq -\frac{2}{7}$ **d.** $a \leq -\frac{2}{7}$

23. **a.** Sample: Adam's total earnings for 10 weeks was $723. How much did he earn each week?

    b. $x = \$72.30$

24. **a.** Sample: If you can read $2\frac{1}{2}$ pages a minute and the chapter is at most 130 pages long, how many minutes will it take to read the chapter?

    b. $130 \geq 2.5x$

    $\frac{1}{2.5} \cdot 130 \geq \frac{1}{2.5} \cdot 2.5x$

    $52 \geq x$

    At most 52 minutes

25. $\frac{3}{8}y < \frac{5}{4}$

    $\frac{8}{3} \cdot \frac{3}{8}y < \frac{8}{3} \cdot \frac{5}{4}$

    $y < \frac{10}{3}$

26. $(2-3)t \leq 8$

    $-t \leq 8$

    $t \geq -8$

27. Multiplication Property of Equality

28. 14 hours $\left(\$101.92 \cdot \frac{1 \text{ hour}}{\$7.28} = 14 \text{ hours}\right)$

29. $16000\frac{\text{grains}}{\text{in}^3} \cdot 1728\frac{\text{in}^3}{\text{ft}^3} \cdot 25 \text{ ft}^3 = 6.912 \cdot 10^8$ or 691,200,000 grains in a 25 cubic-foot sandbox

30. $\frac{233m^5}{50n^3}$

31. Sample: $3 \cdot 4 = 4 \cdot 3$

32. If the volume of one solid is xyz, then the volume of the other is $\frac{1}{2}x \cdot \frac{2}{3}y \cdot \frac{3}{4}z = \frac{1}{4}xyz$ or $\frac{1}{4}$ the volume of the second solid.

33. **a.** Sample: $2 + 5 > 2$

    b. Sample: $2 + -1 > 2$ is not true.

    c. $b > 0$; positive numbers

34. Answers will vary.

35. 10

36. Most calculators will give an error message. n must be an integer.

37. **a.** EQUAL
    RADII
    SPHERE
    ORIGIN

    b. LINE

CHAPTER 2

1. $\frac{22!}{20!} = 22 \cdot 21 = 462$

2. False. $(-5)^{10}$ is positive whereas -5^{10} is negative.
$((-5)^{10} = 9{,}765{,}625$, but $-5^{10} = -9{,}765{,}625)$

3. $\frac{25}{3y}$

4. $\frac{22}{x^3}$

5. $-a^2$

6. Sample: $7 \cdot 5 = 5 \cdot 7 = 35$

7. $50x = 10$; $x = \frac{10}{50} = \frac{1}{5}$

8. $\frac{1}{4}k = -24$; $k = -96$

9. $15 \leq 3m$; $m \geq \frac{15}{3}$; $m \geq 5$

10. $-y \leq -2$; $y \geq 2$

11. a. $-2n < 18$; $n > -9$

   b.
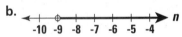

12. $\quad -48 = -\frac{4}{3}n$

$$-\frac{3}{4} \cdot -48 = -\frac{3}{4} \cdot -\frac{4}{3}n$$

$$36 = n$$

Check: $-\frac{4}{3} \cdot 36 = -48$

13. $-\frac{n}{3}$

14. $\frac{1}{3.2} = 0.3125 = \frac{5}{16}$

15. $a \cdot -\frac{1}{a} = -1$

16. 8 in. $= 8 \cdot 2.54$ cm $= 20.32$ cm

17. $205,200 ($24{,}000 \cdot 0.57 \cdot 15 = 205{,}200$)$

18. $4n \cdot 8n \cdot 1.5n = 48n^3$ cubic units

19. 5.45 hours or 5 hr 27 min
$\left(300 \text{ miles} \cdot \frac{1 \text{ hour}}{55 \text{ miles}}\right)$

20. 6175 ft^2 $(80^2 - 15^2 = 6400 - 225 = 6175)$

21. a. positive

   b. negative $\times$ negative = positive

22. a. negative

   b. odd power of negative number

23. a. $\frac{5x}{6}, \frac{3y}{4}$

   b. area: $\frac{5x}{6} \cdot \frac{3y}{4} = \frac{5xy}{8}$

24. a. Sample: $0x = 48$

   b. Sample: For any value of x, $0 \cdot x = 0$. So $0 \cdot x$ cannot equal 48.

25. a. $40r = 600$

   b. There will be 15 rows.

26. $7 \cdot 5 \cdot 3 = 105$ program choices

27. $5! = 120$ possible arrangements

28. $2^{25} = 33{,}554{,}432$

CHAPTER 2

1. $\frac{9x}{10} \cdot \frac{3}{4x} = \frac{27}{40}$

2. $\frac{3}{5} \cdot \frac{n}{2} = \frac{3n}{10}$

3. $\frac{x}{y}$

4. $2x^2$

5. $3n$

6. $\frac{5y^2z}{3}$

7. $\frac{r}{3}$

8. $-\frac{3}{2x^2}$

9. 270

10. -24

11. -8

12. 625

13. negative (odd number of negative factors)

14. positive (even number of negative factors)

15. a. 36

   b. -36

   c. -216

   d. -216

16. False. $(-9)^6 = 531441$, whereas $-9^6 = -531441$.

17. positive

18. If two numbers have the same sign, then their product is positive. Otherwise, the product is negative.

19.
$$2.4m = 360$$
$$\frac{1}{2.4} \cdot 2.4m = 360 \cdot \frac{1}{2.4}$$
$$m = 150$$
Check: $2.4 \cdot 150 = 360$

20.
$$-\frac{1}{2}k = -10$$
$$-2 \cdot -\frac{1}{2}k = -10 \cdot -2$$
$$k = 20$$
Check: $-\frac{1}{2} \cdot 20 = -10$

21.
$$-2 = 0.4h$$
$$\frac{1}{0.4} \cdot -2 = \frac{1}{0.4} \cdot 0.4h$$
$$-5 = h$$
Check: $0.4 \cdot -5 = -2$

22.
$$12 = 36m$$
$$\frac{1}{36} \cdot 12 = \frac{1}{36} \cdot 36m$$
$$\frac{1}{3} = m$$
Check: $12 = 36 \cdot \frac{1}{3}$

23.
$$\frac{5}{3}n = -45$$
$$\frac{3}{5} \cdot \frac{5}{3}n = -45 \cdot \frac{3}{5}$$
$$n = -27$$
Check: $\frac{5}{3} \cdot -27 = -45$

24.
$$4(5x) = 0$$
$$\frac{1}{4} \cdot 4(5x) = \frac{1}{4} \cdot 0$$
$$5x = 0$$
$$\frac{1}{5} \cdot 5x = \frac{1}{5} \cdot 0$$
$$x = 0$$
Check: $4(5 \cdot 0) = 0$

25. $g = \frac{d}{c}$

26. $y = \frac{2z}{k}$

27. Sample: $0 \cdot h = 13$

28. Sample: $0 \cdot t = 0$

29.
$$8m \le 16$$
$$\frac{1}{8} \cdot 8m \le \frac{1}{8} \cdot 16$$
$$m \le 2$$
Check: Does $8 \cdot 2 = 16$? Yes. Pick a value that works in $m \le 2$, we pick -1. Is $8 \cdot -1 < 16$? Yes

30.
$$-250 < 5y$$
$$\frac{1}{5} \cdot -250 < \frac{1}{5} \cdot 5y$$
$$-50 < y$$
$$y > -50$$
Check: Does $5 \cdot -50 = -250$? Yes. Pick a value that works in $y > -50$; we pick 2. Is $-250 < 5 \cdot 2$? Yes, $-250 < 10$.

31.
$$-6u > 12$$
$$-\frac{1}{6} \cdot -6u < 12 \cdot -\frac{1}{6}$$
$$u < -2$$
Check: Does $-6 \cdot -2 = 12$? Yes. Pick a value that works in $u < -2$; we pick -4. Is $-6 \cdot -4 > 12$? Yes, $24 > 12$.

32.
$$-x \ge -1$$
$$-1 \cdot -x \le -1 \cdot -1$$
$$x \le 1$$
Check: Does $-(1) = -1$? Yes. Pick a value that works in $x \le 1$; we pick 0. Is $-(0) \ge -1$? Yes, $0 \ge -1$.

33. a.
$$-\frac{1}{2}g \ge 5$$
$$-2 \cdot -\frac{1}{2}g \le 5 \cdot -2$$
$$g \le -10$$

b.
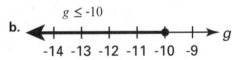

34. a.
$$3.6h < 720$$
$$\frac{1}{3.6} \cdot 3.6h < \frac{1}{3.6} \cdot 720$$
$$h < 200$$

b.
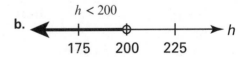

35. $4! + 3! = 24 + 6 = 30$

36. $\frac{16!}{14!} = 16 \cdot 15 = 240$

37. $15! \approx 1.3077 \cdot 10^{12}$

38. $(4!)! = 24! \approx 6.2045 \cdot 10^{23}$

39. **a.** False

   b. $\frac{10!}{10} = 9!$; $9! \neq 1!$

40. **a.** True

   b. $18! = 18 \cdot 17 \cdot 16 \cdot \ldots \cdot 2 \cdot 1 = 18 \cdot 17!$

41. $\frac{102!}{99!} = 102 \cdot 101 \cdot 100 \cdot = 1,030,200$

42. Sample: $2 \cdot (3 \cdot 7) = (2 \cdot 3) \cdot 7$

43. **a.** $2200x$

   b. Commutative and Associative Properties of Multiplication

44. Commutative Property of Multiplication

45. $-\frac{1}{2}$

46. $\frac{5}{3}$

47. $\frac{4}{3x}$

48. $a \cdot \frac{1}{a} = 1$

49. Multiplication Property of Equality

50. $x > -\frac{1}{3}$

51. opposite

52. 48 ft^2 (The dimensions of the colored regions are 3 ft by 8 ft and 4 ft by 6 ft.)

53. **a.** $\frac{1}{2}\ell$ by $\frac{2}{3}w$

   b. The area of the Cohens' garden is ℓw sq units and the area of the Banjerils' garden is $\frac{1}{3}\ell w$ square units. The Banjerils' garden is $\frac{1}{3}$ the size of the Cohens' garden.

54. A strip $83\frac{1}{3}$ ft long can be seeded with one box.

55. 31.25 ft high (If the area of the base is 3200 ft^2, the height should be $\frac{100,000}{3200} = 31.25$ ft.)

56. $12 \cdot 15 \cdot 8 = 1440$ cm^3

57. 720 cubes of sugar would fit. (The volume of the solid would be $10s \cdot 12s \cdot 6s = 720s^3$ and the volume of each sugar cube is s^3, hence $\frac{720s^3}{s^3} = 720$.)

58. $450k$ dollars

59. $\frac{\$1.00}{\text{gallon}} \cdot \frac{1 \text{ gallon}}{30 \text{ miles}} = \frac{\$0.033}{\text{mile}}$ or $3\frac{1}{3}\text{¢}$ per mile

60. $24 \cdot 43560 = 1,045,440$ ft^2

61. $3\frac{\text{cuts}}{\text{hour}} \cdot 5 \text{ hours} \cdot 15\frac{\text{dollars}}{\text{cut}} = 225$ dollars

62. $24B$ books fit on a bookcase; $24BC$ books fit on C bookcases.

63. 446 miles $\cdot \frac{1 \text{ hour}}{50 \text{ miles}} = 8.92$ hours or 8 hr 55 min

64. $\frac{\$550}{\$45} \approx 12.2$; he can stay at most 12 days at the hotel.

65. **a.** $\frac{1}{2}$ second per revolution

   b. It takes a pirouetting ballet dancer $\frac{1}{2}$ second to make one revolution.

66. $\frac{\$75.30}{\text{carton}} \cdot \frac{1 \text{ carton}}{24 \text{ box}} \approx \frac{\$3.14}{\text{box}}$

67. $24^3 = 13,824$ 3-letter monograms

68. $5^{10} = 9765625$ different sets of answers

69. $18! \approx 6.4 \cdot 10^{15}$ different orders

70. $30! \approx 2.65 \cdot 10^{32}$ different ways

71. fs different types are possible.

72. $p!$ different ways

73. Commutative Property of Multiplication

74. $\frac{1}{2} \cdot \frac{2}{3} = \frac{2}{6} = \frac{1}{3}$

75. **a.**

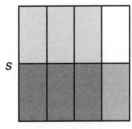

   b. $\frac{s}{2} \cdot \frac{3s}{4} = \frac{3s^2}{8}$

76. 704 ft^2 (Subdivide the region into rectangles with dimensions 36 ft by 16 ft and 16 ft by 8 ft.)

77. $8k \cdot 6k \cdot \frac{k}{2} = 24k^3$

78. $.3m \cdot .45m \cdot 4m = 0.54m^3$

79. 2600 cells

80. 736 dots (32 columns and 23 rows; $32 \cdot 23 = 736$)

CHAPTER 2

REFRESHER
p. 139

1. 7.8

2. 133.56

3. 11.0239

4. $1\frac{1}{2} + 2\frac{1}{4} = 1\frac{2}{4} + 2\frac{1}{4} = 3\frac{3}{4}$

5. $\frac{2}{3} + 8\frac{1}{3} = 8\frac{3}{3} = 9$

6. $\frac{2}{5} + \frac{1}{6} + \frac{3}{7} = \frac{84}{210} + \frac{35}{210} + \frac{90}{210} = \frac{209}{210}$

7. 18%

8. 31.2%

9. 11.03 cm

10. 2.3 km

11. $2'3'' + 9'' = 2'12'' = 3'$

12. $6' + 11'' + 4'' = 6'15'' = 7'3''$

13. 30 oz + 8 lb = 1 lb 14 oz + 8 lb = 9 lb 14 oz or 158 oz

14. 4 lb 13 oz + 2 lb 12 oz = 6 lb 25 oz = 7 lb 9 oz

15. 24

16. -15

17. 1

18. 13

19. -4

20. -16

21. $4 + -7 = -3$

22. $-3 + -4 = -7$

23–31.

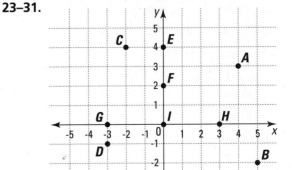

32. $x + 3 = 11$

$x = 11 + -3$

$x = 8$

33. $9 + z = 40$

$z = 40 + -9$

$z = 31$

34. $665 + w = 1072$

$w = 1072 + -665$

$w = 407$

35. $7 = m + 2$

$m = 7 + -2$

$m = 5$

36. $2000 = n + 1461$

$n = 2000 + -1461$

$n = 539$

37. $472 = 173 + s$

$s = 472 + -173$

$s = 299$

38. $n + 75 = 2000$

$n = 2000 + -75$

$n = 1925$

CHAPTER 3
ADDITION IN ALGEBRA

1. $120 + 95 + 2 \cdot 70 + 1.5 \cdot 150 =$
   $120 + 95 + 140 + 225 = 580$ calories

2. The Putting-Together Model for Addition: If a quantity x is put together with a quantity y with the same units, and there is no overlap, then the result is the quantity $x + y$.

3. In 1994, both the New York and New Orleans plants show a decrease in profits.

4. The combined profits of both plants in 1988 were approximately \$110,000.

5. True (Commutative Property of Addition)

6. $72.50 + 23.75 + 20 + E = 150.00$ or
   $E = 150.00 - (72.50 + 23.75 + 20)$

7. **a.**

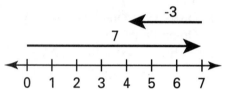

   b. a gain of 4 yards $(7 + -3 = 4)$

8. $T° + 5°$ or $5° + T°$

9. $28 + (k + 30) = k + (28 + 30) = k + 58$

10. $(p + -139) + 639 = p + (-139 + 639) = p + 500$

11. (a)

12. (c)

13. Sample: $5 + 3a = 3a + 5$

14. Sample: $(a + 4) + 1 = a + (4 + 1) = a + 5$

15. $x° + -3° + 5°$

16.

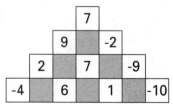

17. **a.** $A + 3$
    b. $A + -4$

18. **a.** about $13 + 17$ million or about 30 million males
    b. about $28 + 32$ million or about 60 million people
    c. Sample: More than half the number of students who completed 4 years of high school completed 4 or more years of college.

19. $50 + x = 54$

20. **a.** $24 \text{ in}^2 + x \text{ in}^2 + 18 \text{ in}^2 = 54 \text{ in}^2$
    b. $42 + x = 54; x = 12$
    c. The rectangle with area 24 in^2 is 6 in. by w in. $(A = 24 = 6w; w = 4 \text{ in.})$
    The rectangle with area 18 in^2 is 5 in. by b in. $(A = 18 = 5b; b = 3.6 \text{ in.})$
    The rectangle with area x or 12 in^2 is 5 in. by t in. $(A = 12 = 5t; t = 2.4 \text{ in.})$

21. $M + 4.25 < 10.5$

22. $(x + 4) + (5 + y) = (x + y) + (4 + 5) = x + y + 9$

23. $(a + -2) + (b + 7) = (a + b) + (-2 + 7) = a + b + 5$

24. $49.95 + 59.28 + 0.05 + 0.72 = (49.95 + 0.05) + (59.28 + 0.72) = 50 + 60 = 110$

25. **a.** The multiplicative identity is 1.
    b. Sample: When you multiply a number by 1, the product is the same as (or identical to) the number.

26. **a.**

x	y
5	25

   b. $y = x^2$

27. $12^2 + 5^2 = x^2$
    $144 + 25 = x^2$
    $169 = x^2$
    $13 = x$

28. perimeter $= 5 + 4 + BD = 9 + \sqrt{41}$
    $\left(BD^2 = 5^2 + 4^2 = 41; BD = \sqrt{41} \right)$

29. **a.** 12.6   **b.** 0
    c. 0

30. **a.** $.16 \cdot 24 = 3.84$
    b. $.16 \cdot 2400 = 384$
    c. $.16 \cdot 24,000,000 = 3,840,000$

31. Sample: When salt is added to water, most of the salt will dissolve in the water. Thus, there won't be a full cup of solution.

1. **a.** -10

   b. Adding zero to a number does not change that number's value.

   c. 1

2. opposite

3. 0

4. $(x + -93.2) + 93.2$
   $= x + (-93.2 + 93.2)$
   $= x + 0$
   $= x$

5. $-(-7) = 7$

6. $-41 + -(-41) = -41 + 41 = 0$

7. **a.** $-(-x) = x$

   b. Any negative value such as -6

8. Property of Opposites

9. Additive Identity Property

10. In four years you will still be the same age as your friend.

11. Five years ago you were the same age as your friend.

12. Addition Property of Equality: For all real numbers a, b, and c, if $a = b$, then $a + c = b + c$.

13. **a.** -42

    b. $m + 42 + -42 = 87 + -42$
    $m + 0 = 45$
    $m = 45$
    Check: $45 + 42 = 87$

14. $\quad -12 + y = -241$
    $12 + -12 + y = 12 + -241$
    $0 + y = -229$
    $y = -229$
    Check: $-12 + -229 = -241$

15. $\quad z + 14 = 60$
    $z + 14 + -14 = 60 + -14$
    $z + 0 = 46$
    $z = 46$
    Check: $46 + 14 = 60$

16. Addition Property of Equality

17. Additive Identity Property

18. **a.** $\$72.95 = n + \$35.00$

    b. $\$72.95 + -\$35.00 = n + \$35.00 + -\$35.00$
    $\$37.95 = n + 0$
    $\$37.95 = n$

19. $\quad\quad x^2 + 15^2 = 17^2$
    $x^2 + 15^2 - 15^2 = 17^2 + 15^2$
    $x^2 = 289 - 225$
    $x^2 = 64$
    $x = \sqrt{64}$
    $x = 8$

20. Sample: If you spend $9, then earn $9, you will have the same amount of money that you started with.

21. **a.** 3.14

    b. Opposite of Opposites Property or the Op-op Property

22. $-(-8 + -10) = -(-18) = 18$

23. $\quad\quad 15.2 = f + 2.15$
    $15.2 + -2.15 = f + 2.15 + -2.15$
    $13.05 = f + 0$
    $13.05 = f$
    Check: $13.05 + 2.15 = 15.2$

24. $\quad C + -8 + -5 = -15$
    $C + -13 = -15$
    $C + -13 + 13 = -15 + 13$
    $C + 0 = -2$
    $C = -2$
    Check: $-2 + -8 + -5 = -15$

25. **a.** $17 + C = -12$

    b. $17 + -17 + C = -12 + -17$
    $C = -29$

    c. $17 + -29 = -12$

26. **a.** $562 + A = 1321$

    b. $562 + -562 + A = 1321 + -562$
    $A = 759$

    c. $562 + 759 = 1321$

27. $40 - n + 2n = (40 + n)$ records

28. a. $9 \text{ cm} \cdot 8 \text{ cm} + k \text{ cm}^2 + 15 \text{ cm}^2$
     $= 72 \text{ cm}^2 + k \text{ cm}^2 + 15 \text{ cm}^2$
     $= 87 \text{ cm}^2 + k \text{ cm}^2$

  b. Putting-Together Model

29. (b)

30. a.

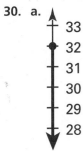

  b. $x \leq 32$

31. Sample: a line that goes neither up nor down; it is level with the horizon.

32. perpendicular

33. $A = (1, 4)$; $B = (5, 2)$; $C = (-2, 2)$;
$D = (-5, 0)$; $E = (0, -2)$; $F = (-5, -3)$;
$G = (3, -3)$; $H = (3, 0)$

34. a. Sample: a fall in the price for a share of stock; a rise in the price for a share of stock

  b. Sample: the number of seconds before a rocket is launched; the number of seconds after a rocket is launched

  c. Sample: three under par in a tournament; three over par in a tournament

  d. Sample: amount of national debt; amount of national profit

---

LESSON 3-3   pp. 155–162

1. The number lines used in a coordinate graph are called the axes.

2. (60, 30)

3. a. 2

  b. Beth spent 60 minutes and Gary spent 90 minutes.

4. The more time students spent watching television, the less time they spent doing homework.

5. to simplify the labeling of the intervals along the vertical axis of the graph

6. 1975   **7.** $141 billion

8. a. (-3, 1)   **b.** Julie

9. Bill lives 1.4 miles east and 2.9 miles south of the Town center.

10. 16 minutes

11. a. L **b.** J

  c. American; the point for the average American student falls in the middle of the scatterplot.

12. a.

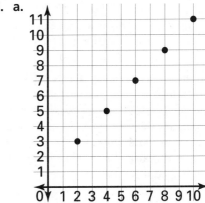

  b. 101

  c. $m + 1$

13. a.

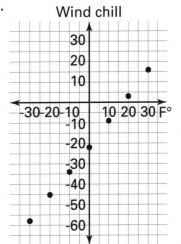

  b. Sample: For every 10° drop in temperature, the wind chill drops about 12°.

14. (a)

15. (c)

16. Sample: The water has temperature of 70° when the pot is placed on the stove. After 5 minutes, it begins to boil and continues boiling for 3 minutes. When the pot is taken off the stove, the water cools to room temperature after another 18 minutes.

17. about $1\frac{3}{4}$ hours

18. record album; in 1972, the average American worked about 2.4 hours to buy an album, while in 1982 about 1.3 hours of work bought an album. This is a change of 1.1 hours. No other item had a greater decrease.

19. (b)

20. **a.** Sample: Long distance rates decreased significantly.

   b. Sample: In 1972 the cost was about 24 minutes of work; in 1982, about 12 minutes of work; and in 1992, about 6 minutes of work. So in 2002, the cost may be about 3 minutes of work.

21. **a.** -17.3

   b. Property of Opposites

22. **a.**
$$x + 3.5 = 10.8$$
$$x + 3.5 + \text{-}3.5 = 10.8 + \text{-}3.5$$
$$x + 0 = 7.3$$
$$x = 7.3$$

   b. Sample: You have a $10.8 million contract to play baseball over a three-year period. How much money remains on your contract if you already received $3.5 million?

23. **a.**
$$n + 10 = 19$$
$$n + 10 + \text{-}10 = 19 + \text{-}10$$
$$n + 0 = 9$$
$$n = 9$$

   b.
$$n + \text{-}10 = 19$$
$$n + \text{-}10 + 10 = 19 + 10$$
$$n + 0 = 29$$
$$n = 29$$

   c.
$$\text{-}10 = n + 19$$
$$\text{-}10 + \text{-}19 = n + 19 + \text{-}19$$
$$\text{-}29 \overset{.}{=} n + 0$$
$$\text{-}29 = n$$

   d.
$$\text{-}10 = 19n$$
$$\frac{1}{19} \cdot \text{-}10 = \frac{1}{19} \cdot 19n$$
$$\frac{\text{-}10}{19} = n$$

24. $\text{-}2\frac{3}{8} + \frac{3}{8} + \frac{3}{8} = \text{-}1\frac{5}{8}$

25. $(\text{-}2 + p + \text{-}q)$ feet

26. $95 + y = 140$

27.
$$\text{-}225 = \text{-}25t$$
$$\frac{\text{-}1}{25} \cdot \text{-}225 = \frac{\text{-}1}{25} \cdot \text{-}25t$$
$$9 = t$$
9 minutes

28. 1458 bricks ($N = 7 \cdot 24.5 \cdot 8.5 = 1457.75$)

29. **a.** -13

   b. 12

   c. -32

30. **a.–c.** Answers will vary.

LESSON 3-4   pp. 163–169

1. **a.** x **b.** y

2. II   **3.** II and III

4. **a.** image   **b.** preimage

5. $(\text{-}2.5, 5)$ **6.** $(0, 45)$

7.

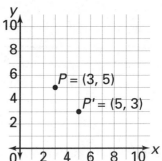

8. **a.**

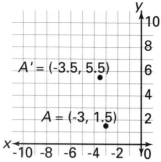

b. II

9. **a.**, **b.**

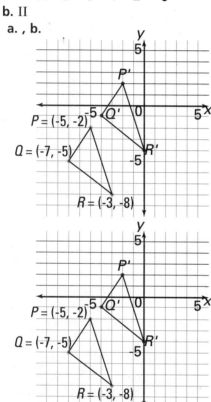

10. **a.**

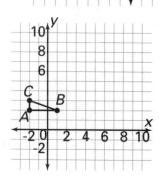

b.

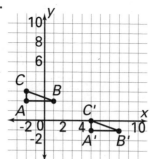

11. **a.** $(x + 3, y + -7)$

b. pick $P = (-3, 4)$ then $P' = (-3 + 3, 4 + -7) = (0, -3)$

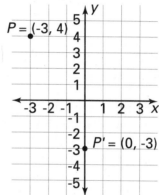

12. **a.** $(x + -3, y + -1)$

b. pick $P = (6, 8)$ then $P' = (6 + -3, 8 + -1) = (3, 7)$

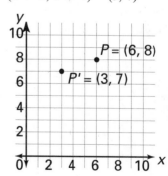

13. a. $Q' = (-6 + 5, -6 + -3) = (-1, -9)$

b.

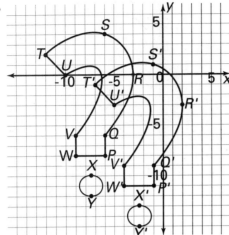

14. a. $(x + -9, y)$

    b. Sample: The identity of the second coordinate stays the same. The second coordinate of the image is $y + 0$, which is y.

15. 8 units to the right; 6 units down

16. Sample: The image of $(x, y) = (x + 1, y + 0)$.

17. a. 9; 8   **b.** 9; 8

18. Sample: 4 blocks east and 4 blocks north; 1 block east, 3 blocks north, 3 blocks east, and 1 block north; 4 blocks north and 4 blocks east

19. $(x + 3, y + 9) = (7, -1)$; $(x, y) = (4, -10)$

20. The person is moving closer to the sensor from 0–2 minutes and from 4–6 minutes.

21. The person was touching the sensor at 6 minutes.

22.

Graph with axis labeled "cost in cents" (y, 50 to 400) and "number of cans" (x, 1 to 7).

23. $(x + 14) + -14 = x + (14 + -14) = x + 0 = x$

24. $(-7 + 5x) + 7 = 5x + (-7 + 7) = 5x + 0 = 5x$

25. $-5 + 3.2 = -1.8$; the net change is a loss of $1.8 million.

26. a.
$$2.75x = 8.25$$
$$\frac{1}{2.75} \cdot 2.75x = \frac{1}{2.75} \cdot 8.25$$
$$x = 3$$

    b. Multiply both sides of the equation by $\frac{1}{a}$.

    c.
$$2.75 + x = 8.25$$
$$-2.75 + 2.75 + x = -2.75 + 8.25$$
$$0 + x = 5.5$$
$$x = 5.5$$

    d. Add $-a$ to both sides of the equation.

27. a. Commutative Property of Addition $(y + x = x + y)$

    b. $x + y$

28. a.
$$\frac{2}{3}x = 24$$
$$\frac{3}{2} \cdot \frac{2}{3}x = \frac{3}{2} \cdot 24$$
$$x = 36$$

    b. Sample: Crystal gave $\frac{2}{3}$ of her money, which was $24, to her sister. How much money did she have to start with?

29. a. EER $= \frac{12600}{1315} \approx 9.58$ or 9.6 to the nearest tenth

    b. EER $= \frac{5000}{850} \approx 5.88$ or 5.9 to the nearest tenth

    c. part **a**, since it has the higher EER number

30. No; $4 \cdot -6 + 15 = -24 + 15 = -9$; $-9 \neq -7$.

31. a. 635,506 feet west or 120.4 miles west and 317,753 feet south or 60.2 miles south (From 1990 to 2020, there are 10,957 days, taking leap years into consideration.
$10,957 \cdot 58 = 635,506$ feet
$10,957 \cdot 29 = 317,753$ feet
$\frac{635,506}{5280} \approx 120.4$ miles
$\frac{317,775}{5280} \approx 60.2$ miles)

    b. near Chesapeake, Missouri, about 20 miles west of Springfield, Missouri

1. a. $2W + 4 = 12$

  b. Remove 4 oz from both sides (1). Divide the remaining number of ounces on the right by the number of boxes on the left (2).

  c. Each box weighs 4 oz.

2. a. -8; multiply; $\frac{1}{4}$

  b.
$$4n + 8 = 60$$
$$4n + 8 + \text{-}8 = 60 + \text{-}8$$
$$4n = 52$$
$$\frac{1}{4} \cdot 4n = \frac{1}{4} \cdot 52$$
$$n = 13$$
Check: $4 \cdot 13 + 8 = 52 + 8 = 60$

3. a. -61 was added to both sides.

  b. Both sides were multiplied by $\frac{1}{55}$.

4.
$$8x + 15 = 47$$
$$8x + 15 + \text{-}15 = 47 + \text{-}15$$
$$8x = 32$$
$$\frac{1}{8} \cdot 8x = \frac{1}{8} \cdot 32$$
$$x = 4$$
Check: $8 \cdot 4 + 15 = 32 + 15 = 47$

5.
$$7y + 11 = 74$$
$$7y + 11 + \text{-}11 = 74 + \text{-}11$$
$$7y = 63$$
$$\frac{1}{7} \cdot 7y = \frac{1}{7} \cdot 63$$
$$y = 9$$
Check: $7 \cdot 9 + 11 = 63 + 11 = 74$

6.
$$\text{-}2z + 32 = 288$$
$$\text{-}2z + 32 + \text{-}32 = 288 + \text{-}32$$
$$\text{-}2z = 256$$
$$\frac{\text{-}1}{2} \cdot \text{-}2z = \frac{\text{-}1}{2} \cdot 256$$
$$z = \text{-}128$$
Check: $\text{-}2 \cdot \text{-}128 + 32 = 256 + 32 = 288$

7.
$$2 = 9x + \text{-}3$$
$$2 + 3 = 9x + \text{-}3 + 3$$
$$5 = 9x$$
$$\frac{1}{9} \cdot 5 = \frac{1}{9} \cdot 9x$$
$$\frac{5}{9} = x$$
Check: $9 \cdot \frac{5}{9} + \text{-}3 = 5 + \text{-}3 = 2$

8. a. Add 3.5 and 5.6.

  b.
$$3.5 + 2x + 5.6 = 10$$
$$2x + 9.1 = 10$$
$$2x + 9.1 + \text{-}9.1 = 10 + \text{-}9.1$$
$$2x = 0.9$$
$$\frac{1}{2} \cdot 2x = \frac{1}{2} \cdot 0.9$$
$$x = 0.45$$
Check: $3.5 + 2 \cdot 0.45 + 5.6 =$
$$3.5 + 0.9 + 5.6 = 10$$

9.
$$9.8h + 8.00 + 3.00 = 89.40$$
$$9.8h + 11.00 = 89.40$$
$$9.8h + 11.00 + \text{-}11.00 = 89.40 + \text{-}11.00$$
$$9.8h = 78.40$$
$$\frac{1}{9.8} \cdot 9.8h = \frac{1}{9.8} \cdot 78.40$$
$$h = 8$$
Val worked 8 hours that day.

10.
$$\frac{3}{4}x + 12 = 27$$
$$\frac{3}{4}x + 12 + \text{-}12 = 27 + \text{-}12$$
$$\frac{3}{4}x = 15$$
$$\frac{4}{3} \cdot \frac{3}{4}x = \frac{4}{3} \cdot 15$$
$$x = 20$$
Check: $\frac{3}{4} \cdot 20 + 12 = 15 + 12 = 27$

11.
$$5 = -4x + 15$$
$$5 + -15 = -4x + 15 + -15$$
$$-10 = -4x$$
$$\tfrac{-1}{4} \cdot -10 = \tfrac{-1}{4} \cdot -4x$$
$$\tfrac{5}{2} = x$$
Check: $-4 \cdot \tfrac{5}{2} + 15 = -10 + 15 = 5$

12.
$$-8n + -18 = 88$$
$$-8n + -18 + 18 = 88 + 18$$
$$-8n = 106$$
$$\tfrac{-1}{8} \cdot -8n = \tfrac{-1}{8} \cdot 106$$
$$n = -13.25$$
Check: $-8(-13.25) + -18 = 106 + -18 = 88$

13.
$$16 = \tfrac{2}{3}a + 20$$
$$16 + -20 = \tfrac{2}{3}a + 20 + -20$$
$$-4 = \tfrac{2}{3}a$$
$$\tfrac{3}{2} \cdot -4 = \tfrac{3}{2} \cdot \tfrac{2}{3}a$$
$$-6 = a$$
Check: $\tfrac{2}{3} \cdot -6 + 20 = -4 + 20 = 16$

14. a. $5 - 3x = 0.53$; where x is the price of a hamburger

b.
$$5 - 3x = 0.53$$
$$-5 + 5 - 3x = -5 + 0.53$$
$$-3x = -4.47$$
$$\tfrac{-1}{3} \cdot 3x = \tfrac{-1}{3} \cdot -4.47$$
$$x = 1.49$$
The price of one hamburger is $1.49.

15. a. $4347.59 + 752.85 + -550.0 + x = 4574.14$
where x represents interest earned during June.

b. $4347.59 + 752.85$
$$+ -550.0 + x = 4574.14$$
$$4550.44 + x = 4574.14$$
$$-4550.44 + 4550.44 + x = 4574.14 + -4550.44$$
$$x = 23.70$$
Carlos earned $23.70 in interest during June.

16. a. $150x + 1500 = 3637.50$; where x is the value of one share of stock

b.
$$150x + 1500 = 3637.5$$
$$150x + 1500 + -1500 = 3637.5 + -1500$$
$$150x = 2137.5$$
$$\tfrac{1}{150} \cdot 150x = \tfrac{1}{150} \cdot 2137.5$$
$$x = 14.25$$
The value of one share of stock is $14.25.

17. a.
$$3\tfrac{1}{4} + x = 10\tfrac{1}{2}$$
$$-3\tfrac{1}{4} + 3\tfrac{1}{4} + x = -3\tfrac{1}{4} + 10\tfrac{1}{2}$$
$$x = 7\tfrac{1}{4}$$

b. Check: $3\tfrac{1}{4} + 7\tfrac{1}{4} = 10\tfrac{1}{2}$

18. a.
$$\tfrac{2}{3}t + \tfrac{1}{3} = 7$$
$$\tfrac{2}{3}t + \tfrac{1}{3} + \tfrac{-1}{3} = 7 + \tfrac{-1}{3}$$
$$\tfrac{2}{3}t = 6\tfrac{2}{3}$$
$$\tfrac{3}{2} \cdot \tfrac{2}{3}t = \tfrac{3}{2} \cdot \tfrac{20}{3}$$
$$t = 10$$

b. Check: $\tfrac{2}{3} \cdot 10 + \tfrac{1}{3} = \tfrac{20}{3} + \tfrac{1}{3} = \tfrac{21}{3} = 7$

19.

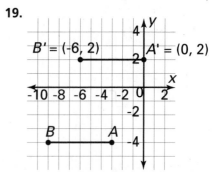

20. The image of (x, y) is $(x, y - 5)$.

21. a. 2 units right; 4 units down

b. $D' = (2, -4)$ and $E' = (3, 0)$

22. a. $-(-39) + -(-(-39)) = 39 + -39 = 0$

b. Sample: The right term is the opposite of the left term, so they add to zero.

23. a. $3.00

b. $.50n = c$

24. $x^2 + x + x = x^2 + 2x$

25. a. $20\% = 0.2$

b. $2\% = 0.02$

c. $102\% = 1.02$

d. $120\% = 1.2$

26. D (Gourmet $= (43, 2)$)

27. B (Select $= (18, -1)$)

28. Merry Berry $(49, -1)$

29. Yes, several of the higher priced ice creams have a high rating.

30. a. Sample: $x + 10 = 7$

b. $x + 10 = 7$

$x + 10 + \text{-}10 = 7 + \text{-}10$

$x = \text{-}3$

31. a. Answers will vary.

b. The key is a step that finds $x = \frac{c - b}{a}$

IN-CLASS ACTIVITY   p. 176

1. a.

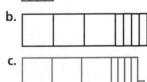

b.

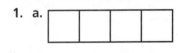

c.

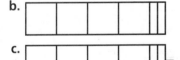

2. a.

b.

c.

3. $x^2 + 4x + 5$

4. $2x^2 + x + 3$

---

5. 3; 4; 2

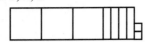

6. a. $3x^2 + 4x + 5$

b. $x^2 + 2x + 5$

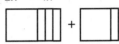

c. $2x^2 + 4x$

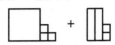

d. $4x^2 + 3x + 5$

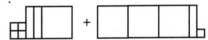

LESSON 3-6   pp. 177–182

1. Distributive Property: For any real numbers a, b, and c, $ac + bc = (a + b)c$ and $ac - bc = (a - b)c$.

2. $7x$ in^2 (Area $= (11 - 4)x = 7x$)

3. $(21 + 8)n = 21n + 8n$

4.

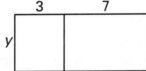

5. a. $-5s + 8s = 3s$

b. Mark the number line in units of s. Start at $0s$ and draw an arrow 5 units to the left followed by an arrow 8 units to the right. The slide ends at $3s$.

6. a. $AB = x + x + y = 2x + y$

b. $BC = y + y + x = 2y + x$

c. $AC = AB + BC = 2x + y + 2y + x = 3x + 3y$

7. $9x + \text{-}3x = (9 - 3)x = 6x$

8. $5z + z = (5 + 1)z = 6z$

9. $5a + 4b$

10. $8p + 7q + 8$

11. $3h + 2h = 40$

$5h = 40$

$\frac{1}{5} \cdot 5h = \frac{1}{5} \cdot 40$

$h = 8$

12. $x + 3x = -20$

$4x = -20$

$\frac{1}{4} \cdot 4x = \frac{1}{4} \cdot -20$

$x = -5$

13. $67.9 = r + r$

$67.9 = 2r$

$\frac{1}{2} \cdot 67.9 = \frac{1}{2} \cdot 2r$

$33.95 = r$

14. $321 = a + 2a + 3a$

$321 = 6a$

$\frac{1}{6} \cdot 321 = \frac{1}{6} \cdot 6a$

$53.5 = a$

15. a. $r + r + \frac{1}{4}r = 90{,}000$

$\frac{9}{4}r = 90{,}000$

$\frac{4}{9} \cdot \frac{9}{4}r = \frac{4}{9} \cdot 90{,}000$

$r = 40{,}000$

Two heirs receive $40,000 each and the third receives $10,000.

b. $r + r + \frac{1}{4}r + 10{,}000 = 90{,}000$

$\frac{9}{4}r = 80{,}000$

$\frac{4}{9} \cdot \frac{9}{4}r = \frac{4}{9} \cdot 80{,}000$

Two heirs receive $35,555.56 each and the third receives $8,888.89.

16. $s + 5s = 6s$

17. $F - \frac{3}{10}F = \frac{7}{10}F = .7F$

18. $(x + -6) + (2x + 4) + (3x + -3)$

$= (1 + 2 + 3)x + -6 + 4 + -3$

$= 6x + -5$

19. $5f + (4f - 6) + (6 + -9f)$

$= (5 + 4 + -9)f + -6 + 6$

$= 0$

20. $x + \frac{1}{5}x = 500{,}000$

$\frac{6}{5}x = 500{,}000$

$\frac{5}{6} \cdot \frac{6}{5}x = \frac{5}{6} \cdot 500{,}000$

$x = 416{,}666.67$

The winner receives $416,666.67 and the loser receives $83,333.33.

21. $\frac{1}{4} \cdot 60 + 2x + 2x + x = 60$, where x is the daughter's share

$15 + 5x = 60$

$-15 + 15 + 5x = -15 + 60$

$5x = 45$

$\frac{1}{5} \cdot 5x = \frac{1}{5} \cdot 45$

$x = 9$

The daughter would receive 9 camels.

22. $-n + 2n + -5n + 7 = -9$

$-4n + 7 = -9$

$-7 + -4n + 7 = -7 + -9$

$-4n = -16$

$\frac{-1}{4} \cdot -4n = \frac{-1}{4} \cdot -16$

$n = 4$

Check: $-4 + 2 \cdot 4 + -5 \cdot 4 + 7 = -9$

23. a. $3W + 2 = 8$

b. $3W + 2 + -2 = 8 + -2$

$3W = 6$

$\frac{1}{3} \cdot 3W = \frac{1}{3} \cdot 6$

$W = 2$

Each box weighs 2 oz.

- 24.
$$93 = \tfrac{2}{3}x + 17$$

$$93 + \text{-}17 = \tfrac{2}{3}x + 17 + \text{-}17$$

$$76 = \tfrac{2}{3}x$$

$$\tfrac{3}{2} \cdot 76 = \tfrac{3}{2} \cdot \tfrac{2}{3}x$$

$$114 = x$$

Check: $\tfrac{2}{3} \cdot 114 + 17 = 76 + 17 = 93$

25. Sample: First add $-b$ to both sides; then multiply both sides by $\tfrac{1}{a}$. To solve $3x + 5 = 11$, add -5 to both sides to get $3x = 6$; then multiply both sides by $\tfrac{1}{3}$ to get $x = 2$.

26. a. rectangle
   b. $7 \cdot 10 = 70$ square units
   c.

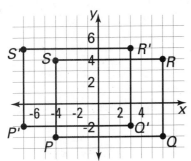

   d. The areas are the same.

27. a. -17   **b.** $\tfrac{1}{17}$

28. a. $\tfrac{39}{2}$ **b.** $\tfrac{-2}{39}$

29. The minus sign indicates the Death Valley area is 282 ft below sea level.

30. a. $\tfrac{4}{10} = \tfrac{2}{5}$

   b. $\tfrac{3}{10} + \tfrac{1}{5} = \tfrac{3}{10} + \tfrac{2}{10} = \tfrac{5}{10} = \tfrac{1}{2}$

   c. $\tfrac{3}{10} + \tfrac{2}{15} = \tfrac{9}{30} + \tfrac{4}{30} = \tfrac{13}{30}$

31. There are 7200 pages to be printed. It will take 7200 pages $\cdot \, \tfrac{1}{8}\tfrac{\text{minutes}}{\text{page}} = 900$ minutes $\cdot$

$\tfrac{1}{60}\tfrac{\text{hour}}{\text{minutes}} = 15$ hours to print.

32. 4.98×10^{-23}

33. a. False; $6 \cdot 3 \cdot 2 \cdot 3 \neq 12 \cdot 3$
   b. False; $\tfrac{6 \cdot 8}{2 \cdot 8} \neq 3 \cdot 8$
   c. False; $6^3 + 2^3 \neq 8^3$
   d. True
   e. True

LESSON 3-7   pp. 183–187

1. Distributive Property: Removing Parentheses form of the Distributive Property: For all real numbers a, b, and c, $c(a + b) = ca + cb$ and $c(a - b) = ca - cb$.

2. a. $5x(x + 2) = 5x^2 + 10x$
   b.

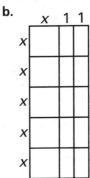

3. a. $5(x + 2) = 5x + 10$
   b.

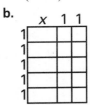

4. $4(n + 6)$
   $= 4n + 4 \cdot 6$
   $= 4n + 24$

5. $12(k - 5)$
   $= 12k - 12 \cdot 5$
   $= 12k - 60$

6. $10b(b + c)$
   $= 10b \cdot b + 10b \cdot c$
   $= 10b^2 + 10bc$

7. $5 \cdot \$9.96$
$= 5(\$10 - 4\cancel{c})$
$= \$50 - 20\cancel{c}$
$= \$49.80$

8. $4(2.00 + 0.07)$
$= 8.00 + 0.28$
$= 8.28$
4 gallons of milk will cost $8.28

9. $21.00

10. $9.75

11. $14.98 or $14.99

12. $2(x + 3.1) = 9.8$
$2x + 6.2 = 9.8$
$2x + 6.2 + \text{-}6.2 = 9.8 + \text{-}6.2$
$2x = 3.6$
$\frac{1}{2} \cdot 2x = \frac{1}{2} \cdot 3.6$
$x = 1.8$
Check: $2(1.8 + 3.1) = 2 \cdot 4.9 = 9.8$

13. $6(m + \text{-}1) = 10$
$6m + \text{-}6 = 10$
$6m + \text{-}6 + 6 = 10 + 6$
$6m = 16$
$\frac{1}{6} \cdot 6m = \frac{1}{6} \cdot 16$
$m = \frac{8}{3}$
Check: $6\left(\frac{8}{3} + \text{-}1\right) = \frac{48}{3} + \text{-}6 = 16 + \text{-}6 = 10$

14. $7(u + \text{-}3) = 0$
$7u + \text{-}21 = 0$
$7u + \text{-}21 + 21 = 0 + 21$
$7u = 21$
$\frac{1}{7} \cdot 7u = \frac{1}{7} \cdot 21$
$u = 3$
Check: $7(3 + \text{-}3) = 7 \cdot 0 = 0$

15. $9 = 2(2x + 2) + 2$
$9 = 4x + 4 + 2$
$9 = 4x + 6$
$9 + \text{-}6 = 4x + 6 + \text{-}6$
$3 = 4x$
$\frac{1}{4} \cdot 3 = \frac{1}{4} \cdot 4x$
$\frac{3}{4} = x$
Check: $9 = 2\left(2 \cdot \frac{3}{4} + 2\right) + 2$
$= 2\left(\frac{3}{2} + 2\right) + 2$
$= 2 \cdot \frac{7}{2} + 2$
$= 7 + 2$

16. $2 + 3(v + 4) = 5$
$2 + 3v + 12 = 5$
$14 + 3v = 5$
$\text{-}14 + 14 + 3v = \text{-}14 + 5$
$3v = \text{-}9$
$\frac{1}{3} \cdot 3v = \frac{1}{3} \cdot \text{-}9$
$v = \text{-}3$
Check: $2 + 3(\text{-}3 + 4) = 2 + 3 \cdot 1$
$= 2 + 3$
$= 5$

17. $\text{-}5(t + 2) + 3t = 8$
$\text{-}5t + \text{-}10 + 3t = 8$
$\text{-}10 + \text{-}2t = 8$
$10 + \text{-}10 + \text{-}2t = 10 + 8$
$\text{-}2t = 18$
$\text{-}\frac{1}{2} \cdot \text{-}2t = \text{-}\frac{1}{2} \cdot 18$
$t = \text{-}9$
Check: $\text{-}5(\text{-}9 + 2) + 3 \cdot \text{-}9 = \text{-}5 \cdot \text{-}7 + \text{-}27$
$= 35 + \text{-}27$
$= 8$

18. n represents a whole number.

19. $.40 + .13(n - 3) = 2.00$

$.40 + .13n - .39 = 2.00$

$.13n + .01 = 2.00$

$.13n + .01 + -.01 = 2.00 + -.01$

$.13n = 1.99$

$\frac{1}{.13} \cdot .13n = \frac{1}{.13} \cdot 1.99$

$n \approx 15.3$

You could talk for 15 minutes.

20. a. $.49 + .16 \cdot 57 = .49 + 9.12$

$= 9.61$

It will cost $9.61 to talk for 1 hour.

b. $.49 + .16(n - 3) < 6.00$

$.49 + .16n - .48 < 6.00$

$.16n + .01 < 6.00$

$.16n + .01 - .01 < 6.00 - .01$

$.16n < 5.99$

$\frac{1}{.16} \cdot .16n < \frac{1}{.16} \cdot 5.99$

$n < 37.4375$

You can talk for at most 37 minutes for less than $6.00.

21. 5,999,994 $(6(1,000,000 - 1) = 6,000,000 - 6)$

22. 51 minutes of commercials

23. a. $60 = \frac{1}{2} \cdot 6(5 + b_2)$

b. $60 = 3(5 + b_2)$

$60 = 15 + 3b_2$

$60 + -15 = 15 + -15 + 3b_2$

$45 = 3b_2$

$\frac{1}{3} \cdot 45 = \frac{1}{3} \cdot 3b_2$

$15 = b_2$

The length of the other base is 15 cm.

24. a. $19.95

b. $19.95

c. $32.45 $(19.95 + .25(150 - 100)$

$= 19.95 + .25(50)$

$= 19.95 + 12.5$

$= 32.45)$

25. $25.70 = 19.95 + .25(m - 100)$

$25.70 = 19.95 + .25m - 25$

$25.70 = -5.05 + .25m$

$25.70 + 5.05 = 5.05 + -5.05 + .25m$

$30.75 = .25m$

$\frac{1}{.25} \cdot 30.75 = \frac{1}{.25} \cdot .25m$

$123 = m$

The sales representative drove 123 miles that day.

26. $3x^2 + 4x + 9$

27. $2a + 6b + -2c$

28. $1.19n$

29. a. $5m + 2m < 84$

$7m < 84$

$\frac{1}{7} \cdot 7m < \frac{1}{7} \cdot 84$

$m < 12$

Check: Does $5 \cdot 12 + 2 \cdot 12 = 60 + 24 = 84$? Yes.

Pick some value that works in $m < 12$, we pick 10.

Is $5 \cdot 10 + 2 \cdot 10 < 84$? Yes, $50 + 20 = 70$ and $70 < 84$.

b. Yes, -5 is less than 12.

30. -24

31. 12

32. Answers will vary.

LESSON 3-8   pp. 188–194

1. a. Suzie will need 31 chips to make the 5th design.

b.

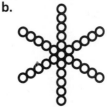

2. a. d represents the number of the design.

b. c represents the number of chips in the design.

3. Suzie needs $1 + 6 \cdot 13 = 79$ chips to make the 13th design.

4.
$$103 = 1 + 6d$$
$$103 - 1 = 1 - 1 + 6d$$
$$102 = 6d$$
$$\tfrac{1}{6} \cdot 102 = \tfrac{1}{6} \cdot 6d$$
$$17 = d$$
It was the 17th design in the sequence.

5. a. h represents the number of hours the car is parked in the lot.

b. $1.25 is the additional charge for each hour of parking.

c. $31.50 $(c = 1.5 + 1.25 \cdot 24$
$$= 1.5 + 30$$
$$= 31.50)$$

6. a. Yes; $c = 1.5 + 1.25 \cdot 1$
$$= 1.5 + 1.25$$
$$= 2.75$$
The cost of 1 hour of parking is $2.75.

b. No, but you would round up to 3 hours anyway.

c. the set of positive integers

7. $c = 1.5 + 1.25 \cdot 10$
$$= 1.5 + 12.5$$
$$= 14$$
She paid $14.00.

8.
$$17.75 = 1.5 + 1.25h$$
$$17.75 - 1.5 = 1.5 - 1.5 + 1.25h$$
$$16.25 = 1.25h$$
$$\tfrac{1}{1.25} \cdot 16.25 = \tfrac{1}{1.25} \cdot 1.25h$$
$$13 = h$$
He parked 13 hours.

9. a. 999 times

b. 7 $(C = 1 + 6 * 1$
$$= 1 + 6$$
$$= 7)$$

c. 5995 $(C = 1 + 6 * 999$
$$= 1 + 5994$$
$$= 5995)$$

d. 517 $(C = 1 + 6 * 86$
$$= 1 + 516$$
$$= 517)$$

10. (a)

11.

n	1	2	3	4
t	3	5	7	9

12. a. 15

b.

13. a. $t = 1 + 2n$

b. 11 $(23 = 1 + 2 \cdot 11)$

14. a. 41 dots

b. $d = 4c + 1$ We begin with one dot. Each new color requires four new dots.

15. a.

Minutes	Cost
100	$ 65.95
200	$ 65.95
300	$ 86.95
400	$107.95
500	$128.95

b. $c = \$65.95 + \$0.21(m - 200)$

c. $m \geq 200$

16. a.

day	gallons
1	7500
2	15,000
3	22,500
4	30,000
5	37,500
6	45,000

b. $g = 7500n$

c. $g = 7500 \cdot 20$
$$= 150,000$$
150,000 gal

d.
$$7,500,000 = 7500n$$
$$\tfrac{1}{7500} \cdot 7,500,000 = \tfrac{1}{7500} \cdot 7500n$$
$$1000 = n$$
1000 days

17.
```
10   PRINT "GALLONS OF GASOLINE
     CONSUMED"
20   PRINT "DAYS", "GALLONS"
30   FOR N = 1 TO 20
40   LET G = 7500 * N
50   PRINT N, G
60   NEXT N
70   END
```

18. $4 \cdot \$9.95 = 4(\$10 - 5¢)$
$$= 4 \cdot \$10 - 4 \cdot 5¢$$
$$= \$40 - 20¢$$
$$= \$39.80$$

19. $25 \cdot \$1.99 = 25(\$2 - 1¢)$
$$= 25 \cdot \$2 - 25 \cdot 1¢$$
$$= \$50 - 25¢$$
$$= \$49.75$$

20. $5L + 5 \cdot 4L + 5 + 5 + 5 = 25L + 15$

21. $3x + \text{-}5x + 12 + \text{-}15 = \text{-}4$
$$\text{-}2x + \text{-}3 = \text{-}4$$
$$\text{-}2x + \text{-}3 + 3 = \text{-}4 + 3$$
$$\text{-}2x = \text{-}1$$
$$\text{-}\frac{1}{2} \cdot \text{-}2x = \text{-}\frac{1}{2} \cdot = \text{-}1$$
$$x = \frac{1}{2}$$

22. $t - 0.1t = 1.8$
$$0.9t = 1.8$$
$$\frac{1}{0.9} \cdot 0.9t = \frac{1}{0.9} \cdot 1.8$$
$$t = 2$$

23. $\frac{5}{2}x + 1 = 26$
$$\frac{5}{2}x + 1 + \text{-}1 = 26 + \text{-}1$$
$$\frac{5}{2}x = 25$$
$$\frac{2}{5} \cdot \frac{5}{2}x = \frac{2}{5} \cdot 25$$
$$x = 10$$

24. $\text{-}3 = \text{-}6n + 1 + 2(n + 1)$
$$\text{-}3 = \text{-}6n + 1 + 2n + 2$$
$$\text{-}3 = \text{-}4n + 3$$
$$\text{-}3 + \text{-}3 = \text{-}4n + 3 + \text{-}3$$
$$\text{-}6 = \text{-}4n$$
$$\frac{\text{-}1}{4} \cdot \text{-}6 = \frac{\text{-}1}{4} \cdot \text{-}4n$$
$$\frac{3}{2} = n$$

25. Quadrant II

26. a. January, February, March, April, May, June, October, and November

b. July and August

c. The average rainfall for April is 0 inches.

d. The greatest change is between June and July.

27. a. $3z < 231$
$$\frac{1}{3} \cdot 3z < \frac{1}{3} \cdot 231$$
$$z < 77$$

b.

28. $53 \frac{\text{miles}}{\text{hour}} \cdot 2\frac{1}{2} \text{ hours} = 132.5 \text{ miles}$

29. Sample: Susie opens a savings account with a $100 deposit. She then deposits $5 per week into her account. What is her bank balance after w weeks, assuming the account earns no interest? Total $= 100 + 5(w - 1)$

LESSON 3-9   pp. 195–199

1. They must be equal.

2. $\frac{3}{10}$ in. $+ \text{-}\frac{2}{5}$ in. $= \frac{3}{10}$ in. $+ \text{-}\frac{4}{10}$ in. $= \text{-}\frac{1}{10}$ in.

3. $\frac{2}{5} + \text{-}\frac{1}{5} + 3\frac{4}{5} = 3\frac{5}{5} = 4$

4. $\text{-}\frac{11}{3} + \text{-}\frac{2}{3} + \text{-}\frac{8}{3} = \text{-}\frac{21}{3} = \text{-}7$

5. $\frac{2a}{3} + \frac{28a}{3} = \frac{30a}{3} = 10a$

6. $\frac{6y + 11}{2y} + \frac{\text{-}11}{2y} = \frac{6y}{2y} = 3$

7. $\frac{x}{5} + \frac{x}{5} + \frac{2x}{5} = \frac{4x}{5}$

8. $\frac{a}{6} + \frac{2a}{6} = \frac{3a}{6} = \frac{a}{2}$

9. a. 20

b. $\frac{x}{5} + \frac{3x}{4} = \frac{4x}{20} + \frac{15x}{20} = \frac{19x}{20}$

10. $\frac{a}{6} + \frac{a}{3} = \frac{a}{6} + \frac{2a}{6} = \frac{3a}{6} = \frac{a}{2}$

47

11. $\frac{2d}{7} + \frac{3d}{4} = \frac{8d}{28} + \frac{21d}{28} = \frac{29d}{28}$

12. $C + \frac{C}{3} + \frac{C}{3} = \frac{3C}{3} + \frac{2C}{3} = \frac{5C}{3}$

13. $B + -\frac{B}{2} = \frac{2B}{2} + -\frac{B}{2} = \frac{B}{2}$

14. $\frac{k}{2} + \frac{2k}{3} + \frac{k}{4} = \frac{6k}{12} + \frac{8k}{12} + \frac{3k}{12} = \frac{17k}{12}$

15. $\frac{5}{x} + \frac{3}{x} - \frac{9}{x} = -\frac{1}{x}$

16. $\frac{2n}{3} + 4 \cdot \frac{n}{3} + 5\left(\frac{1}{3}n\right) = \frac{2n}{3} + \frac{4n}{3} + \frac{5n}{3} = \frac{11n}{3}$

17. $-\frac{2}{x} + \frac{3}{2x} - \frac{1}{x} = -\frac{4}{2x} + \frac{3}{2x} + -\frac{2}{2x} = -\frac{3}{2x}$

18. Sample: Let $a = 1$, $b = 2$, $c = 3$, and $d = 4$
$\frac{a}{b} + \frac{c}{d} = \frac{1}{2} + \frac{3}{4} = \frac{2}{4} + \frac{3}{4} = \frac{5}{4}$ whereas
$\frac{a + c}{b + d} = \frac{1 + 3}{2 + 4} = \frac{4}{6} = \frac{2}{3}$

19. **a.** $W + L + W + L = 2W + 2L$
   b. $\frac{1}{2}W + \frac{1}{2}L + \frac{1}{2}W + \frac{1}{2}L = W + L$

20. $3\frac{1}{2}$ ft $+ -1\frac{2}{3}$ ft $+ -4\frac{5}{6}$ ft $= 3\frac{3}{6} + -1\frac{4}{6} + -4\frac{5}{6} =$
   $-2\frac{6}{6} = -3$; 3 feet on the side of team B.

21. **a.** Sample: after the first slide at 75¢, the cost is 50¢ per slide. The cost is always divisible by 25¢.
   b. $4.25 (75 + 50(n - 1) = c$
$$= 75 + 50(8 - 1)$$
$$= 75 + 50 \cdot 7$$
$$= 75 + 350$$
$$= 425¢)$$
   c. 15 copies $(775 = 75 + 50(n - 1)$
$$775 = 75 + 50n + -50$$
$$775 = 25 + 50n$$
$$775 + -25 = 25 + 50n + -25$$
$$750 = 50n$$
$$15 = n$$

22. **a.** 3 (Their dimensions are 5×3, 5×8, and 5×11.)
   b. $5 \cdot 3 + 5 \cdot 8 = 15 + 40$
$$= 55 \text{ square units}$$
$$5(3 + 8) = 5 \cdot 11$$
$$= 55 \text{ square units}$$
   c. Distributive Property

23. **a.**

n	t
1	4
2	7
3	10
4	13

   b. Sample: t increases by 3 for every increase of one in n.
   c. 181 toothpicks ($60 \cdot 3 + 1 = 180 + 1 = 181$)
   d. $n = 100$; Sample: How many squares are formed by 301 toothpicks arranged side by side in one row?

24. $x + 2x + 3x + 4x = 5$
$$10x = 5$$
$$\frac{1}{10} \cdot 10x = \frac{1}{10} \cdot 5$$
$$x = \frac{1}{2}$$
   Does $.5 + 2 \cdot .5 + 3 \cdot .5 + 4 \cdot .5 = 5$? Yes, it checks.

25. $\quad 8 = 2(n + 3) + 4(5n + 6)$
$$8 = 2n + 6 + 20n + 24$$
$$8 = 22n + 30$$
$$8 + -30 = 22n + 30 + -30$$
$$-22 = 22n$$
$$\frac{1}{22} \cdot -22 = \frac{1}{22} \cdot 22n$$
$$-1 = n$$
   Does $8 = 2(-1 + 3) + 4(5 \cdot -1 + 6)$? Yes, it checks.

26. (c)

27. $u + -d$

28. $7e + -5e + c = 2e + c$

29. $11! = 11 \cdot 10 \cdot 9 \cdot 8 \cdot 7 \cdot 6 \cdot 5 \cdot 4 \cdot 3 \cdot 2 \cdot 1$

30. a. $-2n > 10$ ✗

$$\frac{-1}{2} \cdot -2n < \frac{-1}{2} \cdot 10$$

$$n < -5$$

b.

31. $14.40h > 400$

$$\frac{1}{14.40} \cdot 14.40h > \frac{1}{14.40} \cdot 400$$

$$h > 27.8$$

She must work more than 27.8 hours in a week in order to earn more than $400.

32. Sample: The temperature on a winter day ranged from a high of 4° to a low of -3°.

33. $169,000,000 \text{ dollars} \cdot \frac{1}{9 \text{ years}} =$
$18,777,777.78$ dollars per year

34. a. **i.** $\frac{1}{2} + \frac{1}{4} + \frac{1}{8} = \frac{4}{8} + \frac{2}{8} + \frac{1}{8} = \frac{7}{8}$

ii. $\frac{1}{2} + \frac{1}{4} + \frac{1}{8} + \frac{1}{16} = \frac{8}{16} + \frac{4}{16} + \frac{2}{16} + \frac{1}{16} = \frac{15}{16}$

iii. $\frac{1}{2} + \frac{1}{4} + \frac{1}{8} + \frac{1}{16} + \frac{1}{32} =$

$\frac{16}{32} + \frac{8}{32} + \frac{4}{32} + \frac{2}{32} + \frac{1}{32} =$

$\frac{31}{32}$

b. 1

LESSON 3-10   pp. 200–204

1. Addition Property of Inequality: For all real numbers a, b, and c, if $a > b$, then $a + c > b + c$.

2. a. $4w + 3 > 11$

b. $4w + 3 + -3 > 11 + -3$

$$4w > 8$$

$$\frac{1}{4} \cdot 4w > \frac{1}{4} \cdot 8$$

$$w > 2$$

3. $0.2n + 6 \leq 200$

$$0.2n + 6 + -6 \leq 200 + -6$$

$$0.2n \leq 194$$

$$\frac{1}{0.2} \cdot 0.2n \leq \frac{1}{0.2} \cdot 194$$

$$n \leq 970$$

At most 970 lemons can be put in the crate.

4. $0.5n + 10 < 50$

$$0.5n + 10 + -10 < 50 + -10$$

$$0.5n < 40$$

$$\frac{1}{0.5} \cdot 0.5n < \frac{1}{0.5} \cdot 40$$

$$n < 80$$

At most 79 grapefruits can be packed in the crate.

5. $3x + 4 < 19$

$$3x + 4 + -4 < 19 + -4$$

$$3x < 15$$

$$\frac{1}{3} \cdot 3x < \frac{1}{3} \cdot 15$$

$$x < 5$$

Check: Does $3 \cdot 5 + 4 = 19$? Yes. Pick some value that works in $x < 5$, we pick 4. Is $3 \cdot 4 + 4 < 19$? Yes, $12 + 4 = 16$ and $16 < 19$.

6. $6 \leq 4b + 10$

$$6 + -10 \leq 4b + 10 + -10$$

$$-4 \leq 4b$$

$$\frac{1}{4} \cdot -4 \leq \frac{1}{4} \cdot 4b$$

$$-1 \leq b$$

Check: Does $4 \cdot -1 + 10 = 6$? Yes. Pick some value that works in $b \geq -1$, we pick 0. Is $6 \leq 4 \cdot 0 + 10$? Yes, $0 + 10 = 10$ and $6 \leq 10$.

7. $5 \leq -3n + 2$

$$5 + -2 \leq -3n + 2 + -2$$

$$3 \leq -3n$$

$$-\frac{1}{3} \cdot (3) \geq -\frac{1}{3} \cdot -3n$$

$$-1 \geq n \text{ or } n \leq -1$$

Check: Does $-3 \cdot -1 + 2 = 5$? Yes. Pick some value that works in $n \leq -1$, we pick -2. Is $5 \leq -3 \cdot -2 + 2$? Yes, $6 + 2 = 8$ and $5 \leq 8$.

8.
$$101 + 102x > 103$$
$$101 - 101 + 102x > 103 - 101$$
$$102x > 2$$
$$\frac{1}{102} \cdot 102x > \frac{1}{102} \cdot 2$$
$$x > \frac{1}{51}$$

Check: Does $101 + 102 \cdot \frac{1}{51} = 103$? Yes. Pick some value that works in $x > \frac{1}{51}$, we pick 1. Is $101 + 102 \cdot 1 > 103$? Yes, $101 + 102 = 203$ and $203 > 103$.

9. $n + (n + 1) + (n + 2) > 79$
$$3n + 3 > 79$$
$$3n + 3 - 3 > 79 - 3$$
$$3n > 76$$
$$\frac{1}{3} \cdot 3n > \frac{1}{3} \cdot 76$$
$$n > 25\frac{1}{3}$$

Hence three smallest consecutive integers whose sum is greater than 79 are 26, 27, and 28.

10.
$$3(x + 4) < 12$$
$$3x + 12 < 12$$
$$3x + 12 - 12 < 12 - 12$$
$$3x < 0$$
$$\frac{1}{3} \cdot 3x < \frac{1}{3} \cdot 0$$
$$x < 0$$

11.
$$-0.02y + \frac{1}{2} \geq 0.48$$
$$-0.02y + 0.5 - 0.5 \geq 0.48 - 0.5$$
$$-0.02y \geq -0.02$$
$$-\frac{1}{0.02} \cdot -0.02y \leq -\frac{1}{0.02} \cdot -0.02$$
$$y \leq 1$$

12.
$$15 \geq 12 + \frac{1}{3}y$$
$$15 - 12 \geq 12 - 12 + \frac{1}{3}y$$
$$3 \geq \frac{1}{3}y$$
$$\frac{3}{1} \cdot 3 \geq \frac{3}{1} \cdot \frac{1}{3}y$$
$$9 \geq y$$

13.
$$\frac{-5x}{6} + 30 < 120$$
$$\frac{-5x}{6} + 30 - 30 < 120 - 30$$
$$\frac{-5x}{6} < 90$$
$$\left(\frac{6}{-5}\right)\left(\frac{-5}{6}\right)x > \left(\frac{6}{-5}\right)90$$
$$x > -108$$

14. $-4x + 7(x + -2) > -18$
$$-4x + 7x + -14 > -18$$
$$3x + -14 > -18$$
$$14 + 3x + -14 > 14 + -18$$
$$3x > -4$$
$$x > -\frac{4}{3}$$

Choose any x such that $-\frac{4}{3} < x < 0$. x could be -1.

15. Celsius temperatures greater than 37°C
$$\left(C > \frac{5}{9}(F - 32)\right.$$
$$C > \frac{5}{9}(98.6 - 32)$$
$$C > \frac{5}{9}(66.6)$$
$$\left. C > 37\right)$$

16. temperatures less than 20°C
$$\left(68 > \frac{9}{5}C + 32\right.$$
$$68 - 32 > \frac{9}{5}C + 32 - 32$$
$$36 > \frac{9}{5}C$$
$$\frac{5}{9} \cdot 36 > \frac{5}{9} \cdot \frac{9}{5}C$$
$$\left. 20 > C\right)$$

17. a.
$$350 = -90P + 1200$$
$$350 - 1200 = -90P + 1200 - 1200$$
$$-850 = -90P$$
$$-\frac{1}{90} \cdot -850 = -\frac{1}{90} \cdot -90P$$
$$9\frac{4}{9} = P$$
They should charge $9.45.

b.
$$300 = -90P + 1200$$
$$300 - 1200 = -90P + 1200 - 1200$$
$$-900 = -90P$$
$$-\frac{1}{90} \cdot -900 = -\frac{1}{90} \cdot -90P$$
$$10 = P$$
They should charge $10.00.

18. a. $ax + b < c$
$$ax < c - b$$
$$x < \frac{c-b}{a}$$

b. If $a < 0$, then the direction of the inequality would change: $x > \frac{c-b}{a}$.

19. $\frac{3a}{5} + \frac{7a}{5} = \frac{10a}{5} = 2a$

20. $\frac{3}{x} + \frac{-2}{x} + \frac{4}{x} = \frac{5}{x}$

21. $\frac{x}{3} + \frac{-2x}{5} = \frac{5x}{15} + \frac{-6x}{15} = \frac{-x}{15}$

22. a. Sample: To find y, multiply x by 4 and add 6.

b. $y = 4 \cdot 8 + 6 = 38$

c. $96 = 4x + 6$
$$90 = 4x$$
$$22.5 = x$$
y is never 96.

23. a. 4 cubes   **b.** 10 cubes
c. $2(n+1)$ or $2n + 2$

24. $(4x + 3) + 2x = -9$
$$6x + 3 = -9$$
$$6x = -12$$
$$x = -2$$
Check: $(4 \cdot -2 + 3) + 2 \cdot -2 =$
$$-8 + 3 + -4 = -12 + 3 = -9$$

25. $6(4y + -1) + -2y = 82$
$$24y + -6 + -2y = 82$$
$$22y + -6 = 82$$
$$22y + -6 + 6 = 82 + 6$$
$$22y = 88$$
$$y = 4$$
Check: $6(4 \cdot 4 + -1) + -2 \cdot 4 =$
$$6(16 - 1) + -8 = 6 \cdot 15 + -8 =$$
$$90 + -8 = 82$$

26. In using the Distributive Property, you must multiply each term in the parentheses by -3. Darrell forgot to multiply -6 by -3.

27.
$$\$250 = 40(\$5.25) + h(1.5)(\$5.25)$$
$$250 = 210 + 7.875h$$
$$250 + -210 = 210 + 7.875h + -210$$
$$40 = 7.875h$$
$$\frac{1}{7.875} \cdot 40 = \frac{1}{7.875} \cdot 7.875h$$
$$h \approx 5.08$$
You must work 45 hours and 5 minutes.

28.
$$\frac{2}{3}b = 100 - 2$$
$$\frac{2}{3}b = 98$$
$$\frac{3}{2} \cdot \frac{2}{3}b = \frac{3}{2} \cdot 98$$
$$b = 147$$
They can make 147 banners.

29. a. 75^{75}

b. There are 75 factors of 75 in 75^{75} whereas the factors of 75! are $75(74)(73)\ldots(3)(2)(1)$

30. $x = 10$ (Clue 1: $x > 6$; Clue 2: $x < 11$; Clue 3: $x \neq 8$; Clue 4: x is an integer; Clue 5: x is even. x is between 6 and 11. It could be 7, 8, 9, or 10. It is not 8. It is not 7 or 9 (odd).

31. Samples: $-2x + 5 > -43$; $x + 1 < 25$; $3x + 4 < 76$; $-x > -24$; $100x + 100 < 2500$

PROGRESS SELF-TEST pp. 208–209

1. $m + 3m = 4m$

2. $\frac{5}{2}(4v + 100 + w) = 10v + 250 + \frac{5}{2}w$

3. $-9k + 3(k + 3) = -9k + 3k + 9 = -6k + 9$

4. $(x + 5 + x) + (-8 + -x) = x + -3$

5. $-(-(-p)) = -p$

6. $\frac{2}{n} + \frac{5}{n} + \frac{-3}{n} = \frac{4}{n}$

7. $\frac{3x}{2} + \frac{5x}{3} = \frac{9x}{6} + \frac{10x}{6} = \frac{19x}{6} = 3\frac{1}{6}x$

8.
$$8r + 14 = 74$$
$$8r + 14 + -14 = 74 + -14$$
$$8r = 60$$
$$\frac{1}{8} \cdot 8r = \frac{1}{8} \cdot 60$$
$$r = \frac{15}{2}$$

9.
$$-4q + 3 + 9q = -12$$
$$3 + 5q = -12$$
$$3 + -3 + 5q = -12 + -3$$
$$5q = -15$$
$$\frac{1}{5} \cdot 5q = \frac{1}{5} \cdot -15$$
$$q = -3$$

10.
$$3(x + 2) + 100 = 54$$
$$3x + 6 + 100 = 54$$
$$3x + 106 = 54$$
$$3x + 106 + -106 = 54 + -106$$
$$3x = -52$$
$$\frac{1}{3} \cdot 3x = \frac{1}{3} \cdot -52$$
$$x = -\frac{52}{3} = -17\frac{1}{3}$$

11.
$$85 = x + 2(3x + 4)$$
$$85 = x + 6x + 8$$
$$85 = 7x + 8$$
$$85 + -8 = 7x + 8 + -8$$
$$77 = 7x$$
$$\frac{1}{7} \cdot 77 = \frac{1}{7} \cdot 7x$$
$$11 = x$$

12.
$$30v + -18 > 15$$
$$30v + -18 + 18 > 15 + 18$$
$$30v > 33$$
$$\frac{1}{30} \cdot 30v > \frac{1}{30} \cdot 33$$
$$v > \frac{11}{10}$$

13. Addition Property of Equality

14. Adding Like Terms form of the Distributive Property

15. -100 is not an element of the solution set of $15 \le x + 87$ since $15 > -100 + 87$ or $15 > -13$.

16. $\$137.25 + \$2.50w$

17. $6(\$3 - 1\cent) = 6 \cdot \$3 - 6 \cdot 1\cent = \$18 - 6\cent = \$17.94$

18.
$$50 = \frac{9}{5}C + 32$$
$$18 = \frac{9}{5}C$$
$$\frac{5}{9} \cdot 18 = \frac{5}{9} \cdot \frac{9}{5}C$$
$$10 = C$$
$$50°F = 10°C$$

19. Let j = amount Jill should receive.
$$\$58.50 = 2j + j$$
$$\$58.50 = 3j$$
$$\frac{1}{3} \cdot 58.50 = \frac{1}{3} \cdot 3j$$
$$19.50 = j$$

Jill should receive $19.50.

20. a. The area of the large rectangle can be found by one of two ways: $ac + bc$ and $(a + b)c = ac + bc$.

  b. The total area is also the sum of the areas of the two smaller rectangles ($ac + bc$). So $(a + b)c = ac + bc$.

21. The image is $(5 + -4, -2 + 5)$ or $(1, 3)$.

22. $B' = (5, -4)$ (a slide of 10 units to the right and 2 units down)

23. a. Although the deaths do not decrease every year, the likelihood of being killed by a tornado has generally decreased during the last 70 years.

  b. Sample: Better health care makes it possible for more victims of natural disasters to survive.

24.

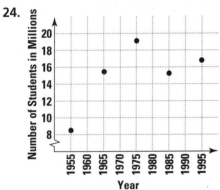

CHAPTER 3

REVIEW   pp. 210–213

1. $8x + -3x + 10x = 15x$

2. $-3m + 4m + -m = 0m = 0$

3. $c + \frac{1}{2}c = \frac{3}{2}c = 1\frac{1}{2}c$

4. $\frac{-2}{3}(6 + -9v + 4v) = \frac{-2}{3}(6 + -5v)$
$$= \frac{-2}{3} \cdot 6 + \frac{-2}{3} \cdot -5v$$
$$= -4 + \frac{10v}{3}$$

5. $11(3x + 2) + 4(5x + 6) = 33x + 22 + 20x + 24$
$$= 53x + 46$$

6. $3w + 4 + 5(4w + 6) = 3w + 4 + 20w + 30$
$$= 23w + 34$$

7. $2.5 = t + 3.1$
$$2.5 + -3.1 = t + 3.1 + -3.1$$
$$-0.6 = t$$
Check: $-0.6 + 3.1 = 2.5$

8. $x + -11 = 12$
$$x + -11 + 11 = 12 + 11$$
$$x = 23$$
Check: $23 + -11 = 12$

9. $(3 + n) + -11 = -5 + 4$
$$n + -8 = -1$$
$$n + -8 + 8 = -1 + 8$$
$$n = 7$$
Check: $(3 + 7) + -11 =$
$$10 + -11 = -1; \ -5 + 4 = -1$$

10. $\left(2\frac{1}{2} + 1\frac{1}{4}\right) + \frac{-3}{4} = (a + 6) + -2$
$$3\frac{3}{4} + \frac{-3}{4} = a + 4$$
$$3 = a + 4$$
$$3 + -4 = a + 4 + -4$$
$$-1 = a$$
Check: $\left(2\frac{1}{2} + 1\frac{1}{4}\right) + \frac{-3}{4} = 3;$
$$(-1 + 6) + (-2) = 5 + -2 = 3$$

11. $4n + 3 = 15$
$$4n + 3 + -3 = 15 + -3$$
$$4n = 12$$
$$\frac{1}{4} \cdot 4n = \frac{1}{4} \cdot 12$$
$$n = 3$$
Check: $4 \cdot 3 + 3 = 12 + 3 = 15$

12. $-470 + 2n = 1100$
$$-470 + 470 + 2n = 1100 + 470$$
$$2n = 1570$$
$$\frac{1}{2} \cdot 2n = \frac{1}{2} \cdot 1570$$
$$n = 785$$
Check: $-470 + 2 \cdot 785 = -470 + 1570 = 1100$

13. $\frac{2}{3}x + 14 = 15$

$\frac{2}{3}x + 14 + \text{-}14 = 15 + \text{-}14$

$\frac{2}{3}x = 1$

$\frac{3}{2} \cdot \frac{2}{3}x = \frac{3}{2} \cdot 1$

$x = \frac{3}{2}$

Check: Does $\frac{2}{3} \cdot \frac{3}{2} + 14 = 15$?

$1 + 14 = 15$?

$15 = 15$

Yes, it checks.

14. $5m + \text{-}3m + 6 = 12$

$2m + 6 = 12$

$2m + 6 + \text{-}6 = 12 + \text{-}6$

$2m = 6$

$\frac{1}{2} \cdot 2m = \frac{1}{2} \cdot 6$

$m = 3$

Check: Does $5 \cdot 3 + \text{-}3 \cdot 3 + 6 = 12$?

$15 + \text{-}9 + 6 = 12$?

$12 = 12$

Yes, it checks.

15. $17r + 12 + 9r = 1312$

$26r + 12 = 1312$

$26r + 12 + \text{-}12 = 1312 + \text{-}12$

$26r = 1300$

$\frac{1}{26}r \cdot 26r = \frac{1}{26} \cdot 1300$

$r = 50$

Check: Does $17 \cdot 50 + 12 + 9 \cdot 50 = 1312$?

$850 + 12 + 450 = 1312$?

$1312 = 1312$

Yes, it checks.

16. $5(x + 3) = 95$

$5x + 15 = 95$

$5x + 15 + \text{-}15 = 95 + \text{-}15$

$5x = 80$

$\frac{1}{5} \cdot 5x = \frac{1}{5} \cdot 80$

$x = 16$

Check: Does $5(16 + 3) = 95$?

$5 \cdot 19 = 95$?

$95 = 95$

Yes, it checks.

17. $2x + 3(1 + x) = 18$

$2x + 3 + 3x = 18$

$5x + 3 = 18$

$5x + 3 + \text{-}3 = 18 + \text{-}3$

$5x = 15$

$\frac{1}{5} \cdot 5x = \frac{1}{5} \cdot 15$

$x = 3$

Check: Does $2 \cdot 3 + 3(1 + 3) = 18$?

$6 + 3 \cdot 4 = 18$?

$6 + 12 = 18$?

$18 = 18$

Yes, it checks.

18. $16 = \frac{3}{4}b + 22$

$16 + \text{-}22 = \frac{3}{4}b + 22 + \text{-}22$

$\text{-}6 = \frac{3}{4}b$

$\frac{4}{3} \cdot \text{-}6 = \frac{4}{3} \cdot \frac{3}{4}b$

$\text{-}8 = b$

Check: Does $16 = \frac{3}{4} \cdot \text{-}8 + 22$?

$16 = \frac{\text{-}24}{4} + 22$?

$16 = \text{-}6 + 22$?

$16 = 16$

Yes, it checks.

19. $\frac{x}{3} + \frac{y}{3} = \frac{x+y}{3}$

20. $\frac{30}{a} + \frac{10}{a} + \frac{20}{a} = \frac{60}{a}$

21. $\frac{2}{3}x + \frac{1}{3}x = \frac{3}{3}x = x$

22. $\frac{x}{3} + \frac{x}{4} = \frac{4x}{12} + \frac{3x}{12} = \frac{7x}{12}$

23. $\frac{x}{5} + \frac{-3x}{2} = \frac{2x}{10} + \frac{-15x}{10} = \frac{-13x}{10}$

24. $\frac{2x}{5} + \frac{3y}{5} + \frac{-3x}{5} = \frac{2x + 3y - 3x}{5} = \frac{3y - x}{5}$

25. $\qquad 2x + 11 < 201$

$\qquad 2x + 11 + \text{-}11 < 201 + \text{-}11$

$\qquad\qquad 2x < 190$

$\qquad \frac{1}{2} \cdot 2x < \frac{1}{2} \cdot 190$

$\qquad\qquad x < 95$

Check: Does $2 \cdot 95 + 11 = 201$? Yes,
$190 + 11 = 201$. Pick some value that works
for $x < 95$. We choose 0. Is $2 \cdot 0 + 11 < 201$?
Yes, $0 + 11 = 11$ and $11 < 201$.

26. $\frac{3}{4}t + 21 > 12$

$\qquad \frac{3}{4}t > \text{-}9$

$\qquad t > \text{-}12$

Check: Does $\frac{3}{4} \cdot \text{-}12 + 21 = 12$? Yes,
$\text{-}9 + 21 = 12$. Pick some value that works
for $t > \text{-}12$. We choose 4. Is $\frac{3}{4} \cdot 4 + 21 > 12$?
Yes, $3 + 21 = 24$ and $24 > 12$.

27. $\text{-}2 + (5 + x) > 4$

$\qquad 3 + x > 4$

$\qquad 3 + x + \text{-}3 > 4 + \text{-}3$

$\qquad\qquad x > 1$

Check: Does $\text{-}2 + (5 + 1) = 4$? Yes, $\text{-}2 + 6 = 4$.
Pick some value that works for $x > 1$. We
choose 2. Is $\text{-}2 + (5 + 2) > 4$? Yes, $\text{-}2 + 7 = 5$
and $5 > 4$.

28. $\qquad \text{-}28 \leq 17 + (y + 5)$

$\qquad \text{-}28 \leq 22 + y$

$\text{-}28 + \text{-}22 \leq 22 + y + \text{-}22$

$\qquad \text{-}50 \leq y$

Check: Does $\text{-}28 = 17 + (\text{-}50 + 5)$? Yes,
$17 + \text{-}45 = \text{-}28$. Pick some value that works
for $y \geq \text{-}50$. We choose $\text{-}5$.
Is $17 + (\text{-}5 + 5) \geq \text{-}28$? Yes, $17 + 0 = 17$ and
$17 \geq \text{-}28$.

29. $\qquad 4 < \text{-}16g + 7g + 5$

$\qquad 4 < \text{-}9g + 5$

$\qquad 4 + \text{-}5 < \text{-}9g + 5 + \text{-}5$

$\qquad \text{-}1 < \text{-}9g$

$\qquad \text{-}\frac{1}{9} \cdot \text{-}1 > \text{-}\frac{1}{9} \cdot \text{-}9g$

$\qquad \frac{1}{9} > g$

Check: Does $\text{-}16 \cdot \frac{1}{9} + 7 \cdot \frac{1}{9} + 5 = 4$?

$\qquad \text{-}\frac{16}{9} + \frac{7}{9} + 5 = 4$?

$\qquad \text{-}\frac{9}{9} + 5 = 4$?

$\qquad \text{-}1 + 5 = 4$?

$\qquad 4 = 4$

Yes, it is true. Pick some value that works
for $g < \frac{1}{9}$. We pick 0. Is $4 < \text{-}16 \cdot 0 + 7 \cdot 0 + 5$?
Yes, $4 < 5$.

30. $p + 2p + 3p + 4p \leq 85$

$\qquad 10p \leq 85$

$\qquad \frac{1}{10} \cdot 10p \leq \frac{1}{10} \cdot 85$

$\qquad p \leq 8.5$

Check:
Does $8.5 + 2 \cdot 8.5 + 3 \cdot 8.5 + 4 \cdot 8.5 = 85$?
Yes, $8.5 + 17 + 25.5 + 34 = 85$.
Pick some value that works for $p \leq 8.5$.
We choose 1.
Is $1 + 2 \cdot 1 + 3 \cdot 1 + 4 \cdot 1 \leq 85$?
Yes, $1 + 2 + 3 + 4 = 10$ and $10 \leq 85$.

31. Commutative Property of Addition

32. Associative Property of Addition

33. Opposite of the Opposites Property

34. Distributive Property Adding Fractions form of the Distributive Property

35. Adding like terms form of the Distributive Property

36. Addition Property of Inequality

37. $x + -21 = 0$

38. a positive integer

39. $7(\$3 + 4¢) = \$21 + 28¢ = \$21.28$

40. $35(100 + 1) = 3500 + 35 = 3535$

41. $3(100 - 5) = 300 - 15 = 285$

42. $9(\$20 - 1¢) = \$180 - 9¢ = \$179.91$

43. $-11 + t = 13$

$$t = 24$$

The temperature must increase by 24°C.

44. $T_1 + C > T_2$

45. The two states produced $w + c$ billion pounds of milk.

46. $\$26 > \$5.40 + \$7.50 + d$

47. $e \geq \$5 + \$4$; at least $9

48.
$$\$320.50 = \$25.00 + \$15.00$$
$$+ \$7.50 + \$7.80h$$
$$320.50 = 47.50 + 7.8h$$
$$320.50 + -47.50 = 47.50 + -47.50 + 7.8h$$
$$273.00 = 7.8h$$
$$\frac{1}{7.8} \cdot 273.00 = \frac{1}{7.8} \cdot 7.8h$$
$$35 = h$$

She worked 35 hours.

49.
$$\$67,500 = x + x + x + x + .5x$$
$$67,500 = 4.5x$$
$$\frac{1}{4.5} \cdot 67,500 = \frac{1}{4.5} \cdot 4.5x$$
$$15,000 = x$$

Each child should receive $15,000 and the grandchild should receive $7,500.

50. a. $\$45 + \$6w$

b.
$$45 + 6w = 195$$
$$45 + -45 + 6w = 195 + -45$$
$$6w = 150$$
$$\frac{1}{6} \cdot 6w = \frac{1}{6} \cdot 150$$
$$w = 25$$

After 25 weeks she will have saved $195.

51. a.

x	y
⋮	⋮
6	25

b. $y = 3x + 7$

52. a. 5 $.29 + .23 + .23 + .23 + .23$ $.29 + .23(4)$

b. $.29 + .23(n - 1)$

53. a. $\$2.95 + .75(4 - 3) = \$2.95 + \$0.75 = \$3.70$

b. $\$2.95 + .75(10 - 3) = \$2.95 + \$5.25 = \$8.20$

c. $\$2.95 + .75(n - 3)$ when $n > 3$

54. a. jobs lost

b.

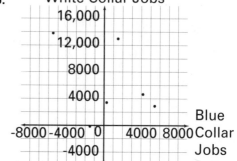

55. halfway up

56. 4

57. Ohio

58. 1960–1970

59. 1950–1960

60.

61. $(2 + -40, -4 + 60) = (-38, 56)$

62. $(x + 4, y - 10)$

63. The image of (x, y) is $(x - 1, y + 8)$.

64. $R' = (-3 + 3, 2) = (0, 2)$

65. The image of A is $(4, 2)$. The image of B is $(3, -3)$.

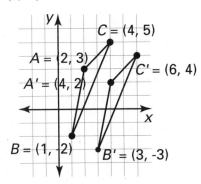

66. a. $3b + 2 = 8$

b. $3b = 6$

$b = 2$

Each box weighs 2 kg.

67. a. $5W + 8 = 13$

b. $5W = 5$

$W = 1$

Each box weights 1 kg.

68.

69. $ad + bd + cd;\ d(a + b + c)$

70. $2x^2 + x;\ x(2x + 1)$

71. $12 + y \le 48$

$-12 + 12 + y \le -12 + 48$

$y \le 36$

72. $-\frac{3}{5} > z + 20$

$-\frac{3}{5} + -20 > z + 20 + -20$

$-20\frac{3}{5} > z$

$-20\frac{3}{5}$

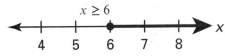

73. $-2x + 4 < 17$

$-2x + 4 + -4 < 17 + -4$

$-2x < 13$

$-\frac{1}{2} \cdot -2x > -\frac{1}{2} \cdot 13$

$x > -\frac{13}{2}$

-6.5

74. $5(2 + 3x) + 6 \ge 106$

$10 + 15x + 6 \ge 106$

$15x + 16 \ge 106$

$15x + 16 + -16 \ge 106 + -16$

$15x \ge 90$

$\frac{1}{15} \cdot 15x \ge \frac{1}{15} \cdot 90$

$x \ge 6$

CHAPTER 3

REFRESHER p. 213

1. $8\frac{2}{3} - 3\frac{1}{3} = 5\frac{1}{3}$

2. $13.96 - 4.89 = 9.07$

3. $12.5 - 6.85 = 5.65$

4. $18\frac{1}{2} - 10\frac{3}{4} = 17\frac{6}{4} - 10\frac{3}{4} = 7\frac{3}{4}$

5. $100\% - 4\% = 96\%$

6. $100\% - 8.5\% = 91.5\%$

7. $40 - 200 = \text{-}160$

8. $76 - 79 = \text{-}3$

9. $\text{-}2 - 6 = \text{-}8$

10. $\text{-}12 - \text{-}11 = \text{-}1$

11. $111 - \text{-}88 = 199$

12. $\text{-}2 - \text{-}3 = 1$

13. $$x - 40 = 11$$
$$x - 40 + 40 = 11 + 40$$
$$x = 51$$

14. $$878 = y - 31$$
$$878 + 31 = y - 31 + 31$$
$$909 = y$$

15. $$w - 64 = 49$$
$$w - 64 + 64 = 49 + 64$$
$$w = 113$$

16. $$\text{-}100 = z - 402$$
$$\text{-}100 + 402 = z - 402 + 402$$
$$302 = z$$

17. (b)

18. (c)

19. $m\angle V = 74°$

20. $m\angle W = 120°$

21.

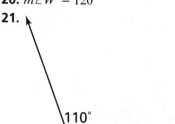

22.

CHAPTER 4
SUBTRACTION IN ALGEBRA

LESSON 4-1   pp. 216–220

1. Algebraic Definition of Subtraction: For all real numbers a and b, $a - b = a + -b$.

2. **a.** $-2 - 7 = -2 + -7$
   b. $-2 - 7 = -2 + -7 = -9$

3. **a.** $28 - -63 = 28 + 63$
   b. $28 - -63 = 28 + 63 = 91$

4. **a.** $\frac{3}{5} - -\frac{7}{10} = \frac{3}{5} + \frac{7}{10}$
   b. $\frac{3}{5} - -\frac{7}{10} = \frac{3}{5} + \frac{7}{10}$
   $\frac{6}{10} + \frac{7}{10} = \frac{13}{10} = 1\frac{3}{10}$

5. **a.** $-3.5 - 0.9 = -3.5 + -0.9$
   b. $-3.5 - 0.9 = -3.5 + -0.9 = -4.4$

6. **a.** $12 + -15 = -3$; the new temperature is $-3°$.
   b. $12 - 15 = -3$; the new temperature is $-3°$.

7. **a.** 73 $\boxed{+/-}$ $\boxed{-}$ 91 $\boxed{+/-}$
   b. 73 $\boxed{+/-}$ $\boxed{+}$ 91

8. **a.** False $((3 - 9) - 1 = -6 - 1$
   $= -7$, whereas
   $3 - (9 - 1) = 3 - 8$
   $= -5)$
   b. The Associative Property of Subtraction is not verified.

9. $20 - 4 - 3$
   $= 20 + -4 + -3$
   $= 16 + -3$
   $= 13$

10. $-7 - 30 - 20$
    $= -7 + -30 + -20$
    $= -37 + -20$
    $= -57$

11. $x - -d = x + d$

12. $-y - -5 = -y + 5 = 5 - y$

13. $10p - 2q + 4 + 8q$
    $= 10p - 2q + 8q + 4$
    $= 10p + 6q + 4$

14. $-2a - 3a + 4b - b$
    $= -2a + -3a + 4b + -b$
    $= -5a + 3b$

15. $= 3 - 5^2$
    $= 3 - 25$
    $= 3 + -25$
    $= -22$

16. $-(-12) - 2$
    $= 12 + -2$
    $= 10$

17. $-1 - (-3) - 2$
    $= -1 + 3 + -2$
    $= 2 + -2$
    $= 0$

18. $-4\frac{7}{8} + 1\frac{3}{4} - 1\frac{3}{4} + 1\frac{1}{4} + 2\frac{1}{8} - \frac{5}{8}$
    $= \left(1\frac{3}{4} + 1\frac{1}{4} + 2\frac{1}{8}\right) - \left(4\frac{7}{8} + 1\frac{3}{4} + \frac{5}{8}\right)$
    $= 5\frac{1}{8} - 7\frac{1}{4}$
    $= -2\frac{1}{8}$
    or,
    $= -4\frac{7}{8} + 1\frac{3}{4} - 1\frac{3}{4} + 1\frac{1}{4} + 2\frac{1}{8} - \frac{5}{8}$
    $= -4\frac{7}{8} + 1\frac{3}{4} + -1\frac{3}{4} + 1\frac{1}{4} + 2\frac{1}{8} + -\frac{5}{8}$
    $= -4\frac{7}{8} + 1\frac{1}{4} + 2\frac{1}{8} + -\frac{5}{8}$
    $= -4\frac{7}{8} + 1\frac{2}{8} + 2\frac{1}{8} + -\frac{5}{8}$
    $= -3\frac{5}{8} + 2\frac{1}{8} + -\frac{5}{8}$
    $= -1\frac{4}{8} + -\frac{5}{8}$
    $= -2\frac{1}{8}$

19. **a.** $-4 + -3 + -3 + 5$
    b. $-4 - 3 - 3 + 5$
    c. -5; He lost 5 pounds.

20. a. Sample: $t = 40$ and $f = 5$
b. Toni
c. Sample: $t = 40$, $f = 5$;
$$f - t = 5 - 40$$
$$= -35$$

21. Clue 1: eliminate -7, -4, -3, and -2.
Clue 2: eliminate 7.
Clue 3: eliminate 3.
Clue 4: eliminate 4.
Hence, $x = 1$.

22. a. $p - q = 5 - -1 = 5 + 1 = 6$
$q - p = -1 - 5 = -6$
b. $p - q = 1 - 3 = 1 + -3 = -2$
$q - p = 3 - 1 = 2$
c. $p - q = -2 - 0 = -2$
$q - p = 0 - -2 = 2$
d. $p - q = -3 - -6 = -3 + 6 = 3$
$q - p = -6 - -3 = -6 + 3 = -3$
e. No, switching p and q when $p \neq q$ gives different answers.
f. $p - q$ is the opposite (additive inverse) of $q - p$.

23. $n + .2(n + 15) = n + .2n + 3 = 1.2n + 3$

24. $\quad -3 = x + -7$
$-3 + 7 = x + -7 + 7$
$\quad\quad 4 = x$

25. $\quad\quad 2.7 + 7y = 3.4$
$2.7 + -2.7 + 7y = 3.4 + -2.7$
$\quad\quad\quad 7y = 0.7$
$\quad \frac{1}{7} \cdot 7y = \frac{1}{7} \cdot 0.7$
$\quad\quad\quad\quad y = 0.1$

26. There are 9 choices for the first digit, 8 choices for the second digit, 7 choices for the third digit, and 6 choices for the fourth digit or $9 \cdot 8 \cdot 7 \cdot 6 = 3024$ possible numbers.

27. 30% of $74.95 = .3 \cdot 74.95 = 22.485$

28. a. graph II (The greatest number of people would be present at breakfast, lunch, and dinner.)
b. graph I (The greatest number of people present would be from 9 A.M. to 3 P.M.)

c. graph III (The number of people remains fairly constant.)

29. a. (i) MDCCXXXI (1731)
b. (ii) MCDXCII (1492)
c. (iv) MCMXVII (1917)
d. (iii) MCMXXVIII (1928)

LESSON 4-2   pp. 221–226

1. $(x - 3)$ feet

2. a. Amount of the discount is $160
b. Percent of discount is 20%
$\left(\frac{160}{800} = .2 = 20\% \right)$
c. The sale price is $640.

3. a. $.25C$ (25% of C)
b. $.75C$ ($C - .25C = .75C$)

4. $J - .4J = .6J$ (40% of J is $.4J$.)

5. a. 4% of P is $.04P$.
b. The total amount paid is $P + .04P = 1.04P$.
c. If $P = \$65$, then total amount paid is $65 + .04 \cdot 65 = 65 + 2.6 = \$67.60$.

6. $40^2 - b^2 = 1600 - b^2$

7. The temperature rose 49°F. ($45 - -4 = 45 + 4 = 49$)

8. The range of temperatures in the U.S. is 214°F. ($134 - -80 = 134 + 80 = 214$)

9. $4x$ square units (The area of the larger rectangle is $7x$ square units; the area of the smaller rectangle is $3x$ square units; their difference is $7x - 3x$.)

10. $14,000 - (S + 2580) = 14,000 - S - 2580 = (11,420 - S)$ ft^2

11. a. Bernie
b. 7 years older

12. a. John
b. 4 years older $((B - 3) - (B - 7) = B + -3 + -B + 7 = -3 + 7 = 4)$

13. a. $.80R$ ($R - .20R = .80R$)
b. $.80R - .10 \cdot .80R = .80R - .0800R = .72R$
c. $.72R + .03 \cdot .72R = .72R + .0216R = .7416R$

60

14. a. The temperature rose $\frac{1}{2}$ degree.
$(100.9 - 100.4 = .5)$

b. The temperature fell 1.5 degrees.
$(100.4 - 98.9 = 1.5)$

15. a. The angles differ by 47 degrees.
$\left(72\frac{1}{2} - 25\frac{1}{2} = 47\right)$

b. $a - b$ or $b - a$

16. a.

Student	Pretest	Posttest	Change
Chui, L.	57	65	8
Fields, S.	43	41	-2
Ivan, J.	63	70	7
Washington, C.	54	51	-3

b. Chui's test scores showed the most improvement.

17. $-3 - -3 = -3 + 3 = 0$

18. $-8.7 - 16.03 = -8.7 + -16.03 = -24.73$

19. $-p - -q = -p + q = q - p$

20. $-7ab + 2a - 5b - 6ab - 4a + b$
$= -7ab + -6ab + 2a + -4a + -5b + b$
$= -13ab + -2a + -4b$

21. a. The coordinate of E is -10. $(-6 - 4 = -10)$

b. The coordinate of F is $-6 + n$ where $n > 0$.

c. Point F could be located anywhere to the right of Point A.

22. $7t + 6 > 41$
$7t + 6 - 6 > 41 - 6$
$7t > 35$
$\frac{1}{7} \cdot 7t > \frac{1}{7} \cdot 35$
$t > 5$

23. $3x + 8 = 5$
$3x + 8 + -8 = 5 + -8$
$3x = -3$
$\frac{1}{3} \cdot 3x = \frac{1}{3} \cdot -3$
$x = -1$

24. $16 + x = 0$
$-16 + 16 + x = -16 + 0$
$x = -16$

25. $-28.3 > -x + 17.5$
$-28.3 + -17.5 > -x + 17.5 + -17.5$
$-45.8 > -x$
$-1 \cdot -45.8 < -1 \cdot -x$
$45.8 < x$

26. $x + 4 = 7; x = 3$
$y - 2 = -1; y = 1$

27. a. $9^2 - 4^2 = 81 - 16 = 65$ and $(9 + 4)(9 - 4) = 13 \cdot 5 = 65$; $31^2 - 29^2 = 961 - 841 = 120$ and $(31 + 29)(31 - 29) = 60 \cdot 2 = 120$; $3.5^2 - 2.5^2 = 12.25 - 6.25 = 6$ and $(3.5 + 2.5)(3.5 - 2.5) = 6 \cdot 1 = 6$

b. $a^2 - b^2 = (a + b)(a - b)$

c. Sample: $3^2 - 2^2 = (3 + 2)(3 - 2)$; True

28. The areas of the triangles are:

a. $\frac{1}{2} \cdot b \cdot b = \frac{1}{2}b^2$ square units

b. $\frac{1}{2} \cdot 3h \cdot 4h = 6h^2$ square units

c. $\frac{1}{2} \cdot \frac{1}{2} \cdot \frac{1}{4} = \frac{1}{16}$ square units

29. a. The smallest number is 1 day; the largest number is 1 day less that 2 years or 729 days.

b. 80 or 81 (If the month of her death precedes the month of her birth, then her last birthday was in 1798, so $1798 - 1718 = 80$. If the month of her death follows the month of her birth, then her birthday in 1799 is past, so $1799 - 1718 = 81$.)

c. 89 years

d. 279 years

LESSON 4-3 pp. 227–231

1. a. $x - -154 = 573$

b. $x + 154 = 573$
$x + 154 + -154 = 573 + -154$
$x = 419$
The maximum temperature was 419°C.

2. In solving equations in this lesson the first step is to change subtraction to adding the opposite.

3.
$$12y + \text{-}9 = \text{-}3$$
$$12y + \text{-}9 + 9 = \text{-}3 + 9$$
$$12y = 6$$
$$\frac{1}{12} \cdot 12y = \frac{1}{12} \cdot 6$$
$$y = \frac{1}{2}$$

4.
$$\frac{1}{2}x + \text{-}7 = 8$$
$$\frac{1}{2}x + \text{-}7 + 7 = 8 + 7$$
$$\frac{1}{2}x = 15$$
$$2 \cdot \frac{1}{2}x = 2 \cdot 15$$
$$x = 30$$

5.
$$5z + \text{-}3.4 = 2.9$$
$$5z + \text{-}3.4 + 3.4 = 2.9 + 3.4$$
$$5z = 6.3$$
$$\frac{1}{5} \cdot 5z = \frac{1}{5} \cdot 6.3$$
$$z = 1.26$$

6.
$$\text{-}9A + \text{-}1 = 0$$
$$\text{-}9A + \text{-}1 + 1 = 0 + 1$$
$$\text{-}9A = 1$$
$$\frac{\text{-}1}{9} \cdot \text{-}9A = \frac{\text{-}1}{9} \cdot 1$$
$$A = \frac{\text{-}1}{9}$$

7.
$$3.01 - c = .54$$
$$\text{-}3.01 + 3.01 - c = \text{-}3.01 + .54$$
$$\text{-}c = \text{-}2.47$$
$$\text{-}1 \cdot \text{-}c = \text{-}1 \cdot \text{-}2.47$$
$$c = 2.47$$
2.47 mm was cut off.

8.
$$\text{-}3 - t = \text{-}1$$
$$\text{-}3 + \text{-}t = \text{-}1$$
$$\text{-}3 + 3 + \text{-}t = \text{-}1 + 3$$
$$\text{-}t = 2$$
$$t = \text{-}2$$

9.
$$\text{-}10 = 400 - A$$
$$\text{-}10 = 400 + \text{-}A$$
$$\text{-}10 + \text{-}400 = 400 + \text{-}400 + \text{-}A$$
$$\text{-}410 = \text{-}A$$
$$A = 410$$

10.
$$5000 - 30x = 1000$$
$$5000 + \text{-}30x = 1000$$
$$5000 + \text{-}5000 + \text{-}30x = 1000 + \text{-}5000$$
$$\text{-}30x = \text{-}4000$$
$$\frac{\text{-}1}{30} \cdot \text{-}30x = \frac{\text{-}1}{30} \cdot \text{-}4000$$
$$x = 133.\overline{3}$$
The area is about 133.4 square units.

11. a.
$$2x - 16 = 20$$
$$2x + \text{-}16 + 16 = 20 + 16$$
$$2x = 36$$
$$\frac{1}{2} \cdot 2x = \frac{1}{2} \cdot 36$$
$$x = 18$$

b.
$$2x - 16 \geq 20$$
$$2x + \text{-}16 + 16 \geq 20 + 16$$
$$2x \geq 36$$
$$\frac{1}{2} \cdot 2x \geq \frac{1}{2} \cdot 36$$
$$x \geq 18$$

c.
$$16 - 2x = 20$$
$$16 + \text{-}2x + \text{-}16 = 20 + \text{-}16$$
$$\text{-}2x = 4$$
$$\frac{\text{-}1}{2} \cdot \text{-}2x = \frac{\text{-}1}{2} \cdot 4$$
$$x = \text{-}2$$

d.
$$16 - 2x \geq 20$$
$$16 + \text{-}2x + \text{-}16 \geq 20 + \text{-}16$$
$$\text{-}2x \geq 4$$
$$\frac{\text{-}1}{2} \cdot \text{-}2x \leq \frac{\text{-}1}{2} \cdot 4$$
$$x \leq \text{-}2$$

12. In the fourth step Ali dropped the negative sign in front of the 3. It should be $-3x = 1$ hence $x = \frac{-1}{3}$.

13. a. $10n - 3 = 84$

   b.
   $$10n - 3 = 84$$
   $$10n + -3 = 84$$
   $$10n + -3 + 3 = 84 + 3$$
   $$10n = 87$$
   $$\frac{1}{10} \cdot 10n = \frac{1}{10} \cdot 87$$
   $$n = 8.7$$

14.
$$x - 3276 \geq 1500$$
$$x + -3276 + 3276 \geq 1500 + 3276$$
$$x \geq 4776$$
Mr. Archer has at least $4776 in his account.

15.
$$11{,}200 - 60x = 8000$$
$$11{,}200 + -60x + -11{,}200 = 8000 + -11{,}200$$
$$-60x = -3200$$
$$\frac{-1}{60} \cdot -60x = \frac{-1}{60} \cdot -3200$$
$$x = 53.\overline{3}$$
It will take over 53 years for the town's population to reach 8000. Hence in the year 2044 the town's population will reach 8,000.

Year	Population
1990	11,200
1991	11,140
1992	11,080
1993	11,020
⋮	⋮
2043	8,020
2044	7,960

16. t = time of her 1988 Olympic race
$$39.25 - t = .15$$
$$39.25 - t + -39.25 = .15 + -39.25$$
$$-t = -39.10$$
$$t = 39.10$$
Bonnie Blair's 1988 Olympic time was 39.10 seconds.

17.
$$-12.2 - p = -0.56$$
$$-12.2 + -p = -0.56$$
$$-12.2 + -p + 12.2 = -0.56 + 12.2$$
$$-p = 11.64$$
$$p = -11.64$$

18.
$$-1 \leq -1 - y$$
$$-1 \leq -1 + -y$$
$$-1 + 1 \leq -1 + -y + 1$$
$$0 \leq -y$$
$$0 \geq y$$

19.
$$\tfrac{3}{4}t - 11 > 7$$
$$\tfrac{3}{4}t - 11 + 11 > 7 + 11$$
$$\tfrac{3}{4}t > 18$$
$$\tfrac{4}{3} \cdot \tfrac{3}{4}t > \tfrac{4}{3} \cdot 18$$
$$t > 24$$

20.
$$-3(2n + 1) - 4 = -11$$
$$-6n + -3 + -4 = -11$$
$$-6n + -7 = -11$$
$$-6n + -7 + 7 = -11 + 7$$
$$-6n = -4$$
$$\tfrac{-1}{6} \cdot -6n = \tfrac{-1}{6} \cdot -4$$
$$n = \tfrac{2}{3}$$

21. They were married in the year $y - 50$.

22. They were married in the year $2000 - n$.

23. a. $22.00 (10% of $20.00 is $.1 \cdot 20 = 2$ and new hourly wage is $20.00 + $2.00 = $22.00.)

   b. $19.80 (10% of $22.00 is $.1 \cdot 22 = 2.2$ and new hourly wage is $22.00 - $2.20 = $19.80.)

   c. The amount subtracted from 22, 10% of 22, is larger than the amount added to 20, 10% of 20, so the net result is less than 20.

24. $120\frac{1}{4} + -9\frac{3}{8} = 110\frac{7}{8}$

25. (a) always negative

26. (d) none of these; it may be positive or negative

27. (a) always negative; taking the sum of two negative numbers

28. $5 - (4 - (3 - (2 - 1)))$

$= 5 - (4 - (3 - 1))$

$= 5 - (4 - 2)$

$= 5 - 2$

$= 3$

29. $1 - (2 - (3 - (4 - 5)))$

$= 1 - (2 - (3 - -1))$

$= 1 - (2 - 4)$

$= 1 - -2$

$= 1 + 2$

$= 3$

30. $\frac{4a}{5} + \frac{a}{3}$

$= \frac{12a}{15} + \frac{5a}{15}$

$= \frac{17a}{15}$

31. $-1(3x + -5)$

$= -1 \cdot 3x + -1 \cdot -5$

$= -3x + 5$

32. (a) the distance traveled in h hours at 30 mph (Using the points on the graph you are 30 miles away after 1 hour, 60 miles away after 2 hours, and 90 miles away after 3 hours.)

33. **a.** There are 42 students in the class. (There are 20 students between 7 and 28; hence, there should be 20 students between them in the other half of the circle of which 6 are the students counting from 1 to 6.)

b. $2n - 14$ (There are $n - 8$ students between 7 and n.)

LESSON 4-4 pp. 232–239

1. Total contract; $355.30 changes to $365.30. Balance due; $130.30 changes to $140.30.

2. Dan Bricklin and Bob Frankston in 1978

3. cells

4. 27 $(18 + (-3)\,{}^\wedge\,2 = 18 + 9 = 27)$

5. D3 = -.6; E3 = -.6

6. **a.** $= A4 * (B4 - C4)$

b. $= A4 * B4 - A4 * C4$

c. Because the property $a(b - c) = ab - ac$ holds true for all real numbers

7. replication

8. **a.** $= A7\,{}^\wedge\,2 + B7\,{}^\wedge\,2$

b. 26 $(1\,{}^\wedge\,2 + 5\,{}^\wedge\,2 = 1 + 25 = 26)$

c. = SQRT(C7)

d. 5.099 $(\sqrt{26} \approx 5.0990195)$

9. 86   **10.** D3

11. Marcel's mean from the first two tests

12. **a.** $= (B5 + C5)/2$

b. D5

13. $= (J5 + J6 + K5 + K6)/4$

14. $(x - y)/(2x + y^3)$

15. No. $(\sqrt{16 + 25} = \sqrt{41}$ which does not equal 9.)

16. In cell B2, $= A2\,{}^\wedge\,2$; in C2, $= A2\,{}^\wedge\,3$; in D2, $= A2\,{}^\wedge\,4$; in E2, $= A2\,{}^\wedge\,5$

17. **a.** $12.00 $(C = 5 + .5(39 - 25)$

$C = 5 + .5(14)$

$C = 5 + 7$

$C = 12)$

b. Sample: In cell A1 enter the label "Number of words." In cell B1 enter the label "Cost of ad." In cell A2 enter 25, and in cell A3 enter the formula $= A2 + 1$. Replicate this formula in cells A4 through A77. Enter the formula $= 5.00 + .50 * (A2 - 25)$ in cell B2. Finally replicate the formula from cell B2 in cells B3 through B77.

18.
$$9x + \text{-}18 = 432$$
$$9x + \text{-}18 + 18 = 432 + 18$$
$$9x = 450$$
$$\frac{1}{9} \cdot 9x = \frac{1}{9} \cdot 450$$
$$x = 50$$

19.
$$9(x - 18) = 432$$
$$9x + \text{-}162 = 432$$
$$9x + \text{-}162 + 162 = 432 + 162$$
$$9x = 594$$
$$\frac{1}{9} \cdot 9x = \frac{1}{9} \cdot 594$$
$$x = 66$$

20.
$$\frac{y}{2} + \text{-}7 = \text{-}6$$
$$\frac{y}{2} + \text{-}7 + 7 = \text{-}6 + 7$$
$$\frac{y}{2} = 1$$
$$2 \cdot \frac{y}{2} = 2 \cdot 1$$
$$y = 2$$

21.
$$\text{-}4 < 8z + \text{-}4$$
$$\text{-}4 + 4 < 8z + \text{-}4 + 4$$
$$0 < 8z$$
$$\frac{1}{8} \cdot 0 < \frac{1}{8} \cdot 8z$$
$$0 < z$$

22. (d)

23. Use the Pythagorean Theorem.
$$385^2 + 2470^2 = (AB)^2$$
$$6{,}249{,}125 = (AB)^2$$
$$\sqrt{6{,}249{,}125} = AB$$
$$2499.825 = AB$$
The distance from A to B is about 2500 ft.

24. 7 and 8; 53 is between the perfect squares 49 and 64, so $\sqrt{49} < \sqrt{53} < \sqrt{64}$.

25. Answers will vary.

1. a. $20 - r - t$ or $20 - (r + t)$
 b. $20 - 3 - 7 = 17 - 7 = 10$ and
  $20 - (3 + 7) = 20 - 10 = 10$

2. $D - L - 10$ or $D - (L + 10)$

3. (c) **4.** (b)

5. $\text{-}(x + 15)$ **6.** $\text{-}(4n + \text{-}3m)$
  $= \text{-}x + \text{-}15$ $= \text{-}(4n + \text{-}3m)$
  $= \text{-}x - 15$ $= \text{-}4n + 3m$

7. $x - (x + 2)$
  $= x + \text{-}(x + 2)$
  $= x + \text{-}x + \text{-}2$
  $= \text{-}2$

8. $3y - 5(y + 1)$
  $= 3y + \text{-}5(y + 1)$
  $= 3y + \text{-}5y + \text{-}5$
  $= \text{-}2y + \text{-}5$

9. $(3k + 4) - (7k - 9)$
  $= 3k + 4 + \text{-}(7k + \text{-}9)$
  $= 3k + 4 + \text{-}7k + 9$
  $= \text{-}4k + 13$

10. $\text{-}(5 + k) + (k - 18)$
  $= \text{-}5 + \text{-}k + k + \text{-}18$
  $= \text{-}23$

11.
$$\text{-}(A - 9) = 11$$
$$\text{-}A + 9 = 11$$
$$\text{-}A + 9 + \text{-}9 = 11 + \text{-}9$$
$$\text{-}A = 2$$
$$A = \text{-}2$$

12.
$$2 - (x + 3) = 4$$
$$2 + \text{-}x + \text{-}3 = 4$$
$$\text{-}x + \text{-}1 = 4$$
$$\text{-}x + \text{-}1 + 1 = 4 + 1$$
$$\text{-}x = 5$$
$$x = \text{-}5$$

13. $12 - (2y - 4) = 18$

$12 + -2y + 4 = 18$

$-2y + 16 = 18$

$-2y + 16 + -16 = 18 + -16$

$-2y = 2$

$\frac{-1}{2} \cdot -2y = \frac{-1}{2} \cdot 2$

$y = -1$

14. $5x - 3(5 - 2x) = -15$

$5x + -15 + 6x = -15$

$11x + -15 = -15$

$11x + -15 + 15 = -15 + 15$

$11x = 0$

$\frac{1}{11} \cdot 11x = \frac{1}{11} \cdot 0$

$x = 0$

15. $\frac{8x}{3} - \frac{3x + 2}{6}$

$= \frac{16x}{6} - \frac{3x + 2}{6}$

$= \frac{16x - (3x + 2)}{6}$

$= \frac{16x - 3x - 2}{6}$

$= \frac{13x - 2}{6}$

16. $\frac{n + 1}{2} - \frac{n - 1}{3}$

$= \frac{3(n + 1)}{6} - \frac{2(n - 1)}{6}$

$= \frac{3(n + 1) - 2(n - 1)}{6}$

$= \frac{3n + 3 - 2n + 2}{6}$

$= \frac{n + 5}{6}$

17. $-(a + 2b - c) = -a + -2b + c$

18. $270 - A_1 - A_2$ or $270 - (A_1 + A_2)$ (The area of the rectangle is $15 \cdot 18 = 270$ square units.)

19. $90 - f - f - p - f - f =$
$90 - p - 4f$ or $90 - (p + 4f)$

20. $3x - 2(x + 6.5) < 25.5$

$3x + -2x + -13 < 25.5$

$x + -13 < 25.5$

$x + -13 + 13 < 25.5 + 13$

$x < 38.5$

21. $3(t + 9) - (9 + t) + 6(t + 9) = 80$

$3t + 27 + -9 + -t + 6t + 54 = 80$

$8t + 72 = 80$

$8t + 72 + -72 = 80 + -72$

$8t = 8$

$\frac{1}{8} \cdot 8t = \frac{1}{8} \cdot 8$

$t = 1$

22. a. In D3, 1232; in E3, 1232; in D4, -807; in E4, -807

b. The results are the same.

c. The results are the same because $I - E = I + -E$. Subtracting a number is the same as adding its opposite.

23. $10 = 3L - 26$

$10 + 26 = 3L + -26 + 26$

$36 = 3L$

$\frac{1}{3} \cdot 36 = \frac{1}{3} \cdot 3L$

$12 = L$

His feet are approximately 12 inches in length.

24. $6\frac{1}{2} = 3L - 22$

$6\frac{1}{2} + 22 = 3L + -22 + 22$

$28\frac{1}{2} = 3L$

$\frac{1}{3} \cdot \frac{57}{2} = \frac{1}{3} \cdot 3L$

$\frac{57}{6} = 9.5 = L$

Her feet are about 9.5 inches in length.

25. $D + .06D + .15D = 1.21D$; the person paid $1.21D$ dollars.

26.
$$15 + .10b \geq 25$$
$$15 + -15 + .1b \geq 25 + -15$$
$$.1b \geq 10$$
$$10 \cdot .1b \geq 10 \cdot 10$$
$$b \geq 100$$

At least 100 bags must be sold.

27. a.

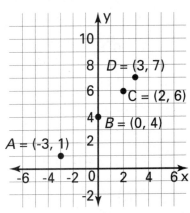

b. Sample: all points lie on a line.

c. Sample: the y-coordinate is 4 more than the x-coordinate.

28. $100(5 \cdot 20 = 100)$; total cost = 5 · number of tapes

29. TABLE OF (X,Y) VALUES

X VALUE	Y VALUE
0	12
1	11
2	10
3	9
4	8
5	7

30. (b)

31. Sample: The answer is equal to twice the second number. If x and y are the numbers, then the quantity we want is $x + y - (x - y)$. By the properties of this lesson, that quantity is $x + y + -x + y$, or $2y$.

32.
$$\frac{x-1}{3} - \frac{2x+5}{4} > \text{-}2$$
$$\frac{4(x-1)}{12} - \frac{3(2x+5)}{12} > \text{-}2$$
$$\frac{4x - 4 - 6x - 15}{12} > \text{-}2$$
$$\frac{\text{-}2x - 19}{12} > \text{-}2$$
$$12 \cdot \frac{\text{-}2x - 19}{12} > 12 \cdot \text{-}2$$
$$\text{-}2x + \text{-}19 > \text{-}24$$
$$\text{-}2x + \text{-}19 + 19 > \text{-}24 + 19$$
$$\text{-}2x > \text{-}5$$
$$\frac{\text{-}1}{2} \cdot \text{-}2x < \frac{\text{-}1}{2} \cdot \text{-}5$$
$$x < \frac{5}{2}$$

LESSON 4-6 pages 246–252

1. 2 bran muffins ($B = 12 - 10 = 2$)

2. True ($0 + 12 = 12$)

3. a. There are 13 solutions to the equation $R + B = 12$.

b. Each solution is represented by a point on the graph.

4. The graph of all pairs of real numbers whose sum is 12 is a line through (0, 12) and (12, 0).

5. a. $x + y = 7$

b.

x	y	(x, y)
4	3	(4, 3)
3	4	(3, 4)
2	5	(2, 5)
1	6	(1, 6)
0	7	(0, 7)
-1	8	(-1, 8)

c.

6. a.

x	y	(x, y)
4	-16	(4, -16)
5	-15	(5, -15)
6	-14	(6, -14)
7.5	-12.5	(7.5, -12.5)

b. These points are graphed in the Example.

7. a. $y - x = 5$

b.

x	y	(x, y)
1	6	(1, 6)
2	7	(2, 7)
3	8	(3, 8)
4	9	(4, 9)
5	10	(5, 10)
6	11	(6, 11)

c.

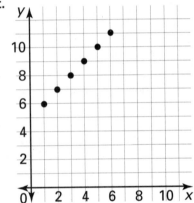

d. No. Sample: Because they cannot earn a fraction of a medal.

8. $(R, B) = (4, 8)$

9. a.

s	a	(s, a)
0	8	(0, 8)
1	7	(1, 7)
2	6	(2, 6)
3	5	(3, 5)
4	4	(4, 4)
5	3	(5, 3)
6	2	(6, 2)
7	1	(7, 1)
8	0	(8, 0)

b. If Sal has two more fish than Al, then Al has 3 fish.

10. a.

x	y	(x, y)
-2	2	(-2, 2)
-1	1	(-1, 1)
0	0	(0, 0)
1	-1	(1, -1)
2	-2	(2, -2)

b.

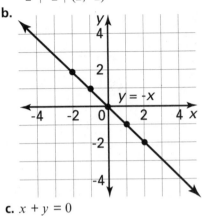

c. $x + y = 0$

11. (c), (d)

12. (b), (d)

13. a.

j	m	(j, m)
0	10	(0, 10)
1	9	(1, 9)
2	8	(2, 8)
3	7	(3, 7)
4	6	(4, 6)
5	5	(5, 5)
6	4	(6, 4)
7	3	(7, 3)
8	2	(8, 2)
9	1	(9, 1)
10	0	(10, 0)

b.

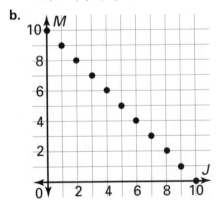

14. Sample: Jack spent x dollars the same day that Joyce spent y dollars. Together they spent 20 dollars.

15. $12a - 3(5a + 4)$

$= 12a + {-15a} + {-12}$

$= {-3a} + {-12}$

$= {-3a} - 12$

16. $\dfrac{11n + 1}{5} - \dfrac{3n + 4}{5}$

$= \dfrac{11n + 1 - 3n - 4}{5}$

$= \dfrac{8n - 3}{5}$

17. **a.**

	A	B
1	Time (hrs)	Distance (mi)
2	1.0	55
3	1.5	82.5
4	2.0	110
5	2.5	137.5
6	3.0	165
7	3.5	192.5

b. $= A6 * 55$

18. $16 - 5x = 21$

$16 + {-5x} + {-16} = 21 + {-16}$

$-5x = 5$

$\dfrac{-1}{5} \cdot {-5x} = \dfrac{-1}{5} \cdot 5$

$x = {-1}$

19. $y - (7 - 4y) = 11$

$y + {-7} + 4y = 11$

$-7 + 5y = 11$

$7 + {-7} + 5y = 11 + 7$

$5y = 18$

$\dfrac{1}{5} \cdot 5y = \dfrac{1}{5} \cdot 18$

$y = \dfrac{18}{5} = 3\dfrac{3}{5}$

20. **a.** The smallest range of temperatures is in Australia.

b. The largest range of temperatures is in North America.

(Ranges:
Africa, $58 - {-24} = 58 + 24 = 82$
Australia, $53 - {-22} = 53 + 22 = 75$
North America, $57 - {-63} = 57 + 63 = 120$
South America, $49 - {-33} = 49 + 33 = 82$)

21. If $c = 1.5$ pounds, then

$p = 2.39 \cdot 1.5 + 1.69(5 - 1.5)$

$= 3.585 + 1.69 \cdot 3.5$

$= 3.585 + 5.915$

$= 9.5$

Hence, the price is $9.50.

22. If the price is $9.95, then

$9.95 = 2.39c + 1.69(5 - c)$

$9.95 = 2.39c + 8.45 + {-1.69c}$

$9.95 = 0.7c + 8.45$

$9.95 + {-8.45} = 0.7c + 8.45 + {-8.45}$

$1.5 = 0.7c$

$\dfrac{10}{7} \cdot 1.5 = \dfrac{10}{7} \cdot \dfrac{7}{10}c$

$2.14 \approx c$

Hence, the package contains about 2.14 pounds of cashews.

23. **a.** $10^3 = 1000$

b. $2 \cdot 10^3 = 2 \cdot 1000 = 2000$

c. $\left(\dfrac{1}{2} \cdot 10\right)^3 = 5^3 = 125$

24. At 3:00, the measure of the angle between the hands of the clock is $90°$.

25. The angle between the top and the back of the case is $60°$. $(180° - 120° = 60°)$

26. **a.** Subtract: $5755 - 1995 = 3760$. Add 3760 to obtain the Jewish year. $1066 + 3760 = 4826$ in the Jewish calendar.

b. The line slants up since as you increase J, the value for G also increases.

c. Sample: Islamic, Chinese, Julian

27. The sum of Democrats and Republicans in the U.S. Senate is usually 100. Even though there are 100 Senators, some may belong to a third party.

LESSON 4-7 pp. 253–258

1. $x + y = 180°$

2. If $x = 42°$, then $y = 180 - 42 = 138°$.

3. If $y = 137.5°$, then $x = 180 - 137.5 = 42.5°$.

4. Angles F and G are not supplementary since the sum of their measures is 190°, not 180°.

5. The supplement of angle J measures $180 - 115 = 65°$.

6. a. $m\angle A = 53°$, $m\angle B = 53°$, and $m\angle C = 74°$; $m\angle P = 17°$; $m\angle Q = 140°$, and $m\angle R = 23°$

b. The sum of the three angles in each of the triangles is 180° as is stated in the Triangle Sum Theorem.

7. The third angle measures $180 - (114 + 46) = 180 - 160 = 20°$.

8. a. The third angle measures $180 - (37 + 53) = 180 - 90 = 90°$.

b. This is a right triangle.

9. $w = 90 - 13 = 77°$

10.
$$180 = x + x + 36 = 2x + 36$$
$$180 + \text{-}36 = 2x + 36 + \text{-}36$$
$$144 = 2x$$
$$\tfrac{1}{2} \cdot 144 = \tfrac{1}{2} \cdot 2x$$
$$72° = x$$

11.
$$180 = 12 + d + 6d$$
$$180 = 12 + 7d$$
$$180 + \text{-}12 = 12 + \text{-}12 + 7d$$
$$168 = 7d$$
$$\tfrac{1}{7} \cdot 168 = \tfrac{1}{7} \cdot 7d$$
$$24° = d$$

12. True (65° and 25° are measures of complementary angles since their sum is 90°.)

13. If $m\angle Q = 29°$, then the measure of its complement is 61°. $(90 - 29 = 61)$

14. a. Sample: (10, 80); (25, 65); (35, 55); (70, 20); (89, 1)

b. Answers will vary.

c.
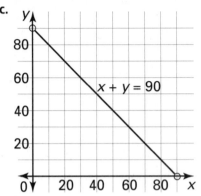

d. $x + y = 90$

15. If $m\angle A = x$, then $m\angle B = 90 - x$.

16. a.–c.
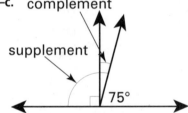

d. The supplement of 90° more than the complement of the angle. $(105 - 15 = 90)$

17. Sample: The angle formed by the jumper's legs and the back part of the skis measures 165°.

18. $x = 58°$; $y = 58°$

$i + x = 90$	$r + y = 90$
$x = 90 - i$	$y = 90 - r$
$x = 90 - 32$	$y = 90 - 32$
$x = 58$	$y = 58$

19.
$$x + x + x - 12 = 180$$
$$3x - 12 = 180$$
$$3x = 192$$
$$x = 64$$
$$x - 12 = 52$$
The measures are 64°, 64°, and 52°.

20. a.
$$180 = x + x - 17$$
$$180 = 2x - 17$$
$$180 + 17 = 2x + -17 + 17$$
$$197 = 2x$$
$$\frac{1}{2} \cdot 197 = \frac{1}{2} \cdot 2x$$
$$98.5 = x$$

b. $(x - 17)^\circ = (98.5 - 17)^\circ$
$$= 81.5^\circ$$

21. $m\angle C = 180 - m\angle A - m\angle B$

22. a. Sample:

savings	checking
2	23
5	20
8	17
21	4
22	3

b. $x + y = 25$

c.

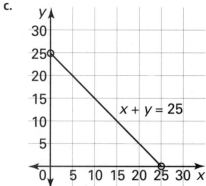

23.

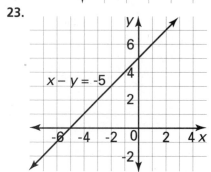

24.
$$50 + x > 30$$
$$50 + -50 + x > 30 + -50$$
$$x > -20$$

25.
$$12n + 5 - (2n + 20) = -20$$
$$12n + 5 + -2n + -20 = -20$$
$$10n + -15 = -20$$
$$10n + -15 + 15 = -20 + 15$$
$$10n = -5$$
$$\frac{1}{10} \cdot 10n = \frac{1}{10} \cdot -5$$
$$n = \frac{-1}{2}$$

26. (b)

27. $\frac{1}{2}x - \frac{1}{3}x - \frac{3}{4}x = \frac{6}{12}x - \frac{4}{12}x - \frac{9}{12}x$
$$= -\frac{7}{12}x$$

28. $\frac{y}{2} - \frac{y}{3} - \frac{3y}{4} = \frac{6y}{12} - \frac{4y}{12} - \frac{9y}{12}$
$$= -\frac{7}{12}y$$

29. a.

time	charge
$\frac{1}{2}$ h	$70
1 h	$90
$1\frac{1}{2}$ h	$110
2 h	$130
$2\frac{1}{2}$ h	$150
3 h	$170

b. $c = 50 + 20n$

30. $-4 \le x \le 8$

31. $0 \le x \le 2$

32. The theater could be on any corner of any of the intersections marked with a dot on the diagram.

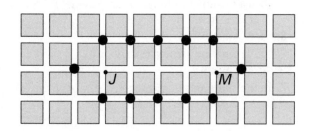

1.

	Length of Straws (in.)			Triangle?	Compare, Use <, >, or =.		
	r	s	t		$r+s$ $\underset{?}{}t$	$s+t$ $\underset{?}{}r$	$r+t$ $\underset{?}{}s$
a.	1	2	2	Yes	>	>	>
b.	3	3	6	No	=	>	>
c.	3	6	1	No	>	>	<
d.	2	3	4	Yes	>	>	>
e.	2	2	3	Yes	>	>	>
f.	5	2	3	No	>	=	>
g.	3	4	5	Yes	>	>	>
h.	1	2	5	No	<	>	>

2. greater than

LESSON 4-8 pp. 260–266

1. $BC = 10 + d$

2. $PQ = PM + MQ$

$\quad 7 = 5 + MQ$

$\quad 7 - 5 = MQ$

$\quad MQ = 2$

3. Triangle Inequality:
Part 1: If A, B, and C are any three points, then $AB + BC \geq AC$
Part 2: If A, B, and C are vertices of a triangle, then $AB + BC > AC$.

4. **a.** $k + n > m$
b. $n + m > k$
c. $k + m > n$

5. **a.** PQ can be no shorter than 12 cm.
$(32 - 20 = 12)$
b. PQ can be no longer than 52 cm.
$(32 + 20 = 52)$

6. **a.** x must be less than 9.
b. x must be greater than 1.
c. $1 < x < 9$

7. If the third side is x, then $1.7 < x < 14.7$.
$(8.2 - 6.5 < x < 8.2 + 6.5)$

8. The distance May lives from school must be greater than or equal to 0.5 km but less than 2.1 km. $(1.3 - .8 \leq \text{distance} \leq 1.3 + .8)$

9. The third side must be greater than 0 inches but less than 6 inches.

10. $100x^2 - 75x^2 < \text{third side} < 100x^2 + 75x^2$
The third side can have any length between $25x^2$ and $175x^2$.

11. There is no triangle with sides of lengths 1 cm, 2 cm, and 4 cm since 1 cm + 2 cm is not greater than 4 cm.

12. **a.** $(8x + 1) + (13x + 12) > 223$
b. $\quad 21x + 13 > 223$
$\quad 21x + 13 + \text{-}13 > 223 + \text{-}13$
$\quad\quad 21x > 210$
$\quad\quad \frac{1}{21} \cdot 21x > \frac{1}{21} \cdot 210$
$\quad\quad\quad x > 10$

13. $11.3 - 8.7 = 2.6$;
$11.3 + 8.7 = 20$
2.6 light-years $\leq m \leq 20$ light-years

14. $25 - 10 = 15$;
$25 + 10 = 35$
15 minutes $\leq t \leq 35$ minutes

15. Sample: The flying distance will be less because you can fly in a straight line from one city to another; while on land the Triangle Inequality may be applied many times between cities.

16. $(180 - 2a)°$

17. Let x be the measure of the smallest angle.
$x + 2x + 4x = 180$
$\quad\quad 7x = 180$
$\quad \frac{1}{7} \cdot 7x = \frac{1}{7} \cdot 180$
$\quad\quad\quad x = 25\frac{5}{7}$
The three angles measure $25\frac{5}{7}°, 51\frac{3}{7}°$, and $102\frac{6}{7}°$.

18. $5b + 4b = 90$
$\quad\quad 9b = 90$
$\quad \frac{1}{9} \cdot 9b = \frac{1}{9} \cdot 90$
$\quad\quad b = 10$

The measures of these two angles are 50° and 40°.

19.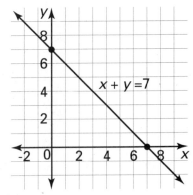

20. $15c - 200 \geq 350$

$\qquad 15c \geq 550$

$\qquad c \geq 36\frac{2}{3}$

They must cut at least 37 lawns.

21. $4x + -3(u + 2x + v^2) + 2x$

$\quad = 4x + -3u + -6x + -3v^2 + 2x$

$\quad = -3u + -3v^2$

22. a. $p + p + p = 3p$

b. $p \cdot p \cdot p = p^3$

23. The image $P' = (3 + 4, 6 + 6) = (7, 12)$

24. a. nonwhite females

b. Answers will vary.

c. Sample: Females live longer than males; people are living longer; white females live longer than nonwhite females.

25. There are 7 possible combinations for a perimeter of 15, but only three with all sides different lengths: 2, 6, 7; 3, 5, 7; and 4, 5, 6.

LESSON 4-9   pp. 267–273

1. a. After 3 weeks Beth will have $10 + 5 \cdot 3 = 10 + 15 = \$25$.

b. After 6 weeks Beth will have $10 + 5 \cdot 6 = 10 + 30 = \$40$.

2. a.

weeks (w)	total (t)
0	5
1	7
2	9
3	11
4	13

b.

c. $t = 2w + 5$

d. The domain of w is the set of whole numbers.

3. After two hours the stream will be 10 inches above normal.

$\quad (10 = 14 - 2x$

$\quad 10 + -14 = 14 + -14 - 2x$

$\qquad -4 = -2x$

$\quad -\frac{1}{2} \cdot -4 = -\frac{1}{2} \cdot -2x$

$\qquad 2 = x)$

4. After 4 hours the stream will be 6 inches above normal.

$\quad (6 = 14 - 2x$

$\quad 6 + -14 = 14 + -14 - 2x$

$\qquad -8 = -2x$

$\quad -\frac{1}{2} \cdot -8 = -\frac{1}{2} \cdot -2x$

$\qquad 4 = x)$

5. After 7 hours the stream level will be back to normal.

$\quad (0 = 14 - 2x$

$\quad -14 = 14 + -14 - 2x$

$\qquad 2x = 14$

$\quad \frac{1}{2} \cdot 2x = \frac{1}{2} \cdot 14$

$\qquad x = 7)$

6. The points in Quadrant IV represent the times and heights when the stream is below its normal level.

7. a. $y = -2x + 1$

$$y = -2 \cdot \frac{1}{2} + 1$$

$$y = -1 + 1$$

$$y = 0$$

b. This point lies on the line graphed.

8.
$$-2 = -2x + 1$$
$$-2 + -1 = -2x + 1 + -1$$
$$-3 = -2x$$
$$\frac{-1}{2} \cdot -3 = \frac{-1}{2} \cdot -2x$$
$$\frac{3}{2} = x$$

9. a. 30 FOR X = 0 TO 7

b. 10 PRINT "TABLE OF (X, Y)
        VALUES"
   20 PRINT "X VALUE", "Y VALUE"
   30 FOR X = -5 TO 5
   40 LET Y = 8 * X − 3
   50 PRINT X, Y
   60 NEXT X
   70 END

10. a. Change cell A2 to 0, change the formula in cell A3 to = A2 + 2, and copy A3 into A4 through A7.

b. Change the formula in B2 to = 3 * A2 + 40.

11. a.

w	b
0	30
1	25
2	20
3	15
4	10

b. $b = 30 - 5w$

c.

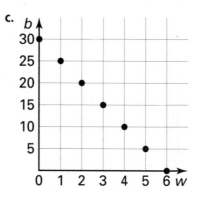

d. In the 6th week Oprah will withdraw her last dollar.

12. a. Sample

x	y
0	-2
1	2
2	6

b.

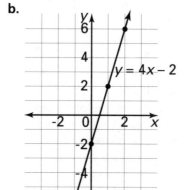

13. a. Sample

x	y
0	10
1	10.5
2	11
3	11.5
4	12

13. b. The domain of x is the set of nonnegative real numbers.

c.

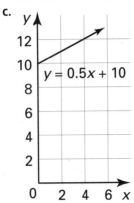

$y = 0.5x + 10$

d. After 20 years the radius will equal 20 cm.

$$(20 = 10 + .5x$$
$$20 + \text{-}10 = 10 + \text{-}10 + .5x$$
$$10 = .5x$$
$$\tfrac{1}{.5} \cdot 10 = \tfrac{1}{.5} \cdot .5x$$
$$20 = x)$$

14.

x	y
-2	-75
-1	-25
0	25
1	75

15. a, b.

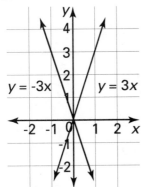

$y = \text{-}3x$ $y = 3x$

c. The graphs intersect at $(0, 0)$.

d. Sample: The graphs are reflection images of each other over the y-axis.

16. a. $y = \text{-}0.6x + 39.1$

b.

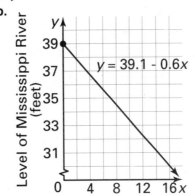

$y = 39.1 - 0.6x$

Days after August 16, 1993

c. Sample: In about 16 days, September 1, 1993, the river is expected to drop to the lowest "flood level stage."

17. The minimum number of points needed to graph a straight line is 2.

18. Samples: They are all straight lines or parts of straight lines. They pass through different points on the x-axis and y-axis. Some slant to the right and some slant to the left.

19. $27 - 20 = 7$; $20 + 27 = 47$
$7 < \text{length} < 47$

20. $2 - 1.4 = .6$; $2 + 1.4 = 3.4$
$.6 < \text{distance from Tokyo Bay} < 3.4$

21. $x - 10 + x + 10 + x + 30 = 180$
$$3x + 30 = 180$$
$$3x + 30 + \text{-}30 = 180 + \text{-}30$$
$$3x = 150$$
$$\tfrac{1}{3} \cdot 3x = \tfrac{1}{3} \cdot 150$$
$$x = 50$$
The measures of the three angles are 40°, 60°, and 80°.

22. a. The supplement measures $(180 - x)°$.
b. The complement measures $(90 - x)°$.
c. $(180 - x)° - (90 - x)°$
$= 180 - x - 90 + x$
$= (180 - 90)° - (x + \text{-}x)°$
$= 90° - 0°$
$= 90°$

23. d

24.
$$3(w - 4) = 48$$
$$3w + -12 = 48$$
$$3w + -12 + 12 = 48 + 12$$
$$3w = 60$$
$$\frac{1}{3} \cdot 3w = \frac{1}{3} \cdot 60$$
$$w = 20$$

25. $\frac{x}{7} - \frac{2x}{5}$
$$= \frac{5x}{35} - \frac{14x}{35}$$
$$= -\frac{9x}{35}$$

26. 3.3264×10^6
$$\left(\frac{12!}{3!4!} = \frac{12 \cdot 11 \cdot 10 \cdot 9 \cdot 8 \cdot 7 \cdot 6 \cdot 5 \cdot 4 \cdot 3 \cdot 2 \cdot 1}{3 \cdot 2 \cdot 1 \cdot 4 \cdot 3 \cdot 2 \cdot 1} = \right.$$
$$12 \cdot 11 \cdot 10 \cdot 9 \cdot 8 \cdot 7 \cdot 5 =$$
$$\left. 3,326,400 \right)$$

27. a. 0.25
   b. 2.5
   c. 25
   d. 250,000

28. Area of $\triangle RST = \frac{1}{2} \cdot 8.4 \cdot 11 = 46.2$ in^2

29. Sample: a skydiver initially picks up speed while falling and then reaches a terminal velocity. When the chute opens, velocity drops sharply; then the diver floats at a relatively constant rate.

CHAPTER 4

PROGRESS SELF-TEST
p. 277

1. Adding -7 to a number is the same as subtracting 7 from a number.

2. Today it is $(D - 53)°$ warmer than yesterday.

3. $9p - 7q - (-14z)$
$$= 9p + -7q + 14z$$

4. $n - 16 - 2n - (-12)$
$$= n + -16 + -2n + 12$$
$$= -n - 4$$

5. $-8x - (2x - x)$
$$= -8x + -2x + x$$
$$= -9x$$

6. $-(2b - 6) = -2b + 6$

7. $\frac{1}{2}m - \frac{7m}{2}$
$$= \frac{m}{2} + \frac{-7m}{2}$$
$$= \frac{-6m}{2}$$
$$= -3m$$

8. $S - .2S = .8S$ is the sale price of the skis.

9.
$$5n - 6 = 54$$
$$5n + -6 + 6 = 54 + 6$$
$$5n = 60$$
$$\frac{1}{5} \cdot 5n = \frac{1}{5} \cdot 60$$
$$n = 12$$

10.
$$8 < 6 - 3p$$
$$8 + -6 < 6 + -6 + -3p$$
$$2 < -3p$$
$$\frac{-1}{3} \cdot 2 > \frac{-1}{3} \cdot -3p$$
$$\frac{-2}{3} > p$$

11.
$$\frac{3}{4} - \frac{1}{4}m = 12$$
$$\frac{3}{4} + -\frac{3}{4} - \frac{1}{4}m = \frac{48}{4} + -\frac{3}{4}$$
$$\frac{-1}{4}m = \frac{45}{4}$$
$$-4 \cdot \frac{-1}{4}m = -4 \cdot \frac{45}{4}$$
$$m = -45$$

12.
$$201 = 15f - 2(3 + 6f)$$
$$201 = 15f - 6 - 12f$$
$$201 = 3f - 6$$
$$201 + 6 = 3f + -6 + 6$$
$$207 = 3f$$
$$\frac{1}{3} \cdot 207 = \frac{1}{3} \cdot 3f$$
$$69 = f$$

13.
$$C = \frac{5}{9}(F - 32)$$
$$50 = \frac{5}{9}(F - 32)$$
$$\frac{9}{5} \cdot 50 = \frac{9}{5} \cdot \frac{5}{9}(F - 32)$$
$$90 = F - 32$$
$$90 + 32 = F + -32 + 32$$
$$122 = F$$
$$50°C = 122°F$$

14.
$$1100 - 6m > 350$$
$$-1100 + 1100 - 6m > 350 + -1100$$
$$-6m > -750$$
$$\frac{-1}{6} \cdot 6m < \frac{-1}{6} \cdot -750$$
$$m < 125$$

When the copier has been running 125 minutes, there will be exactly 350 sheets of paper left. Since one page is copied every 10 seconds, there will be more than 350 sheets of paper left during the first 124 minutes 50 seconds of continuous copying.

15.

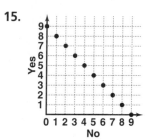

16. a.

x	y
-1	-5
0	-3
1	-1
2	1
3	3

b.

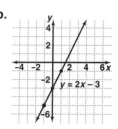

17. The greatest possible distance from Los Angeles to San Antonio is $786 + 582 = 1368$ miles.

18. a. The supplement has measure $(180 - 18)° = 162°$.

b. The complement has measure $(90 - 18)° = 72°$.

19.

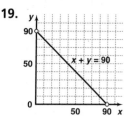

20. By the Triangle Sum Theorem:
$$n + 2n + 2n - 4 = 180$$
$$5n - 4 = 180$$
$$5n + -4 + 4 = 180 + 4$$
$$5n = 184$$
$$\frac{1}{5} \cdot 5n = \frac{1}{5} \cdot 184$$
$$n = 36\frac{4}{5}$$

Hence, $m\angle L = 2 \cdot 36\frac{4}{5}° = 73\frac{3}{5}°$.

21. $7 - 3 < p < 7 + 3$;
$4 < p < 10$ by the Third Side Property

22. a. 428.75   **b.** A4
c. 143.02   **d.** $= B2 - C2 - D2$

CHAPTER 4

REVIEW   pp. 278–281

1. $3x - 4x + 5x = 3x + -4x + 5x = 4x$

2. $\frac{-2}{3} - \frac{4}{5}$
$$= \frac{-10}{15} + \frac{-12}{15}$$
$$= \frac{-22}{15}$$

3. $\frac{3a}{2} - \frac{9a}{2}$
$$= \frac{3a}{2} + \frac{-9a}{2}$$
$$= -\frac{6a}{2}$$
$$= -3a$$

4. $\frac{1}{3}x - \frac{5x}{3} = \frac{x}{3} + \frac{-5x}{3}$
$$= -\frac{4x}{3}$$

5. $c - \frac{c}{3} - 2c - 2 = \frac{3c}{3} + \frac{-c}{3} + \frac{-6c}{3} - 2 = -\frac{4}{3}c - 2$

6. $3x + y - 4x - 7y$
$$= 3x + y + -4x + -7y$$
$$= -x - 6y$$

7. $z^3 - 7 + 8 - 4z^3$
$= z^3 + -7 + 8 + -4z^3$
$= -3z^3 + 1$

8. $3(x - 6) - 5x$
$= 3x - 18 - 5x = 3x - 18 + -5x$
$= -2x - 18$

9. $x - 47 = -2$
$x + -47 + 47 = -2 + 47$
$x = 45$

10. $2.5 = t - 3.34$
$2.5 + 3.34 = t + -3.34 + 3.34$
$5.84 = t$

11. $\frac{3}{2} + y - \frac{1}{4} = \frac{3}{4}$
$y + \frac{6}{4} + -\frac{1}{4} = \frac{3}{4}$
$y + \frac{5}{4} = \frac{3}{4}$
$y + \frac{5}{4} + -\frac{5}{4} = \frac{3}{4} + -\frac{5}{4}$
$y = -\frac{2}{4}$
$y = -\frac{1}{2}$

12. $8 = \frac{3}{4}a - 10$
$8 + 10 = \frac{3}{4}a + -10 + 10$
$18 = \frac{3}{4}a$
$\frac{4}{3} \cdot 18 = \frac{4}{3} \cdot \frac{3}{4}a$
$24 = a$

13. $4n - 3 = 17$
$4n + -3 + 3 = 17 + 3$
$4n = 20$
$\frac{1}{4} \cdot 4n = \frac{1}{4} \cdot 20$
$n = 5$

14. $470 - 2n = 1100$
$470 + -470 + -2n = 1100 + -470$
$-2n = 630$
$\frac{-1}{2} \cdot -2n = \frac{-1}{2} \cdot 630$
$n = -315$

15. $m - 3m = 10$
$-2m = 10$
$\frac{-1}{2} \cdot -2m = \frac{-1}{2} \cdot 10$
$m = -5$

16. $46n - 71n - 6 = 144$
$-25n - 6 = 144$
$-25n + -6 + 6 = 144 + 6$
$-25n = 150$
$\frac{-1}{25} \cdot -25n = \frac{-1}{25} \cdot 150$
$n = -6$

17. $0 = 4a - 6$
$0 + 6 = 4a + -6 + 6$
$6 = 4a$
$\frac{1}{4} \cdot 6 = \frac{1}{4} \cdot 4a$
$\frac{3}{2} = a$

18. $18(2x - 4) - 6 = -168$
$36x + -72 + -6 = -168$
$36x + -78 = -168$
$36x + -78 + 78 = -168 + 78$
$36x = -90$
$\frac{1}{36} \cdot 36x = \frac{1}{36} \cdot -90$
$x = -2.5$

19. $2x - 11 < 201$
$2x + -11 + 11 < 201 + 11$
$2x < 212$
$\frac{1}{2} \cdot 2x < \frac{1}{2} \cdot 212$
$x < 106$
Check:
Does $201 = 2 \cdot 106 - 11$? Yes, $212 - 11 = 201$.
Check a value smaller than 106, say 100. Is
$2 \cdot 100 - 11 < 201$? Yes, $200 - 11 = 189$ which
is less than 201.

20.
$$-8y + 4 \le 12$$
$$-8y + 4 + \text{-}4 \le 12 + \text{-}4$$
$$-8y \le 8$$
$$\tfrac{-1}{8} \cdot -8y \ge \tfrac{-1}{8} \cdot 8$$
$$y \ge \text{-}1$$

Check:
Does $-8 \cdot \text{-}1 + 4 = 12$? Yes, $8 + 4 = 12$.
Check a value larger than -1, say 1. Is
$-8 \cdot 1 + 4 \le 12$? Yes, $-8 + 4 = \text{-}4$ which is
less than or equal to 12.

21.
$$32 - y > 45$$
$$32 - 32 - y > 45 - 32$$
$$-y > 13$$
$$y < \text{-}13$$

Check:
Does $32 - \text{-}13 = 45$? Yes, $32 + 13 = 45$.
Check a value less than -13, say -15. Is
$32 - \text{-}15 > 45$? Yes $32 + 15 = 47$ which is
greater than 45.

22. $0.9(90n - 14) - 3n \ge 455.4$
$$81n - 12.6 - 3n \ge 455.4$$
$$78n - 12.6 \ge 455.4$$
$$78n - 12.6 + 12.6 \ge 455.4 + 12.6$$
$$78n \ge 468$$
$$\tfrac{1}{78} \cdot 78n \ge \tfrac{1}{78} \cdot 468$$
$$n \ge 6$$

Check:
Does $0.9(90 \cdot 6 - 14) - 3 \cdot 6 = 455.4$?
Yes, $0.9(540 - 14) - 18 = .9(526) - 18 =$
$473.4 - 18 = 455.4$.
Check a value greater than 6, say 10. Is
$0.9(90 \cdot 10 - 14) - 3 \cdot 10 \ge 455.4$?
$0.9(900 - 14) - 30 = 0.9 \cdot 886 - 30 =$
$797.4 - 30 = 767.4$ which is greater than
455.4.

23. $-(4a + 7) = \text{-}4a - 7$

24. $-(3f - 4g + 6) = \text{-}3f + 4g - 6$

25. $1 - (z - 1)$
$$= 1 + \text{-}z + 1$$
$$= 2 - z$$

26. $3x - (2x - 9)$
$$= 3x + \text{-}2x + 9$$
$$= x + 9$$

27. $2(a - 3) - 5(a + 2)$
$$= 2a + \text{-}6 + \text{-}5a + \text{-}10$$
$$= \text{-}3a - 16$$

28. $-3(n + 6) - 6(n - 3)$
$$= \text{-}3n + \text{-}18 + \text{-}6n + 18$$
$$= \text{-}9n$$

29.
$$-(p - 6) = 14$$
$$-p + 6 = 14$$
$$-p + 6 - 6 = 14 - 6$$
$$-p = 8$$
$$p = \text{-}8$$

30.
$$-(r + 3) > 9$$
$$-r + \text{-}3 > 9$$
$$-r + \text{-}3 + 3 > 9 + 3$$
$$-r > 12$$
$$r < \text{-}12$$

31.
$$5 - 2(x - 3) < \text{-}9$$
$$5 - 2x + 6 < \text{-}9$$
$$11 + \text{-}2x < \text{-}9$$
$$11 + \text{-}11 + \text{-}2x < \text{-}9 + \text{-}11$$
$$-2x < \text{-}20$$
$$\tfrac{-1}{2} \cdot -2x > \tfrac{-1}{2} \cdot -20$$
$$x > 10$$

32. $1\tfrac{1}{2} - \left(\tfrac{3}{4} - y\right) = 7$
$$1\tfrac{1}{2} - \tfrac{3}{4} + y = 7$$
$$\tfrac{3}{4} + y = 7$$
$$\tfrac{3}{4} - \tfrac{3}{4} + y = 7 - \tfrac{3}{4}$$
$$y = 6\tfrac{1}{4}$$

33. $(5x - 8) - (3x + 1) = 36$

$5x + \text{-}8 + \text{-}3x + \text{-}1 = 36$

$2x + \text{-}9 = 36$

$9 + 2x + \text{-}9 = 36 + 9$

$2x = 45$

$\frac{1}{2} \cdot 2x = \frac{1}{2} \cdot 45$

$x = 22.5$

34. $75 = 4e - 5(3 + 2e)$

$75 = 4e + \text{-}15 + \text{-}10e$

$75 = \text{-}6e + \text{-}15$

$75 + 15 = \text{-}6e + \text{-}15 + 15$

$90 = \text{-}6e$

$\text{-}\frac{1}{6} \cdot 90 = \text{-}\frac{1}{6} \cdot \text{-}6e$

$\text{-}15 = e$

35. $x - y + z = x + \text{-}y + z$

36. $\text{-}8 - v = 42$

$\text{-}8 + \text{-}v = 42$

37. True (The sum of $m - k$ and $k - m$ is 0.)

38. (d) (It is the additive inverse of (a), (b), and (c).)

39. **a.** The complement is $(90 - 17)° = 73°$

    b. The supplement is $(180 - 17)° = 163°$

40. If the angles are complements, then $x + z = 90$.

41. True (The supplement of any angle with measure $x°$ is $180 - x$. The complement is $90 - x$. $180 - x$ is greater than $90 - x$.)

42. Since the angles are complements,

$(3x - 6) + (4x - 16) = 90$

$7x + \text{-}22 = 90$

$7x + \text{-}22 + 22 = 90 + 22$

$7x = 112$

$\frac{1}{7} \cdot 7x = \frac{1}{7} \cdot 112$

$x = 16$

The angles measure $3 \cdot 16 - 6 = 42°$ and $4 \cdot 16 - 16 = 48°$.

43. By the Triangle Sum Theorem, the third angle measures

$180 - (75 + 32)$

$= 180 - 107$

$= 73°$.

44. The angles can be expressed by x, $10x$, and $x + 10$.

$x + 10x + x + 10 = 180$

$12x + 10 = 180$

$12x + 10 + \text{-}10 = 180 + \text{-}10$

$12x = 170$

$\frac{1}{12} \cdot 12x = \frac{1}{12} \cdot 170$

$x = 14\frac{1}{6}$

The angles measure $14\frac{1}{6}°$, $24\frac{1}{6}°$, and $141\frac{2}{3}°$.

45. 40°, 40°, 100° or 40°, 70°, 70° (The sum of the measures is 180 where two angles have the same measure.)

46. $(x - 29) + x + (x - 39) = 180$

$3x + \text{-}68 = 180$

$3x + \text{-}68 + 68 = 180 + 68$

$3x = 248$

$\frac{1}{3} \cdot 3x = \frac{1}{3} \cdot 248$

$x = 82\frac{2}{3}$

$m\angle M = 82\frac{2}{3}°$, $m\angle C = 43\frac{2}{3}°$, and $m\angle A = 53\frac{2}{3}°$

47. 16, 3, 5 cannot be the sides of a triangle since $3 + 5$ is not greater than 16.

48. 16, 8, 10 can be the sides of a triangle by the Triangle Inequality.

49. $7 + m > 8$, $8 + m > 7$, and $7 + 8 > m$

50. $a + b > c$, $a + c > b$, and $b + c > a$

51. $3 < y < 25$ by the Third Side Property

52. $0.2 < y < 4.6$ by the Third Side Property

53. $S = E - P$

54. Let $w =$ the weight of the other passengers.

$w + 80 > L$

$w + 80 - 80 > L - 80$

$w > L - 80$

55. The second floor's area is
$$3500 - (F + 1000)$$
$$= 3500 - F - 1000$$
$$= (2500 - F) \text{ ft}^2$$

56. $S - 40 < 3$ or $S < 43$

57. Eileen is $D - 5$ years old.

58. $30,000 - -1,500 = 30,000 + 1,500 = 31,500$ feet.

59. a. 30% off V is $.3V$, hence the amount of the discount is $.3V$ dollars.

   b. The sale price is $V - .3V = .7V$ dollars.

60. a. The tip is 15% of F or $.15F$ dollars. The cost of the food and tip is $F + .15F = 1.15F$ dollars.

   b. The cost of the food and tip is now $1.15(F - 5) = 1.15F - 5.75$.

61.
$$750 + 15w > 1500$$
$$750 - 750 + 15w > 1500 - 750$$
$$15w > 750$$
$$\frac{1}{15} \cdot 15w > \frac{1}{15} \cdot 750$$
$$w > 50$$
She must save for 51 weeks.

62. $F = \frac{9}{5}C + 32$; If $F = 100$,
$$100 = \frac{9}{5}C + 32$$
$$100 - 32 = \frac{9}{5}C + 32 - 32$$
$$68 = \frac{9}{5}C$$
$$\frac{5}{9} \cdot 68 = \frac{5}{9} \cdot \frac{9}{5}C$$
$$\frac{340}{9} = C$$
$$100°F = 37\frac{7}{9}° C$$

63.
$$200 + 92d \le 1400$$
$$200 - 200 + 92d \le 1400 - 200$$
$$92d \le 1200$$
$$\frac{1}{92} \cdot 92d \le \frac{1}{92} \cdot 1200$$
$$d \le \frac{1200}{92} \text{ or } \approx 13 \text{ days}$$

64. a. After m minutes there are $1500 - 8m$ sheets left.

   b.
$$1500 - 8m = 200$$
$$1500 - 1500 - 8m = 200 - 1500$$
$$-8m = -1300$$
$$\frac{-1}{8} \cdot -8m = \frac{-1}{8} \cdot -1300$$
$$m = 162.5$$
After 162.5 minutes there will be 200 sheets left.

65. The greatest possible distance from Dallas to El Paso is $346 + 887 = 1233$ miles.

66. Let m represent the number of minutes that Malinda travels from Roger's place to Charles' place. $10 \le m \le 50$

67. a. = A6 ^ 2 + A6
   b. $6 ((-3)^2 + -3 = 9 + -3 = 6)$
   c. B6 would change to 380. $((-20)^2 + -20 = 400 + -20 = 380)$

68. a. = A2 ∗ 180 − 360
   b. = A6 ∗ 180 − 360
   c. In B4, 360; in B5, 540; in B6, 720; in B7, 900

69. a. In D3, 740; in D4, 586; in D5, 1118; in D6, 1180; in D7, 520
   b. = B4 ∗ 6 + C4 ∗ 4
   c. August 30

70. a. In E2, 17; in E3, 9; in E5, 23; in E6, 6; in E7, 5
   b. C5
   c. = B5 ∗ 1 + C5 ∗ 2 + D5 ∗ 3
   d. = C2 + C3 + C4 + C5 + C6 + C7

71.

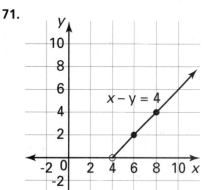

72.

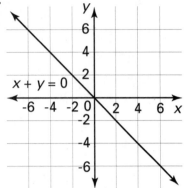

$x + y = 0$

73.

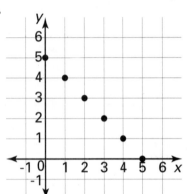

74.

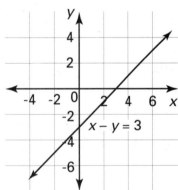

$x - y = 3$

75.

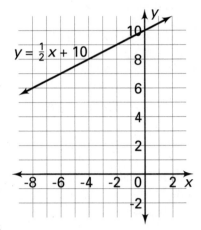

$y = \frac{1}{2}x + 10$

76.

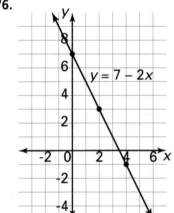

$y = 7 - 2x$

77.

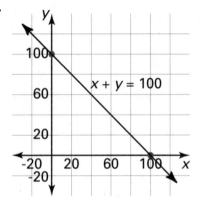

$x + y = 100$

LINEAR SENTENCES

LESSON 5-1   pp. 284–290

1. There was no national speed limit before 1/1/74.

2. The national speed limit on July 1, 1987, was 65 miles per hour.

3. $y = 55$ mph.

4. $y = 65$ mph.

5. All points on a horizontal line have the same y-coordinate.

6. All points on a vertical line have the same x-coordinate.

7. $x = 1$

8. $y = -1$

9. a.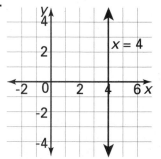

b.

10. a.

b.

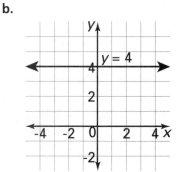

11. a.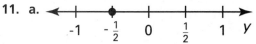

b.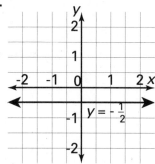

12. a.

b.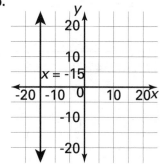

13. a. Mac would not have to pay the service fee for 9 weeks.

   b. Mac would not have to pay the service fee when $580 - 20x \geq 400$.

14.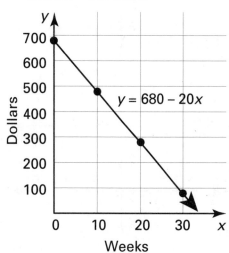

15. a.

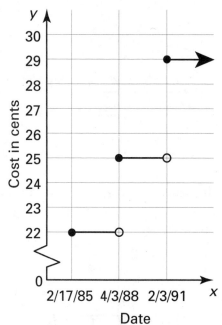

Date

b. Let x = the date and y = the cost in cents.

For $2/17/85 \leq x \leq 4/2/88$, $y = 22$;
for $4/3/88 \leq x \leq 2/2/91$, $y = 25$;
for $x \geq 2/3/91$, $y = 29$.

16. $y = 12$

17. $x = -6$

18. The point of intersection is $(15, -4)$.

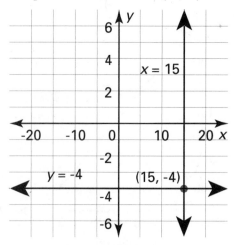

19. a. A horizontal line through $(7, -13)$ has equation $y = -13$.

b. A vertical line through $(7, -13)$ has equation $x = 7$.

20. x; y; horizontal lines are parallel to the x-axis and perpendicular to the y-axis.

21. a. An equation to relate the repair cost y to the time spent x is $y = 25 + 35x$.

b., c.

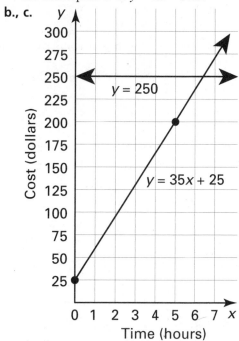

Time (hours)

d. The maximum number of hours that Ron could work and still keep Sasha's bill under $250 is 6.

e.
$$250 \geq 25 + 35x$$
$$250 - 25 \geq 25 - 25 + 35x$$
$$225 \geq 35x$$
$$\left(\tfrac{1}{35}\right)225 \geq \left(\tfrac{1}{35}\right)35x$$
$$6.43 \geq x$$
Ron could work for 6 whole hours.

22. $w = 90°$; $x = 46°$; $y = 46°$; $z = 136°$

23. The sale price is $d - .20d = .80d$.

24. $t = 25 + 2w$

25. $25(9.8 + 14.2)$ or $9.8 \cdot 25 + 14.2 \cdot 25$

26. $(-a \cdot b) \cdot -a = a^2 b$

27. $-\frac{3}{2} \cdot -\frac{2}{3}a = \frac{6}{6}a = a$

28. $232 \frac{\text{miles}}{\text{h}} \cdot 5280 \frac{\text{ft}}{\text{mile}} \cdot .043 \sec \cdot \frac{1}{3600} \frac{\text{h}}{\text{sec}} = 14.63 \, \text{ft}$
To the nearest tenth of a foot, Al reached the destination 14.6 feet ahead of Scott.

29. a. Sample: Any real number multiplied by one equals the same real number.
 b. Sample: $1 \cdot 5 = 5$

30. Answers may vary.

LESSON 5-2   pp. 291–296

1. a. It costs less at Phil's for less than three copies.
 b. It costs less at Peggy's for more than three copies.

2. $70 + 0.03 \cdot 4292 = 70 + 128.76 = \$198.76$

3. If your company averaged 4500 copies per month, you would choose Best. Best is cheaper if fewer than 9,000 copies are needed per month.

4. = 250 + .01 * A10

5. = 70 + .03 * A11

6. a. Acme provides the better deal for 9100 copies in one month.
 b. Acme: $250 + .01 \cdot 9100 = 250 + 91 = \$341$
 Best: $70 + .03 \cdot 9100 = 70 + 273 = \$343$

7. a.

Number of copies	Acme's Charges	Best's Charges
10,000	300	270
11,000	310	290
12,000	320	310
13,000	330	330
14,000	340	350
15,000	350	370

 b. It will cost the same with each company for 13,000 copies.

8. At Acme 35,000 copies could be copied at $600 per month. $(600 = 250 + 0.01 \cdot 35,000)$

9. a. Amount Kim has after w weeks:
 $m = 20 + 6w$
 b. Amount Jenny has after w weeks:
 $m = 150 - 4w$
 c. After 13 weeks, Kim and Jenny will have the same amount of money.

10. a. Selling about $10,000 worth of goods, Rufus should work for Company A.
 (Company A earnings:
 $800 + .05 \cdot 10,000 =$
 $800 + 500 = \$1300$
 Company B earnings:
 $600 + .06 \cdot 10,000 =$
 $600 + 600 = \$1200$)

 b.

Sales	Earnings at Company A	Earnings at Company B
20,000	1800	1800
22,000	1900	1920
24,000	2000	2040

 He must have sales of more than $20,000.

11. Sample: (-3, -6); (0, -6); (17, -6)

12. $x = 6$

13. a.

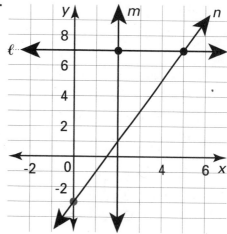

 b. ℓ and m intersect at (2, 7).
 c. ℓ and n intersect at (5, 7).
 d. The two perpendicular sides have lengths 3 and 6 so the area of the triangle is $\left(\frac{1}{2}\right) \cdot 3 \cdot 6 = 9$ square units.

14. The longest possible air distance from Miami to Seattle is $1061 + 1724 = 2785$ miles.

15. a.

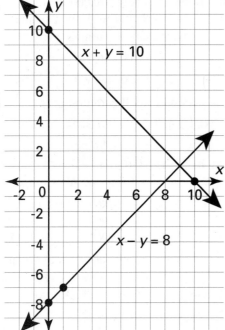

$x + y = 10$

$x - y = 8$

b. The lines intersect at $(9, 1)$.

16.
$$1 = 9 - (c - 2)$$
$$1 = 9 - c + 2$$
$$1 = 11 - c$$
$$1 - 11 = 11 - 11 - c$$
$$-10 = -c$$
$$10 = c$$

17.
$$42(m - 4) + 210 < 252$$
$$42m - 168 + 210 < 252$$
$$42m + 42 < 252$$
$$42m + 42 + -42 < 252 + -42$$
$$42m < 210$$
$$m < 5$$

18.
$$50 \leq 5.40 \cdot 8 + .28b$$
$$50 \leq 43.2 + .28b$$
$$50 + -43.2 \leq 43.2 + -43.2 + .28b$$
$$6.8 \leq .28b$$
$$\left(\tfrac{1}{.28}\right)6.8 \leq \left(\tfrac{1}{.28}\right).28b$$
$$24.29 \leq b$$

The farm worker must pick 25 boxes to earn at least $50.00 for the day.

19. $x + y - 3(z + w) = x + y - 3z - 3w$
Sample: Multiplication by -3 was not distributed over the w-term.

20. a. $5! = 120$ ways
b. $4! = 24$ ways

21. $(\sqrt{37})^2 = \sqrt{37} \cdot \sqrt{37} = 37$

22. $(8c)^2 = 8c \cdot 8c = 64c^2$

23. 3.46 trillion $= 3.46 \cdot 10^{12}$

24. $12 \cdot 9.95 \approx 120$ ($12 \cdot 10 = 120$)

25. $\tfrac{5}{6} + \tfrac{7}{8} + \tfrac{13}{12} \approx 3$ $(1 + 1 + 1 = 3)$

26. Sample:

```
10 PRINT "Week", "Kim", "Jenny"
20 FOR W = 1 TO 20
30 LET X = 20 + 9 * W
40 LET Y = 150 − 4 * W
50 PRINT W, X, Y
60 IF X = Y THEN GO TO 80
70 NEXT W
80 PRINT "Weeks = "; W
90 END
```

LESSON 5-3 pp. 297–303

1. a. $5W + 6 = 3W + 10$
b. Sample: Remove 3 boxes from both sides; remove 6 ounces from both sides; remove half the remaining contents of both sides.
c. The weight of each box is 2 oz.

2. a. You could add -2x or -8x to both sides.
b.
$$8x + 7 = 2x + 9$$
$$8x + -2x + 7 = 2x + -2x + 9$$
$$6x + 7 = 9$$
$$6x + 7 + -7 = 9 + -7$$
$$6x = 2$$
$$\tfrac{1}{6} \cdot 6x = \tfrac{1}{6} \cdot 2$$
$$x = \tfrac{1}{3}$$

3.

$$250 + 0.01n = 70 + 0.03n$$

$$250 + 0.01n - 0.03n = 70 + 0.03n - 0.03n$$

$$250 - 0.02n = 70$$

$$250 - 250 - 0.02n = 70 - 250$$

$$-0.02n = -180$$

$$-\frac{1}{0.02} \cdot -0.02n = -\frac{1}{0.02} \cdot -180$$

$$n = 9000$$

4. Sample: Adding $7y$ saves one step in the solution.

5.

$$2p + 38 = 5p + 5$$

$$2p + -5p + 38 = 5p + -5p + 5$$

$$-3p + 38 = 5$$

$$-3p + 38 + -38 = 5 + -38$$

$$-3p = -33$$

$$-\frac{1}{3} \cdot -3p = -\frac{1}{3} \cdot -33$$

$$p = 11$$

Check: Does $2 \cdot 11 + 38 = 5 \cdot 11 + 5$?

$$22 + 38 = 55 + 5?$$

$$60 = 60$$

Yes, it checks.

6.

$$4n = -2n + 3$$

$$4n + 2n = -2n + 2n + 3$$

$$6n = 3$$

$$\frac{1}{6} \cdot 6n = \frac{1}{6} \cdot 3$$

$$n = \frac{1}{2}$$

Check: Does $4 \cdot \frac{1}{2} = -2 \cdot \frac{1}{2} + 3$?

$$2 = -1 + 3?$$

$$2 = 2$$

Yes, it checks.

7.

$$12x + 1 = 3x - 8$$

$$12x + 1 + -3x = 3x + -3x + -8$$

$$9x + 1 = -8$$

$$9x + 1 + -1 = -8 + -1$$

$$9x = -9$$

$$\frac{1}{9} \cdot 9x = \frac{1}{9} \cdot -9$$

$$x = -1$$

Check: Does $12 \cdot -1 + 1 = 3 \cdot -1 - 8$?

$$-12 + 1 = -3 - 8?$$

$$-11 = -11$$

Yes, it checks.

8.

$$43 - 8w = 25 + w$$

$$43 - 8w - w = 25 + w - w$$

$$43 - 9w = 25$$

$$43 - 43 - 9w = 25 - 43$$

$$-9w = -18$$

$$\frac{-1}{9} \cdot -9w = \frac{-1}{9} \cdot -18$$

$$w = 2$$

Check: Does $43 - 8 \cdot 2 = 25 + 2$?

$$43 - 16 = 27?$$

$$27 = 27$$

Yes, it checks.

9.

$$7y = 5y - 3$$

$$7y + -5y = 5y + -5y - 3$$

$$2y = -3$$

$$\frac{1}{2} \cdot 2y = \frac{1}{2} \cdot -3$$

$$y = \frac{-3}{2}$$

Check: Does $7 \cdot \frac{-3}{2} = 5 \cdot \frac{-3}{2} - 3$?

$$\frac{-21}{2} = \frac{-15}{2} - 3?$$

$$\frac{-21}{2} = \frac{-21}{2}$$

Yes, it checks.

10.
$$2 - z = 3 - 4z$$
$$2 - z + 4z = 3 - 4z + 4z$$
$$2 + 3z = 3$$
$$2 - 2 + 3z = 3 - 2$$
$$3z = 1$$
$$\frac{1}{3} \cdot 3z = \frac{1}{3} \cdot 1$$
$$z = \frac{1}{3}$$

Check: Does $2 - \frac{1}{3} = 3 - 4 \cdot \frac{1}{3}$?
$$\frac{5}{3} = 3 - \frac{4}{3}?$$
$$\frac{5}{3} = \frac{5}{3}$$

Yes, it checks.

11.
$$12 + 0.6f = 1.2f$$
$$12 + 0.6f + \text{-}0.6f = 1.2f + \text{-}0.6f$$
$$12 = 0.6f$$
$$\frac{1}{0.6} \cdot 12 = \frac{1}{0.6} \cdot 0.6f$$
$$20 = f$$

Check: Does $12 + 0.6 \cdot 20 = 1.2 \cdot 20$?
$$12 + 12 = 24?$$
$$24 = 24$$

Yes, it checks.

12.
$$2.85p - 3.95 = 9.7p + 9.75$$
$$2.85p + \text{-}9.7p - 3.95 = 9.7p + \text{-}9.7p + 9.75$$
$$\text{-}6.85p - 3.95 = 9.75$$
$$\text{-}6.85p - 3.95 + 3.95 = 9.75 + 3.95$$
$$\text{-}6.85p = 13.7$$
$$\frac{1}{\text{-}6.85} \cdot \text{-}6.85p = \frac{1}{\text{-}6.85} \cdot 13.7$$
$$p = \text{-}2$$

Check: Does
$$2.85 \cdot \text{-}2 - 3.95 = 9.7 \cdot \text{-}2 + 9.75?$$
$$\text{-}5.7 - 3.95 = \text{-}19.4 + 9.75?$$
$$\text{-}9.65 = \text{-}9.65$$

Yes, it checks.

13. In Alaska, n years after 1990 the population will be $550{,}000 + 15{,}000n$. In Delaware, n years after 1990 the population will be $666{,}000 + 7{,}000n$.

$$550{,}000 + 15{,}000n = 666{,}000 + 7000n$$
$$550{,}000 + 15{,}000n + \text{-}7000n = 666{,}000 + 7000n + \text{-}7000n$$
$$550{,}000 + 8000n = 666{,}000$$
$$\text{-}550{,}000 + 550{,}000 + 8000n = \text{-}550{,}000 + 666{,}000$$
$$8000n = 116{,}000$$
$$\frac{1}{8000} \cdot 8000n = \frac{1}{8000} \cdot 116{,}000$$
$$n = 14.5$$

At these rates, about 14.5 years after 1990, that is, in 2004 or 2005, the populations would be the same.

14. In Jacksonville, n years before 1990 the population was $673{,}000 - 13{,}200n$. In El Paso, n years before 1990 the population was $515{,}000 - 9000n$.

$$673{,}000 - 13{,}200n = 515{,}000 - 9000n$$
$$673{,}000 - 13{,}200n + 13{,}200n = 515{,}000 - 9000n + 13{,}200n$$
$$673{,}000 = 515{,}000 + 4200n$$
$$673{,}000 - 515{,}000 = 515{,}000 - 515{,}000 + 4200n$$
$$158{,}000 = 4200n$$
$$\frac{1}{4200} \cdot 158{,}000 = \frac{1}{4200} \cdot 4200n$$
$$37.6 = n$$

At these rates, about 37.6 years before 1990, that is, in 1952 or 1953, the populations would have been the same.

15. a. $2x$
   b. Add 1
   c. Multiply
   d. $\frac{1}{3}$

16.
$$1.5c + 17 = 0.8c - 32$$
$$-0.8c + 1.5c + 17 = -0.8c + 0.8c - 32$$
$$0.7c + 17 = -32$$
$$0.7c + 17 + -17 = -32 + -17$$
$$.7c = -49$$
$$\frac{1}{.7} \cdot .7c = \frac{1}{.7} \cdot -49$$
$$c = -70$$

17.
$$3d + 4d + 5 = 6d + 7d + 8$$
$$7d + 5 = 13d + 8$$
$$-13d + 7d + 5 = -13d + 13d + 8$$
$$-6d + 5 = 8$$
$$-6d + 5 + -5 = 8 + -5$$
$$-6d = 3$$
$$-\frac{1}{6} \cdot -6d = -\frac{1}{6} \cdot 3$$
$$d = -\frac{1}{2}$$

18.
$$3(x - 4) = 4(x - 3)$$
$$3x - 12 = 4x - 12$$
$$3x - 12 + 12 = 4x - 12 + 12$$
$$3x = 4x$$
$$3x + -4x = 4x + -4x$$
$$-1x = 0$$
$$\frac{1}{-1} \cdot -1x = \frac{1}{-1} \cdot 0$$
$$x = 0$$

19.
$$7(3y - 6) = 14y$$
$$21y - 42 = 14y$$
$$-21y + 21y - 42 = -21y + 14y$$
$$-42 = -7y$$
$$-\frac{1}{7} \cdot -42 = -\frac{1}{7} \cdot -7y$$
$$6 = y$$

20. Let n = the number.
$$5 + 2n = 3 + 4n$$
$$5 + 2n + -2n = 3 + 4n + -2n$$
$$5 = 3 + 2n$$
$$-3 + 5 = -3 + 3 + 2n$$
$$2 = 2n$$
$$\frac{1}{2} \cdot 2 = \frac{1}{2} \cdot 2n$$
$$1 = n$$

21. a. women's record x years after 1992:
   $54.64 - .33x$
   b. men's record x years after 1992:
   $49.36 - .18x$
   c.
$$54.64 - .33x = 49.36 - .18x$$
$$54.64 - .33x + .33x = 49.36 - .18x + .33x$$
$$54.64 = 49.36 + .15x$$
$$-49.36 + 54.64 = -49.36 + 49.36 + .15x$$
$$5.28 = .15x$$
$$\frac{1}{.15} \cdot 5.28 = \frac{1}{.15} \cdot .15x$$
$$35.2 = x$$
   After about 35 years, at the Olympics in the year 2028.

22.
$$x + 3 + 3x + x + 6 = 4 \cdot 2x$$
$$5x + 9 = 8x$$
$$-5x + 5x + 9 = -5x + 8x$$
$$9 = 3x$$
$$\frac{1}{3} \cdot 9 = \frac{1}{3} \cdot 3x$$
$$3 = x$$
   The length of a side of the square is $2 \cdot 3 = 6$.

23. a.

Hours	Lamont's distance	Chris's distance
0	24	0
1	33	13
2	42	26
3	51	39
4	60	52
5	69	65
6	78	78

   b. It takes Chris 6 hours to catch up to Lamont.

24. $y = n$

25.

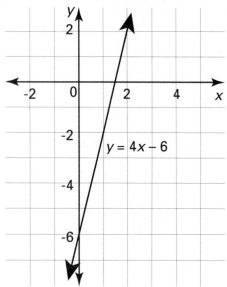

$y = 4x - 6$

26. a. $2 < x < 14 \ (8 - 6 < x < 8 + 6)$

b. If $\angle A$ is a right angle, then $x = 10$ by the Pythagorean Theorem. $(6^2 + 8^2 = 10^2)$

c.

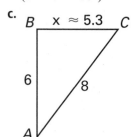

$$6^2 + x^2 = 8^2$$
$$36 + x^2 = 64$$
$$x^2 = 28$$
$$x \approx 5.3$$

27. a. $3(2 + x)$

b. $(x + 2)3$

c. $3x + 6$

28. $-4 + \frac{1}{4} = -3\frac{3}{4}$ or $-\frac{15}{4}$

29. a. Yes, $3 \cdot 6 = 18$ and $2 \cdot 6 + 6 = 18$

b. No, $3 \cdot 10 = 30$ and $2 \cdot 10 + 6 = 26$

c. Yes, $3\sqrt{31} \approx 16.7$ and $2\sqrt{31} + 6 \approx 11.14 + 6 \approx 17.4$

30. 1 bottle + 1 glass = 1 pitcher; given
1 glass + 1 plate + 1 glass = 1 pitcher;
use 1 bottle = 1 glass + 1 plate
2 glasses + 1 plate = 1 pitcher; simplified
3(2 glasses + 1 plate) = 3(1 pitcher);
Distributive Property
6 glasses + 3 plates = 3 pitchers; simplified;
6 glasses + 2 pitchers = 3 pitchers;
use 3 plates = 2 pitchers
6 glasses = 1 pitcher;
subtract 2 pitchers from each side
6 glasses = 1 bottle + 1 glass;
use 1 bottle + 1 glass = 1 pitcher
1 bottle = 5 glasses;
subtract 1 glass from each side

LESSON 5-4   pp. 304–309

1. Distance from starting point after 12 seconds
hare: $d = 5 \cdot 12 = 60$ feet
tortoise: $d = 100 + .1 \cdot 12 = 100 + 1.2$
$= 101.2$ feet

2. Distance from starting point after 60 seconds
hare: $d = 5 \cdot 60 = 300$ feet
tortoise: $d = 100 + .1 \cdot 60 = 100 + 6$
$= 106$ feet

3. The hare reaches the tortoise after about 20.4 seconds.
$5 \cdot 20.4 = 102$ feet or
$100 + .1(20.4) = 100 + 2.04 \approx 102$ feet

4. a. If the race course is 110 ft long, the hare will win.

b. It will take the hare $110 = 5t$ or 22 seconds to finish, whereas it will take the tortoise $110 = 100 + .1t$; $10 = .1t$ or 100 seconds to finish.

5. a. the rat's distance in the race is:
$d = 50 + 2t$

b.

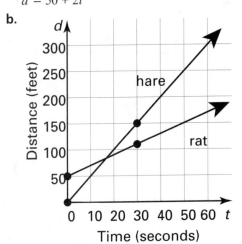

c. The hare reaches the rat after about 17 seconds.

6. a. The price is the same for about 3000 copies per month.

b. The cost of 3000 copies is about $160.

c. $10 + 0.05x = 70 + 0.03x$
$10 + 0.02x = 70$
$0.02x = 60$
$x = 3000$

7. a. Carlson's and Acme charge the same price for 6000 copies per month.

b. It will cost approximately $310 for the 6000 copies per month.

c. $10 + 0.05x = 250 + 0.01x$
$10 + 0.04x = 250$
$0.04x = 240$
$x = 6000$

8. a. Cost of car rental
American Rental: $y = 70 + 0.1x$
Coast-to-Coast Rent-a-Car:
$y = 50 + 0.13x$

b. The cost to rent a car from American for 1 week if you drove 600 miles would be $130.

$y = 70 + .1 \cdot 600$
$= 70 + 60$
$= 130$

c.

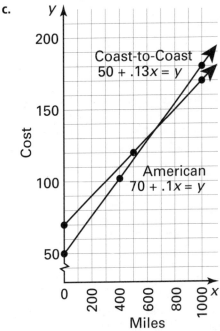

d. The two rental agencies will charge the same for about 700 miles.

e. $70 + 0.1x = 50 + 0.13x$
$70 = 50 + .03x$
$20 = .03x$
$x = 666.\overline{6}$
$x \approx 667$ miles
The two rental agencies will charge the same for about 667 miles.

f. Rent a car from American Rental, because their cost is less when you drive more than 667 miles.

9. a. At about 9000 copies costs are equal.

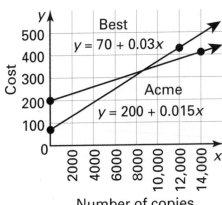

9. b. The costs will be equal for 8667 copies.

$$200 + 0.015x = 70 + 0.03x$$
$$200 = 70 + .015x$$
$$130 = .015x$$
$$x = 8666.\overline{6}$$

10. a. Drucilla arrived first; the graph shows she reached 1250 miles in about 36 hours and Phil arrived about 8 hours later.

b. Phil's plane trip took about 4 hours.

11. Using a table, you get 312.5 pu.

$x =$ distance dog travels	$y =$ distance hare is ahead
0	50
125	30
250	10
312.5	0

Using a graph, you may approximate the answer. Graph the line from (0, 50) through (125, 30). When the distance (y) the hare is ahead reaches zero, the x-value tells the total distance traveled by the dog.

12. $3p - 5 = 2p + 12$
$$p - 5 = 12$$
$$p = 17$$

13. $-7r + 54 = 2r - 36$
$$-9r + 54 = -36$$
$$-9r = -90$$
$$r = 10$$

14. $6(x + 3) + 4(3x - 75) = 258$
$$6x + 18 + 12x - 300 = 258$$
$$18x - 282 = 258$$
$$18x = 540$$
$$x = 30$$

15. $\quad 6m = 2m + 2$
$$6m - 2m = 2$$
$$4m = 2$$
$$m = \frac{1}{2}$$

16. a. A new Soft White bulb costs $0.59.

b. A new Energy Choice bulb is $.92 - .59$ or $0.16 more.

c. After about 300 hours of use for the two bulbs, the total costs are the same.

d. If a bulb lasts for 1000 hours of use, you would be saving $5.39 - 4.95 = \$0.44$ by buying an Energy Choice bulb.

17. a.

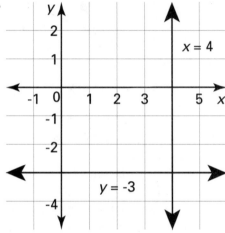

b. The two lines intersect at (4, -3).

18. (d) $\frac{4x}{10} = \frac{2x}{5} \neq \frac{x}{6}$

19. SQUARE ROOTS AND SQUARES

1	1	1
1.41421356	2	4
1.73205081	3	9
2	4	16
2.23606789	5	25
2.44948974	6	36

20. Answers will vary.

LESSON 5-5 pp. 310–316

1. a. The window is the part of the coordinate grid shown on the screen.

b. The default window is the window that appears automatically when you turn on the grapher.

2. Answers will vary.

3. $-15 < x < 15$; $-10 < y < 10$

4. Yes   **5.** Yes

6. No

7. Samples: Both graphs intersect the y-axis at -5. Both graphs slant in the same direction.

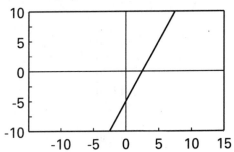

8. Sample:

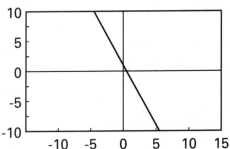

9. Sample:

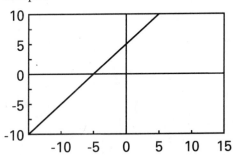

10. a. Answers will vary. Sample:
($-200 < x < 200$; $-300 < y < 300$)

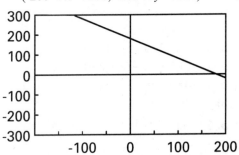

b. Samples: (0, 180); (60, 120); (90, 90)

11. a. Answers will vary. Sample graph:

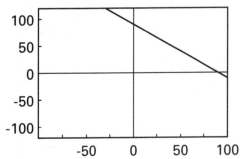

b. True

c. As the x-coordinate increases, the y-coordinate decreases.

12. a. Sample:

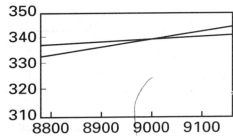

b. Answers will vary but should be close to (9000, 340).

13. a.

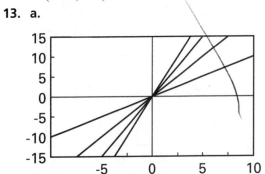

b. Sample: All lines pass through (0, 0). Some lines are steeper than others. The higher the coefficient of x, the steeper the graph is.

c. Sample: It will pass through the origin and be steeper than the other graphs.

14. Tonelli's price is cheaper for pizza with more than 4 toppings. Sample graph:

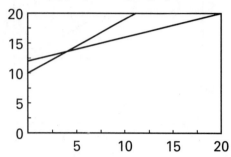

15. a.

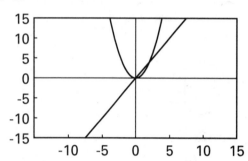

b. Sample: The graphs are not equal. One is a line and one is a curve.

16. a.

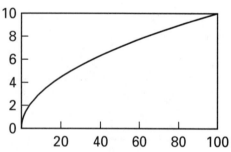

b. Samples: (1, 1); (2, 1.41); (3, 1.73); (4, 2); (5, 2.24)

17. $7(d + 5) = 11(2d - 20)$

$7d + 35 = 22d - 220$

$35 = 15d - 220$

$255 = 15d$

$17 = d$

18.

Number of Extra Items x	Battaglia's Charges $y = 10 + .9x$	Tonelli's Charges $y = 12 + .4x$
0	$10.00	$12.00
1	$10.90	$12.40
2	$11.80	$12.80
3	$12.70	$13.20
4	$13.60	$13.60
5	$14.50	$14.00
6	$15.40	$14.40
7	$16.30	$14.80

19. (c)

20. $(17a + 12) - (a - 4)$

$= 17a + 12 + \text{-}a + 4$

$= 16a + 16$

21. $(4x - 1) - 3(x + 2) = 2$

$4x - 1 - 3x - 6 = 2$

$x - 7 = 2$

$x = 9$

22. a. $2W - 7 < 1$

$2W < 8$

$W < 4$

b. $7 - 2x < 1$

$\text{-}2x < \text{-}6$

$x > 3$

c. $2y - 7 < \text{-}1$

$2y < 6$

$y < 3$

d. $7 - 2z < \text{-}1$

$\text{-}2z < \text{-}8$

$z > 4$

23. a. $x - s - 2m$

b. $x - (s + 2m)$

24. a. $x - (3s + m) - (s + 2m)$

b. $x - 4s - 3m$

25. (b)

26. a. $20 \text{ feet} \cdot \frac{1}{3} \frac{\text{minute}}{\text{feet}} \approx 6.7 \text{ minutes}$

b. $\frac{f}{3}$ min

27. a. $x + 3 = 5$

$x = 2$

b. $\sqrt{y} + 3 = 5$

$\sqrt{y} = 2$

$y = 4$

c. $2\sqrt{z} = 8$

$\sqrt{z} = 4$

$z = 16$

28. Sample: $y = 7 - x$; $y = 7 + x$; $y = -7 - x$; $y = -7 + x$

29. a. Sample: It magnifies the graph around the cursor. Press the ZOOM key for access.

b. Sample: It displays a greater portion of the graph that is centered around the cursor location. To access it, select ZOOM OUT from the ZOOM menu.

c. It draws each data point as a coordinate on the display. To access, it, press ⟨2nd⟩ [STAT] ← to display the STAT DATA menu. Select <Edit>. Enter the value for x and press ENTER. Enter the value for y and press ENTER. When finished entering all data values, press ⟨2nd⟩ [STAT] → to display the STAT DRAW menu. Select <scatter>. Press ENTER. Then the scatterplot is displayed on the screen.

LESSON 5-6   pp. 317–321

1. When they were planted, the beech was taller.
2. After 7 years the beech tree was taller.
3. After 20 years the maple tree will be taller.

4. a. $8 + 0.5t < 3 + t$

$8 + 0.5t + -0.5t < 3 + t + -0.5t$

$8 < 3 + 0.5t$

$-3 + 8 < -3 + 3 + 0.5t$

$5 < 0.5t$

$\frac{1}{0.5} \cdot 5 < \frac{1}{0.5} \cdot 0.5t$

$10 < t$

b. Sample: More than 10 years after they were planted, the maple tree was taller than the beech tree.

5. The elm tree will be taller than the maple 4 years from now. It will be taller by 3 feet.
elm: $7 + 3 \cdot 4 = 7 + 12 = 19$ feet
maple: $12 + 4 = 16$ feet

6. The maple is taller than the elm for the first $2\frac{1}{2}$ years.

$12 + t > 7 + 3t$

$12 + t + -t > 7 + 3t + -t$

$12 > 7 + 2t$

$-7 + 12 > -7 + 7 + 2t$

$5 > 2t$

$\frac{1}{2} \cdot 5 > \frac{1}{2} \cdot 2t$

$\frac{5}{2} > t$

7. a. $4k + 3 > 9k + 18$

$4k + -4k + 3 > 9k + -4k + 18$

$3 > 5k + 18$

$3 - 18 > 5k + 18 - 18$

$-15 > 5k$

$\frac{1}{5} \cdot -15 > \frac{1}{5} \cdot 5k$

$-3 > k$

b. $4k + 3 > 9k + 18$

$4k + -9k + 3 > 9k + -9k + 18$

$-5k + 3 > 18$

$-5k + 3 - 3 > 18 - 3$

$-5k > 15$

$-\frac{1}{5} \cdot -5k < -\frac{1}{5} \cdot 15$

$k < -3$

c. Yes, you should get the same answer for parts **a** and **b**.

d. Sample: In part **a**, the sense of the inequality does not change; in part **b**, the sense of the inequality is reversed.

8. a. $5n + 7 \geq 2n + 19$

$$5n + \text{-}2n + 7 \geq 2n + \text{-}2n + 19$$

$$3n + 7 \geq 19$$

$$3n + 7 - 7 \geq 19 - 7$$

$$3n \geq 12$$

$$\tfrac{1}{3} \cdot 3n \geq \tfrac{1}{3} \cdot 12$$

$$n \geq 4$$

b. Does $5 \cdot 4 + 7 = 2 \cdot 4 + 19$? Yes, $20 + 7 = 27$ and $8 + 19 = 27$. Try a number that satisfies $n \geq 4$; try $n = 10$. Is $5 \cdot 10 + 7 > 2 \cdot 10 + 19$? $57 > 39$; yes, it checks.

9. a. $\qquad \text{-}48 + 10a \leq \text{-}8 + 20a$

$$\text{-}48 + 10a + \text{-}10a \leq \text{-}8 + 20a + \text{-}10a$$

$$\text{-}48 \leq \text{-}8 + 10a$$

$$\text{-}48 + 8 \leq \text{-}8 + 10a + 8$$

$$\text{-}40 \leq 10a$$

$$\tfrac{1}{10} \cdot \text{-}40 \leq \tfrac{1}{10} \cdot 10a$$

$$\text{-}4 \leq a$$

b. Does $\text{-}48 + 10 \cdot \text{-}4 = \text{-}8 + 20 \cdot 4$? Yes, $\text{-}48 + \text{-}40 = \text{-}88$ and $\text{-}8 + \text{-}80 = \text{-}88$. Try a number that satisfies $\text{-}4 \leq a$; try $a = 0$. Is $\text{-}48 + 10 \cdot 0 < \text{-}8 + 20 \cdot 0$? $\text{-}48 < \text{-}8$; yes, it checks.

10. a. $\qquad 4x + 12 < \text{-}2x - 6$

$$4x + 12 + 2x \leq \text{-}2x - 6 + 2x$$

$$6x + 12 < \text{-}6$$

$$6x + 12 + \text{-}12 < \text{-}6 + \text{-}12$$

$$6x < \text{-}18$$

$$\tfrac{1}{6} \cdot 6x < \tfrac{1}{6} \cdot \text{-}18$$

$$x < \text{-}3$$

b. Does $4 \cdot \text{-}3 + 12 = \text{-}2 \cdot \text{-}3 - 6$? Yes, $\text{-}12 + 12 = 0$ and $6 - 6 = 0$. Try a number that satisfies $x < \text{-}3$; try $x = \text{-}5$. Is $4 \cdot \text{-}5 + 12 < \text{-}2 \cdot \text{-}5 - 6$? Yes, $\text{-}20 + 12 = \text{-}8$ and $10 - 6 = 4$; $\text{-}8 < 4$.

11. a. $\qquad 12 - 3y > 27 + 7y$

$$12 - 3y + 3y > 27 + 7y + 3y$$

$$12 > 27 + 10y$$

$$12 + \text{-}27 > 27 + 10y + \text{-}27$$

$$\text{-}15 > 10y$$

$$\tfrac{1}{10} \cdot \text{-}15 > \tfrac{1}{10} \cdot 10y$$

$$\text{-}\tfrac{3}{2} > y$$

b. Does $12 - 3 \cdot \text{-}\tfrac{3}{2} = 27 + 7 \cdot \text{-}\tfrac{3}{2}$? Yes, $12 + 4.5 = 16.5$ and $27 - 10.5 = 16.5$. Try a number that satisfies $\text{-}\tfrac{3}{2} > y$; try $y = \text{-}2$. Is $12 - 3 \cdot \text{-}2 > 27 + 7 \cdot \text{-}2$? Yes, $12 + 6 = 18$ and $27 - 14 = 13$; $18 > 13$.

12. $\qquad 5x < 3x$

$$5x + \text{-}3x < 3x + \text{-}3x$$

$$2x < 0$$

$$\tfrac{1}{2} \cdot 2x < \tfrac{1}{2} \cdot 0$$

$$x < 0$$

Any negative number is part of the solution set.

13. $\qquad 5 - 3(x + 2) < 10x$

$$5 - 3x + \text{-}6 < 10x$$

$$\text{-}3x + \text{-}1 < 10x$$

$$3x + \text{-}3x + \text{-}1 < 10x + 3x$$

$$\text{-}1 < 13x$$

$$\tfrac{1}{13} \cdot \text{-}1 < \tfrac{1}{13} \cdot 13x$$

$$\text{-}\tfrac{1}{13} < x$$

14. $\qquad \text{-}3t \geq \text{-}t + 3 + 9t$

$$\text{-}3t \geq 8t + 3$$

$$\text{-}3t + \text{-}8t \geq 8t + \text{-}8t + 3$$

$$\text{-}11t \geq 3$$

$$\text{-}\tfrac{1}{11} \cdot \text{-}11t \leq \text{-}\tfrac{1}{11} \cdot 3$$

$$t \leq \text{-}\tfrac{3}{11}$$

15. The Gazette's rates are cheaper for ads with more than 25 words.
$$2 + .08x < 1.50 + .10x$$
$$2 + .08x + -.08x < 1.50 + .10x + -.08x$$
$$2 < 1.5 + .02x$$
$$2 + -1.5 < 1.5 + .02x + -1.5$$
$$.5 < .02x$$
$$\frac{1}{.02} \cdot .5 < \frac{1}{.02} \cdot .02x$$
$$25 < x$$

16. a. Speedy Service is cheaper.
Fast Fellows: $3.5 + .25 \cdot 20 = \$8.50$
Speedy Service: $4.75 + .10 \cdot 20 = \$6.75$

b. Packages 8 oz or less are cheaper at Fast Fellows; packages 9 oz or more are cheaper at Speedy Service.

17. a.

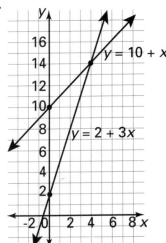

b. When $x = 4$, $10 + x = 2 + 3x$. On the graph the lines intersect at $x = 4$.

18. $4x + 12 = -2(x + 3)$
$$4x + 12 = -2x + -6$$
$$6x + 12 = -6$$
$$6x = -18$$
$$x = -3$$

19. $60t - 1 = 48t$
$$-1 = 48t - 60t$$
$$-1 = -12t$$
$$\frac{1}{12} = t$$

20. $109 - m = 18m - 5$
$$109 = 19m - 5$$
$$114 = 19m$$
$$6 = m$$

21. $3n - n + 5 = 4n - n + 20$
$$2n + 5 = 3n + 20$$
$$5 = n + 20$$
$$-15 = n$$

22. a. The intersection is about $(5, 8)$.

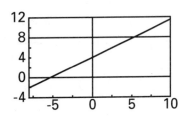

b.
$$8 = 4 + 0.75x$$
$$4 = .75x$$
$$\frac{1}{.75} \cdot 4 = \frac{1}{.75} \cdot .75x$$
$$\frac{16}{3} = x \text{ or } 5.33 \approx x$$

23. $\frac{t}{4} + \frac{t}{3} = \frac{3t}{12} + \frac{4t}{12} = \frac{7t}{12}$

24. It will take 3.35 hours, or 3 hours 21 minutes, to drive from San Antonio to Houston.
$1946 = 386 + 400 + 582 + x + 377$; $x = 201$;
$201 \text{ miles} \cdot \frac{1}{60} \frac{\text{hour}}{\text{miles}} = 3.35$ hours.

25. No; Sample: because
$12! = (12 \cdot 11 \cdot 10 \cdot 9 \cdot 8 \cdot 7) \cdot 6! \neq 2 \cdot 6!$

26. (d) $4\left(\frac{1}{3x}\right) = \frac{4}{3x}$

27. a. $30 \cdot \frac{1}{6} = \frac{30}{6} = 5$

b. $30 \cdot \frac{5}{6} = \frac{150}{6} = 25$

c. $30 \cdot \frac{x}{6} = \frac{30x}{6} = 5x$

d. $30 \cdot \frac{5}{6}x = \frac{150}{6}x = 25x$

28. a. $-(a - b) = b - a$

b. The pattern is true for all real numbers. Use the Distributive Property, Definition of Subtraction, and Commutative Property of Addition: $-(a - b) =$ $-1 \cdot (a-b) = -1 \cdot (a + -b) = -1 \cdot a + -1 \cdot -b =$ $-a + b = b - a$

29. $x^2 < (x - 1)(x + 2)$

    a. Sample: 3; $3^2 < (3 - 1)(3 + 2)$

$$9 < 2 \cdot 5$$
$$9 < 10$$

    b. any number x such that $x > 2$

LESSON 5-7   pp. 322–326

1. $100°F = 37.8°C$
$$\left(\tfrac{5}{9}(100 - 32) = \tfrac{5}{9} \cdot 68 = 37.\overline{7}\right)$$

2. $200°C = 392°F$ $\left(\tfrac{9}{5} \cdot 200 + 32 = 392\right)$

3. $5x + y = 6$
$$y = -5x + 6$$

4. $3x - 6y = 12$
$$-6y = -3x + 12$$
$$y = -\tfrac{1}{6}(-3x + 12) = \tfrac{1}{2}x - 2$$

5. Sample: To use automatic graphers, you need to enter equations that give y in terms of x.

6. $A = p + pr$

7. a. Multiplicative Identity

    b. Distributive

    c. $\frac{1}{1+r}$

8. $d = rt$

9. $P = 2(L + W)$
$$P = 2L + 2W$$
$$P - 2W = 2L$$
$$\tfrac{1}{2}(P - 2W) = L$$
$$\tfrac{1}{2}P - W = L$$

10. $a = \frac{F}{M}$

11. $A = \tfrac{1}{2}(b_1 + b_2)h$
$$2A = (b_1 + b_2)h$$
$$\frac{2A}{b_1 + b_2} = h$$

12. $C = K - 273$
$$C + 273 = K$$

13. a. $\pi = \frac{C}{d}$

    b. Sample: If you know the circumference and diameter of a circle, you can substitute those values in the equation to find an approximation for π.

    c. Answers may vary.

14. $V = 2\pi r^2 + 2\pi rh$
$$V = 2\pi r(r + h)$$
$$\frac{V}{2\pi r} = r + h$$
$$\frac{V}{2\pi r} - r = h$$

15. a. $D = \tfrac{9}{10}G$

    b. 100 grads = 90 degrees
$$\left(\tfrac{9}{10} \cdot 100 = 90\right)$$

16. The graphs are parallel.

17. a. -40 degrees has the same reading on both the Fahrenheit and Celsius scales.

    b. Solve $\quad C = \tfrac{9}{5}C + 32$:
$$-\tfrac{4}{5}C = 32$$
$$C = -40$$

    or solve $\quad F = \tfrac{5}{9}(F - 32)$:
$$\tfrac{9}{5}F = F - 32$$
$$\tfrac{4}{5}F = -32$$
$$F = -40$$

18. $-3z - 4 > 2z - 24$
$$-5z - 4 > -24$$
$$-5z > -20$$
$$z < 4$$

19. $7(x-2)+5(2-x) \geq 4(3x-4)$

$$7x-14+10-5x \geq 12x-16$$
$$2x-4 \geq 12x-16$$
$$\text{-}10x-4 \geq \text{-}16$$
$$\text{-}10x \geq \text{-}12$$
$$x \leq \frac{6}{5}$$

20. a. Sample: Jack opened a bank account with a deposit of $150. Every week he deposited $2 to his account. At the same time, Mary opened an account with a deposit of $100. Every week she added $5 to her account. After how many weeks will they have the same amount of money in the bank (ignoring interest)?

b. $150+2x=100+5x$

$$150=100+3x$$
$$50=3x$$
$$\frac{50}{3}=x \text{ or } 16.67 \approx x$$

c. Sample: They will have the same amount of money after about 17 weeks.

21.

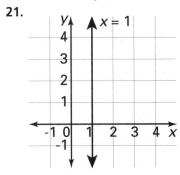

22. a. $y=0$
b. $x=0$

23. In over three years, or the year 1993, the population of Lagos would first exceed the population of London.

$$8,487,000+395,000x > 9,170,000-55,000x$$
$$8,487,000+450,000x > 9,170,000$$
$$450,000x > 683,000$$
$$x > 1.52$$

24. a. $\frac{2}{3}+\frac{1}{8}=\frac{16}{24}+\frac{3}{24}=\frac{19}{24}$

b. $\frac{2}{3}a+\frac{1}{8}a=\frac{16}{24}a+\frac{3}{24}a=\frac{19}{24}a$

c. $\frac{2a}{3}+\frac{a}{8}=\frac{16a}{24}+\frac{3a}{24}=\frac{19a}{24}$

25. a. 40 dots make up Figure 10.
b. $4n$ dots make up Figure n.

26. 5,999,994 $(6 \cdot 1,000,000-6 \cdot 1 = 6,000,000-6)$

27. Answers will vary. Sample: The formula to find the volume of a pyramid is $V=\frac{1}{3}Bh$, where B is the area of the base and h is the altitude. Solve for h. $3V=Bh$

$$\frac{3V}{B}=h$$

LESSON 5-8 pp. 327–332

1. a. $12\left(\frac{1}{3}x+5\right)=12\left(\frac{5}{12}x\right)$

$$\frac{12}{3}x+12 \cdot 5 = \frac{60}{12}x$$
$$4x+60=5x$$

b. $60=x$

c. Does $\frac{1}{3} \cdot 60+5 = \frac{5}{12} \cdot 60$?

$$20+5=\frac{300}{12}?$$
$$25=25$$

Yes, it checks.

2. a. $12 \cdot \frac{a}{4}=12\left(20-\frac{a}{6}\right)$

$$3a=240-2a$$
$$5a=240$$
$$a=48$$

b. $24 \cdot \frac{a}{4}=24\left(20-\frac{a}{6}\right)$

$$6a=480-4a$$
$$10a=480$$
$$a=48$$

c. Sample: Fractions in an equation can be cleared by multiplying any common multiple of the denominators in the equation.

3. Does $\frac{1}{4} \cdot 36 = 21 - \frac{1}{3} \cdot 36$?

$9 = 21 - 12$?

$9 = 9$

Yes, it checks.

4. Multiplication Properties of Equality and Inequality

5. a. $\frac{1}{5}t + \frac{1}{2}t + 18 = t$

  b. $10\left(\frac{1}{5}t + \frac{1}{2}t + 18\right) = 10 \cdot t$

  $2t + 5t + 180 = 10t$

  $7t + 180 = 10t$

  $180 = 3t$

  $60 = t$

  The commute takes 60 minutes.

6. a. $15\left(\frac{8a}{15} - 2\right) = 15 \cdot \frac{a}{5}$

  $8a - 30 = 3a$

  b. $-30 = -5a$

  $6 = a$

7. a. $18\left(\frac{x}{2} + \frac{x}{6} + 10\right) < 18 \cdot \frac{5}{9}x$

  $9x + 3x + 180 < 10x$

  b. $12x + 180 < 10x$

  $12x - 10x < -180$

  $2x < -180$

  $x < -90$

8. $5150 + 90n = 6280 - 8n$

  $5150 + 98n = 6280$

  $98n = 1130$

  $n = \frac{1130}{98} \approx 11.53$

9. $\frac{5}{6}x + \frac{1}{2} = \frac{2}{3}$

  $6 \cdot \left(\frac{5}{6}x + \frac{1}{2}\right) = 6 \cdot \frac{2}{3}$

  $5x + 3 = 4$

  $5x = 1$

  $x = \frac{1}{5}$

Check: Does $\frac{5}{6} \cdot \frac{1}{5} + \frac{1}{2} = \frac{2}{3}$?

$\frac{1}{6} + \frac{3}{6} = \frac{2}{3}$?

$\frac{2}{3} = \frac{2}{3}$

Yes, it checks.

10. $\frac{a}{5} - 1 = \frac{a}{30}$

$30 \cdot \left(\frac{a}{5} - 1\right) = 30 \cdot \frac{a}{30}$

$6a - 30 = a$

$-30 = -5a$

$6 = a$

Check: Does $\frac{6}{5} - 1 = \frac{6}{30}$?

$\frac{1}{5} = \frac{1}{5}$

Yes, it checks.

11. $0.03y - 1.5 = 0.09y - 0.48$

$100(0.03y - 1.5) = 100(0.09y - 0.48)$

$3y - 150 = 9y - 48$

$-6y - 150 = -48$

$-6y = 102$

$y = -17$

Check: Does

$0.03 \cdot -17 - 1.5 = 0.09 \cdot -17 - 0.48$?

$-0.51 - 1.5 = -1.35 - 0.48$?

$-2.01 = -2.01$

Yes, it checks.

12. $6000n + 9000 = 11,000 - 2000n$

$\frac{1}{1000}(6000n + 9000) = \frac{1}{1000}(11,000 - 2000n)$

$6n + 9 = 11 - 2n$

$8n + 9 = 11$

$8n = 2$

$n = \frac{1}{4}$

Check: Does

$6000 \cdot \frac{1}{4} + 9000 = 11,000 - 2000 \cdot \frac{1}{4}$?

$1500 + 9000 = 11,000 - 500$?

$10,500 = 10,500$

Yes, it checks.

13. $\frac{3x}{5} - \frac{x}{10} < 5$

$10\left(\frac{3x}{5} - \frac{x}{10}\right) < 10 \cdot 5$

$6x - x < 50$

$5x < 50$

$x < 10$

Check: Does $\frac{3 \cdot 10}{5} - \frac{10}{10} = 5$?

$6 - 1 = 5$?

$5 = 5$

Yes, so choose $x < 10$; we choose $x = 0$.

Is $\frac{3 \cdot 0}{5} - \frac{0}{10} < 5$?

$0 - 0 < 5$?

$0 < 5$

Yes, it checks.

14. $\frac{n}{2} - 1 \geq \frac{4}{5} + \frac{3n}{10}$

$10\left(\frac{n}{2} - 1\right) \geq 10\left(\frac{4}{5} + \frac{3n}{10}\right)$

$5n - 10 \geq 8 + 3n$

$2n - 10 \geq 8$

$2n \geq 18$

$n \geq 9$

Check: Does $\frac{9}{2} - 1 = \frac{4}{5} + \frac{3 \cdot 9}{10}$?

$\frac{45}{10} - \frac{10}{10} = \frac{8}{10} + \frac{27}{10}$?

$\frac{35}{10} = \frac{35}{10}$

Yes, so choose $n > 9$; we choose $n = 10$.

Is $\frac{10}{2} - 1 \geq \frac{4}{5} + \frac{3 \cdot 10}{10}$?

$\frac{50}{10} - \frac{10}{10} \geq \frac{8}{10} + \frac{30}{10}$?

$\frac{40}{10} \geq \frac{38}{10}$

Yes, it checks.

15. a. $\frac{3}{8}x + \frac{1}{4}x = 25{,}400$

$8\left(\frac{3}{8}x + \frac{1}{4}x\right) = 8 \cdot 25{,}400$

$3x + 2x = 203{,}200$

$5x = 203{,}200$

$x = 40{,}640$

The total amount of dividends paid to the stockholders was \$40,640.

b. Stockholders, other than the Bigbears, received \$15,240 in dividends ($40{,}640 - 25{,}400 = 15{,}240$).

16. $\frac{1}{4}x + \frac{2}{5}x = 660\,\text{billion}$

$20\left(\frac{1}{4}x + \frac{2}{5}x\right) = 20 \cdot 660\,\text{billion}$

$5x + 8x = 13{,}200\,\text{billion}$

$13x = 13{,}200\,\text{billion}$

$x \approx 1015.4\,\text{billion}$

The world's total crude oil reserves is about 1015.4 billion barrels.

17. No; the term $\frac{1}{1000}x$ would appear in the equation, which would not simplify the solution.

18. $\frac{n}{3} - 5 = \frac{n}{4} - 2n$

$12\left(\frac{n}{3} - 5\right) = 12\left(\frac{n}{4} - 2n\right)$

$4n - 60 = 3n - 24n$

$4n - 60 = -21n$

$-60 = -25n$

$\frac{12}{5} = n$

19. $\frac{1}{4}(x + 6) + \frac{1}{8}x = \frac{1}{2}(x + 1)$

$8\left(\frac{1}{4}(x + 6) + \frac{1}{8}x\right) = 8\left(\frac{1}{2}(x + 1)\right)$

$2(x + 6) + x = 4(x + 1)$

$2x + 12 + x = 4x + 4$

$12 + 3x = 4x + 4$

$12 = x + 4$

$8 = x$

20. $\dfrac{a+3}{3} = \dfrac{2a-3}{6} + \dfrac{a+2}{4}$

$12\left(\dfrac{a+3}{3}\right) = 12\left(\dfrac{2a-3}{6} + \dfrac{a+2}{4}\right)$

$4(a+3) = 2(2a-3) + 3(a+2)$

$4a + 12 = 4a - 6 + 3a + 6$

$4a + 12 = 7a$

$12 = 3a$

$4 = a$

21. $\dfrac{y-2}{6} - \dfrac{1}{15} < \dfrac{2y+1}{10}$

$30\left(\dfrac{y-2}{6} - \dfrac{1}{15}\right) < 30\left(\dfrac{2y+1}{10}\right)$

$5(y-2) - 2 < 3(2y+1)$

$5y - 10 - 2 < 6y + 3$

$5y - 12 < 6y + 3$

$-12 < y + 3$

$-15 < y$

22. $x = \dfrac{2uv}{g}$

$g \cdot x = g \cdot \dfrac{2uv}{g}$

$g \cdot x = 2uv$

$\dfrac{gx}{2u} = v$

23. $d = \dfrac{1}{2}gt - vt$

$d - \dfrac{1}{2}gt = -vt$

$-\dfrac{1}{t}\left(d - \dfrac{1}{2}gt\right) = -\dfrac{1}{t} \cdot -vt$

$\dfrac{-d}{t} + \dfrac{1}{2}g = v$

$\dfrac{1}{2}g - \dfrac{d}{t} = v$

24. a. $3(x-9) < 9(3-x)$

$3x - 27 < 27 - 9x$

$12x - 27 < 27$

$12x < 54$

$x < 4.5$

b.

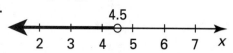

25. a. A

   b. \$2,000

26. a. After about 3 years the cars are the same in value.

   b. After 4 years car B will get about \$1,000 more than car A.

27. a.

Years from now	Town A pop.	Town B pop.
0	25000	35500
1	26200	35200
2	27400	34900
3	28600	34600
4	29800	34300
5	31000	34000
6	32200	33700
7	33400	33400
8	34600	33100

   b. In about 7 years the population of the towns will be equal.

28. $\sqrt{9} \cdot x + 3! \cdot x - 50\% \cdot x$

$= 3 \cdot x + 6 \cdot x - .5x$

$= 8.5x$

29. $p^2 = 10000$

$p = 100$ or $p = -100$

30. Diophantus lived 84 years.

$\dfrac{1}{2}x = x - 4 - \left(\dfrac{1}{6}x + \dfrac{1}{12}x + \dfrac{1}{7}x + 5\right)$

$84 \cdot \dfrac{1}{2}x = 84\left(x - 4 - \dfrac{1}{6}x - \dfrac{1}{12}x - \dfrac{1}{7}x - 5\right)$

$42x = 84x - 336 - 14x - 7x - 12x - 420$

$42x = 51x - 756$

$-9x = -756$

$x = 84$

Diophantus lived 84 years.

LESSON 5-9   pp. 333–337

1. Chunking is a term psychologists use to describe the process of grouping small bits of information into a single piece of information.

2. $8(12t - 7) - 3(12t - 7) = 5(12t - 7)$
$= 60t - 35$

3. $12(10 - a) - 4(10 - a) = 8(10 - a)$
$= 80 - 8a$

4. a. Think of $2y - 6$ as a chunk.
b. $\dfrac{11}{2y - 6} + \dfrac{4}{2y - 6} = \dfrac{15}{2y - 6}$
c. $2y - 6$ cannot equal 0.

5. a. $\dfrac{x}{x + 8} - \dfrac{5}{x + 8} = \dfrac{x - 5}{x + 8}$
b. x cannot have the value -8.

6. a. $10(2a + 3) - 7(2a + 3) = 39$
$3(2a + 3) = 39$
$2a + 3 = 13$
$2a = 10$
$a = 5$

b. $10(2a + 3) - 7(2a + 3) = 39$
$20a + 30 - 14a - 21 = 39$
$6a + 9 = 39$
$6a = 30$
$a = 5$

c. Answers may vary.

7. If $3x = 8.5$, then $6x = 2 \cdot 8.5 = 17$ and $6x - 1 = 17 - 1 = 16$.

8. If $18a = 12$, then $9a = .5 \cdot 12 = 6$ and $9a + 7 = 6 + 7 = 13$.

9. a. $(x + 1)^2 = 81$
$x + 1 = 9$ or $x + 1 = $ -9
$x = 8$ or $x = $ -10

b. $(4x + 1)^2 = 81$
$4x + 1 = 9$ or $4x + 1 = $ -9
$4x = 8$ or $4x = $ -10
$x = 2$ or $x = -\dfrac{5}{2}$

10. a. Then $m - 11 = 8$ or $m - 11 = $ -8.
b. $(m - 11)^2 = 64$
$m - 11 = 8$ or $m - 11 = $ -8
$m = 19$ or $m = 3$

11. $(p + 3)^2 = 225$
$p + 3 = 15$ or $p + 3 = $ -15
$p = 12$ or $p = $ -18

12. $7\sqrt{5}$

13. $-2\sqrt{a}$

14. $7(x^2 - 9) - 4(x^2 - 9) = 3(x^2 - 9) = 3x^2 - 27$

15. $3(x^2 - 2y) + 6(x^2 - 2y) - 4(x^2 - 2y) =$
$5(x^2 - 2y) = 5x^2 - 10y$

16. $\dfrac{8(x + 7)}{5a} \cdot \dfrac{3a}{2(x + 7)} = \dfrac{8 \cdot 3a(x + 7)}{2 \cdot 5a \cdot (x + 7)} = \dfrac{4 \cdot 3}{5} = \dfrac{12}{5}$

17. $\dfrac{x + 10}{x + 5} + \dfrac{2x + 5}{x + 5} = \dfrac{3x + 15}{x + 5}$
$= \dfrac{3(x + 5)}{x + 5}$
$= 3$

18. $(d + 11)^2 = 57$
$d + 11 \approx 7.55$ or $d + 11 \approx $ -7.55
$d \approx $ -3.45 or $d \approx $ -18.55

19. $7^2 + 3 = 49 + 3 = 52$

20. If $a + 7 = 91$, then $2a + 14 = 2(a + 7) = 2 \cdot 91 = 182$.

21. If $18y - 12t = 25$, then $9y - 6t = .5(18y - 12t) = .5 \cdot 25 = 12.5$.

22. If $5x + 4y = 32$ and $2y = 1$, then
a. $5x = 32 - 4y$
$= 32 - 2 \cdot 2y$
$= 32 - 2 \cdot 1$
$= 30$
b. $x = 6$

23. $(3p + 5)^2 = 625$
$3p + 5 = 25$ or $3p + 5 = $ -25
$3p = 20$ or $3p = $ -30
$p = \dfrac{20}{3}$ or $p = $ -10

24. $(x^2)^2 = 256$
$x^2 = 16$ or $x^2 = $ -16
$x = 4$ or $x = $ -4 or $\varnothing$
Hence $x = 4$ or $x = $ -4.

25. Multiplication Property of Equality

26. $\dfrac{3w}{4} - 2 \le \dfrac{1}{2}$

$4\left(\dfrac{3w}{4} - 2\right) \le 4 \cdot \dfrac{1}{2}$

$3w - 8 \le 2$

$3w \le 10$

$w \le \dfrac{10}{3}$

27. $\dfrac{x}{2} + \dfrac{x}{3} - \dfrac{1}{4} = \dfrac{1}{6}$

$12\left(\dfrac{x}{2} + \dfrac{x}{3} - \dfrac{1}{4}\right) = 12 \cdot \dfrac{1}{6}$

$6x + 4x - 3 = 2$

$10x - 3 = 2$

$x = \dfrac{5}{10} = \dfrac{1}{2}$

28. $\dfrac{7}{8}x - \dfrac{1}{8}x = 450$

$8\left(\dfrac{7}{8}x - \dfrac{1}{8}x\right) = 8 \cdot 450$

$7x - x = 3600$

$6x = 3600$

$x = 600$

The tank holds 600 gallons.

29. Let x represent half his monthly earnings.

$\dfrac{1}{4}x + \dfrac{1}{3}x + \dfrac{1}{4}x + 40 = x$

$12\left(\dfrac{1}{4}x + \dfrac{1}{3}x + \dfrac{1}{4}x + 40\right) = 12x$

$3x + 4x + 3x + 480 = 12x$

$10x + 480 = 12x$

$480 = 2x$

$240 = x$

Bertrand's monthly savings are \$480.

30. $v^2 = ar$

$\dfrac{v^2}{a} = r$

31. a. $2x + 5y = 10$

$5y = -2x + 10$

$y = \left(\dfrac{1}{5}\right)(-2x + 10)$

$y = \left(-\dfrac{2}{5}\right)x + 2$

b.

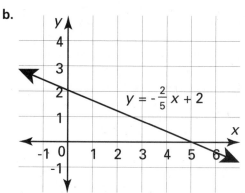

$y = -\dfrac{2}{5}x + 2$

32. a. Sample: One balloonist is 200 ft above the ground and is descending at a rate of 3 ft per second. Another is at 240 ft and is descending 5 ft per second. When will they be at the same altitude?

b. $200 - 3x = 240 - 5x$

$200 + 2x = 240$

$2x = 40$

$x = 20$

33. Sample: $44 + 31 = 31 + 44$

34. $26^3 = 17{,}576$

35. $3(x + 4) = 2x + 2(x + 5)$

$3x + 12 = 2x + 2x + 10$

$3x + 12 = 4x + 10$

$12 = x + 10$

$2 = x$

The length of each side of the triangle is $2 + 4 = 6$ units.

36. Students memorize by chunking.

CHAPTER 5

PROGRESS SELF-TEST
pp. 341–342

1. a. In solving the equation $5y - 9 = 12 - 3y$ an effective first step is to add $-5y$ or $3y$ to each side of the equation.

b. Addition Property of Equality

2. Each side of the equation can be multiplied by 15 to clear the fractions.

3. $4x - 3 = 3x + 14$

$x - 3 = 14$

$x = 17$

4. $3.9z - 56.9 = 6.1 - 4.7z$

$8.6z - 56.9 = 6.1$

$8.6z = 63.0$

$z \approx 7.33$

5. $5n \geq 2n + 12$

$3n \geq 12$

$n \geq 4$

6. $5(10 - y) = 6(y + 1)$

$50 - 5y = 6y + 6$

$50 = 11y + 6$

$44 = 11y$

$4 = y$

7. $-5a + 6 < -11a + 24$

$6a + 6 < 24$

$6a < 18$

$a < 3$

8. $\frac{1}{2}m - \frac{3}{4} = \frac{2}{3}$

$12\left(\frac{1}{2}m - \frac{3}{4}\right) = 12 \cdot \frac{2}{3}$

$6m - 9 = 8$

$6m = 17$

$m = \frac{17}{6}$

9. $5000 - 4000v = 11{,}000v + 680{,}000$

$5 - 4v = 11v + 680$

$5 - 15v = 680$

$-15v = 675$

$v = -45$

10. If $4y = 2.6$, then $20y = 5 \cdot 2.6 = 13$ and
$20y + 3 = 13 + 3 = 16.$

11. $\frac{4}{t+7} + \frac{5}{t+7} = \frac{9}{t+7}$

12. $8(x^2 - 5) + 3(x^2 - 5) = 11(x^2 - 5) = 11x^2 - 55$

13. $(n + 3)^2 = 49$

$n + 3 = 7$ or $n + 3 = -7$

$n = 4$ or $n = -10$

14. $3x + 5y = 15$

$5y = -3x + 15$

$y = \frac{1}{5}(-3x + 15)$

$y = -\frac{3}{5}x + 3$

15. $\frac{C}{n} = p$

16.

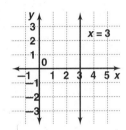

17. Perimeter of triangle:
$24 + 4x + (6x - 6) = 18 + 10x$

Perimeter of square: $4 \cdot 3x = 12x$

$12x = 18 + 10x$

$2x = 18$

$x = 9$

The lengths of the sides of the triangle are
24, $4 \cdot 9 = 36$, and $6 \cdot 9 - 6 = 54 - 6 = 48$.
The length of a side of the square is $3 \cdot 9 = 27$.

18. **a.** After 12 months, the graph of the
younger child's savings is higher than the
graph of the older child's savings.

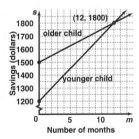

b. $1200 + 50m > 1500 + 25m$

$1200 + 25m > 1500$

$25m > 300$

$m > 12$

19. a.

Monthly Sales	Sun Fashions Total Salary	Today's Outerwear Total Salary
$ 0	$ 400	$ 750
$ 5000	$1000	$1250
$10000	$1600	$1750
$15000	$2200	$2250
$20000	$2800	$2750
$25000	$3400	$3250

b. Sun Fashions will pay Jolisa a greater total salary for sales at least $20,000.

c. Jolisa should take a job with Today's Outerwear because they pay more for sales less than or equal to $15,000.

20. a.

	A	B	C
1	yrs from now	house value	car value
2	0	80,000	14,000
3	1	83,500	12,200
4	2	87,000	10,400
5	3	90,500	8,600
6	4	94,000	6,800
7	5	97,500	5,000
8	6	101,000	3,200

b. $v = \$80{,}000 + 3500t$

21. a. For more than 7 photos it is cheaper to go to Picture Perfect.

b. For less than 7 photos it is more expensive to go to Picture Perfect.

c. The two stores charge the same price for exactly 7 photos.

22. a.

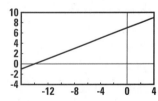

b. $x = -14$

c. The y-coordinate increases.

1. $A + 5 = 9A - 11$

$5 = 8A - 11$

$16 = 8A$

$2 = A$

2. $-12k + 144 = 3k - 45$

$-15k + 144 = -45$

$-15k = -189$

$k = 12.6 \text{ or } \frac{63}{5}$

3. $2a - 6 = -2a$

$-6 = -4a$

$a = \frac{3}{2}$

4. $3n = 2n + 4 + 5n$

$3n = 7n + 4$

$-4n = 4$

$n = -1$

5. $4x - 11.7 = -.3x$

$-11.7 = -4.3x$

$x = \frac{117}{43}$

$x \approx 2.721$

6. $10e = 4e - 5(3 + 2e)$

$10e = 4e - 15 - 10e$

$10e = -6e - 15$

$16e = -15$

$e = -\frac{15}{16}$

7. $3(x + 10) = -2(2x - 1)$

$3x + 30 = -4x + 2$

$7x + 30 = 2$

$7x = -28$

$x = -4$

8. $5(4 - y) = 2(y + 10)$

$20 - 5y = 2y + 20$

$20 - 7y = 20$

$-7y = 0$

$y = 0$

9. $\frac{n}{2} + \frac{3}{2} = 3$

$2\left(\frac{n}{2} + \frac{3}{2}\right) = 2 \cdot 3$

$n + 3 = 6$

$n = 3$

10. $\frac{1}{4}a - 1 = -2a$

$4\left(\frac{1}{4}a - 1\right) = 4 \cdot -2a$

$a - 4 = -8a$

$-4 = -9a$

$\frac{4}{9} = a$

11. $\frac{x}{3} + \frac{x}{5} + 21 = x$

$15\left(\frac{x}{3} + \frac{x}{5} + 21\right) = 15x$

$5x + 3x + 315 = 15x$

$8x + 315 = 15x$

$315 = 7x$

$45 = x$

12. $193.4x + 193.4 = 1934$

$193.4x = 1740.6$

$x = 9$

13. $11h + 71 \geq 13h - 219$

$71 \geq 2h - 219$

$290 \geq 2h$

$145 \geq h$

14. $4x - 1 < 2x + 1$

$2x - 1 < 1$

$2x < 2$

$x < 1$

15. $5(5 + z) < 3(2 + 2z)$

$25 + 5z < 6 + 6z$

$25 < 6 + z$

$19 < z$

16. $-3x + 7 \geq -9x + 25$

$6x + 7 \geq 25$

$6x \geq 18$

$x \geq 3$

17. a. $9(x + 3) + 2 \leq 4 - x$

$9x + 27 + 2 \leq 4 - x$

$9x + 29 \leq 4 - x$

$10x + 29 \leq 4$

$10x \leq -25$

$x \leq -\frac{5}{2}$

b.

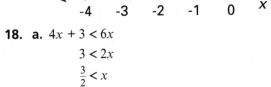

18. a. $4x + 3 < 6x$

$3 < 2x$

$\frac{3}{2} < x$

b.

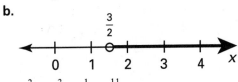

19. $\frac{3}{10}n + \frac{3}{5} < -\frac{1}{2}n - \frac{11}{5}$

$10\left(\frac{3}{10}n + \frac{3}{5}\right) < 10\left(-\frac{1}{2}n - \frac{11}{5}\right)$

$3n + 6 < -5n - 22$

$8n + 6 < -22$

$8n < -28$

$n < -\frac{7}{2}$

20. $\frac{x}{2} + \frac{5}{3} > \frac{2x}{3} - 2$

$6\left(\frac{x}{2} + \frac{5}{3}\right) > 6\left(\frac{2x}{3} - 2\right)$

$3x + 10 > 4x - 12$

$10 > x - 12$

$22 > x$

21. $5000x - 9000 > 3500x - 15{,}000$

$\frac{1}{100}(5000x - 9000) > \frac{1}{100}(3500x - 15{,}000)$

$50x - 90 > 35x - 150$

$15x - 90 > -150$

$15x > -60$

$x > -4$

22.
$$0.12x + 4 \leq 0.2x - 0.32$$
$$100(0.12x + 4) \leq 100(0.2x - 0.32)$$
$$12x + 400 \leq 20x - 32$$
$$400 \leq 8x - 32$$
$$432 \leq 8x$$
$$54 \leq x$$

23. If $7y = 21.2$, then $21y = 3 \cdot 21.2 = 63.6$ and $21y + 4 = 63.6 + 4 = 67.6$.

24. If $11x + 5 = 29.5$, then $2(11x + 5) = 22x + 10 = 2 \cdot 29.5 = 59$

25. $13(x - 7) - 10(x - 7) = 3(x - 7) = 3x - 21$

26. $99(12a + 19) - 98(12a + 19) = 1(12a + 19) = 12a + 19$

27. $\frac{-8(x + y)}{z} + \frac{9(x + y)}{z} = \frac{1(x + y)}{z} = \frac{x + y}{z}$

28. $\frac{4(n + 3)}{n - 7} \cdot \frac{n - 7}{n + 3} = \frac{4(n + 3)(n - 7)}{(n - 7)(n + 3)} = 4$

29.
$$(m + 2)^2 = 64$$
$$m + 2 = 8 \quad \text{or} \quad m + 2 = \text{-}8$$
$$m = 6 \quad \text{or} \qquad m = \text{-}10$$

30.
$$(z - 4)^2 = 144$$
$$z - 4 = 12 \quad \text{or} \quad z - 4 = \text{-}12$$
$$z = 16 \quad \text{or} \qquad z = \text{-}8$$

31.
$$(2x)^2 = 400$$
$$2x = 20 \quad \text{or} \quad 2x = \text{-}20$$
$$x = 10 \quad \text{or} \qquad x = \text{-}10$$

32.
$$(3x + 7)^2 = 676$$
$$3x + 7 = 26 \quad \text{or} \quad 3x + 7 = \text{-}26$$
$$3x = 19 \quad \text{or} \qquad 3x = \text{-}33$$
$$x = \frac{19}{3} \quad \text{or} \qquad x = \text{-}11$$

33. $A = \left(\frac{1}{2}\right)bh$
$$2A = bh$$
$$\frac{2A}{h} = b$$

34. $V = lwh$
$$\frac{V}{lw} = h$$

35.
$$P = 2(l + w)$$
$$\tfrac{1}{2}P = l + w$$
$$\tfrac{1}{2}P - l = w$$

36.
$$S = 2\pi r^2 + 2\pi rh$$
$$S - 2\pi r^2 = 2\pi rh$$
$$\frac{S - 2\pi r^2}{2\pi r} = h$$

37. $y = \frac{x}{z}$
$$yz = x$$

38.
$$T = a + (n - 1)d$$
$$T - a = (n - 1)d$$
$$\frac{T - a}{d} = n - 1$$
$$\frac{T - a}{d} + 1 = n$$

39. $10x + 8y = 40$
$$8y = \text{-}10x + 40$$
$$y = \left(\tfrac{1}{8}\right)(\text{-}10x + 40)$$
$$y = \text{-}\tfrac{5}{4}x + 5$$

40. $6y - 5x = 12$
$$6y = 5x + 12$$
$$y = \left(\tfrac{1}{6}\right)(5x + 12)$$
$$y = \tfrac{5}{6}x + 2$$

41. a. $6x + 3 = 8x + 5$
$$3 = 8x + \text{-}6x + 5$$
$$3 = 2x + 5$$
$$\text{-}5 + 3 = 2x$$
$$\text{-}2 = 2x$$
$$\text{-}1 = x$$

41. b.
$$6x + 3 = 8x + 5$$
$$6x + \text{-}8x + 3 = 5$$
$$\text{-}2x + 3 = 5$$
$$\text{-}2x = 5 + \text{-}3$$
$$\text{-}2x = 2$$
$$x = \text{-}1$$

c. They are equal.

42. a. $a + 2 < 3a + 4$
$$2 < 3a + \text{-}a + 4$$
$$2 < 2a + 4$$
$$2 + \text{-}4 < 2a$$
$$\text{-}2 < 2a$$
$$\text{-}1 < a$$

b. $a + 2 < 3a + 4$
$$a + \text{-}3a + 2 < 4$$
$$\text{-}2a + 2 < 4$$
$$\text{-}2a < 4 + \text{-}2$$
$$\text{-}2a < 2$$
$$a > \text{-}1$$

c. They are equal.

43. *Multiply* each side by *16*.
Apply the *distributive* property.
Add -2x to each side.
Add 80 to each side.

44. Add *5y* to each side.
Add -8 to each side.
Multiply each side by $\frac{1}{8}$.

45. Sample: Multiply by 12;
$$\frac{1}{4} - 2x = \frac{5}{6}x + 9$$
$$12\left(\frac{1}{4} - 2x\right) = 12\left(\frac{5}{6}x + 9\right)$$
$$3 - 24x = 10x + 108$$

46. Sample: Multiply by 100;
$$3.6y = 0.15 - 0.04y$$
$$100 \cdot 3.6y = 100(0.15 - 0.04y)$$
$$360y = 15 - 4y$$

47. Sample: Multiply by $\frac{1}{100}$;
$$\left(\tfrac{1}{100}\right)(4800t - 120{,}000) = \left(\tfrac{1}{100}\right)(3600t)$$
$$48t - 1200 = 36t$$

48. Sample: Multiply by $\frac{1}{7}$;
$$\left(\tfrac{1}{7}\right)(35w + 21) = \left(\tfrac{1}{7}\right) \cdot 105(w + 2)$$
$$5w + 3 = 15(w + 2)$$

49. a. Kate has $1500 + $45n.
Melissa has $2000 + 20n.

b. After 20 months they have the same amount of money in their accounts.
$$1500 + 45n = 2000 + 20n$$
$$1500 + 25n = 2000$$
$$25n = 500$$
$$n = 20$$

50. a. $25 + 9x > 100 - 5x$

b. $25 + 14x > 100$
$$14x > 75$$
$$x > \frac{75}{14} \approx 5\frac{5}{14}$$

After 6 weeks have passed Len will have more money than Basil.

51. Let x represent the number of years since the trees have been planted.
$$8 + 3x > 12 + 1.5x$$
$$8 > 12 + \text{-}1.5x$$
$$\text{-}4 > \text{-}1.5x$$
$$2\frac{2}{3} < x$$

After 3 years the willow tree will be taller than the elm.

52. Let n represent the number of miles driven.
$$100 + .15n = 150 + .12n$$
$$100 + .03n = 150$$
$$.03n = 50$$
$$n = 1666\frac{2}{3}$$

The costs will be the same at the two rental agencies for driving about 1666.7 miles.

53. Let x represent the number of days since the new factory has been producing loaves of bread.

$$550x > 109,000 + 200x$$

$$350x > 109,000$$

$$x > 311.43$$

After 312 days the new factory will have made more bread than the old one.

54. Let n represent the number of seconds since Angie starts the race.

$$50 + 3n = 5n$$

$$50 = 2n$$

$$25 = n$$

It will take Angie 25 seconds to catch up with her sister.

55. Let x represent the number of gallons the gas tank holds.

$$\frac{7}{8}x = 10.4$$

$$x = 11.886$$

The capacity of the tank to the nearest gallon is 12 gallons.

56. Let x represent their after-tax income.

$$x - (.25x + .15x + .12x +$$
$$.10x + .10x + .10x + .10x) \geq 3000$$

$$x - 0.92x \geq 3000$$

$$0.08x \geq 3000$$

$$x \geq 37,500$$

Their after-tax income must be at least $37,500.

57. a.

Number of CD's	Charges First Club	Second Club
2	$ 33	$ 30
4	$ 51	$ 49
6	$ 69	$ 68
8	$ 87	$ 87
10	$105	$106

b. You must buy 8 CD's for the two clubs' charges to be equal.

c. The first club's price is better when purchasing more than 8 CD's.

d. The second club's price is better when purchasing less than 8 CD's.

58. a.

Sales	Appliance World Total Salary	Better Kitchens Total Salary
$ 0	$1000	$ 600
$ 5,000	$1200	$ 900
$10,000	$1400	$1200
$15,000	$1600	$1500
$20,000	$1800	$1800
$25,000	$2000	$2100
$30,000	$2200	$2400

b. Better Kitchens will pay a greater total salary for sales over $20,000.

59. a.

	A	B	C
1	yrs. from now	bu. corn	bu. soybeans
2	0	10200	6750
3	1	10300	7250
4	2	10400	7750
5	3	10500	8250
6	4	10600	8750
7	5	10700	9250
8	6	10800	9750
9	7	10900	10250
10	8	11000	10750
11	9	11100	11250
12	10	11200	11750

b. In B5: $= 10200 + A5 * 100$
In C5: $= 6750 + A5 * 500$

c. Nine years from now the number of bushels of soybeans will exceed the number of bushels of corn.

59. d.

	D	E
1	corn value	soybean value
2	$26520	$51975
3	$26780	$55825
4	$27040	$59675
5	$27300	$63525
6	$27560	$67375
7	$27820	$71225
8	$28080	$75075
9	$28340	$78925
10	$28600	$82775
11	$28860	$86625
12	$29120	$90475

e. This year the soybean crop is worth about twice the corn crop's value. Ten years from now, it will be worth about three times as much.

60.

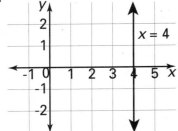

61.

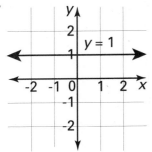

62. True

63. True

64. Sample: The graph contains all the solutions to $y = -2$.

65. $x = 5$

66. a. $h = 35,000 - 1500m$

b.

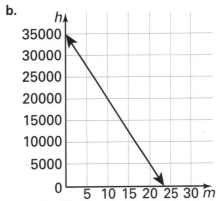

c. It will take about 23 minutes to land the plane.

67.

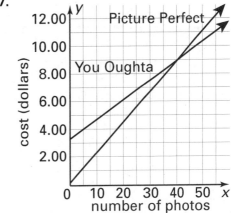

68. a.

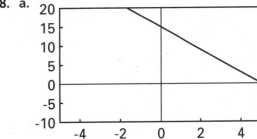

b. $x < 5$

69.

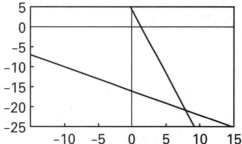

  a. true when $x = 8.48$

  b. true when $x < 8.48$

  c. true when $x > 8.48$

70. The *window* on the automatic grapher is the visible portion of the coordinate grid.

71. $-5 \leq x \leq 15$; $-8 \leq y \leq 12$

72. The trace command on an automatic grapher moves the cursor along the graph and identifies the coordinates of the point it is on.

73.

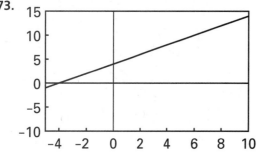

$x = -4$ when $y = 0$

74. **a.** Answers may vary.

  b. Sample: A different part of the line may become visible, and the line may be less steep.

75.

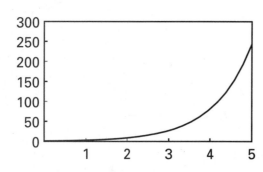

$x = 4$ when $3^x = 81$

CHAPTER 5

REFRESHER   p. 347

p. 347

1. **a.** 3   **b.** 21   **c.** 7

2. **a.** 100   **b.** 20   **c.** 0.2

3. **a.** 7   **b.** 56   **c.** 8

4. **a.** 9   **b.** 11.7   **c.** 1.3

5. **a.** $40 \div 100 = 0.40$

  b. $100 \div 40 = 2.5$

6. **a.** $30 \div \frac{1}{2} = 60$

  b. $\frac{1}{2} \div 30 = \frac{1}{60} = .01\overline{6}$

7. **a.** $\frac{1}{4} \div \frac{1}{5} = \frac{5}{4}$ or 1.25

  b. $\frac{1}{5} \div \frac{1}{4} = \frac{4}{5}$ or 0.8

8. $7.2 \div 3 = 2.4$

9. $80 \div 0.05 = 1600$

10. $\frac{0.06}{0.3} = 0.2$

11. $\frac{6.8}{34} = 0.2$

12. $\frac{12}{7} \div \frac{2}{7} = \frac{12}{7} \cdot \frac{7}{2} = 6$

13. $\frac{3}{5} \div \frac{3}{4} = \frac{3}{5} \cdot \frac{4}{3} = \frac{4}{5}$

14. $\frac{2}{9} \div \frac{1}{3} = \frac{2}{9} \cdot \frac{3}{1} = \frac{2}{3}$

15. $\frac{3}{2} \div \frac{4}{5} = \frac{3}{2} \cdot \frac{5}{4} = \frac{15}{8}$

16. $6\,\text{ft} \div 2 = 3\,\text{ft}$

17. $10\,\text{m} \div 4 = 2.5\,\text{m}$

18. $100\,\text{kg} \div 7 = 14\frac{2}{7}\,\text{kg}$

19. $6\,\text{lb} \div 25 = 0.24\,\text{lb}$

20. $-8 \div -4 = 2$

21. $-40 \div 5 = -8$

22. $60 \div -120 = -\frac{1}{2}$

23. $2 \div -80 = -\frac{1}{40} = -0.025$

24. $\frac{-3}{-6} = \frac{1}{2}$

25. $\frac{400}{-4} = -100$

26. $\frac{3}{4} = 0.75 = 75\%$

27. $\frac{1}{40} = 0.025 = 2.5\%$

28. $\frac{73}{100} = 0.73 = 73\%$

29. $\frac{1}{7} = 0.14$

30. $\frac{20}{3} = 6.67$

31. $\frac{110}{17} = 6.47$

32. $\frac{11}{5} = 2.2 = 220\%$

33. $\frac{27}{100} = 0.27 = 27\%$

34. $\frac{8}{9} = .0889 = 89\%$

35. **a.** 0.3   **b.** $\frac{3}{10}$

36. **a.** 0.01   **b.** $\frac{1}{100}$

37. **a.** 3.0   **b.** $\frac{300}{100}$

38. **a.** 0.0246   **b.** $\frac{123}{5000}$

39. **a.** 0.0003   **b.** $\frac{3}{10,000}$

40. **a.** 0.0025   **b.** $\frac{25}{10,000}$

41. $.32 \cdot 750 = 240$

42. $.94 \cdot 72 = 67.68$ or 68 questions

43. $.073 \cdot 40,296 = 2941.61$ or 2942 voters

44. 100% of 12,000 square miles is 12,000 square miles.

45. 0% of 60 is 0.

46. $1.5 \cdot 10,000 = \$15,000$

47. $\frac{(14 + 9 + 47 + 17)}{4} = \frac{87}{4} = 21\frac{3}{4}$ or 21.75

48. $\frac{(3 + 3.1 + \text{-}6 + 0 + 14 + 5.5)}{6} = \frac{19.6}{6} = 3.267$

49. $\pi \cdot 5^2 = 25\pi \text{ cm}^2 \approx 78.54 \text{ cm}^2$

50. $\pi \cdot 4^2 = 16\pi \text{ in}^2 \approx 50.27 \text{ in}^2$

DIVISION IN ALGEBRA

LESSON 6-1 pp. 350–355

1. If Abe divided a quart of orange juice equally among his five children and himself, they each received $5\frac{1}{3}$ ounces.

$$32 \div 6 = 5.\overline{3}$$

$$32 \cdot \frac{1}{6} = 5.\overline{3}$$

2. The Algebraic Definition of Division: For any real numbers a and b, $b \neq 0$, $a \div b = a \cdot \frac{1}{b}$.

3. **a.** $\frac{m}{n} = m \div n$

   b. $\frac{m}{n} = m \cdot \frac{1}{n}$

4. **a.** $\frac{\frac{p}{q}}{\frac{r}{s}} = \frac{p}{q} \div \frac{r}{s}$

   b. $\frac{p}{q} \div \frac{r}{s} = \frac{p}{q} \cdot \frac{s}{r}$

5. $\dfrac{\frac{3}{4}}{\frac{-4}{5}} = \frac{3}{4} \div \frac{-4}{5} = \frac{3}{4} \cdot \frac{5}{-4} = \frac{15}{-16} = -\frac{15}{16}$

6. $\dfrac{\frac{x}{4}}{-\frac{4}{y}} = \frac{x}{4} \div \frac{-4}{y} = \frac{x}{4} \cdot \frac{y}{-4} = \frac{xy}{-16} = -\frac{xy}{16}$

7. $\frac{5}{6} \div \frac{n}{10} = \frac{5}{6} \cdot \frac{10}{n} = \frac{50}{6n} = \frac{25}{3n}$

8. $-\frac{12\pi}{5} \div \frac{\pi}{4} = -\frac{12\pi}{5} \cdot \frac{4}{\pi} = \frac{-48}{5}$

9. $1\frac{2}{3} \div 3\frac{1}{3} = \frac{5}{3} \div \frac{10}{3} = \frac{5}{3} \cdot \frac{3}{10} = \frac{1}{2}$

10. $\dfrac{\frac{3\pi}{5}}{\frac{6}{\pi}} = \frac{3\pi}{5} \div \frac{6}{\pi} = \frac{3\pi}{5} \cdot \frac{\pi}{6} = \frac{3\pi^2}{30\pi} = \frac{\pi^2}{10}$

11. **a.** You could multiply both sides by $-\frac{1}{3}$.

    b. You could divide both sides by -3.

12. (c) $\frac{-7}{-2}$ is not equivalent to the others; it is equal to $\frac{7}{2}$.

13. **a.** $\frac{-3}{11} = -0.273$

    b. $\frac{3}{-11} = -0.273$

    c. $-\frac{3}{11} = -0.273$

14. $\frac{-a}{b} = -\frac{a}{b} = \frac{a}{-b}$

15. $\qquad -143 = 13x$

    $\qquad -143 = 13x$

    $\frac{1}{13} \cdot -143 = \frac{1}{13} \cdot 13x$

    $\qquad -11 = x$

16. $\qquad -1.5q = -75$

    $-\frac{1}{1.5} \cdot -1.5q = -\frac{1}{1.5} \cdot -75$

    $\qquad q = 50$

17. $\qquad 2.5k = -0.7$

    $\left(\frac{1}{2.5}\right)2.5k = \left(\frac{1}{2.5}\right)(-0.7)$

    $\qquad k = -0.28$

18. $-1900 = -0.2n$

    $\left(\frac{1}{-0.2}\right)(-1900) = \left(\frac{1}{-0.2}\right)(-0.2n)$

    $\qquad 9500 = n$

19. $\qquad \frac{2}{3}t = \frac{5}{6}$

    $\frac{3}{2} \cdot \frac{2}{3}t = \frac{3}{2} \cdot \frac{5}{6}$

    $\qquad t = \frac{5}{4}$

20. $\qquad 3x = -\frac{5}{3}$

    $\frac{1}{3} \cdot 3x = \frac{1}{3} \cdot -\frac{5}{3}$

    $\qquad x = -\frac{5}{9}$

21. **a.** $200 \div \frac{1}{4}$

    b. $200 \div \frac{1}{4} = 200 \cdot \frac{4}{1} = 800$

    800 bottles will be filled by a batch.

22. Each person received $\frac{128}{x}$ ounces of milk.

23. $\frac{1}{2} \div 3 = \frac{1}{2} \cdot \frac{1}{3} = \frac{1}{6}$ pizza

24. $b \div \frac{1}{b} = b \cdot \frac{b}{1} = b^2$

25. $\frac{xy}{21} \div \frac{x}{4y} = \frac{xy}{21} \cdot \frac{4y}{x} = \frac{4y^2}{21}$

26. a. i. $12 \div 2 = 6; \ 2 \div 12 = \frac{1}{6}$

    ii. $20 \div -5 = -4; \ -5 \div 20 = -\frac{1}{4}$

    iii. $\frac{2}{3} \div \frac{4}{5} = \frac{2}{3} \cdot \frac{5}{4} = \frac{10}{12} = \frac{5}{6}$,

         $\frac{4}{5} \div \frac{2}{3} = \frac{4}{5} \cdot \frac{3}{2} = \frac{12}{10} = \frac{6}{5}$

  b. Division is not commutative, the answers are different.

  c. $x \div y$ and $y \div x$ are reciprocals of each other; $x \div y = \dfrac{1}{y \div x}$

27. a. A positive number divided by a positive number is positive.

  b. A negative number divided by a negative number is positive.

  c. A negative number divided by a positive number is negative.

  d. A positive number divided by a negative number is negative.

28. a. The investment grew in value $8.01 between years 2 and 3. ($122.50 − $114.49 = $8.01)

  b. The growth in the investment is the largest in year 5.

29. a. $3B + 2 = 10$

  b. $\quad 3B = 8$

     $\frac{1}{3} \cdot 3B = \frac{1}{3} \cdot 8$

     $\quad B = \frac{8}{3}$

    The weight of each box is $2\frac{2}{3}$ kg.

30. $\quad V + 0.06V + 100 = 14{,}289.16$

$\quad\quad\quad 1.06V + 100 = 14{,}289.16$

$1.06V + 100 + \text{-}100 = 14{,}289.16 + \text{-}100$

$\quad\quad\quad\quad\quad 1.06V = 14{,}189.16$

$\quad \frac{1}{1.06} \cdot 1.06V = \frac{1}{1.06} \cdot 14{,}189.16$

$\quad\quad\quad\quad\quad\quad V = 13{,}386$

31. If $100 < n! < 200$, then $n = 5$.
(5! = 120 and $100 < 120 < 200$)

32. a. $y \le 0$

  b. $-1470 \le y \le 0$

  c.

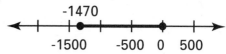

33. The area of the circle is πr^2.

    $\pi \cdot 1.2^2 = \pi \cdot 1.44$

            $= 4.5 \text{ m}^2$

34.

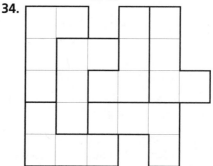

LESSON 6-2   pp. 356–361

1. a. $\dfrac{300 \text{ miles}}{8 \text{ hours}} = 37.5$ miles per hour

  b. $\dfrac{8 \text{ hours}}{300 \text{ miles}} = \frac{2}{75}$ hours per mile $= 0.02\overline{6}$ hour per mile or 1.6 minutes per mile

2. Rate Model for Division: If a and b are quantities with different units, then $\frac{a}{b}$ is the amount of quantity a per quantity b.

3. a. $\dfrac{24 \text{ miles}}{\frac{2}{3} \text{ hour}} = 24 \text{ miles} \cdot \frac{3}{2} \cdot \frac{1}{\text{hour}} =$ 36 miles per hour

  b. $\dfrac{m \text{ miles}}{\frac{2}{3} \text{ hour}} = m \text{ miles} \cdot \frac{3}{2} \cdot \frac{1}{\text{hour}} = 1.5m$ mph $= \dfrac{3m}{2}$ miles per hour

  c. $\dfrac{24 \text{ miles}}{h \text{ hours}} = \frac{24}{h}$ miles per hour

  d. $\dfrac{m \text{ miles}}{h \text{ hours}} = \frac{m}{h}$ miles per hour

4. $\frac{495 \text{ dollars}}{9 \text{ days}} = \$55$ per day

5. $\frac{2.10 \text{ dollars}}{c \text{ cans}} = \frac{2.10}{c}$ dollars per can

6. $\frac{270 \text{ miles}}{7.8 \text{ gallons}} \approx 34.6$ miles per gallon

7. $\frac{6799 \text{ students}}{931 \text{ faculty members}} = 7.3$ students per faculty member

8. $\frac{\text{-11 degrees}}{5 \text{ hours}} = -2.2$ degrees per hour

9. $\frac{6 \text{ degrees}}{12 \text{ hours}} = \frac{1}{2}$ degree per hour

10. $\frac{0 \text{ degrees}}{4 \text{ hours}} = 0$ degrees per hour

11. An error message (E) appears.

12. $k \neq 4$

13. $x \neq -1$

14. w can have any value.

15. $\$300 \div \$120$ per week $= 2.5$ weeks. They had enough money for $2\frac{1}{2}$ weeks.

16. 500 words $\div$ 35 words per minute $= 14.3$ minutes. He needs 14.3 minutes to type the essay.

17. a. $178\cent \div 20$ oz $= 8.9\cent$ per oz
   b. $78\cent \div 6$ oz $= 13\cent$ per oz
   c. Based on the unit cost, the 20-ounce can is the better buy.

18. a. Bangladesh population density:
   $122{,}255{,}000 \div 55{,}813 \approx 2190$ people per square mile
   Greenland population density:
   $57{,}000 \div 840{,}000 \approx 0.068$ people per square mile
   b. Bangladesh's population density is about 32,206 times as large as Greenland's. ($2190 \div 0.068 \approx 32{,}206$)

19. a. $\frac{.5 \text{ mile}}{2 \text{ minutes}} = \frac{.25 \text{ mile}}{1 \text{ minute}} = 0.25$ mile per minute
   $= \frac{1}{4}$ mile per minute
   b. $\frac{.25 \text{ mile}}{1 \text{ minute}} \cdot \frac{60 \text{ minutes}}{\text{hour}} = 15$ mph

20. (b) $\frac{60n}{t} \left(\frac{n \text{ copies}}{t \text{ minutes}} \cdot \frac{60 \text{ minutes}}{\text{hour}} = \frac{60n}{t} \text{ copies per hour.} \right)$

21. John Olerud had the better batting average. (John Olerud's batting average $= 200 \div 551 = 0.363$; Frank Thomas's batting average $= 174 \div 549 = 0.317$)

22. a. the set of all real numbers, n, such that $n \neq \frac{-3}{2}$
   b. the set of all real numbers
   c. the set of all real numbers, n, such that $n \neq \frac{-3}{2}$

23. a. An error message will be printed because division by 0 is undefined.
   b. 0, because $\frac{0}{100} = 0$

24. $\frac{\frac{5}{2}}{3} = 5 \cdot \frac{3}{2} = \frac{15}{2} = 7.5$

25. $\frac{-3}{4} \div \frac{-3}{2} = \frac{-3}{4} \cdot \frac{2}{-3} = \frac{1}{2}$

26. $\frac{x}{2y} \div \frac{11y}{3} = \frac{x}{2y} \cdot \frac{3}{11y} = \frac{3x}{22y^2}$

27. $6x \div \frac{x}{2} = 6x \cdot \frac{2}{x} = 12$

28. The cook can make $4x$ hamburgers. $\left(x \div \frac{1}{4} = x \cdot 4 = 4x \right)$

29. a. The supplement has measure $180 - a$.
   b. No. If a supplement were less than 90°, then the angle would be obtuse and not have a complement.
   c. The supplement of an angle can be 4 times the complement of the angle. When an angle measure is 60°, its complement is 30° and its supplement is 120°.

30. a.
$$5 \cdot 10 - 4y = 40$$
$$50 - 4y = 40$$
$$-50 + 50 - 4y = -50 + 40$$
$$-4y = -10$$
$$\frac{1}{-4} \cdot -4y = \frac{1}{-4} \cdot -10$$
$$y = 2.5$$
   b. The point on the graph is (10, 2.5).

31. **a.** $-x > 8$

$$-1 \cdot -x < -1 \cdot 8$$

$$x < -8$$

b. $-2x > 8$

$$\frac{1}{-2} \cdot -2x < \frac{1}{-2} \cdot 8$$

$$x < -4$$

c. $-3x + 4 > 8$

$$-3x + 4 + -4 > 8 + -4$$

$$-3x > 4$$

$$\frac{1}{-3} \cdot -3x < \frac{1}{-3} \cdot 4$$

$$x < \frac{-4}{3}$$

d. $-5x + 6 > 8 - 7x$

$$2x + 6 > 8$$

$$2x > 2$$

$$x > 1$$

32. **a.**

K	Value of $7/(K-5)$
8	$2.\overline{3}$
7.5	2.8
7	3.5
6.5	$4.\overline{6}$
6	7
5.5	14
5	NONE

b.

K	Value of $7/(K-5)$
4.5	-14
4	-7
3.5	$-4.\overline{6}$
3	-3.5
2.5	-2.8
2	$-2.\overline{3}$

c. Sample: Values for K that are the same distance from 5 give values for $\frac{7}{K-5}$ that are opposites.

33. Answers will vary. Sample: In 1992, the debt per capita was about $15,900.

34. Answers will vary.

LESSON 6-3 pp. 362–367

1. A woman runs an increased risk of heart disease if her waist and hip measurements are 32 inches and 37 inches. $\left(\frac{32}{37} = 0.8649 \text{ and } 0.8649 > 0.8\right)$

2. If a man's waist measures more than his hips, then he is at an increased risk of heart disease. $\left(\frac{w}{h} > 1 \text{ or } w > h \text{ or } w - h > 0\right)$

3. A man does not run an increased risk of heart disease if his waist is 34 in. and his hips are 36 in. $\left(\frac{34}{36} = \frac{17}{18} \text{ and } \frac{17}{18} < 1\right)$

4. $\frac{x}{y}$ compares x to y.

$\frac{y}{x}$ compares y to x.

5. A rate is a comparison of quantities with different units. A ratio is a comparison of quantities with the same unit.

6. (b) $\frac{150 \text{ miles}}{3 \text{ hours}}$ (The units are not the same.)

7. **a.** 25 minutes to 30 minutes or $\frac{25 \text{ minutes}}{30 \text{ minutes}} = \frac{5}{6}$

b. 30 minutes to 25 minutes or $\frac{30 \text{ minutes}}{25 \text{ minutes}} = \frac{6}{5}$

8. **a.** The discount in dollars is $21 - $15 = $6.

b. The percent of discount is $\frac{6}{21} \approx 29\%$.

9. **a.** $0.64 to $16.00 or $\frac{\$0.64}{\$16.00} = \frac{1}{25}$

b. The percent of tax is $\frac{.64}{16} = 4\%$.

10. **a.** Yes   **b.** No   **c.** Yes
d. No   **e.** Yes   **f.** No

11. To make 2 quarts of lemonade where the ratio is 3 to 1: Let x be the number of quarts of concentrate and $3x$ be the number of quarts of water.

$$3x + x = 2$$

$$4x = 2$$

$$\frac{1}{4} \cdot 4x = \frac{1}{4} \cdot 2$$

$$x = \frac{1}{2}$$

You will need $\frac{1}{2}$ quart of concentrate and $1\frac{1}{2}$ quarts of water.

12. a. 36 games to 40 games or $\frac{36}{40} = \frac{9}{10}$

  b. It won 90% of the games.

  c. 0.900

13. The 1991–92 salary is about 182 times the 1870 salary. ($34,413 \div 189 = 182.08$)

14. a. Fred owns $\frac{y}{x}$ times as many sweaters as Frieda does.

  b. The answer in part **a** is a ratio.

15. The ratio of x to y is the reciprocal of the ratio of y to x.

16. Let x be the number of children and $4x$ be the number of adults.

$$4x + x = 200$$
$$5x = 200$$
$$\tfrac{1}{5} \cdot 5x = \tfrac{1}{5} \cdot 200$$
$$x = 40$$

There are 40 children and 160 adults expected at the concert.

17. a to b is equal to ax to bx; hence the second quantity is bx.

18. $7x + 5x + x = 50$
$$13x = 50$$
$$\tfrac{1}{13} \cdot 13x = \tfrac{1}{13} \cdot 50$$
$$x = \tfrac{50}{13} \approx 3.8$$

To make 50 gallons of paint you need 26.9 gallons of linseed oil and 19.2 gallons of solvent, and 3.8 gallons of pigment.

19. a. ratio of the diameter of Circle I to the diameter of Circle II is 6 to 4 or 3 to $2 = \frac{3}{2}$

  b. ratio of the area of Circle I to the area of Circle II is 9π to $4\pi = \frac{9}{4}$

  c. $\frac{9}{4} = 2.25$

20. a. $1,500,000,000,000 is one trillion five hundred billion dollars.

  b. The amount of increase per year is about $300,000,000,000 or three hundred billion dollars.
  ($1500 billion $\div$ 5 = $300 billion)

21. The average rate in meters per second is $200 \div 118.47 = 1.69$ meters per second.

22. The expression is undefined for $x = -\frac{5}{2}$ because that would make the denominator zero.

23. $\frac{3x}{4} \div \frac{x}{2} = \frac{3x}{4} \cdot \frac{2}{x} = \frac{3}{2}$

24. (c) $\frac{-a}{-b} = \frac{a}{b}$

25. If $5a = 36$, then $\sqrt{5a} + 7\sqrt{5a} = \sqrt{36} + 7\sqrt{36} = 6 + 7 \cdot 6 = 6 + 42 = 48$

26. a. $5x = 19$
$$\tfrac{1}{5} \cdot 5x = \tfrac{1}{5} \cdot 19$$
$$x = \tfrac{19}{5} = 3.8$$

  b. $0.05x = 19$
$$\tfrac{1}{0.05} \cdot 5x = \tfrac{1}{0.05} \cdot 19$$
$$x = 380$$

  c. $x + 0.05x = 19$
$$1.05x = 19$$
$$\tfrac{1}{1.05} \cdot 1.05x = \tfrac{1}{1.05} \cdot 19$$
$$x = 18.1$$

27. The student's test average is 81.8.
($(75 + 90 + 86 + 78 + 80) \div 5 = 409 \div 5 = 81.8$)

28. a. The ratios are $\frac{5}{4}, \frac{5}{3}, \frac{4}{5}, \frac{4}{3}, \frac{3}{5}$, and $\frac{3}{4}$.

  b. $\sin 37° = 0.601815$; $\frac{3}{5} = 0.6$

  c. $\cos 37° = 0.798636$; $\frac{4}{5} = 0.8$

  d. $\tan 37° = 0.753554$; $\frac{3}{4} = 0.75$

IN-CLASS ACTIVITY   pp. 368–369

1. Sample: 7, since there are more ways to get 7: 1, 6; 2, 5; 3, 4.

2. Answers will vary.

3. Answers will vary.

4. Answers will vary.

5. a.

sum	probability
2	$\frac{1}{36} \approx 0.028$
3	$\frac{2}{36} \approx 0.056$
4	$\frac{3}{36} \approx 0.083$
5	$\frac{4}{36} \approx 0.111$
6	$\frac{5}{36} \approx 0.139$
7	$\frac{6}{36} \approx 0.167$
8	$\frac{5}{36} \approx 0.139$
9	$\frac{4}{36} \approx 0.111$
10	$\frac{3}{36} \approx 0.083$
11	$\frac{2}{36} \approx 0.056$
12	$\frac{1}{36} \approx 0.028$

    b. Answers will vary.

6. a. Answers will vary.

    b. Answers will vary.

LESSON 6-4   pp. 370–375

1. a. The number of girls born in 1990 was $4{,}158{,}000 - 2{,}129{,}000 = 2{,}029{,}000$.

    b. The relative frequency of female births in 1990 is $\frac{2{,}029{,}000}{4{,}158{,}000} \approx 0.488$.

2. a. The percentage of horses tested that had rabies was $\frac{22}{474} \approx 0.046 = 4.6\%$.

    b. The percentage that did not have rabies was $100\% - 4.6\% = 95.4\%$.

3. A relative frequency of 0 means that a particular event did not occur.

4. A relative frequency of 1 means that a particular event occurred every time it could.

5. a. The relative frequency of households with a television that also have a VCR is $\frac{67 \text{ million}}{93 \text{ million}} \approx 0.72 = 72\%$.

    b. The relative frequency of households with a television that have no VCR is $100\% - 72\% = 28\%$.

6. (b)

7. a. If there are 4 choices, then the probability that you will get the question correct is $\frac{1}{4} = .25$.

    b. $E = \{C\}$; $N(E) = 1$; $S = \{A,\ B,\ C,\ D\}$; $N(S) = 4$; $P(E) = \frac{1}{4} = .25$

    c. $1 - .25 = .75$

    d. The events in parts **a** and **c** are called complements.

8. a. $P(x > 32) = \frac{18}{50} = \frac{9}{25}$

    b. $P(x < 32) = \frac{31}{50}$

    c. $P(x = 32) = \frac{1}{50}$

9. P (selecting the 7 of clubs) $= \frac{1}{52}$

10. P (selecting a king) $= \frac{4}{52} = \frac{1}{13}$

11. P (selecting a diamond) $= \frac{13}{52} = \frac{1}{4}$

12. When a probability equals 0, it means the event is impossible.

13. When a probability equals 1, it means the event is sure to happen.

14. $p + q = 1$

15. The probability of picking a vowel from the English alphabet or $P(A, E, I, O, \text{or } U) = \frac{5}{26}$.

16. The event is winning; the number of possible outcomes is the number of people who enter.

17. a. You would expect X to have the largest relative frequency since it has the greatest probability of occurring.

    b. Y doesn't have to have the smallest relative frequency. The relative frequency can vary from experiment to experiment; probability is what is expected to occur in the long run.

18. The relative frequency of a tire lasting less than 25,000 miles is $\frac{10}{50} = \frac{1}{5}$.

19. The relative frequency of a tire lasting at least 10,000 miles is $\frac{50}{50} = 1$.

20. (a) $\frac{c}{t} = 0.3$

21. (d) $16n$ since $\frac{4}{9} = \frac{4}{9} \cdot \frac{4n}{4n} = \frac{16n}{36n}$

22. **a.** The percent of discount is $20 \div 79.95 \approx .2502 = 25\%$ where \$20 is the discount.

   b. The percent of discount is $\frac{(F-S)}{F}$.

   c. The tax rate is $\frac{3.3}{59.95} = 0.055 = 5.5\%$.

23. Let x represent the number of gallons needed for one part.

$$2x + 3x = 6 \text{ gallons} \cdot 4\frac{\text{quarts}}{\text{gallon}}$$
$$5x = 24 \text{ quarts}$$
$$\tfrac{1}{5} \cdot 5x = \tfrac{1}{5} \cdot 24 \text{ quarts}$$
$$x = 4.8 \text{ quarts}$$
$$2 \cdot 4.8 = 9.6 \text{ quarts of orange juice}$$
$$3 \cdot 4.8 = 14.4 \text{ quarts of ginger ale}$$

24. the set of all real numbers, t, such that $t \neq 0$

25. If the area of square S is 9 square units, then each side has length 3 units. If the perimeter of square T is 20 units, then each side has length 5 units. Then the length of each side of square R is 8 units and the area of square R is 64 square units.

26. **a.** $\frac{2a}{5} + \frac{a}{b} = \frac{2ab}{5b} + \frac{5a}{5b} = \frac{2ab + 5a}{5b}$

   b. $\frac{2a}{5} - \frac{a}{b} = \frac{2ab}{5b} - \frac{5a}{5b} = \frac{2ab - 5a}{5b}$

   c. $\frac{2a}{5} \cdot \frac{a}{b} = \frac{2a^2}{5b}$

   d. $\frac{2a}{5} \div \frac{a}{b} = \frac{2a}{5} \cdot \frac{b}{a} = \frac{2b}{5}$

27.
$$\tfrac{5}{8}m = \tfrac{10}{3}$$
$$\tfrac{8}{5} \cdot \tfrac{5}{8}m = \tfrac{8}{5} \cdot \tfrac{10}{3}$$
$$m = \tfrac{16}{3}$$

28.
$$P - 0.06P - 14 = 98.8$$
$$0.94P - 14 = 98.8$$
$$0.94P - 14 + 14 = 98.8 + 14$$
$$0.94P = 112.8$$
$$\tfrac{1}{0.94} \cdot 0.94P = \tfrac{1}{0.94} \cdot 112.8$$
$$P = 120$$

29. **a.** $b - .25b = .75b$

   b. $b + .04b = 1.04b$

   c. $.75b + .04 \cdot .75b = .75b + .03b = .78b$

30. **a., b., c.** Answers will vary.

LESSON 6-5   pp. 376–380

1. $1.23 \cdot 780 = 959.4$

2. $.40x = 440$
$$\frac{.40x}{.40} = \frac{440}{.40}$$
$$x = 1100$$

3. $4.7x = 0.94$
$$\frac{4.7x}{4.7} = \frac{0.94}{4.7}$$
$$x = 0.2$$
0.94 is 20% of 4.7.

4. $y = .62 \cdot 980 = 607.6$

5. **a.** In 1991 there were 52.5 million married couples in the U.S.

   b. $100\% - 59\% = 41\%$ or 21.5 million did not have two incomes.

6. **a.** $100\% - 11.5\% = 88.5\%$ of America's military personnel in 1992 were men.

   b. $.885 \cdot 1,807,200 = 1,599,372$

7. **a.** $0.131N = 67,000$

   b. $\frac{0.131N}{0.131} = \frac{67,000}{0.131}$
$$N = 511,450$$

8. $x + .06x = 42.39$
$$1.06x = 42.39$$
$$\frac{1.06x}{1.06} = \frac{42.39}{1.06}$$
$$x = 39.99$$
The price without sales tax was \$39.99.

9. $x + .085x = 59$
$$1.085x = 59$$
$$\frac{1.085x}{1.085} = \frac{59}{1.085}$$
$$x = 54.378$$
The tax paid was $59 - 54.38 = \$4.62$.

10. $x + .05x = 14{,}064.75$

$1.05x = 14{,}064.75$

$\dfrac{1.05x}{1.05} = \dfrac{14{,}064.75}{1.05}$

$x = 13{,}395$

The price of the car before sales tax was added was $13,395.

11. On the mathematics test, 8 out of 32 students received A's. This was 25%.

$(32x = 8$

$\dfrac{32x}{32} = \dfrac{8}{32}$

$x = .25)$

12. a. $.14 \cdot 1850 = 259$

The school will gain 259 students.

b. The expected enrollment next year is 2109. $(1850 + 259 = 2109)$

13. $.38x = 250$

$\dfrac{.38x}{.38} = \dfrac{250}{.38}$

$x = 657.9$

658 laws were passed per session.

14. There were 2.9 grams of carbon in 68.4 grams of sucrose. $(.042 \cdot 68.4 = 2.8728)$

15. $68.4x = 35.2$

$\dfrac{68.4x}{68.4} = \dfrac{35.2}{68.4}$

$x = .5146$

51% of the 68.4 grams is oxygen.

16. Let x represent the cost of the clothes before the discount.

$x - .30x = 73.50$

$.70x = 73.50$

$\dfrac{.70x}{.70} = \dfrac{73.50}{.70}$

$x = 105$

The cost of the clothes before the discount was $105.

17. The discount is $320 - $208 = $112.

$320x = 112$

$\dfrac{320x}{320} = \dfrac{112}{320}$

$x = .35$

The discount for the TV was 35%.

18. Area of the square is 100 square units. Area of the circle is $\pi \cdot 5^2 = 25\pi$ square units.

$100x = 25\pi$

$\dfrac{100x}{100} = \dfrac{25\pi}{100}$

$x \approx .785 = 78.5\%$

19. $365 - 156 = 209$ days per year without rain or snow $\dfrac{209 \cdot 30}{365 \cdot 30} = \dfrac{209}{365}$

$= 0.57$

20. a. It is more likely that the number showing is even.

b. The probability of the number being divisible by 3 is $\dfrac{2}{6} = \dfrac{1}{3}$.

The probability of the number being even is $\dfrac{3}{6} = \dfrac{1}{2}$.

21. $1\frac{1}{4}$ hours $= (60 + 15)$ minutes $= 75$ minutes

a. $\dfrac{35 \text{ min}}{75 \text{ min}} = \dfrac{7}{15}$

b. $\dfrac{75 \text{ min}}{35 \text{ min}} = \dfrac{15}{7}$

22. x/y

23. a. Income per acre:

$\dfrac{\$19{,}600}{80 \text{ acres}} = \$245$ per acre

b. The income per acre is a rate because the quantities being compared have different units.

24. $b \neq 7$

25. $(m - 6)^2 = 10$

$m - 6 = 10 \quad \text{or} \quad m - 6 = \text{-}10$

$m = 16 \quad \text{or} \qquad m = \text{-}4$

26. a. $\text{-}4x + 3y = 10$

$3y = 4x + 10$

$\dfrac{1}{3} \cdot 3y = \left(\dfrac{1}{3}\right)(4x + 10)$

$y = \dfrac{4}{3}x + \dfrac{10}{3}$

26. b.

$$y = \frac{4}{3}x + \frac{10}{3}$$

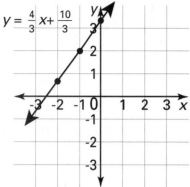

27. Let x be the number.

$$\left(\frac{2}{3}\right)x = 87$$

$$\frac{3}{2} \cdot \frac{2}{3}x = \left(\frac{3}{2}\right)87$$

$$x = 130.5$$

28. A turn of $45°$ is $\frac{1}{8}$ of a complete turn.

$$\left(\frac{45}{360} = \frac{1}{8}\right)$$

29. 0.325823224 is 33% to the nearest percent.

30. a. No

   b. Answers will vary.

   c. Sample: The final result will be 0.91 times the original: $x + .30x = 1.30x$ and $1.30x - .30(1.30x) = 0.91x$.

LESSON 6-6   pp. 381–386

1. a. $\pi \cdot 4^2 = 16\pi = 50.3$ in^2

   b. $25 \cdot 25 = 625$ in^2

   c. P (hitting board and landing in bull's eye) $= \frac{16\pi}{625} = 0.08$

   d. P (hitting board and landing on target outside circle) $= \frac{625 - 16\pi}{625} = 0.92$ (or, since it is the complement of part **c**, $1 - 0.08 = 0.92$)

2. P (the accident is in $\overline{BE}$) $= \frac{\text{length of } \overline{BE}}{\text{length of } \overline{AE}} =$

$\frac{33 \text{ miles}}{50 \text{ miles}} = .66$ or 66%

3. P (the accident is in $\overline{CE}$) $= \frac{\text{length of } \overline{CE}}{\text{length of } \overline{AE}} =$

$\frac{25 \text{ miles}}{50 \text{ miles}} = .50$ or 50%

4. P (spinner will land in region B) $= \frac{90°}{360°} = \frac{1}{4} = .25$

5. P (spinner will land in region C) $= \frac{130°}{360°} = \frac{13}{36}$

6. P (spinner will not land in region C) $=$

$\frac{100° + 30° + 90°}{360°} = \frac{230°}{360°} = \frac{23}{36}$ or, since it is the complement of landing in region C,

$1 - \frac{13}{36} = \frac{23}{36}$.

7. The probability of an event involving a geometric region is the measure of the region in the event divided by the measure of the entire region.

8. P (point lies inside the bull's eye)

$= \frac{\pi \cdot 2^2}{\pi \cdot 8^2} = \frac{4\pi}{64\pi}$

$= \frac{1}{16}$

9. P (point lies in outermost ring)

$= \frac{\pi \cdot 8^2 - \pi \cdot 6^2}{\pi \cdot 8^2}$

$= \frac{64\pi - 36\pi}{64\pi}$

$= \frac{28\pi}{64\pi}$

$= \frac{7}{16}$

10. The surface area of the earth is $57,510,000 + 139,440,000 = 196,950,000$ square miles.

   a. P (meteor will fall on land)

$= \frac{57,510,000}{196,950,000} = .29$

   b. P (meteor will fall on water)

$= \frac{139,440,000}{196,950,000}$

$= 0.71$

11. P (newspaper lands in garden) $= \frac{ab}{pq}$

12. a. P (second hand stopped between 12 and 3) $= \frac{3}{12} = \frac{1}{4}$

   b. P (second hand stopped between 1 and 5) $= \frac{4}{12} = \frac{1}{3}$

   c. P (second hand stopped between 11 and 1) $= \frac{2}{12} = \frac{1}{6}$

13. a. P (dart lands inside the larger circle) =
$$\frac{\pi \cdot 17.5^2}{40^2} = \frac{306.25\pi}{1600} = \frac{962.1}{1600} = 0.60$$

b. P (dart lands inside larger circle but outside bull's eye) $= \frac{306.25\pi - 7.5^2\pi}{1600} =$
$$\frac{306.25\pi - 56.25\pi}{1600} = \frac{250\pi}{1600} = .49$$

c. P (dart lands outside either circle) =
$$\frac{1600 - 962.1}{1600} = \frac{637.9}{1600} = 0.40 \text{ or, since it is}$$
the complement of part **a**, $1 - 0.60 = 0.40$

14. P (rebound landing in NBA lane also lands in high school lane) $= \frac{12 \cdot 19}{16 \cdot 19} = 0.75$

15.

Grade Level Groups

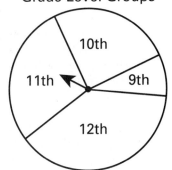

Angle sizes: 9th is 30°; 10th is 90°; 11th is 102°; 12th is 138°.

16. a. 25% of 60 is $\frac{1}{4} \cdot 60 = 15$.

b. 50% of 26 is 13.

c. 8 is $33\frac{1}{3}\%$ of 24.

17. a. $\frac{c}{s}$

b. $\dfrac{d}{n + c + d + s + x}$

c. P (turning on a news program) $=$
$$\dfrac{n}{n + c + d + s + x}$$

18. $5x + 3x = 10$
$$8x = 10$$
$$\frac{8x}{8} = \frac{10}{8}$$
$$x = \frac{5}{4}$$

The shorter piece is $3\left(\frac{5}{4}\right) = \frac{15}{4} = 3.75$ ft.

The longer piece is $5\left(\frac{5}{4}\right) = \frac{25}{4} = 6.25$ ft.

19. a. average number of meters per second

100-meter dash:
$$\frac{100 \text{ meters}}{9.8 \text{ sec}} = 10.152 \text{ meters per sec}$$

200-meter dash:
$$\frac{200 \text{ meters}}{19.72 \text{ sec}} = 10.142 \text{ meters per sec}$$

b. By this measure Burrell is about 0.01 $\frac{m}{sec}$ faster.

20. $1\frac{5}{9} \div 2\frac{1}{7} = \frac{14}{9} \div \frac{15}{7} = \frac{14}{9} \cdot \frac{7}{15} = \frac{98}{135}$

21. $\frac{2x}{s} \div \frac{x}{10} = \frac{2x}{s} \cdot \frac{10}{x} = \frac{20}{s}$

22. $\frac{q}{2} + \frac{q}{3} = \frac{3q}{6} + \frac{2q}{6} = \frac{5q}{6}$

23.
$$\frac{x}{2} - 4 = \frac{3x}{4}$$
$$4\left(\frac{x}{2} - 4\right) = 4 \cdot \frac{3x}{4}$$
$$2x - 16 = 3x$$
$$-2x + 2x - 16 = -2x + 3x$$
$$-16 = x$$

24. $x + 10y = 15$
$$10y = -x + 15$$
$$y = \left(\frac{1}{10}\right)(-x + 15)$$
$$y = \frac{-1}{10}x + \frac{3}{2}$$

25.

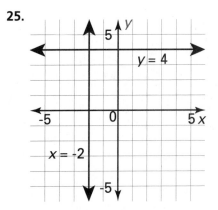

26.
$$V > 1700 \text{ cm}^3$$
$$B \cdot h > 1700$$
$$8 \cdot 15 \cdot h > 1700$$
$$120h > 1700$$
$$\frac{120h}{120} > \frac{1700}{120}$$
$$h > 14.1\overline{6} \text{ cm}$$

27. The number of enlisted personnel in a field army is $10 \cdot 4 \cdot 4 \cdot 4 \cdot 3 \cdot 3 \cdot 2 \cdot 2 = 23{,}040$.

28. Answers will vary.

LESSON 6-7   pp. 387–393

1. The magnitudes of the size change factors are 75%, 64%, and 120%.

2. larger

3. the same size

4. smaller

5. $10 \cdot .64 = 6.4$ in. by $15 \cdot .64 = 9.6$ in.

6. $5.5 \cdot 1.2 = 6.6$ cm

7. **a.** $1.20L = 18$
   b. $1.2L = 18$
$$\frac{1.2L}{1.2} = \frac{18}{1.2}$$
$$L = 15$$
   The length of the original figure is 15 cm.

8. $(-7 \cdot 3, -7 \cdot -9) = (-21, 63)$

9. $(8x, 8y)$

10. a.–c.

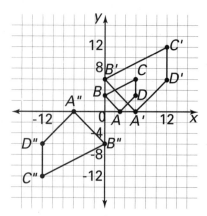

d. The size changes in parts **b** and **c** are expansions.

11. a.–c.

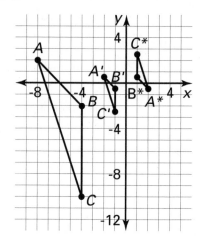

d. Samples: The triangles in parts **b** and **c** are contractions of the triangle in part **a**. The triangle in part **c** seems to be rotated a half turn from the triangle in part **b**.

12. a. contraction
   b. expansion
   c. expansion
   d. neither

13. a.
$$J' = \left(\tfrac{3}{2} \cdot -2, \tfrac{3}{2} \cdot 0\right) = (-3, 0);$$
$$K' = \left(\tfrac{3}{2} \cdot -2, \tfrac{3}{2} \cdot 4\right) = (-3, 6);$$
$$L' = \left(\tfrac{3}{2} \cdot 0, \tfrac{3}{2} \cdot 7\right) = (0, 10.5);$$
$$M' = \left(\tfrac{3}{2} \cdot 6, \tfrac{3}{2} \cdot 4\right) = (9, 6);$$
$$\text{and } N' = \left(\tfrac{3}{2} \cdot 6, \tfrac{3}{2} \cdot 0\right) = (9, 0)$$

b.

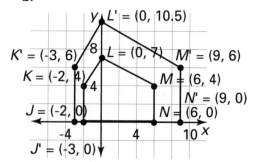

14. $1.5x = 30.98$

$$\frac{1.5x}{1.5} = \frac{30.98}{1.5}$$

$$x = 20.65\overline{3}$$

The average hourly wage was $20.65.

15. $3.5x = 10$

$$\frac{3.5x}{3.5} = \frac{10}{3.5}$$

$$x = 2.86$$

His weight at birth was 2.86 kg.

16. $.1x = 15$

$$\frac{.1x}{.1} = \frac{15}{.1}$$

$$x = 150$$

The hair was magnified 150 times.

17. If $P' = (9, -42)$, then $P = \left(\frac{9}{6}, \frac{-42}{6}\right) = (1.5, -7)$.

18. a. Under a size change of magnitude 1 the graph of the image remains the same.

b. This represents the Multiplicative Identity Property of 1.

19. a. area of original figure:
8 cm · 1 cm = 8 cm^2
area of image A: 6 cm · .75 cm = 4.5 cm^2
area of image B:
5.12 cm · 0.64 cm = 3.2768 cm^2
area of image C:
9.6 cm · 1.2 cm = 11.52 cm^2

b. False. The area of the image is k^2 times the area of the preimage.

20. a., b.

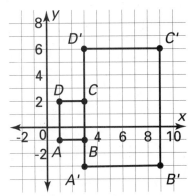

c. Perimeter of the larger figure:
6 + 9 + 6 + 9 = 30 units
Perimeter of the smaller figure:
2 + 3 + 2 + 3 = 10 units
ratio: $\frac{30}{10} = \frac{3}{1}$

d. Area of the larger figure:
6 · 9 = 54 square units
Area of the smaller figure:
2 · 3 = 6 square units
ratio: $\frac{54}{6} = \frac{9}{1}$

21. a. Area irrigated:
$\pi \cdot 100^2 = 10,000\pi = 31,415$ ft^2
area of crops:
200 · 200 = 40,000 ft^2
percent of crops irrigated:
$\frac{31,415.9}{40,000} = 0.785 = 78.5\%$

b. P (point in square is irrigated) = 0.785

22. area of field:
(160 ft)(120 yd) = 160(360) = 57,600 ft^2
darker area:
(20 yd)(160 ft − 30 ft) = 60(130) = 7800 ft^2
P (land in darker area) = $\frac{7800}{57,600} \approx 0.135 = 13.5\%$

23. $195.7x = 73.4$

$$\frac{195.7x}{195.7} = \frac{73.4}{195.7}$$

$$x = .375$$

37.5% of the total waste is paper.

24. a. A customer pays 70% of the price.

b. $.70 \cdot 23.95 = c$

c. $c = 16.765$ The customer pays $16.77.

25. a. The relative frequency of having twins is $\frac{1}{86} \approx 0.012$.

b. P (having twins) = $\frac{1}{86}$

26. A probability of 0 means it is impossible for the event to occur.

27. Answers will vary.

28. a. $\frac{x}{2} + \frac{x}{3} = \frac{3x}{6} + \frac{2x}{6} = \frac{5x}{6}$

b. $\frac{x}{2} - \frac{x}{3} = \frac{3x}{6} - \frac{2x}{6} = \frac{x}{6}$

c. $\frac{x}{2} \cdot \frac{x}{3} = \frac{x^2}{6}$

d. $\frac{x}{2} \div \frac{x}{3} = \frac{x}{2} \cdot \frac{3}{x} = \frac{3}{2}$

29. a. 16 of the small rectangles can fit in the large rectangle.

b. 36 of the small rectangles can fit in the large rectangle.

c. 9 of the small rectangles can fit in the large rectangle.

d. Sample: The number of rectangles

$$= \left(\frac{1}{\text{magnitude}}\right)^2.$$

LESSON 6-8   pp. 394–400

1. A proportion is a statement that two fractions are equal.

2. (b)

3. According to the Means-Extremes Property, if $\frac{x}{y} = \frac{z}{w}$, then $xw = yz$.

4. $\frac{x}{12} = \frac{3}{18}$

$18x = 36$

$x = 2$

Check: Does $\frac{2}{12} = \frac{3}{18}$?

$\frac{1}{6} = \frac{1}{6}$

Yes, it checks.

5. $\frac{-15}{12} = \frac{x}{-20}$

$-15 \cdot -20 = 12x$

$25 = x$

Check: Does $\frac{-15}{12} = \frac{25}{-20}$?

$\frac{-5}{4} = \frac{5}{-4}$

Yes, it checks.

6. $\frac{216 \text{ miles}}{13.8 \text{ gallons}} = \frac{x \text{ miles}}{21 \text{ gallons}}$

$21 \cdot \frac{216}{13.8} = x$

$\frac{4536}{13.8} = x$

$328.7 \approx x$

He can drive about 328.7 miles.

7. a. $5n = 21$

b. $7n = 15$

c. $5n = 21$

d. The proportion in part **b** has a different solution.

8. a. $\frac{1 \text{ in.}}{800 \text{ mi}} = \frac{2\frac{7}{8} \text{ in.}}{x \text{ mi}}$

b. $1 \cdot x = 2\frac{7}{8} \cdot 800$

$x = 2300$ miles

c. Sample: $\frac{1}{2\frac{7}{8}} = \frac{800}{x}$

d. $1 \cdot x = 800 \cdot 2\frac{7}{8}$

$x = 2300$ miles

9. On the map the distance between Chicago and San Francisco is about $2\frac{5}{8}$ in.

$\frac{1 \text{ in.}}{800 \text{ mi}} = \frac{2\frac{5}{8} \text{ in.}}{x \text{ mi}}$

$1 \cdot x = 2\frac{5}{8} \cdot 800$

$x = 2100$ miles

10. $\frac{2}{a} = \frac{-14}{15}$

$-14a = 30$

$a = \frac{30}{-14} = -\frac{15}{7}$

11. $\frac{15}{2a} = \frac{3}{10}$

$6a = 150$

$a = \frac{150}{6} = 25$

12. $\frac{g+3}{4} = \frac{g-2}{2}$

$2(g + 3) = 4(g - 2)$

$2g + 6 = 4g - 8$

$6 = 2g - 8$

$14 = 2g$

$7 = g$

13. $\frac{3x}{4} = \frac{3x+1}{6}$

$6 \cdot 3x = 4(3x+1)$

$18x = 12x + 4$

$6x = 4$

$x = \frac{4}{6} = \frac{2}{3}$

14. $\frac{x}{4} = \frac{9}{x}$

$x^2 = 36$

$x = 6 \text{ or } x = -6$

15. $\frac{98}{x} = \frac{x}{8}$

$x^2 = 784$

$x = 28 \text{ or } x = -28$

16. $\frac{17 \text{ points}}{6 \text{ minutes}} = \frac{x \text{ points}}{32 \text{ minutes}}$

$6x = 544$

$x = 90\frac{2}{3}$

The team will score 91 points in a 32-minute game at this rate.

17. $\frac{173 \text{ cm}}{19 \text{ hours}} = \frac{x \text{ cm}}{24 \text{ hours}}$

$19x = 4152$

$x = 218.53$

About 218.5 cm of snow would fall in 24 hours at this rate.

18. $\frac{68.4 \text{ miles}}{42 \text{ minutes}} = \frac{x \text{ miles}}{60 \text{ minutes}}$

$42x = 4104$

$x = 97.7$

The train would cover 97.7 miles in an hour at this rate.

19. $\frac{1 \text{ face}}{1000 \text{ ships}} = \frac{x \text{ faces}}{5 \text{ ships}}$

$1 \cdot 5 = 1000x$

$\frac{5}{1000} = x$

$.005 = x$

It would take 0.005 of a face to launch 5 ships.

20. a. $\frac{10}{16} \cdot \frac{15}{x} = \frac{5}{8} \cdot \frac{15}{x} = \frac{75}{8x}$

b. $\frac{10}{16} = \frac{15}{x}$

$10x = 240$

$x = 24$

21. $\frac{2}{d} = \frac{d}{11}; d^2 = 22$

a. $d = \sqrt{22} \text{ or } d = -\sqrt{22}$

b. $d = 4.69 \text{ or } d = -4.69$

22. $\frac{4 \text{ pedal}}{7 \text{ wheel}} = \frac{15 \text{ pedal}}{x \text{ wheel}}$

$4x = 7 \cdot 15$

$4x = 105$

$x = 26\frac{1}{4}$

The rear wheel turned $26\frac{1}{4}$ times.

23. $\frac{1}{3} \neq \frac{33}{100}$ since $1 \cdot 100 \neq 33 \cdot 3$

24. $\frac{4.5}{-5} = \frac{-153}{170}$ since $4.5 \cdot 170 = -5 \cdot -153$

25. $\frac{388,162}{171,958} \neq \frac{430,262}{190,603}$ since

$388,162 \cdot 190,603 \neq 430,262 \cdot 171,958$

26. $\frac{13x - 78}{x} = \frac{0}{7953}$

$\frac{13x - 78}{x} = 0$

$13x - 78 = 0 \cdot x$

$13x - 78 = 0$

$13x = 78$

$x = 6$

27. Yes, the fraction would be $\frac{-15}{-20}$; see the following proportion.

$\frac{3}{4} = \frac{x+5}{x}$

$3x = 4(x+5)$

$3x = 4x + 20$

$-x = 20$

$x = -20$

$x + 5 = -20 + 5 = -15$

28. a., b.

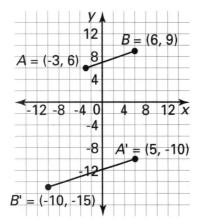

The image of $\overline{AB}$ under a size change of magnitude $-\frac{5}{3}$ would be $A'B'$.

$A' = \left(-3 \cdot \frac{-5}{3},\ 6 \cdot \frac{-5}{3}\right) = (5, -10)$ and

$B' = \left(6 \cdot \frac{-5}{3},\ 9 \cdot \frac{-5}{3}\right) = (-10, -15)$

c. The size change is an expansion.

29. a.

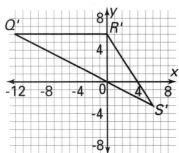

b. $QR = 4$

c. $Q'R' = 12$

d. The perimeter of the image is 3 times as large as the perimeter of the preimage. The area of the image is nine times as large as the area of the preimage.

30. The area of $ABCD$ is $4x$ and the area of the small rectangle is $3y$. The probability of a point falling in the shaded region is $\frac{4x - 3y}{4x}$.

31. The bracelet is 75% gold. $\left(\frac{18}{24} = \frac{3}{4} = .75\right)$

32. $\frac{10}{24} = \frac{5}{12}$ or $41\frac{2}{3}\%$ pure gold

5 oz $\cdot \frac{5}{12} = \frac{25}{12}$ or about 2.1 oz of gold

33. $m \neq -5$

34. a.

State	Number of Vehicles Registered per 100 People
New Mexico	85.9
New Hampshire	85.3
New Jersey	73.1
New York	56.7

b. Answers will vary. Sample: New York and New Jersey are states with large cities where public transportation is frequently used.

35. a.
  i. glass
  ii. pound
  iii. moon
  iv. calf
  v. basketball
  vi. conductor or composer
  vii. Annapolis
  viii. bicyclist

b. Samples:
Japan is to Asia as France is to Europe.
Shoes are to feet as hat is to head.

IN-CLASS ACTIVITY   p. 401

1. a., b.

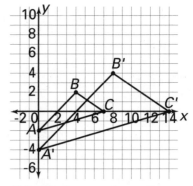

c. Side lengths vary depending upon size of graph paper.
Sample:
$AB = 3.5$ cm, $BC = 2.3$ cm, $AC = 4.2$ cm,
$m\angle A = 30°$, $m\angle B = 100°$, $m\angle C = 50°$
$A'B' = 7$ cm, $B'C' = 4.6$ cm,
$A'C' = 8.4$ cm,
$m\angle A' = 30°$, $m\angle B' = 100°$, $m\angle C' = 50°$

1. d. All ratios are equal to $\frac{2}{1}$.

  e. The measures of corresponding angles are equal.

  f. Answers will vary.

  g. All ratios are equal to k.

  h. The measures of corresponding angles are equal.

  i. Sample: Under every size change, ratios of the sides of the image to the sides of the preimage are equal to each other and are equal to k. The corresponding angles of the image and preimage have equal measures.

2. a., c.

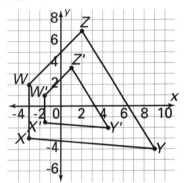

  b. Sample: The ratios of the sides of the image to the sides of the preimage are equal to each other and they are equal to k. The corresponding angles of the image and preimage have equal measures.

  d. Answers will vary.

  e. Sample: Under every size change, the ratios of the sides of the image to the sides of the preimage are equal to each other and they are equal to k. The corresponding angles of the image and preimage have equal measures.

LESSON 6-9   pp. 402–407

1. Their ratios are equal.

2. a. $\overline{BG}$

  b. $\overline{IG}$

  c. $\overline{BI}$

3. $\frac{AC}{BI} = \frac{CT}{IG} = \frac{AT}{BG}$

4. a. $\frac{AC}{BI} = \frac{CT}{IG}, \frac{15}{30} = \frac{8}{IG}$

$15 \cdot IG = 240$

$IG = 16$

  b. $\frac{AC}{BI} = \frac{AT}{BG}, \frac{15}{30} = \frac{17}{BG}$

$15 \cdot BG = 510$

$BG = 34$

5. The only other length that can be found is $AT = 4$.

6. a. Sample: $\frac{2}{1.2} = \frac{3}{x}$

  b. $2x = 3.6$

$x = 1.8$

  c. $\frac{2}{1.2} = \frac{5}{3}, \frac{1.2}{2} = \frac{3}{5}$

7. a. Sample: $\frac{16}{20} = \frac{AB}{16}$

  b. $\frac{AB}{16} = \frac{16}{20}$

$20 \cdot AB = 256$

$AB = 12.8$

8. a.

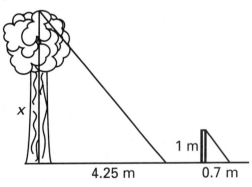

  b. Sample: $\frac{x}{4.25} = \frac{1}{0.7}$

  c. $0.7x = 1 \cdot 4.25$

$.7x = 4.25$

$x = 6.1$ m

9. a. Samples: $\frac{t}{p}; \frac{w}{k}; \frac{e}{r}$

  b. $\frac{p}{t} = \frac{a}{s} = \frac{r}{e} = \frac{k}{w}$

10. $\frac{x}{x+9} = \frac{10}{16}$

$\frac{x}{x+9} = \frac{5}{8}$

$8x = 5(x+9)$

$8x = 5x + 45$

$3x = 45$

$x = 15$

The larger rectangle has width 15 and length 24.

11. a. Drawings will vary.

b. Sample: $\frac{6}{t} = \frac{10}{25}$

c. $10t = 150$

$t = 15$

The building is 15 feet tall.

12.

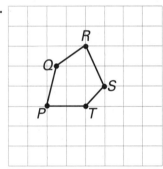

13. a. $\frac{8.7 \text{ cm}}{9 \text{ m}}$

b. $\frac{8.7}{9} = \frac{5.5}{x}$

c. $8.7x = 9 \cdot 5.5$

$8.7x = 49.5$

$x = 5.7$ m

The distance from the ground to the peak of the roof is 5.7 meters.

14. a. (c)

b. $\frac{24}{30} = \frac{x}{40}$

$\frac{4}{5} = \frac{x}{40}$

$160 = 5x$

$32 = x$

c. $\frac{24}{30} = \frac{1.5x}{y}$

$\frac{4}{5} = \frac{1.5 \cdot 32}{y}$

$\frac{4}{5} = \frac{48}{y}$

$4y = 240$

$y = 60$

d. The ratio of the perimeter of $\triangle ABC$ to the perimeter of $\triangle DEF$ is $\frac{24}{30} = \frac{4}{5}$.

15. $\frac{48}{2x} = \frac{9}{5}$

$9 \cdot 2x = 48 \cdot 5$

$18x = 240$

$x = \frac{40}{3}$

16. $\frac{1}{x-1} = \frac{3}{x-2}$

$x - 2 = 3(x-1)$

$x - 2 = 3x - 3$

$3 - 2 = 3x - x$

$1 = 2x$

$\frac{1}{2} = x$

17. a. $\frac{9}{n} \cdot \frac{n}{25} = \frac{9n}{25n} = \frac{9}{25}$

b. $\frac{9}{n} = \frac{n}{25}$; $n^2 = 9 \cdot 25$

$n^2 = 225$

$n = 15$ or $n = -15$

18. a., b.

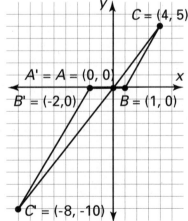

19. Within $\frac{1}{2}$ km of the bicycle shop is a total of 1 km.

P (flat within $\frac{1}{2}$ km of bicycle shop) $= \frac{1}{38}$

20. $x + .15x = 38.81$

$1.15x = 38.81$

$x = 33.75$

The original bill was \$33.75.

21. $21 - 21x = 17$

$21 - 17 = 21x$

$4 = 21x$

$x = \frac{4}{21} = .1904$

The percent of discount is 19%.

22. P (letter in the word MATH) $= \frac{4}{26} = \frac{2}{13} \approx 0.15$

23. $3x \div \frac{1}{2}x = 3x \div \frac{x}{2}$

$= 3x \cdot \frac{2}{x}$

$= 6$

$3x$ is 6 times as large as $\frac{1}{2}x$.

24. $\frac{3\pi}{y^2} \div \frac{\pi}{5} = \frac{3\pi}{y^2} \cdot \frac{5}{\pi} = \frac{15}{y^2}$

25. $\frac{5-2}{3-4} = \frac{3}{-1} = -3$

26. If $a = 7$ and $d = 8$, the expression is not defined for $b = 7$.

27. a. $p + 8 = 23$

$p = 15$

b. $8p = 23$

$p = \frac{23}{8}$

c. $8 - p = 23$

$-p = 15$

$p = -15$

d. $\frac{1}{8}p = 23$

$p = 184$

28. Light travels at $186{,}000 \frac{\text{miles}}{\text{second}} \cdot 60 \frac{\text{seconds}}{\text{minute}} \cdot 60 \frac{\text{minutes}}{\text{hour}} = 669{,}600{,}000$ miles per hour.

29. Answers will vary.

CHAPTER 6

PROGRESS SELF-TEST   p. 411

1. $15 \div -\frac{3}{2} = 15 \cdot -\frac{2}{3} = -10$

2. $\frac{x}{9} \div \frac{2}{3} = \frac{x}{9} \cdot \frac{3}{2} = \frac{3x}{18} = \frac{x}{6}$

3. $\dfrac{\frac{2b}{3}}{\frac{b}{3}} = \frac{2b}{3} \div \frac{b}{3} = \frac{2b}{3} \cdot \frac{3}{b} = 2$

4. $\frac{y}{11} = \frac{2}{23}$

$23y = 22$

$y = \frac{22}{23}$

5. $\frac{b}{49} = \frac{25}{b}$

$b^2 = 25 \cdot 49$

$b^2 = 1225$

$b = 35$ or $b = -35$

6. $\frac{4g - 3}{26} = \frac{g}{8}$

$8(4g - 3) = 26g$

$32g - 24 = 26g$

$-24 = -6g$

$4 = g$

7. $.14x = 60$

$\frac{.14x}{.14} = \frac{60}{.14}$

$x \approx 428.6$

8. $\frac{1}{2}$ is what percent of $\frac{4}{5}$?

$\frac{1}{2} = x\left(\frac{4}{5}\right)$

$\left(\frac{5}{4}\right)\left(\frac{1}{2}\right) = x$

$x = \frac{5}{8} = 62.5\%$

9. P (at least a 5 will show) $= \frac{2}{6} = \frac{1}{3}$

(possibilities include a 5 or a 6)

10. $v \neq -1$; when the denominator is zero, the fraction is undefined.

11. 3 and x are the means.

12. a. $\frac{36}{30} = 1.2 = 120\%$

Horatio's time is 120% of Mary Ellen's time

b. Horatio studied 20% longer than Mary Ellen.

13. $\frac{d}{c+d}$; the total number of animals is $c + d$.

14. a. Two possible ratios of similitude are $\frac{9}{4}$ and $\frac{4}{9}$.

b. $\frac{4}{9} = \frac{z}{12}$

$9z = 48$

$z = 5.\overline{3}$

15. $x - .20x = 236$

$.80x = 236$

$x = 295$

The television originally cost $295.

16. It is faster to read p pages in $7y$ minutes. The same number of pages are read in less time.

17. $\frac{\text{no. with Alzheimer's}}{\text{no. surveyed}} = \frac{36}{400} = 0.09 = 9\%$

The relative frequency of Alzheimer's disease in this group is 9%. Relative frequency is the ratio of people who have Alzheimer's to the number of people in the survey.

18. P (second hand is between 2 and 3) $= \frac{1}{12}$

19. $\frac{280 \text{ miles}}{12 \text{ gallons}} = \frac{x \text{ miles}}{14 \text{ gallons}}$

$\frac{70}{3} = \frac{x}{14}$

$980 = 3x$

$326.\overline{6} = x$

To the nearest mile the car can travel 327 miles.

20. a., b.

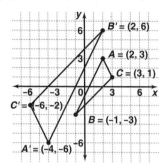

21. a. $\left(\frac{2}{3} \cdot -6, \frac{2}{3} \cdot 4\right) = \left(-4, \frac{8}{3}\right)$

b. The size change is a contraction.

22. Since they are similar:

$\frac{x}{7} = \frac{x+2}{10}$; $10x = 7(x + 2)$

$10x = 7x + 14$

$3x = 14$

$x = \frac{14}{3}$

width $= 4\frac{2}{3}$; length $= 6\frac{2}{3}$

23. Area of total video screen $14 \cdot 16 = 224$

Area of shaded area $6 \cdot 8 = 48$

P (not be able to destroy villain) $= \frac{48}{224} \approx 0.21$

CHAPTER 6

REVIEW   pp. 412–415

1. $-25 \div \frac{1}{5} = -25 \cdot \frac{5}{1} = -125$

2. $\frac{a}{14} \div \frac{7}{2} = \frac{a}{14} \cdot \frac{2}{7} = \frac{2a}{98} = \frac{a}{49}$

3. $\frac{2\pi}{9} \div \frac{\pi}{6} = \frac{2\pi}{9} \cdot \frac{6}{\pi} = \frac{4}{3}$

4. $\frac{x}{z} \div \frac{x}{y} = \frac{x}{z} \cdot \frac{y}{x} = \frac{y}{z}$

5. $\frac{\frac{3x}{2}}{\frac{-15x}{16}} = \frac{3x}{2} \div \frac{-15x}{16} = \frac{3x}{2} \cdot \frac{16}{-15x} = \frac{48x}{-30x} = \frac{8}{-5}$

6. $\frac{\frac{a}{b}}{\frac{c}{d}} = \frac{a}{b} \div \frac{c}{d} = \frac{a}{b} \cdot \frac{d}{c} = \frac{ad}{bc}$

7. $\dfrac{60}{\frac{1}{4}} = 60 \div \dfrac{1}{4} = 60 \cdot \dfrac{4}{1} = 240$

8. $\dfrac{x}{-\frac{x}{4}} = x \div \dfrac{-x}{4} = x \cdot \dfrac{-4}{x} = -4$

9. $x \neq -4$

10. $x \neq 0.2$

11. $.75 \cdot 32 = 24$

12. $.2 \cdot 18 = 3.6$

13. $10 = 5x$

$\dfrac{10}{5} = \dfrac{5x}{5}$

$2 = x$

10 is 200% of 5.

14. $1.2 = 0.8x$

$\dfrac{1.2}{0.8} = \dfrac{0.8x}{0.8}$

$1.5 = x$

1.2 is 150% of 0.8.

15. $.85x = 170$

$\dfrac{.85x}{.85} = \dfrac{170}{.85}$

$x = 200$

85% of 200 is 170.

16. $.30x = \dfrac{3}{4}$

$.30x = .75$

$x = \dfrac{.75}{.30}$

$x = 2.5$

30% of 2.5 is $\dfrac{3}{4}$.

17. $\dfrac{x}{130} = \dfrac{6}{5}$

$5x = 780$

$x = 156$

18. $\dfrac{6}{25} = \dfrac{-10}{m}$

$6m = -250$

$m = \dfrac{-250}{6} = -\dfrac{125}{3}$

19. $\dfrac{4}{x} = \dfrac{x}{225}$

$x^2 = 900$

$x = 30 \text{ or } x = -30$

20. $\dfrac{y}{7} = \dfrac{10}{y}$

$y^2 = 70$

$y = \sqrt{70} \text{ or } y = -\sqrt{70}$

21. $\dfrac{2m-1}{21} = \dfrac{m-5}{24}$

$24(2m-1) = 21(m-5)$

$48m - 24 = 21m - 105$

$27m - 24 = -105$

$27m = -81$

$m = -3$

22. $\dfrac{5+r}{3} = \dfrac{r+2}{2}$

$2(5+r) = 3(r+2)$

$10 + 2r = 3r + 6$

$10 = r + 6$

$4 = r$

23. **a.** The means are 8 and 15.

b. The extremes are 5 and 24.

24. If $\dfrac{m}{n} = \dfrac{p}{q}$, then by the Means-Extremes Property $mp = np$.

25. If $\dfrac{2}{3} = \dfrac{x}{5}$, then $\dfrac{5}{x} = \dfrac{3}{2}$.

26. If $\dfrac{a}{b} = \dfrac{c}{d}$, then $\dfrac{c}{a} = \dfrac{d}{b}$.

27. **a.** $\dfrac{22 \text{ miles}}{2 \text{ hours}} = \dfrac{11 \text{ miles}}{1 \text{ hour}} = 11$ miles per hour

b. $\dfrac{2 \text{ hours}}{22 \text{ miles}} = \dfrac{1 \text{ hour}}{11 \text{ miles}} = \dfrac{1}{11}$ hour per mile

28. $\dfrac{48.1 \text{ miles}}{\frac{1}{2} \text{ hour}} = \dfrac{x}{1 \text{ hour}}$

$48.1 = \dfrac{1}{2}x$

$96.2 = x$

96.2 miles per hour

29. $\dfrac{3\frac{1}{2} \text{ hours}}{\$21} = \dfrac{7}{2} \div 21$

$= \dfrac{7}{2} \cdot \dfrac{1}{21}$

$= \dfrac{1}{6}$

$\dfrac{1}{6}$ hour per dollar is 10 minutes per dollar.

30. Sample: What was the average speed?

$30 \div \frac{3}{4} = 30 \cdot \frac{4}{3} = 40$ miles per hour

31. Sample: How much did Tony spend per day?

$\$400 \div d = \frac{400}{d}$; Tony spent $\frac{400}{d}$ dollars per day.

32. Sample: How much did the puppy gain per week?

$\frac{3 \text{ kg}}{4 \text{ wk}} = \frac{3}{4}$ kg per week

33. **a.** 46-ounce can: $\frac{177¢}{46 \text{ ounces}} = 3.8¢$ per ounce

6-ounce can: $\frac{28¢}{6 \text{ ounces}} = 4.7¢$ per ounce

b. The 46-ounce is a better buy since it is cheaper per ounce.

34. It is faster to read $6w$ words in $2m$ minutes. (The rates are $\frac{w}{m}$ words per minute and $\frac{3w}{m}$ words per minute respectively.)

35. There are 17 boys in the class. The number of boys is $\frac{17}{10} = 1.7$ times the number of girls.

36. **a.** $\frac{76}{18}$

b. $\frac{76}{18} = 4.\overline{2} = 422\%$

37. $\frac{6}{36} = \frac{1}{6} = .1\overline{6}$ The discount is 16.7%.

38. $\frac{8}{20} = \frac{2}{5} = .40$
The profit is 40%.

39. $\frac{x}{x + y}$

40. The number of heads is $m + n$ and the number of feet is $4m + 2n$.
Ratio of heads to feet is $\frac{m + n}{4m + 2n}$.

41. There are 11 numbers to pick from of which 9 are less than 4.
P (number less than 4) $= \frac{9}{11}$

42. P (odd number on die) $= \frac{3}{6} = \frac{1}{2}$

43. P (drawing a club) $= \frac{13}{52} = \frac{1}{4}$

44. P (drawing a jack or king) $= \frac{8}{52} = \frac{2}{13}$

45. P (not winning) $= 1 - \frac{1}{1,000,000} = \frac{999,999}{1,000,000}$

46. **a.** Event B is most likely to happen since $\frac{4}{9} = .\overline{4}$.

b. Event A is least likely to happen.

47. The relative frequency of pet owners is $\frac{116}{200} = \frac{29}{50} = .58 = 58\%$.

48. $100\% - 14.2\% = 85.8\%$.

49. $\frac{1 + 2 + 5}{40} = \frac{8}{40} = \frac{1}{5}$

50. $\frac{40}{40} = 1 = 100\%$

51. Let x be the percent of the original price.
$562.52x = 450$

$x = \frac{450}{562.52}$

$x = 80\%$

52. $\$15.99 - \$11.99 = \$4$ discount

$\frac{4}{15.99} = .25$

25% discount

53. Let x represent the weight of the prior year's aluminum cover.
$x - .37x = 3.7$

$.63x = 3.7$

$x = 5.9$

The wheel covers previously weighed 5.9 pounds.

54. $.48 \cdot 86,000 = 41,280$ people

55. Let x be the price of the shirt before the discount.
$x - .30x + .05(x - .30x) = 7.30$

$.70x + .05x - .015x = 7.30$

$.735x = 7.30$

$x = 9.93$

The price of the shirt before the discount was $9.93.

56. $87 \cdot 30 = 2610$ cm

57. $x + .054x = 437$

$1.054x = 437$

$x = 414.61$

The average 1990 salary was $414.61.

58. Let x be the September 1991 price.
$$x - .553x = 89$$
$$.447x = 89$$
$$x = 199.11$$
The September 1991 price was $199.11.

59. Let n be the number of times Anne earned $35.
$$35n = 245$$
$$n = 7$$
Her mother added $7 \cdot 15 = \$105$.

60. $\dfrac{\frac{3}{4}}{12} = \dfrac{3}{x}$

$$\frac{3}{4}x = 36$$

$$x = 36 \cdot \frac{4}{3}$$

$$x = 48$$
There are 48 tablespoons in 3 cups of sugar.

61. $\dfrac{7}{45} = \dfrac{30}{x}$

$$7x = 1350$$

$$x = 192.9$$
About 193 phone calls will be made in the month at this rate.

62. $\dfrac{1}{1.60} = \dfrac{x}{120}$

$$1.6x = 120$$

$$x = 75$$
The vase would cost $75.

63. (b)

64. (c)

65. area of large square: 16 cm^2
area of shaded region: $16 - 9 = 7 \text{ cm}^2$
P (point is in shaded region) $= \dfrac{7}{16}$

66. length of road: $1 + 8 + 2 + 5 = 16$ km
P (accident on 8 km of road) $= \dfrac{8}{16} = \dfrac{1}{2}$

67. a. area of square: $24^2 = 576 \text{ in.}^2$
area of bull's eye: $\pi \cdot 3^2 = 9\pi$
P (hits bull's eye) $= \dfrac{9\pi}{576} = 0.049$

b. area of second smallest circle: 36π
area of largest circle: 144π
area of two outer rings:
$144\pi - 36\pi = 108\pi$
P (hits two outer rings) $= \dfrac{108\pi}{576} = 0.589$

68. P (lands in region A or B) $= \dfrac{k + 40}{360}$

69. P (second hand will stop between 5 and 7) $= \dfrac{2}{12} = \dfrac{1}{6} = 0.167$

70. $6 \cdot 1.2 = 7.2$ cm

71. $(2 \cdot 3, 4 \cdot 3) = (6, 12)$

72. $\left(-8 \cdot -\frac{1}{4}, -12 \cdot -\frac{1}{4}\right) = (2, 3)$

73. a.

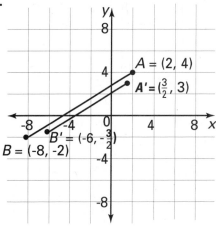

b. See part **a** where $A' = \left(\frac{3}{4} \cdot 2, \frac{3}{4} \cdot 4\right) = \left(\frac{3}{2}, 3\right)$
and $B' = \left(\frac{3}{4} \cdot -8, \frac{3}{4} \cdot -2\right) = \left(-6, -\frac{3}{2}\right)$.

c. This size change is a contraction.

74. $A' = \left(-\frac{1}{2}, \frac{3}{2}\right)$, $B' = (1, 0)$, $C' = \left(1, -\frac{1}{2}\right)$ and $D' = \left(-\frac{3}{2}, -\frac{1}{2}\right)$

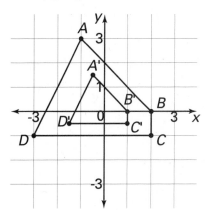

75. $A' = (3, -9)$, $B' = (-6, 0)$, $C' = (-6, 3)$ and $D' = (9, 3)$

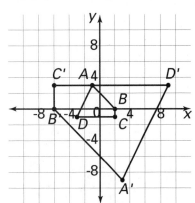

76. Sample: Same size as original; coordinates of preimage are opposites.

77. (c)

78. $\dfrac{a}{e} = \dfrac{b}{f}$

$\dfrac{12}{10} = \dfrac{15}{f}$

$12f = 150$

$f = 12.5$

79. No; ratios of sides are not equal.

80. a. $\dfrac{1}{5}$ or $\dfrac{5}{1}$

b. $AB = 19$

$\left(\dfrac{x}{95} = \dfrac{1}{5}\right.$

$5x = 95$

$x = 19\Big)$

c. $DF = 200$

$\left(\dfrac{40}{y} = \dfrac{1}{5}\right.$

$y = 200\Big)$

81. a. $y = 5.5$

$\left(\dfrac{y}{11} = \dfrac{9}{18}\right.$

$\dfrac{y}{11} = \dfrac{1}{2}$

$2y = 11$

$y = 5.5\Big)$

b. $x = 30$

$\left(\dfrac{\frac{1}{4}x}{15} = \dfrac{1}{2}\right.$

$\dfrac{1}{2}x = 15$

$x = 30\Big)$

82. a. Sketches will vary.

b. Let x represent the height of the tree.

$\dfrac{6}{15} = \dfrac{x}{140}$

$\dfrac{2}{5} = \dfrac{x}{140}$

$5x = 280$

$x = 56$

The tree is 56 feet tall.

83. a. Sketches will vary.

b. $\dfrac{1 \text{ yard}}{n \text{ feet}} = \dfrac{x \text{ feet}}{9 \text{ feet}}$

$\dfrac{3}{n} = \dfrac{x}{9}$

$nx = 27$

$x = \dfrac{27}{n}$

The tree is $\dfrac{27}{n}$ feet tall.

CHAPTER 7
SLOPES AND LINES

LESSON 7-1   pp. 418–424

1. The rate of change in height per year is the change in *height* divided by the change in *years*.

2. a. Height

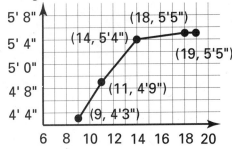

b. The segment connecting $(9, 4'3'')$ to $(11, 4'9'')$ is steeper.

3. a. Karen's rate of change from age 14 to age 18 is $\frac{5'5'' - 5'4''}{(18-14)\ \text{years}} = \frac{1\ \text{inch}}{4\ \text{years}} = 0.25$ inches per year.

b. The rate of change of her height was greater from age 9 to 11.

4. The rate of change in her height from age 18 to 19 is $\frac{5'5'' - 5'5''}{(19-18)\ \text{years}} = \frac{0\ \text{inch}}{1\ \text{year}} = 0$ inches per year.

5. increased

6. 1910–1920, 1920–1930, 1950–1960, 1960–1970, and 1970–1980

7. decrease

8. $\frac{1,487,536 - 1,428,285}{1990 - 1980} = \frac{59,251\ \text{people}}{10\ \text{years}} =$ 5925.1 people per year

9. $\frac{1,487,536 - 1,850,093}{1990 - 1900} = \frac{-362,557\ \text{people}}{90\ \text{years}} =$ -4028.4 people per year

10. During 1850 to 1860 the population changed more rapidly.
Sample: The slope of the line connecting these points is steeper than the slope of the line connecting 1860 to 1870. Therefore, the population increased faster between 1850 and 1860.

11. In terms of coordinates, the rate of change between two points is the *difference* of the *y*-coordinates divided by the difference of the *x*-coordinates.

12. a.

	A	B	C
			Rate of Change in
1	Year	Deer	Previous 5-Yr. Period
2	1975	60	
3	1980	60	0
4	1985	70	2
5	1990	40	-6

b. = (B4 − B3) / (A4 − A3)

c. 2 deer per year

d. C2 (There was no previous 5-year period.)

13. a. The graph slants upward from left to right.

b. The graph slants downward from left to right.

c. The graph is horizontal.

14. a. $A = (6, 32)$

b. $B = (7, 24)$

c. rate of change between A and B:
$$\frac{24 - 32\ \text{meters}}{7 - 6\ \text{seconds}} = \frac{-8\ \text{meters}}{1\ \text{second}}$$
$$= \text{-8 meters per second}$$

15. Rate of change between C and D:
$$\frac{(2-2)\ \text{meters}}{(17-11)\ \text{seconds}} = \frac{0\ \text{meters}}{6\ \text{seconds}}$$
$$= \text{0 meters per second}$$

16. After about 15.5 seconds the altitude of the vulture begins to increase.

17. positive

18. a.

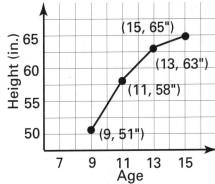

18. b. In the two-year period from age 9 to age 11 the boy grew the fastest. You can tell because the slope of the line is steepest.

c. Rate of growth:
$$\frac{58'' - 51''}{(11 - 9)\ \text{years}} = \frac{7''}{2\ \text{years}} = 3.5\ \text{inches per year}$$

19. $\dfrac{73'' - 74''}{(65 - 55)\ \text{years}} = \dfrac{-1''}{10\ \text{years}} = -0.1$ inch per year

20. a. Rate of change:
$$\frac{(H - h)\ \text{cm}}{(15 - 12)\ \text{years}} = \frac{(H - h)\ \text{cm}}{3\ \text{years}} =$$
$$\frac{H - h}{3}\ \text{cm per year}$$

b. The rate of change is 0 cm per year.

21. Rate of change:
$$\frac{(2y - y)\ \text{meters}}{(6 - 2)\ \text{minutes}} = \frac{y\ \text{meters}}{4\ \text{minutes}} =$$
$$\frac{y}{4}\ \text{meters per minute}$$

22. a. $\overline{CD}$
b. $\overline{AB}$
c. $\overline{DE}$

23. a. $\dfrac{2}{a} - \dfrac{1}{a} = \dfrac{1}{a}$

b. $\dfrac{2}{3 + 4x} - \dfrac{1}{3 + 4x} = \dfrac{1}{3 + 4x}$

c. $\dfrac{2}{3 + 4x} - \dfrac{1}{3 + 4x} = \dfrac{4}{x}$
$$\frac{1}{3 + 4x} = \frac{4}{x}$$
$$x = 4(3 + 4x)$$
$$x = 12 + 16x$$
$$-15x = 12$$
$$x = -\frac{12}{15} = -\frac{4}{5}$$

24. $\dfrac{-\frac{2}{5}}{4} = \dfrac{-2}{5} \div 4$
$$= -\frac{2}{5} \cdot \frac{1}{4}$$
$$= -\frac{1}{10}$$

25. a. $33 - 4y = 12$
$$-4y = -21$$
$$y = \frac{21}{4}$$

b. $3x - 4y = 12$
$$-4y = -3x + 12$$
$$y = \left(-\frac{1}{4}\right)(-3x + 12)$$
$$y = \frac{3}{4}x - 3$$

c. $ax - 4y = 12$
$$-4y = -ax + 12$$
$$y = \left(-\frac{1}{4}\right)(-ax + 12)$$
$$y = \frac{a}{4}x - 3$$

26. a.

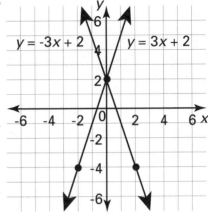

b. They intersect at the point (0, 2).

27. $10{,}000 + 1000x$

28. True; by the Rate Model for Division, if 3 pizzas are divided among 4 people, the result is $\frac{3}{4}$ pizza per person.

29. $\dfrac{y_2 - y_1}{x_2 - x_1} = \dfrac{5 - 6}{-2 - -4} = \dfrac{-1}{2} = -\dfrac{1}{2}$

30. $\dfrac{y_2 - y_1}{x_2 - x_1} = \dfrac{8 - 4}{2 - \frac{1}{3}} = \dfrac{4}{1\frac{2}{3}} = 4 \div \dfrac{5}{3} = 4 \cdot \dfrac{3}{5} = \dfrac{12}{5}$ or 2.4

31. a., b. Answers will vary.

LESSON 7-2   pp. 425–431

1. In a constant increase or decrease situation, all points lie on the same line.

2. slope

3. a. Sample: $\left(7, 7\frac{1}{3}\right)$; $(9, 6)$

b. Rate of change:
$$\frac{\left(7\frac{1}{3} - 6\right)\ \text{feet}}{(7 - 9)\ \text{minutes}} = \frac{\frac{4}{3}\ \text{feet}}{-2\ \text{minutes}}$$
$$= -\frac{2}{3}\ \text{ft per minute}$$

4. a.

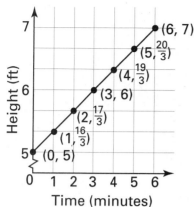

Height (ft) vs Time (minutes)

Points: (0, 5), $(1, \frac{16}{3})$, $(2, \frac{17}{3})$, (3, 6), $(4, \frac{19}{3})$, $(5, \frac{20}{3})$, (6, 7)

b. Rate of change using points (6, 7) and (3, 6)

$\frac{7-6}{6-3} = \frac{1}{3}$ foot per minute

5. slope: $\frac{7-1}{2-0} = \frac{6}{2} = 3$

6. slope: $\frac{4-1}{-2-4} = \frac{3}{-6} = -\frac{1}{2}$

7. a. slope: $\frac{11-2}{6-1} = \frac{9}{5}$

b. slope: $\frac{-16-11}{-10-6} = \frac{-27}{-16} = \frac{27}{16}$

c. The points do not lie on the same line. The slope of the line through (1, 2) and (6, 11) is different from the slope through (6, 11) and (-10, -16).

8. slope using (3, 3) and (2, 1): $\frac{3-1}{3-2} = \frac{2}{1} = 2$

9. slope using (-3, 4) and (-2, 0): $\frac{4-0}{-3--2} = \frac{4}{-1} = -4$

10. a. Sample:

Let $x = 0$: $5 \cdot 0 - 2y = 10$

$-2y = 10$

$y = -5$

Let $y = 0$: $5x - 2 \cdot 0 = 10$

$5x = 10$

$x = 2$

Two points on the line are (0, -5) and (2, 0).

b. slope: $\frac{0--5}{2-0} = \frac{5}{2}$ or 2.5

c.

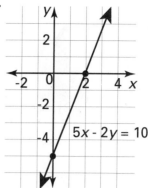

$5x - 2y = 10$

11. a. Sample:

Let $x = 0$: $0 + y = 6$; $y = 6$

Let $y = 0$: $x + 0 = 6$

$x = 6$

Two points on the line are (0, 6) and (6, 0).

b. slope: $\frac{0-6}{6-0} = \frac{-6}{6} = -1$

c.

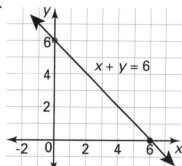

$x + y = 6$

12. C

13. The slope determined by C and D is negative.

14. The slope determined by B and D is zero.

15. a. r

b. q

c. p

16. a. $\frac{585-565}{19-17} = \frac{20}{2} = 10$

$\frac{565-535}{17-14} = \frac{30}{3} = 10$

$\frac{585-535}{19-14} = \frac{50}{5} = 10$

b. The slope represents an increase in rent of $10 per floor.

17. $y - 5 = -2$

$y = -2 + 5$

$y = 3$

18. a.

	A	B	C
1	x	y	rate of change
2	-5	19	
3	0	9	-2
4	7	-5	-2
5	10	-11	-2

b. Yes; the rate of change is constant.

19. a.

	A	B	C
1	x	y	rate of change
2	0	1	
3	4	6	1.25
4	8	7	0.25
5	12	11	1.00

b. No; The rate of change is not constant.

20. a. slope: $\frac{2-2}{-3-2} = \frac{0}{-5} = 0$

b. slope: $\frac{-3--3}{-3-1} = \frac{0}{-4} = 0$

c. The slope of all horizontal lines is zero.

21. a. When you try to find the slope of $x = 3$, zero is in the denominator; division by zero is impossible.

b. Vertical lines do not have slope.

22. line 30: 0, 1
line 50: 2, 7

23. a. 1980–1985

b. 1960–1965 and 1965–1970

c. $\frac{10¢ - 5¢}{1975 - 1965} = \frac{5¢}{10 \text{ yr}} = \frac{1}{2}$ cent per year

d. Sample: The cost of stamps did not gradually rise over each 5-year period. For example, the cost was never 4.3 cents.

24. $\frac{9}{18} = \frac{AB}{FG}$

$\frac{1}{2} = \frac{x+1}{3x}$

$3x = 2(x + 1)$

$3x = 2x + 2$

$x = 2$

$AB = 2 + 1 = 3$ and $FG = 3 \cdot 2 = 6$

25.

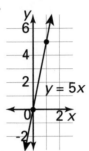

26.

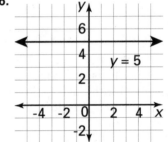

27. No. If you substitute 7 for x in the equation $y = 2x - 5$, then $y = 14 - 5 = 9$. $y \neq 6$.

28. $100 - 4x$

29. $5x - 350$

30. Answers will vary.

LESSON 7-3   pp. 432–438

1. slope: $\frac{0 - 0.5}{1 - 0} = -0.5$

2.

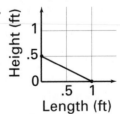

3. Slope is the amount of change in the *height* of a graph for every change of one unit to the right.

4. If the slope of a line is 8, then you move *8 units up* as you move one to the right.

5. slope = $\frac{-3}{1}$ = -3

6. slope = $\frac{1}{1}$ = 1

7. a.

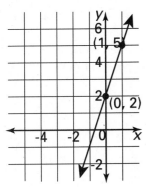

b. Sample: (1, 5)

8. a.

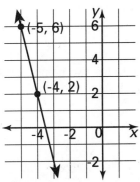

b. Sample: (-4, 2)

9. a.

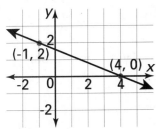

b. Sample: (4, 0)

10. a.

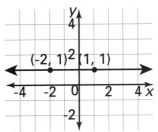

b. Sample: (1, 1)

11. Sample: (-1, -1) Every point on the line has coordinates (-4+3n, -2+n) where n is any real number. This shows that the vertical change is 3 times the horizontal change.

12. .29 + 8 · .23 = $2.13

13.

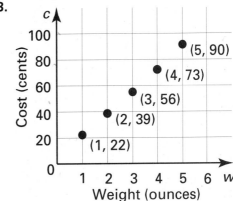

14. Sample: Slope is defined to be the amount of change in height of a line for every change of one unit to the right; vertical lines do not change to the left or right. The slope of the line through (-5, 2) and (-5, 12) is $\frac{10}{0}$, which is not defined.

15.

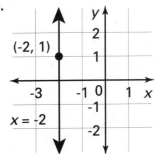

16.

	A	B
1	x	y
2	-5	2
3	-4	9
4	-3	16
5	-2	23

17.

	A	B
1	x	y
2	6	10
3	7	2
4	8	-6
5	9	-14

18.

	A	B
1	x	y
2	0	0
3	1	1.25
4	2	2.5
5	3	3.75

19. The slope of $\overline{UP}$ is $\frac{1}{1.266} \approx 0.79$.

20.

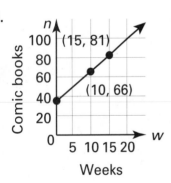

21. a., b.

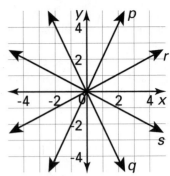

c. Sample: Lines with positive slopes slant upward from left to right. Lines with negative slopes slant downward from left to right.

22. slope: $\frac{3--2}{5-8} = \frac{5}{-3}$

23. slope: $\frac{5--9}{-13--6} = \frac{14}{-7} = -2$

24. Find two points on $3x - y = 15$.

Let $x = 0$: $3(0) - y = 15$
$$y = -15$$
$(0, -15)$

Let $y = 0$:
$$3x - 0 = 15$$
$$3x = 15$$
$$x = 5$$

$(0, -15)$ and $(5, 0)$ are two points on the line.

Slope: $\frac{0-15}{5-0} = \frac{15}{5} = 3$

25. a. $y = .25x + 39$

b.

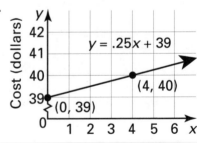

c. slope: $\frac{40-39}{4-0} = \frac{1}{4}$

26. a. 1981–1982
b. 1992–1993

27. a. 1987–1988
b. 1987–1988

28. a. $\frac{1.56-1.42}{1990-1981} = \frac{0.17}{9} \approx 0.019$

   b. $\frac{1.59-1.12}{1990-1981} = \frac{0.44}{9} \approx 0.049$

29. If $4a = 15$, then $12a = 3 \cdot 15 = 45$ and $12a - 5 = 45 - 5 = 40$.

30. $z + 4 + 3z - 2 + 4z - 3 = 71$
$$8z - 1 = 71$$
$$8z = 72$$
$$z = 9$$

31. a. $.15 \cdot 8 = .1 \cdot 8 + .05 \cdot 8 = .80 + .40$
$$= \$1.20$$

   b. $2 \cdot x$ dollars $= \$2x$

32. $-4 = 3 \cdot 2 + b$
$$-4 = 6 + b$$
$$-10 = b$$

33. 13 days; on the 12th day, he has gone 12 feet. On the 13th day, he starts at 12 feet, goes up 3 feet and is out of the well before he slides back down.

LESSON 7-4   pp. 439–444

1. slope-intercept form

2. a. slope: 4   **b.** y-intercept: 2

c.

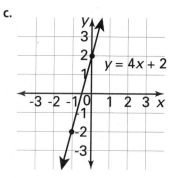

$y = 4x + 2$

3. a. slope: $-\frac{1}{3}$ **b.** y-intercept: 6

c.

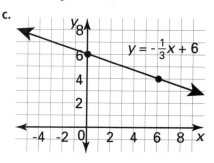

$y = -\frac{1}{3}x + 6$

4. a. $y = -1.2x + 7.3$

   b. slope: -1.2

   c. y-intercept: 7.3

5. a. $x + 6y = 7$
$$6y = -x + 7$$
$$y = -\frac{1}{6}x + \frac{7}{6}$$

   b. slope: $-\frac{1}{6}$

   c. y-intercept: $\frac{7}{6}$

6. a. $3x + 2y = 10$
$$2y = -3x + 10$$
$$y = \frac{-3}{2}x + 5$$

   b. slope: $-\frac{3}{2}$

   c. y-intercept: 5

7. a. $y = x$
$$y = x + 0$$

   b. slope: 1

   c. y-intercept: 0

8. $y = -3x + 5$

9. $y = \frac{2}{3}x - 1$

10. a. $y = 5x + 100$

   b.

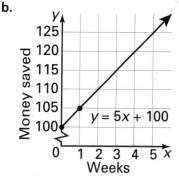

$y = 5x + 100$

   c. slope: 5; y-intercept: 100

11. When a constant increase situation is graphed, the y-intercept can be interpreted as the *starting point*.

12. Equations of *vertical* lines cannot be written in slope-intercept form.

143

13. **a.** (ii)
    b. slope: 4
    c. y-intercept: 100
14. **a.** (i)
    b. slope: -4
    c. y-intercept: 100
15. **a.** (iii)
    b. slope: 4
    c. y-intercept: -100
16. $y = -4$
17. **a.** $y = .50x + 8$
    b. Dollars

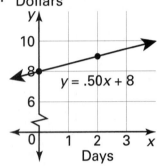

18. **a.** $y = -6x + 9$
    b.

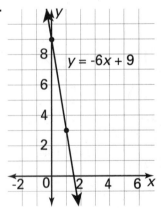

19. **a.** q
    b. p
    c. n
    d. r

20. **a.** u
    b. v
    c. t
    d. s
21. **a.**

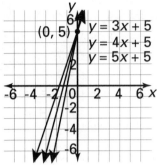

    b. The graph is a line that passes through (0, 5) with slope m.
    c. Yes

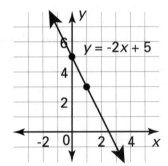

22. slope: $\frac{1}{0.82} \approx 1.22$
23. slope: $\frac{1}{11} \approx .09$
24. Vertical lines have no slope, since you cannot divide by 0.
25. $\frac{-3-7}{5-2} = \frac{-10}{3} = -\frac{10}{3}$
26.
$$\frac{3x + 5}{2 - 4x} = \frac{2}{3}$$
$$3(3x + 5) = 2(2 - 4x)$$
$$9x + 15 = 4 - 8x$$
$$17x + 15 = 4$$
$$17x = -11$$
$$x = -\frac{11}{17}$$

27. $\frac{z+2}{2} = 2z - 2$

$z + 2 = 2(2z - 2)$

$z + 2 = 4z - 4$

$2 = 3z - 4$

$6 = 3z$

$2 = z$

28. a. length: $2w + 5$

b. $2w + 2(2w + 5) = 58$

$2w + 4w + 10 = 58$

$6w = 48$

$w = 8$

width: 8 cm
length: 21 cm

c. area: $8 \cdot 21 = 168$ cm^2

29. Sample: $y = \frac{1}{2}x + 2$; $y = \frac{1}{2}x - 4$; $y = -2x - 4$; $y = -2x + 2$.
The slopes of the lines that form parallel sides of the rectangle are equal. The slopes of the lines that form perpendicular sides are negative reciprocals of one another; their product is -1.

LESSON 7-5 pp. 445–449

1. Step 1: In the equation $y = mx + b$, substitute the slope m and the coordinates of the point (x, y).

Step 2: Solve the equation from step 1 for b.

Step 3: Substitute the values of m and b into the equation $y = mx + b$.

2. Does $0 = -4 \cdot 6 + 24$?

$0 = -24 + 24$?

$0 = 0$

Yes, it checks.

3. $3 = 4 \cdot 2 + b$

$3 = 8 + b$

$-5 = b$

$y = 4x + -5$

4. $3 = -10 \cdot -2 + b$

$3 = 20 + b$

$-17 = b$

$y = -2x + -17$

5. $0 = \frac{1}{3} \cdot -6 + b$

$0 = -2 + b$

$2 = b$

$y = \frac{1}{3}x + 2$

6. $-\frac{1}{2} = 0 \cdot 4 + b$

$-\frac{1}{2} = b$

$y = 0 \cdot x + -\frac{1}{2}$

$y = -\frac{1}{2}$

7. $0 = -4 \cdot 7 + b$

$0 = -28 + b$

$28 = b$

$y = -4x + 28$

8. $y = 80,000 \cdot 2005 - 149,195,000$

$y = 160,400,000 - 149,195,000$

$y = 11,205,000$

A prediction for the population in the year 2005 is 11,205,000.

9. a. $226,300 = 1990 \cdot 5200 + b$

$226,300 = 10,348,000 + b$

$-10,121,700 = b$

$y = 5200x - 10,121,700$

b. $y = 5200 \cdot 2002 - 10,121,700$

$y = 10,410,400 - 10,121,700$

$y = 288,700$

A prediction for the population in the year 2002 is 288,700.

c. $500,000 = 5200x - 10,121,700$

$10,621,700 = 5200x$

$2042.6 = x$

In the year 2042

10. a. $y = 1.5 \cdot 48 + 2$

$y = 72 + 2$

$y = 74$ cm

b. $m = 1.5$: $(x, y) = (0, 2)$

c. $y = 1.5x + 2$

d. $y = 1.5 \cdot 6 + 2$

$y = 9 + 2$

$y = 11$ cm

11. a. slope $= \frac{\text{rise}}{\text{run}} = \frac{3}{1} = 3$

$2 = 3 \cdot 3 + b$

$2 = 9 + b$

$-7 = b$

$y = 3x - 7$

b. The line crosses the y-axis when $x = 0$.

$y = 3 \cdot 0 - 7$

$y = 0 - 7$

$y = -7$

The point is $(0, -7)$.

c. The coordinates of P are $(3 + 1, 2 + 3) = (4, 5)$.

d. Does $5 = 3 \cdot 4 - 7$?

$5 = 12 - 7$?

$5 = 5$

Yes, it checks.

12. a. The slope of the second line is $\frac{1}{2}$.

b. slope $\frac{1}{2}$ and point $(2, 3)$

$3 = \frac{1}{2} \cdot 2 + b$

$3 = 1 + b$

$2 = b$

$y = \frac{1}{2}x + 2$

13. a. slope -3; point $(14, 68)$

b. $68 = -3(14) + b$

$68 = -42 + b$

$110 = b$

$y = -3x + 110$

14. a. slope .10; point $(3, .25)$

b. $.25 = .10(3) + b$

$.25 = .3 + b$

$b = -.05$

$y = .1x - .05$ or

$y = 0.10(x - 3) + .25$

15. a. p

b. n

c. q

16. a. s

b. v

c. u

d. t

17.

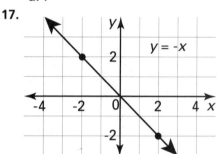

18. Sample: Adam has $45 in a savings account and adds $15 to it each week. After x weeks, he has y total dollars.

19. Compare slopes:

$\frac{3 - -5}{1 - -3} = \frac{8}{4} = 2$; $\frac{3 - 6}{1 - 3} = \frac{-3}{-2} = \frac{3}{2}$

No; $(1, 3)$ and $(-3, -5)$ lie on a line with slope 2, while $(1, 3)$ and $(3, 6)$ lie on a line with slope $\frac{3}{2}$.

20. slope: $\frac{10.86 - 5.91}{10 - 5} = \frac{4.95}{5} = 0.99$

The average cost of long-distance calls between 5 and 10 minutes long is $0.99 per minute.

21. a. A

b. C

22. Elevation (feet)

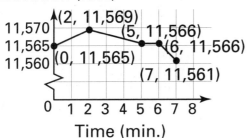

Time (min.)

23. $\frac{7}{10} = \frac{x}{650}$

$10x = 7 \cdot 650$

$10x = 4550$

$x = 455$

Expect 455 adults to drink coffee in the morning.

24. a. $\frac{15}{2} \div \frac{15}{3} = \frac{15}{2} \cdot \frac{3}{15} = \frac{3}{2}$

b. $\frac{a}{2} \div \frac{a}{3} = \frac{a}{2} \cdot \frac{3}{a} = \frac{3}{2}$

c. $\frac{a}{b} \div \frac{a}{c} = \frac{a}{b} \cdot \frac{c}{a} = \frac{c}{b}$

25. a. $n^2 = 24$

$n = \sqrt{24}$ or $n = -\sqrt{24}$

b. $\sqrt{n} = 24$

$n = 24^2$

$n = 576$

c. $n! = 24$

$n = 4$

26. a.–d. Answers will vary.

LESSON 7-6   pp. 450–455

1. slope: $\frac{15-0}{4-1} = \frac{15}{3} = 5$

$0 = 5(1) + b$

$0 = 5 + b$

$b = -5$

$y = 5x + -5$

Check: Substitute (1, 0) to see if it works.

Does $0 = 5(1) + -5$?

$0 = 5 - 5$?

$0 = 0$

Yes, it checks.

2. slope: $\frac{9-3}{1-7} = \frac{6}{-6} = -1$

$9 = -1 \cdot 1 + b$

$9 = -1 + b$

$b = 10$

$y = -x + 10$

Check: Substitute (7, 3) to see if it works.

Does $3 = -1 \cdot 7 + 10$?

$3 = -7 + 10$?

$3 = 3$

Yes, it checks.

3. slope: $\frac{-3--10}{6--8} = \frac{7}{14} = \frac{1}{2}$

$-3 = \frac{1}{2} \cdot 6 + b$

$-3 = 3 + b$

$b = -6$

$y = \frac{1}{2}x + -6$

Check: Substitute (-8, -10) to see if it works.

Does $-10 = \frac{1}{2} \cdot -8 + -6$?

$-10 = -4 + -6$?

$-10 = -10$

Yes, it checks.

4. slope: $\frac{11-0}{0-13} = \frac{11}{-13} = -\frac{11}{13}$

$11 = \frac{-11}{13} \cdot 0 + b$

$11 = b$

$y = \frac{-11}{13}x + 11$

Check: Substitute (13, 0) to see if it works.

Does $0 = \left(\frac{-11}{13}\right)(13) + 11$?

$0 = -11 + 11$?

$0 = 0$

Yes, it checks.

5. René Descartes

6. An 8-minute call would cost $8.88.

$y = 0.99 \cdot 8 + 0.96 = 7.92 + 0.96 = 8.88$

7. slope: $\frac{8.5-4.5}{10-5} = \frac{4}{5} = 0.8$

$8.5 = .8 \cdot 10 + b$

$8.5 = 8 + b$

$.5 = b$

$y = 0.80x + 0.50$

8. linear

9. $70 = \frac{1}{4}x + 37$

$33 = \frac{1}{4}x$

$x = 132$

If the temperature is 70°F, you would expect about 132 chirps per minute.

10. **a.** about 60°F

b. Using the formula:

$y = \frac{1}{4} \cdot 90 + 37$

$y = 22.5 + 37 = 59.5$

The temperature is about 59.5°F.

11. points: (0, 5) and (6, 0)

slope: $\frac{5-0}{0-6} = \frac{5}{-6} = -\frac{5}{6}$

equation: $y = -\frac{5}{6}x + 5$

12. **a.** slope of $\overline{AB}$: $\frac{7-5}{-4-1} = \frac{2}{-5}$

slope of $\overline{BC}$: $\frac{5--1}{1-16} = \frac{6}{-15} = \frac{2}{-5}$

Since the slopes are equal, the points lie on the same line.

b. $7 = \left(-\frac{2}{5}\right) \cdot -4 + b$

$7 = \frac{8}{5} + b$

$b = \frac{27}{5}$

$y = -\frac{2}{5}x + \frac{27}{5}$

13. **a.** slope: $\frac{100-0}{212-32} = \frac{100}{180} = \frac{5}{9}$

$100 = \frac{5}{9} \cdot 212 + b$

$100 = \frac{1060}{9} + b$

$\frac{-160}{9} = b$

$C = \frac{5}{9}F - \frac{160}{9}$

b. When it is 150°F, it is about 65.5°C.

$C = \left(\frac{5}{9}\right)(150) - \frac{160}{9}$

$= \frac{750-160}{9}$

$= \frac{590}{9} \approx 65.5$

c. When it is 150°C, it is 302°F.

$150 = \frac{5}{9}F - \frac{160}{9}$

$1350 = 5F - 160$

$1510 = 5F$

$302 = F$

14. **a.** slope: $\frac{1050-455}{140-60} = \frac{595}{80} \approx 7.4$

b. $455 = 7.4 \cdot 60 + b$

$455 = 444 + b$

$11 = b$

$y = 7.4x + 11$

c. Check: Does $1050 = 7.4 \cdot 140 + 11$?

$1050 = 1036 + 11$?

$1050 = 1047$?

7.4 is an approximation of the actual slope; 1047 is close enough to 1050.

d. If a female has a tail of length 100 mm, then the snake would be about 751 mm long.

$y = 7.4 \cdot 100 + 11$

$= 740 + 11$

$= 751$

15. $S = 180n - 360$

16. **a.** $C = 1.20m + 1.50$

b. Sample: How much would a 10-mile cab ride cost if one uses this cab company?

Solution: $C = 1.20 \cdot 10 + 1.50$

$C = 12.00 + 1.50$

$C = \$13.50$

17. $7 = 7 \cdot 7 + b$

$7 = 49 + b$

$b = -42$

$y = 7x - 42$

18.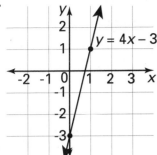

$y = 4x - 3$

19. $\dfrac{5 - -4}{a - -2} = \dfrac{3}{4}$

$\dfrac{9}{a + 2} = \dfrac{3}{4}$

$36 = 3(a + 2)$

$36 = 3a + 6$

$30 = 3a$

$10 = a$

20. a. Between the signs for 15 and 20 miles from Salida the elevation is negative.

b. The rate of change for the entire distance is $\dfrac{1757 - 1744}{20 - 0} = \dfrac{13}{20} \approx .65$ foot per mile.

21. a. $x^2 = 64$

$x = 8$ or $x = -8$

b. $(y - 7)^2 = 64$

$y - 7 = 8$ or $y - 7 = -8$

$y = 15$ or $y = -1$

c. $(3y - 7)^2 = 64$

$3y - 7 = 8$ or $3y - 7 = -8$

$3y = 15$ or $3y = -1$

$y = 5$ or $y = -\dfrac{1}{3}$

22. a. $\dfrac{12}{144} = \dfrac{1}{12}$

b. $\dfrac{3}{3^2} = \dfrac{3}{9} = \dfrac{1}{3}$

c. $\dfrac{d}{d^2} = \dfrac{1}{d}$

23. a.-c. Answers will vary.

IN-CLASS ACTIVITY   pp. 456–457

1.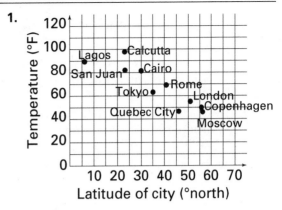

2. Answers will vary. Sample: As the latitude increases the temperature decreases.

3. Samples:

a. 90°; Singapore would probably be like Lagos.

b. 85°; Bombay is at about the same latitude as San Juan.

c. 70°; Madrid is near Rome.

d. 40°; Helsinki is farther north than Moscow and should be colder.

LESSON 7-7   pp. 458–462

1. Latitude signifies how far north or south of the equator a place is located.

2. The latitude of the equator is 0°.

3. Cairo, Egypt, is north of Calcutta, India.

4. To "fit a line by eye" means to take a ruler and draw a line that seems closest to all of the data points in the graph.

5. Estimate the coordinates of two points on the line.

6. a. about 81°F

b. $y = -1.06(25) + 107.6$

$= 81.1$

c. Answers will vary. Sample: 82.8°F

d. They are all close to 82°F.

7. Answers may vary. Sample: My prediction differed from the actual mean temperature by 1.6°F.

8. a. $y = -1.06 \cdot 17 + 107.6$
   $= 89.58$
   The average April high temperature is about 90°F.
   b. Sample: Acapulco is at sea level.
9. a. The latitude of the North Pole is 90° North.
   b. The predicted mean high temperature in April at the North Pole is about 12.2°F. ($y = -1.06(90) + 107.6 = 12.2$)
10. About 26° north; substitute 80 for y in the equation in Example 1.
   $80 = 1.06x + 107.6$
   $-27.6 = 1.06x$
   $26 = x$
11. No; negative values of x would result in values of y that are always greater than 107.6°F.
12. No
13. Yes
14. Yes
15. No
16. a, b.

Temperature F°

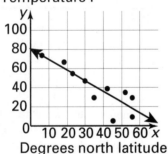

Degrees north latitude

   c. Sample: (6, 74); (30, 47)
   d. slope: $\frac{74-47}{6-30} = \frac{27}{-24} = -\frac{9}{8} = -1.125$
   $74 = -1.125 \cdot 6 + b$
   $74 = -6.75 + b$
   $80.75 = b$
   $y = -1.125x + 80.75$
   e. As you go one degree north, the January low temperature tends to *be about 1° colder*.

f. about 81°F ($y = -1.125 \cdot 0 + 80.75$
   $y = 80.75$)
g. about -21°F ($y = -1.125 \cdot 90 + 80.75$
   $y = -101.25 + 80.75$
   $y = -20.5$)
h. about 62°F ($y = -1.125 \cdot 17 + 80.75$
   $y = -19.125 + 80.75$
   $y = 61.625$)
17. y-intercept: (0, 7); x-intercept: (4, 0)
   slope: $\frac{7-0}{0-4} = -\frac{7}{4}$
   $y = -\frac{7}{4}x + 7$
18. a. $2 = \frac{3}{5} \cdot 3 + b$
   $2 = \frac{9}{5} + b$
   $\frac{1}{5} = b$
   $y = \frac{3}{5}x + \frac{1}{5}$
   b. Sample: $\left(0, \frac{1}{5}\right)$
19. a. $3x + 5y = 2$
   $5y = -3x + 2$
   $y = \frac{-3}{5}x + \frac{2}{5}$
   slope: $\frac{-3}{5}$
   y-intercept: $\frac{2}{5}$
   b.

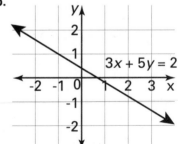

$3x + 5y = 2$

20. **a.** slope: $\frac{-1}{2}$

    b. y-intercept: 0

21. **a.** slope: 0

    b. y-intercept: -2

22. **a.**

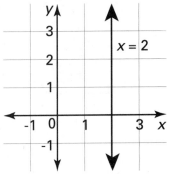

    b. no slope or undefined

23. $\frac{17 \text{ points}}{9 \text{ minutes}} = \frac{x \text{ points}}{48 \text{ minutes}}$

    $816 = 9x$

    $90.\overline{6} = x$

    They would score about 91 points in a 48-minute game.

24. **a.** $8y = 2 + y$

        $7y = 2$

        $y = \frac{2}{7}$

    b. $By = C + y$

       $By - y = C$

    $(B - 1)y = C$

          $y = \frac{C}{B-1}$

25. $2a + 4c$

26. **a.**

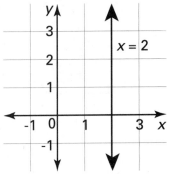

    b.

27. **a.–c.** Answers will vary.

28. Longitude is the distance, east or west, from the great circle through the North Pole and the South Pole passing through Greenwich, England.

1. **a.** $4(3.75) + 3y = 24$

        $15 + 3y = 24$

            $3y = 9$

             $y = 3$

    Each salad cost $3.00.

    b. (3.75, 3)

2. Sample: (3, 4); a sandwich cost $3.00 and a salad cost $4.00.

3. standard form

4. $A = 4$, $B = 2$, and $C = 5$

5. $A = 1$, $B = -8$, and $C = 2$

6. **a.** x-intercept: 10

    $(3x + 5 \cdot 0 = 30$

          $3x = 30$

          $y = 10)$

    y-intercept: 6

    $(3 \cdot 0 + 5y = 30$

          $5y = 30$

          $y = 6)$

    b.

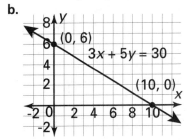

7. **a.** x-intercept: 6

    $(2x - 3 \cdot 0 = 12$

          $2x = 12$

          $x = 6)$

    y-intercept: -4

    $(2 \cdot 0 - 3y = 12$

        $-3y = 12$

          $y = -4)$

7. b.

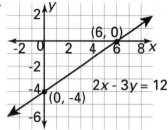

8. vertical lines

9. Every line has an equation in standard form.

10. Sample: (4, 6); (6, 5); (8, 4)

11. a. $4x + 10y = 96$

b. 24 lb of roast beef

$$(4x + 10 \cdot 0 = 96$$
$$4x = 96$$
$$x = 24)$$

c. 9.6 lb of shrimp

$$(4 \cdot 0 + 10y = 96$$
$$10y = 96$$
$$y = 9.6)$$

d.

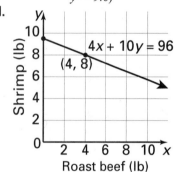

12. a.
$$y = \frac{2}{3}x + 12$$
$$3y = 2x + 36$$
$$-2x + 3y = 36$$

b. $A = -2$, $B = 3$, and $C = 36$

13. a.
$$y = 4x$$
$$-4x + y = 0$$

b. $A = -4$, $B = 1$, and $C = 0$

14. a.
$$y = -8x - 3$$
$$8x + y = -3$$

b. $A = 8$, $B = 1$, and $C = -3$

15. a. $2x + 4y = 100$

b. Samples: (2, 24); (10, 20); (30, 10)

16. a. $5f + s = 36$

b. Samples: (0, 36); (1, 31); (2, 26)

c.

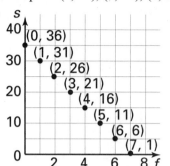

17. a.
$$Ax + By = C$$
$$By = -Ax + C$$
$$y = \frac{-A}{B}x + \frac{C}{B}$$

b. slope: $\frac{-A}{B}$

y-intercept: $\frac{C}{B}$

18. a. x-intercept: 2

y-intercept: 4

b. slope: -2

$$y = -2x + 4$$
$$2x + y = 4$$

19. a.

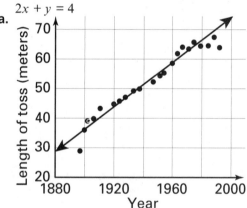

b. We choose points (1900, 36) and (1960, 59).

slope: $\frac{59 - 36}{1960 - 1900} = \frac{23}{60} \approx 0.38$

$$36 = 1900(0.38) + b$$
$$36 = 722 + b$$
$$-686 = b$$
$$y = .38x - 686$$

19. **c.** about 74 meters
    ($y = .38 \cdot 2000 - 686$
      $y = 760 - 686$
      $y = 74$)
  d. Sample: The line is not exact, or there may be a threshold distance beyond which it is physically impossible to throw.

20. slope: $\frac{7-1}{-1-1} = \frac{6}{-2} = -3$
  $7 = (-3)(-1) + b$
  $4 = b$
  $y = -3x + 4$

21. **a.** No; $\frac{0--2}{10-8} = \frac{2}{2} = 1 \neq 2$

  b. Yes; $\frac{18--2}{18-8} = \frac{20}{10} = 2$

22. **a.**

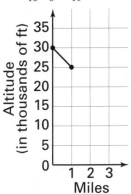

  b. $\frac{-5000 \text{ ft}}{1 \text{ mile}}$

23.

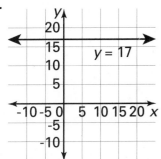

24. No; (Is $0 + 0 < -4$?
               $0 < -4$? No)

25. Yes; (Is $6 \cdot 0 - 0 > -6$?
                  $0 > -6$? Yes)

26. $n > 23$

27. **a.**

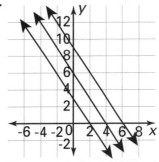

  b. The graph remains parallel to the first line, and slides to the upper-right.

  c. Sample: Try $3x + 2y = -6$. The graph is still parallel to the first line, but slides to the lower-left.

LESSON 7-9   pp. 469–475

1. **a.**

  b.

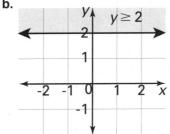

2. **a.**

  b.

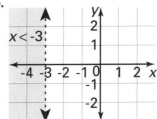

3. $x \geq -3$
4. $y < -100$
5. dashed
6. dashed

7. a. $(0, 0)$

b. You should not choose $(0, 0)$ when it lies on the boundary line.

8.

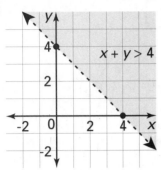

$x + y > 4$

9.

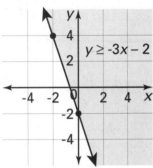

$y \geq -3x - 2$

10.

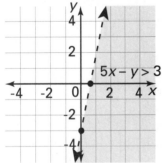

$5x - y > 3$

11.

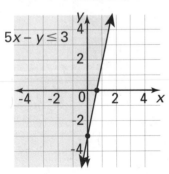

$5x - y \leq 3$

12. a. $.25x + .10y < 4.00$

b.

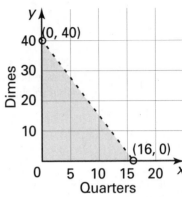

13. a. $2W + T \geq 20$

b.

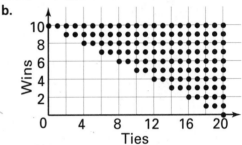

14. a. $10x + 8y \leq 40$

b. Tapes

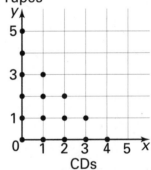

CDs

c. $(1, 0)$; $(1, 1)$; $(1, 2)$; $(1, 3)$; $(2, 0)$; $(2, 1)$; $(2, 2)$; $(3, 0)$; $(3, 1)$

15. a. 6 points

b.

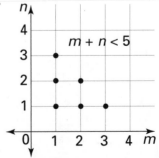

$m + n < 5$

16. a. $4x - 28 = 3y$

$4x - 3y = 28$

b. $A = 4$, $B = -3$, $C = 28$

17. a. Sample: Average annual snowfall is linearly related to latitude.

b. Sample: $y = 5x - 172$

c. Sample: 8 inches

d. Sample: altitude, geographic position

18. $AC^2 = 100^2 + 300^2$

$AC^2 = 10,000 + 90,000$

$AC^2 = 100,000$

$AC \approx 316.2$ yards

$AB + BC = 100 + 300 = 400$

Walking diagonally across the field is shorter by about 83.8 yards $(400 - 316.2 = 83.8)$.

19. $\frac{-100}{300} = -\frac{1}{3}$

20. 4,920,472 men $(.452 \cdot 10,886,000 = 4,920,472)$

21. a. $\frac{50.2\% - 35.8\%}{10} = 1.44\%$

b. $\frac{62.8\% - 50.2\%}{10} = 1.26\%$

c. No

22. a. 125

b. -243

c. 1024

23. a. 0.1

b. 0.03

c. $10 \cdot 10^{-6} = 10^{-5} = 0.00001$

24. Sample: $3 \le x \le 5$ and $8 \le y \le 9.5$

CHAPTER 7

PROGRESS SELF-TEST
p. 479

1. y-intercept: 5

2. x-intercept: 2

3. slope: $\frac{0-5}{2-0} = \frac{-5}{2}$

4. No; the slope of the line between the first two points $\left(\frac{1--5}{-2-4} = \frac{6}{-6} = -1\right)$ is not the same as the slope of the line between the last two points $\left(\frac{1--20}{-2-20} = \frac{21}{-22} = -\frac{21}{22}\right)$.

5. slope: -4

y-intercept: 8

6. slope: $\frac{-5}{2}$

y-intercept: $\frac{1}{2}$

7. $y = \frac{3}{4}x + 13$

8. $-5x + y = -2$

$A = -5$; $B = 1$; $C = -2$

9. The slope of every horizontal line is zero.

10. As you go 1 unit to the right, the height will go up $\frac{3}{5}$ of a unit.

11. 1942 and 1943

12. $\frac{1,889,690 - 3,074,184}{1946 - 1942} = \frac{-1,184,494}{4} =$

-296,123.5 persons per year

13. $2x + y = 67$

14. a.

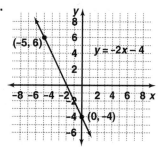

b. $6 = (-2)(-5) + b$

$6 = 10 + b$

$-4 = b$

$y = -2x - 4$

15. slope: $\frac{50-43}{14-12} = \frac{7}{2}$

$50 = \frac{7}{2} \cdot 14 + b$

$50 = 49 + b$

$1 = b$

$y = \frac{7}{2}x + 1$

16.

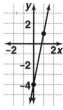

$y = 5x - 4$

17.

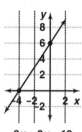

$-3x + 2y = 12$

18.

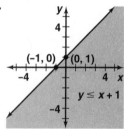

(-1, 0) **(0, 1)**

$y \leq x + 1$

19. c

20. a. $\overline{AB}$
   b. $\overline{DE}$

21. Sample answers for **a.-d.:**
   a. (60, 70); (120, 140)
   b. Slope: $\frac{140 - 70}{120 - 60} = \frac{7}{6}$
   c. $70 = \frac{7}{6} \cdot 60 + b$

   $70 = 70 + b$

   $0 = b$

   $y = \frac{7}{6}x$

   d. $y = \frac{7}{6} \cdot 100$

   $y \approx 117$ ft

---

1. slope: $\frac{2-4}{6-2} = \frac{-2}{4} = -\frac{1}{2}$

2. slope: $\frac{5--2}{1--2} = \frac{7}{3}$

3. slope: $\frac{2--1}{2.5--3} = \frac{3}{5.5} = \frac{6}{11}$ or $.\overline{54}$

4. slope: $\frac{\frac{1}{2}--1}{-3-0} = \frac{1\frac{1}{2}}{-3} = -\frac{1}{2}$

   slope: $\frac{-1--3}{0-4} = \frac{2}{-4} = -\frac{1}{2}$

5. $-2 = \frac{y-10}{8-4}$

   $-2(4) = y - 10$

   $-8 = y - 10$

   $2 = y$

6. $\frac{5}{4} = \frac{y-10}{8-4}$

   $\frac{5}{4} \cdot 4 = y - 10$

   $5 = y - 10$

   $15 = y$

7. $y = 4x + 3$

8. $y = px + q$

9. $1 = (-2)(-4) + b$

   $1 = 8 + b$

   $-7 = b$

   $y = -2x - 7$

10. Horizontal lines have zero slope.
   $y = 10$

11. $\frac{1}{4} = 30(3) + b$

   $\frac{1}{4} = 90 + b$

   $-\frac{359}{5} = b$

   $y = 30x - \frac{359}{4}$

12. Vertical lines have undefined slope.
   $x = 3$

13. slope: $\frac{-2-8}{5--7} = \frac{6}{12} = \frac{1}{2}$

$-2 = \frac{1}{2} \cdot 5 + b$

$-2 = \frac{5}{2} + b$

$-\frac{9}{2} = b$

$y = \frac{1}{2}x - \frac{9}{2}$

14. slope: $\frac{6-4}{0.5-0} = \frac{2}{0.5} = 4$

(0, 4) means $b = 4$ (y-intercept)

$y = 4x + 4$

15. slope: $\frac{9-0}{6-6} = \frac{9}{0}$

The slope is undefined and the line is vertical.

$x = 6$

16. slope: $\frac{2-2}{3--5} = \frac{0}{8} = 0$

The line is horizontal.

$y = 2$

17. $x - 5y = 22$

$A = 1$, $B = -5$, and $C = 22$

18. $y = \frac{2}{5}x + 7$

$5y = 2x + 35$

$-2x + 5y = 35$

$A = -2$, $B = 5$, and $C = 35$

19. $y = -2x + 4$

20. $x + 3y = 11$

$3y = -x + 11$

$y = -\frac{1}{3}x + \frac{11}{3}$

21. slope: 7
y-intercept: -3

22. $4x + 5y = 1$

$5y = -4x + 1$

$y = -\frac{4}{5}x + \frac{1}{5}$

slope: $-\frac{4}{5}$

y-intercept: $\frac{1}{5}$

23. slope: -1
y-intercept: 0

24. $48x - 3y = 30$

$-3y = -48x + 30$

$y = 16x + -10$

slope: 16
y-intercept: -10

25. slope: $\frac{d-b}{c-a}$ or $\frac{b-d}{a-c}$

26. The slope determined by two points is the change in the y-coordinates divided by the *change* in the x-coordinates.

27. Slope is the amount of change in the *height* of the graph for every change of one unit to the *right*.

28. u

29. l and n

30. The slope of any horizontal line is 0.

31. It is undefined.

32. Sample: Check to see if the slope between points A and B is the same as the slope between points B and C.

33. a.

0.46 km

1 km

b. $\frac{0.46 \text{ km}}{1 \text{ km}} = 0.46$

34. slope: $\frac{-250}{1000} = -\frac{1}{4}$

35. $\frac{147.3 - 137.1}{12 - 10} = \frac{10.2}{2} = 5.1$ cm per year

36. $\frac{157.5 - 83.8}{14 - 2} = \frac{73.7}{12} = 6.14$ cm per year

37. a. from birth to 2 years

b. $\frac{83.8 - 50.8}{2 - 0} = \frac{33}{2} = 16.5$ cm per year

38. $\frac{-11 - -3}{8 - 0} = \frac{-8}{8} = -1°$ per hour

39. $\frac{-5 - -3}{24 - 8} = \frac{-2}{16} = -\frac{1}{8} \approx -0.1°$ per hour

40. a. 4 A.M.–6 A.M.

b. $\frac{-11 - -4}{6 - 4} = \frac{-7}{2} = -3.5°$ per hour

41. $y = .25x + 15$
slope: .25
y-intercept: 15
42. $y = -5x + 50$
slope: -5
y-intercept: 50
43. $y = 3x + 50$
44. $y = -5x + 8500$
45. $40 = .2(14) + b$

$40 = 2.8 + b$

$37.2 = b$

$w = .2d + 37.2$
46. $25,500 = 50(3) + b$

$25,500 = 150 + b$

$25,350 = b$

$p = 50m + 25,350$
47. $2.5B + 5L = 25$
48. $1976 = 4(21) + b$

$1976 = 84 + b$

$1892 = b$

$y = 4n + 1892$
49. Sample answers for **a.-e.:**
a.

Women's 400-Meter Freestyle Olympic Winners

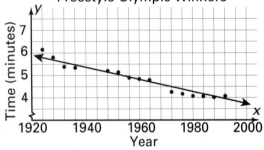

b. about -0.29
c. The Olympic winning times for this event drop (improve) by about .03 $\frac{min}{year}$.
d. $y = -0.029x + 61.7$
e. $y = -0.029(1996) + 61.7$

$y = -57.88 + 61.7$

$y = 3.82$ min or $3:49.2$ min

50. a.

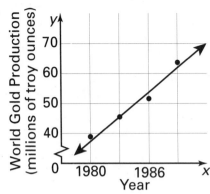

b. Sample: $y = 2.96x - 5824.5$
c. Sample: 80.7 million troy ounces

51.

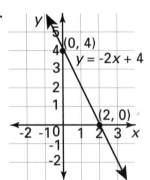

52.

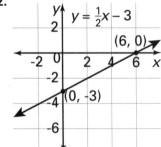

53.

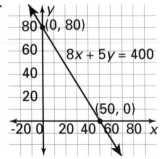

54.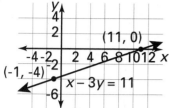

$x - 3y = 11$

55.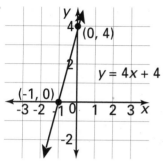

$y = 4x + 4$

56.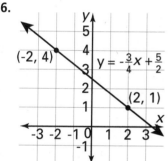

$y = -\frac{3}{4}x + \frac{5}{2}$

57.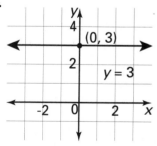

$y = 3$

58.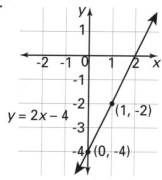

$y = 2x - 4$

59. half-planes

60. Quarters

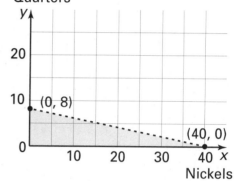

Nickels

61.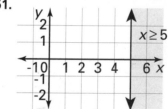

$x \geq 5$

62.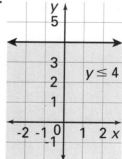

$y \leq 4$

63.

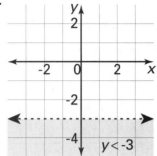

$y < -3$

64.

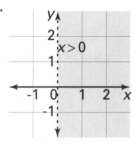

$x > 0$

65.

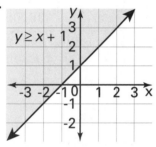

$y \geq x + 1$

66.

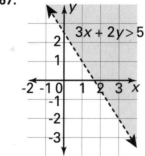

$y < -3x + 2$

67.

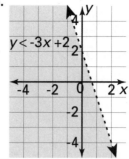

$3x + 2y > 5$

68.

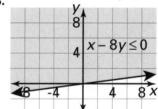

$x - 8y \leq 0$

CHAPTER 8
EXPONENTS AND POWERS

LESSON 8-1
pp. 486–491

1. **a.** $6^3 = 6 \cdot 6 \cdot 6 = 216$
   b. 6 $\boxed{\times}$ 6 $\boxed{\times}$ 6 $\boxed{=}$ 216; or

   6 $\boxed{y^x}$ 3 $\boxed{=}$ 216

2. (1) 100,000
   (2) $100,000 + 2000(50) = 100,000 + 100,000$
   $= 200,000$
   (3) $100,000 \cdot 1.02^{50} = 100,000 \cdot 2.691588$
   $\approx 269,159$

3. **a.** x
   b. x^{10}
   c. 10
   d. 50

4. **a.** (iii)
   b. (ii)
   c. (i)

5. $P(1.06)$

6. $P(1.0275)$

7. **a.** $100(1.03)^5 = 115.93$
   b. \$15.93

8. Each year, the amount in the bank is multiplied by $1 + 0.054 = 1.054$. So, at the end of 1 year, there will be $100(1.054)$; after 2 years, there will be $100(1.054)(1.054) = 100(1.054)^2$; and after 3 years, there will be $100(1.054)(1.054)(1.054) = 100(1.054)^3$.

9. **a.** Compound Interest Formula: If a principal P earns an annual yield of i, then after n years there will be a total T, where $T = P(1 + i)^n$.
   b. T represents the total amount in the account.
   c. P represents the principal, the amount invested.
   d. i is the annual yield.
   e. n represents the number of years the money is invested.

10. Sample: 573 $\boxed{\times}$ 1.063 $\boxed{y^x}$ 24 $\boxed{=}$

11. $150(1 + .04)^5 = 150(1.04)^5 = \$182.50$

12. $2000(1 + .0381)^6 = 2000(1.0381)^6 = \$2503.02$

13. \$232.18 is earned in interest.
    $500(1 + .056)^7 = 500(1.056)^7 = \$732.18$
    $732.18 - 500 = \$232.18)$

14. **a.** Susan: $100(1.05)^2 = \$110.25$
    $110.25 - 100 = \$10.25$ in interest
    Jake: $100(1.10)^2 = \$121$
    $121 - 100 = \$21$ in interest
    b. No; Jake earned more than twice the interest that Susan earned.

15. (a) $P(1.06)^5 \approx P(1.3382)$
    (b) $P(1.10)^3 = P(1.331)$
    More interest can be earned by the conditions in (a).

16. **a.** = 1000 * 1.015 ^ A8
    b. 1109.84
    c. 18%
    $(1180 = 1000(1 + i)^1$
    $1180 = 1000 + 1000i$
    $180 = 1000i$
    $0.18 = i)$

17. **a.** = 1000 * 1.015 ^ A4 − 1000 * 1.015 ^ A3
    b. 15.45

18. It will take about 9 years for the principal to double in value.

19. **a.** $T = 2W + 7$
    b.
    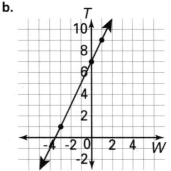

20. $P(\text{prime number: 2, 3, or 5}) = \frac{3}{6} = \frac{1}{2}$

21. $P(\text{jack, queen, or king}) = \frac{12}{52} = \frac{3}{13}$

22. $(1 + x)^2 = 1.1664$

$1 + x = 1.08$ or $1 + x = $ -1.08
$x = 0.08$ or $x = $ -2.08

23. a. $36n$

b. $36n - 84$

c. $-36n + 84$

d. $3n^2 - 7n$

24. (d)

25. $-4\left(\frac{1}{2}\right)^5 = -4\left(\frac{1}{32}\right) = -\frac{1}{8}$

26. $V = \frac{\pi}{6} \cdot 8^3$

$V = \frac{\pi}{6} \cdot 512$

$V = 268 \text{ mm}^3$

27. $t = 6$

28. Answers will vary.

29. a. 1

b. Error

c. Most calculators read "Error." Others will correctly answer "1."

d. Answers may vary depending on the calculator.

LESSON 8-2   pp. 492–497

1. a. 14 times

b. $25(2)^{14} = 25(16,384) = 409,600$ rabbits

2. $25(2)^{20} = 25(1,048,576) = 26,214,400$ rabbits

3. $25(3)^{10} = 25(59,049) = 1,476,225$ rabbits

4. $22(2)^{30} = 22(1,073,741,824) \approx 23,622,000,000$ rabbits

5. Growth Model for Powering: If a quantity is multiplied by a positive number g (the growth factor) in each of x time periods, the quantity will be multiplied by g^x.

6. a. 1.035

b. 1 year

c. $1.035^2 = 1.071225$

7. False; the amount will be multiplied by $10^7 = 10,000,000$.

8. Zero Exponent Property: If g is any nonzero real number, then $g^0 = 1$.

9. $17^0 = 1$

10. A period of length 0 means no time has elapsed, so a quantity multiplied by g^0 doesn't change. This means $g^0 = 1$.

11. a.

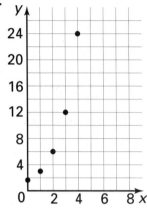

b. The curve is the exponential growth curve.

12. 1.32

13. a. The growth factor would be 1.2.

b. $29,760,021(1.2) = 35,712,025$

14. a.

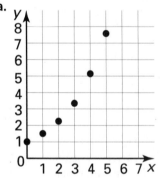

b. rate of change: $\frac{1.5^1 - 1.5^0}{1 - 0} = \frac{1.5 - 1}{1} = .5$

c. rate of change:

$\frac{1.5^5 - 1.5^4}{5 - 4} = \frac{7.59375 - 5.0625}{1} = 2.53125$

d. Sample: the rate of change is increasing as x increases.

15. a. 20 minutes

b. 6 times

c. $2000(3)^6 = 1,458,000$ bacteria

d. $2000(3)^{12} \approx 1,062,882,000$ bacteria

16. a. $2,466,000(1.011)^5 = 2,604,647$
b. $2,466,000(1.011)^{20} = 3,069,136$

17. $4.065(1.125)^2 \approx \$5.14$ trillion

18. $\left(4 \cdot \frac{1}{2}\right)^0 = 1$

19. $7^0 \cdot 7^1 \cdot 7^2 = 1 \cdot 7 \cdot 49 = 343$

20. $6(3 + \text{-}8)^0 = 6 \cdot 1 = 6$

21. $\frac{2}{3} \cdot 1 + \frac{1}{2} \cdot \frac{4}{9} = \frac{2}{3} + \frac{2}{9}$
$= \frac{6}{9} + \frac{2}{9}$
$= \frac{8}{9}$

22. a. $2200(1.06)^6 = \$3120.74$
b. $3120.74 - 2200 = \$920.74$

23. $P(a, e, \text{or } i) = \frac{3}{26}$

24. a. $y^2 = 144$
$y = 12$ or $y = \text{-}12$
b. $(4y)^2 = 144$
$4y = 12$ or $4y = \text{-}12$
$y = 3$ or $y = \text{-}3$
c. $(4y - 20)^2 = 144$
$4y - 20 = 12$ or $4y - 20 = \text{-}12$
$4y = 32$ or $4y = 8$
$y = 8$ or $y = 2$
d. $y^2 + 80 = 144$
$y^2 = 64$
$y = 8$ or $y = \text{-}8$

25. $6(n + 8) + 4(2n - 1) = 6n + 48 + 8n - 4 = 14n + 44$

26. $13 - (2 - x) = 13 - 2 + x = 11 + x$

27. $4 \cdot \left(\frac{1}{2}\right)^9 = 4 \cdot \frac{1}{512} = \frac{1}{128}$

28. $11^2 \cdot 11^3 = 121 \cdot 1331 = 161,051$

29. a. $1^0 = 1; 0.1^0 = 1; 0.01^0 = 1; 0.001^0 = 1.$
This suggests $0^0 = 1$.
b. $0^1 = 0; 0^{0.1} = 0; 0^{0.01} = 0; 0^{0.001} = 0.$
This suggests $0^0 = 0$
c. Error message. 0^0 cannot equal both 0 and 1, so 0^0 is undefined.

30. $2^{63} \approx 9.22 \times 10^{18}$ grains of wheat

1. Sample: In constant-increase situations, a number is repeatedly added; in exponential-growth situations, a number is repeatedly multiplied.

2. $y = 100(1.06)^x$

3. (1): $10 + 50(30) = 10 + 1500 = \$1510$
(2): $10(1.5)^{30} = 1,917,510.59$

4. the tenth day

5. | 18 | 15 | 760 | 4378.94 |

6. The graph of $y = 10 + 5x$ is a line.
The graph of $y = 10 \cdot 1.5^x$ is a curve.

7. a. $y = mx + b$ where $m > 0$
b. $y = b \cdot g^x$ where $g > 1$

8. $\$240 - \$190 = \$50$

9. about 27.5 years

10. a. linear
b. line

11. a. linear
b. line

12. a. exponential
b. curve

13. a. exponential
b. curve

14. $2(1.2)^6 \approx 6$ cm
$3(1.2)^6 \approx 9$ cm
The picture can be enlarged to about 6 cm by 9 cm.

15. a.

	A	B	C
1	years from now	constant increase	exponential
2	0	2520	2520
3	1	2640	2646
4	2	2760	2778
5	3	2880	2917
6	4	3000	3063
7	5	3120	3216

15. b. There are 96 more students if the growth is exponential.

c. 2520 + 120(15) = 4320 students

d. $2520(1.05)^{15}$ = 5239 students

16. (d)   **17.** (c)

18. (a)   **19.** (b)

20. a. $-4(1.2)^3 = -4(1.728) = -6.912$

b. $4(-1.2)^0 = 4(1) = 4$

21. a. 100 * 1.06 ^ YEAR

b. 20   320.7135

c. 30 FOR YEAR = 1 TO 100

d. 100   33930.2084

22. $x \cdot x \cdot x \cdot x \cdot x$

23. a. Sample:

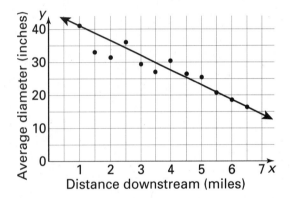

b. Sample: (1, 41) and (6, 19)

c. slope: $\frac{41-19}{1-6} = \frac{22}{-5} = -4.4$

$41 = -4.4(1) + b$

$45.4 = b$

$y = -4.4x + 45.4$

d. $y = -4.4(7.5) + 45.4$

$y = -33 + 45.4$

$y = 12.4$ in.

24. $1.3d + 5.2 = 9.4d - 9.0$

$5.2 = 8.1d - 9$

$14.2 = 8.1d$

$1.75 = d$

25. $4a^2(a + 3) + 2a(a^2 - 1)$

$= 4a^3 + 12a^2 + 2a^3 - 2a$

$= 6a^3 + 12a^2 - 2a$

26. $b(b + 3) - b(b + 1) = b^2 + 3b - b^2 - b = 2b$

27. a. $\frac{9}{x}$ **b.** $\frac{8}{2y} + \frac{5}{2y} = \frac{13}{2y}$

c. $\frac{8z}{2z} + \frac{5}{2z} = \frac{8z + 5}{2z}$

28. a. 200(.90) = $180   **b.** 200(.80) = $160

c. 200(.67) = $134

29. $(2 \cdot 4)^2(3 \cdot -2)^3 = 8^2 \cdot (-6)^3$

$= 64 \cdot (-216)$

$= -13,824$

30. $y = 100(1.06)^{-1} = 94.34$

$y = 100(1.06)^{-2} = 89$

The answers give the amount in the account 1 and 2 years ago respectively.

LESSON 8-4   pp. 505–509

1. $100(.80)^8 = 16.78$

approximately 17 words

2. $100(.80)^3 = 51.2$ The student forgot about $100 - 51 = 49$ words the first 3 days.

3. $100(.80)^6 = 26.2$ The student forgot about $51 - 26 = 25$ words the second 3 days.

4. $100(.80)^5 \approx 33$ About 33 words will be remembered on the 5th day if 20% of the words are forgotten each day.

5. Exponential Decay: $y = b \cdot g^x$, $0 < g < 1$

6. The shape of the constant decrease graph is linear, while the shape of the exponential decay graph is curved.

7. (c) since $0 < g < 1$

8. The growth factor must be greater than 0 and less than 1. $(0 < g < 1)$

9. $67,000(0.95)^1 = 63,650$

10. $67,000(0.95)^n$

11. Multiply by .937 each year to find the population. $(100 - 0.063 = 0.937)$

12. a. Multiply by 0.97. $(100 - 0.03 = 0.97)$

b. $2500(.97)^n$

c. $2500(.97)^{10} \approx 1843.56$ or about 1844 students

13. True; $0 < \frac{1}{2} < 1$

14.

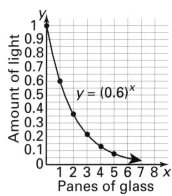

15. a. As f increases, A decays exponentially; the growth factor is $\frac{1}{2}$.

b. As f increases, t grows exponentially; the growth factor is 2.

16. a.

x	y as a fraction	y as a decimal
0	1	1
1	$\frac{1}{2}$	0.5
2	$\frac{1}{4}$	0.25
3	$\frac{1}{8}$	0.125
10	$\frac{1}{1024}$	≈ 0.001
20	$\frac{1}{1,048,576}$	≈ 0.000001

b.

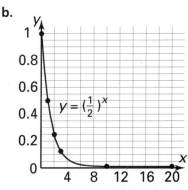

c. No; there is no power of $\frac{1}{2}$ that equals 0.

17. a. 5832 ($8 * 3 \wedge 6 = 8 * 729 = 5832$)

b. 1.033174×10^{-2} ($8 * 0.33 \wedge 6 =$ $8 * 0.00129 = 1.033174 \times 10^{-2}$)

c. $P = 100,000$; $X = 1.02$; $N = 10$

18. The last child received $0.07 or 7 cents.

$\left(\text{Inheritance} = 300,000 \cdot \left(\frac{1}{4}\right)^{n-1} \text{ where}\right.$

n represents the birth number of the child.

$\left. 300,000 \cdot \left(\frac{1}{4}\right)^{11} = 0.07152\right)$

19. $k = 30(1.05)^n$ increases more rapidly since it is exponential and the other graph is linear.

20. $k = 30(1.05)^n$ could represent compound interest because compound interest is an example of exponential growth.

21. $5,170,000(1.027)^7 \approx 6,230,000$ people

22. a. $6 \cdot 2^4 = 6 \cdot 16 = 96$ guppies

b. $6 \cdot 2^{12} = 6 \cdot 4096 = 24,576$ guppies

23. 1

24. $500(1.061)^5 - 500 = 500(1.3445499) - 500 =$ $672.27495 - 500 = \$172.27$

25. a. $V = y \cdot \frac{3}{4}y \cdot \frac{2}{3}y = \frac{1}{2}y^3$ cubic units

b. Sample: $\frac{1}{2}y, y, y$

26. a. $14 = 2 \cdot 7$

b. $40 = 2 \cdot 2 \cdot 2 \cdot 5$

c. $81 = 3 \cdot 3 \cdot 3 \cdot 3$

27. a. The half-life of an element is the time it takes for one half the amount of the element to decay.

b. Originally, the bone had C units of carbon-14 and was found with $\frac{1}{16}$ units,

so $\frac{1}{16}C = C\left(\frac{1}{2}\right)^n$.

This gives $n = 4$. The bone is $4(5600) =$ 22,400 years old.

LESSON 8-5 pp. 510–514

1. a. $b^6 = b \cdot b \cdot b \cdot b \cdot b \cdot b$

b. b^6 is the growth factor after 6 unit periods if there is growth by a factor b in each of 6 unit periods.

2. $3^{2+4} = 3^6$

3. $10^{5+2} = 10^7$

4. a. a^5

   b. Does $(-2)^2 \cdot (-2)^3 = (-2)^5$?

              $4 \cdot -8 = -32$?

              $-32 = -32$

     Yes, it checks.

5. Product of Powers Property: For all m and n, and all nonzero b, $b^m \cdot b^n = b^{m+n}$.

6. a. $2000 \cdot 2^{11}$

   b. $2000 \cdot 2^{17}$

   c. $x^{11} \cdot x^6 = x^{17}$

7. Power of a Power Property: For all m and n, and nonzero b, $(b^m)^n = b^{mn}$.

8. $2^{12} = 4096$

9. $(7^2)^3 = 7^6 = 117,649$

10. $x = 15$ $(3 \cdot 5 = 15$; Power of a Power Property)

11. $x^{5+50} = x^{55}$

12. $k^{10 \cdot 3} = k^{30}$

13. $n^{2 \cdot 6} = n^{12}$

14. $a^{3+5+2} \cdot b^{0+9} = a^{10}b^9$

15. $a^3 b^{3+5} = a^3 b^8$

16. $4n^{3+2 \cdot 10} = 4n^{23}$

17. $a = 7$ $(5 + a = 12$

            $a = 7)$

18. $x = 4$ $(2x = 8$

           $x = 4)$

19. Sample: x^1, x^6; x^3, x^4; x^0, x^7

20. a. 2^{10}

   b. 2^5

   c. 2^{15}

   d. $2^{10} \cdot 2^5 = 2^{15}$ uses the Product of Powers Property.

21. a. $P \cdot 3^5$

   b. Twelve days after the fifth day the bacteria will be $P \cdot 3^{17}$.

22. $x^6 - x^6 = 0$

23. $2x^{3+4} = 2x^7$

24. $15m^{4+2} = 15m^6$

25. $(x^{3+4})^2 = x^{7 \cdot 2} = x^{14}$

26. $a^{3+2} + 4a^{4+2} = a^5 + 4a^6$

27. $y^{7+1} - y^{2+1} = y^8 - y^3$

28. True; the tenth power of x^2 is $(x^2)^{10} = x^{20}$ and the square of x^{10} is $(x^{10})^2 = x^{20}$.

29.

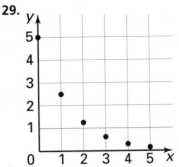

30. a. $2,500,000(1.045)^y$

   b. $2,500,000(0.97)^y$

   c. $2,500,000 - 2500y$

31. Sample: the population T of a city of 5000 that is growing at a rate of 3.5% per year, n years from now

32. a. $7y - 2x + 9x = 19 + 7$

         $7x + 7y = 26$

   b. $7y - 7 = -7x + 19$

        $7y = -7x + 26$

        $y = -x + \frac{26}{7}$

33. The club should charge $4.49 per pound to break even on their costs.

   $(50 \cdot 3.49 + 20 \cdot 6.99 = 174.5 + 139.80 = 314.3$

          $\frac{314.3}{70} = 4.49)$

34. $2^{15} = 32,768$ ways

35. a.

n	$(-1)^n$
1	-1
2	1
3	-1
4	1
5	-1
6	1
7	-1
8	1

   b. 1

36. $4,000,000,000 = 4 \times 10^9$

37. $0.00036 = 3.6 \times 10^{-4}$

38. a. milli-   **b.** mega-
   c. micro-   **d.** giga-
   e. nano-   **f.** tera-
   g. pico-   **h.** peta-
   i. femto-   **j.** exa-
   k. atto-

LESSON 8-6   pp. 515–520

1. a. $4^{-1} = \frac{1}{4}$

   $4^{-2} = \frac{1}{4^2} = \frac{1}{16}$

   $4^{-3} = \frac{1}{4^3} = \frac{1}{64}$

   $4^{-4} = \frac{1}{4^4} = \frac{1}{256}$

b. False

2. (d)

3. a. $10^{-9} = 0.000000001$

   b. $10^{-9} = \frac{1}{10^9} = \frac{1}{1,000,000,000}$

4. reciprocal

5. $\frac{1}{5^2} = \frac{1}{25}$

6. $\frac{1}{3^6} = \frac{1}{729}$

7. $\frac{1}{\frac{1}{2}} = 1 \div \frac{1}{2} = 2$

8. $\frac{x^5}{y^2}$

9. $\frac{3}{a^2 b^4}$

10. $\frac{1}{2^n}$

11. P (red 5 times in 5 spins) $= \left(\frac{1}{3}\right)^5 = \frac{1}{243}$ or about 0.004

12. True

13. $5^{3+-3} = 5^0 = 1$

14. $c^{j+-j} = c^0 = 1$

15. $x^{4 \cdot -2} = x^{-8} = \frac{1}{x^8}$

16. $a^{-3 \cdot 4} = a^{-12} = \frac{1}{a^{12}}$

17. Mr. Cabot's CD was worth about $3434.58 one year ago. $(3675(1.07)^{-1} = 3675(0.9345794) = 3434.5794)$

18. Theresa had $821.12 in her account 8 years ago. $(1236.47(1.0525)^{-8} = 1236.47(0.6640842) = 821.12023)$

19. a.

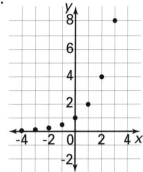

   b. As x becomes smaller and smaller, the y-coordinate approaches zero.

20. $n = -11$

21. $3^{10} \cdot 3^{-12} = 3^z$

      $3^{-2} = 3^z$

      $-2 = z$

   Check: Does $3^{10} \cdot 3^{-12} = 3^{-2}$

      $59,049 \cdot \frac{1}{531,441} = \frac{1}{9}$?

                 $\frac{1}{9} = \frac{1}{9}$

   Yes, it checks.

22. $5^6 \cdot 5^y = 5^{-9}$

      $5^{6+y} = 5^{-9}$

      $6 + y = -9$

         $y = -15$

   Check: Does $5^6 \cdot 5^{-15} = 5^{-9}$?

      $15,625 \cdot \frac{1}{30,517,578,125} = \frac{1}{1,953,125}$?

           $\frac{1}{1,953,125} = \frac{1}{1,953,125}$

   Yes, it checks.

23. $t^{-2+-4} = t^{-6}$

24. $x^{5+-3} y^{3+-5} = x^2 y^{-2}$

25. a. $P = 5 \cdot (1.017)^{1994-1985}$
      $P = 5 \cdot (1.017)^9$
      $P = 5.819$
   The estimated population is 5.82 billion.

   b. $P = 5 \cdot (1.017)^{1980-1985}$
      $P = 5 \cdot (1.017)^{-5}$
      $P = 4.5958$
   The estimated population is 4.60 billion.

26. a. $30{,}000 + 500 + 60 + 2 + .4 + .007 = 30{,}562.407$
   b. $9000 + 800 + 70 + 6 + .5 + .04 + .0009 =$ 9876.5409

27. $12x^3$

28. a^8

29. $12c^7 + 10c^7 = 22c^7$

30. y^{m+n+p}

31. (c)

32. a. The population doubles 16 times in 2 days.
   b. $25 \cdot 2^{16} = 25 \cdot 65{,}536 = 1{,}638{,}400$

33. $y - {-1} = -5(x - 2)$
   $y + 1 = -5x + 10$
     $y = -5x + 9$

34. a. slope: 2
   b. y-intercept: -3
   c.

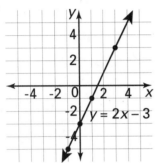

35. a. $28a - 8$
   b. $28a - 8 - (15a + 3) = 13a - 11$
   c. $13a - 11 = 15$
      $13a = 26$
        $a = 2$

36. $\frac{9x}{12x} = \frac{3}{4}$

37. a. Samples: $\left(\frac{1}{2}\right)^3 = \frac{1}{2} \cdot \frac{1}{2} \cdot \frac{1}{2} = \frac{1}{8}$
               $\left(\frac{1}{2}\right)^4 = \frac{1}{2} \cdot \frac{1}{2} \cdot \frac{1}{2} \cdot \frac{1}{2} = \frac{1}{16}$
               $\left(\frac{1}{2}\right)^{-3} = \frac{1}{\left(\frac{1}{2}\right)^3} = \frac{1}{\frac{1}{8}} = 8$
   b. Powers of $\frac{1}{2}$ are reciprocals of the corresponding powers of 2.
   c. $\left(\frac{1}{x}\right)^n = x^{-n}$

1. $2^6 \cdot 2^8 = 2^{14}$

2. $2^{10} \div 2^4 = 2^6$

3. Quotient of Powers Property: For all m and n, and all nonzero b, $\frac{b^m}{b^n} = b^{m-n}$.

4. a. $3^{8-2} = 3^6$
   b. Check: By calculator $\frac{3^8}{3^2} = 729$ and
      $3^6 = 729$. It checks.

5. a. $3^{2-8} = 3^{-6}$
   b. Check: By calculator $\frac{3^2}{3^8} = 0.0013717$ and
      $3^{-6} = 0.0013717$. It checks.

6. $x^{12-6} = x^6$

7. $y^{5-5} = y^0 = 1$

8. $19.2^{4-6} = 19.2^{-2} = \frac{1}{368.64}$

9. $\frac{9.5}{1.9} \cdot 10^{12-4} = 5 \cdot 10^8$

10. $\frac{3}{42} \cdot w^{2-2} \cdot z^{6-3} = \frac{1}{14} \cdot 1 \cdot z^3 = \frac{z^3}{14}$

11. $\frac{4}{28} \cdot a^{1-2} \cdot b^{1-5} \cdot c^{10-1} = \frac{1}{7} \cdot a^{-1} \cdot b^{-4} \cdot c^9 = \frac{c^9}{7ab^4}$

12. The bases are different.

13. $\frac{1.11 \cdot 10^9}{2.56 \cdot 10^8} \approx 0.434 \cdot 10^1 \approx 4.3 \, \frac{\text{five-dollar bills}}{\text{person}}$

14. $b^0 = 1$

15. $\frac{6 \cdot 10^9}{2.56 \cdot 10^8} \approx 2.34 \cdot 10^1 \approx 23 \, \frac{\text{pounds}}{\text{person}}$

16. $3^{-8--2} = 3^{-6}$

17. $3^{-2--8} = 3^6$

18. $x^{-2--8} = x^6$

19. $x^{-2n--3n} = x^n$

20. $(7m)^{2-3} = (7m)^{-1}$

21. $(x + 3)^0 = 1$

22. $3 \cdot x^{2-9} \cdot y^{5-3} = 3x^{-7}y^2$

23. $\frac{5p^5}{p^4} = 5p$

24. Sample: $\frac{16x^7}{2x^2}$

25. $\frac{5.87 \cdot 10^5}{1.48 \cdot 10^6} \approx 4 \cdot 10^{-1} \approx 0.40 \, \frac{\text{people}}{\text{km}^2}$

26. a. $\frac{1}{2^6} = \frac{1}{64}$

    b. 0.015625

27. 4^{x+y}

28. $-2y^{12}$

29. $-2y^{4 \cdot 3 + 4} = -2y^{16}$

30. a. $\left(\frac{1}{6}\right)^5 = \frac{1}{7776}$

    b. 6^{-5}

31. $x^{5+5+5} = x^{15}$

    Check: Does $3^5 \cdot 3^5 \cdot 3^5 = 3^{15}$?

          $243 \cdot 243 \cdot 243 = 14{,}348{,}907$?

                $14{,}348{,}907 = 14{,}348{,}907$

    Yes, it checks.

32. Milo: $3000(1.10)^{10} = 3000(2.59374)$

                      $= \$7781.23$

    Sylvia: $6000(1.05)^5 = 6000(1.27628)$

                      $= \$7657.69$

    Milo would have more money.

33. a. slope: -2; y-intercept: 54; the elevator descends at a rate of 2 floors per second and started on the 54th floor.

    b.

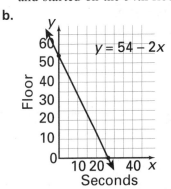

34. $\frac{2^2}{3^2} = \frac{4}{9}$

35. ratio of sides: $\frac{40}{4} = \frac{10}{1}$

    ratio of volumes: $\frac{10^3}{1^3} = \frac{1000}{1}$

    The larger box holds 1000 times as much as the smaller box.

36. a. $2(12 + 2x + 4) = 2(2x + 16) = 4x + 32$ units

    b. $12(2x + 4) = 24x + 48$ square units

    c. $312 = 24x + 48$

        $264 = 24x$

         $11 = x$

37. a. Answers will vary.

    b. people: $5.5 \cdot 10^9 \cdot 4 \text{ ft}^3 = 2.2 \cdot 10^{10} \text{ ft}^3$
cubic mile: $5280^3 \text{ ft}^3 = 1.47 \cdot 10^{11} \text{ ft}^3$
$1.47 \cdot 10^{11} - 2.2 \cdot 10^{10} = 1.47 \cdot 10^{11} - 0.22 \cdot 10^{11} \approx 1.25 \cdot 10^{11} \text{ ft}^3$
The volume of all the people is less by about $1.25 \cdot 10^{11} \text{ ft}^3$.

LESSON 8-8   pp. 527–532

1. a. $5^3 x^3 = 125 x^3$

    b. $(5 \cdot 2)^3 = 10^3 = 1000$;
$125 \cdot 2^3 = 125 \cdot 8 = 1000$

2. a. $12.5^3 = 1953.125 \text{ ft}^3$

    b. $25^3 = 15{,}625 \text{ ft}^3$ or $(2 \cdot 12.5)^3 = 8 \cdot 12.5^3 = 8 \cdot 1953.125 = 15{,}625 \text{ ft}^3$

3. a. $k^3 \text{ in}^3$

    b. $(5k)^3 \text{ in}^3 = 125 k^3 \text{ in}^3$

4. $1.3^5 \cdot 10^{4 \cdot 5} \approx 3.7 \cdot 10^{20}$

5. a. $V = \frac{4}{3}\pi r^3$

        $V = \frac{4}{3}\pi(1.738 \cdot 10^3)^3$

        $V = 21.99 \cdot 10^9 \text{ km}^3$

        $V = 2.1991 \cdot 10^{10} \text{ km}^3$

    b. $V = 21{,}991{,}000{,}000 \text{ km}^3$

6. $\frac{1}{16}$

7. $\frac{343}{1000}$

8. True

9. True

10. a. $-1 \cdot 3^2 = -9$

    b. $-3 \cdot -3 = 9$

    c. $-1 \cdot 5^3 = -125$

    d. $-5 \cdot -5 \cdot -5 = -125$

    e. $-5 \cdot -5 \cdot -5 \cdot -5 = 625$

    f. $-1 \cdot 5^4 = -625$

11. $a^3 b^3$

12. $3^2 x^{3 \cdot 2} = 9x^6$

13. $\dfrac{l^3}{s^3}$

14. $8^3 y^3 = 512 y^3$

15. $(-1)^9 \cdot a^9 \cdot b^9 = -a^9 b^9$

16. $\dfrac{a^3}{b^{5 \cdot 3}} = \dfrac{a^3}{b^{15}}$

17. $\dfrac{1}{2} \cdot 36x^2 = 18x^2$

18. 1

19. $\dfrac{u^t}{3^t}$

20. $4L \cdot \dfrac{25k^2}{L^2} = \dfrac{100k^2}{L}$

21. $\left(\dfrac{2^4}{7^4} z^4\right) \cdot z = \dfrac{16}{2401} z^4 \cdot z = \dfrac{16z^5}{2401}$

22. $32q^5 \cdot 9q^{4 \cdot 2} = 288q^{5+8} = 288q^{13}$

23. **a.** $\left(1 - \dfrac{1}{3}\right)^5 = \left(\dfrac{2}{3}\right)^5 = \dfrac{32}{243} \approx 0.13$

   b. Example 4

24. (e)

25. (a)

26. (d)

27. $(4x)^{8-5} = (4x)^3 = (4 \cdot 3)^3 = 12^3 = 1728$

28. **a.** Sample: Let $x = 1$. Then $3(5(1)^4)^2$

$$= 3(5 \cdot 1)^2$$
$$= 3(5)^2$$
$$= 3 \cdot 25$$
$$= 75;$$

however, $15(1)^6 = 15 \cdot 1 = 15$.

   b. Sample: To simplify correctly, use the Power of a Product Property and the Power of a Power Property as follows:

$$3(5x^4)^2 = 3 \cdot 5^2 \cdot (x^4)^2$$
$$= 3 \cdot 25x^{4 \cdot 2}$$
$$= 75x^8$$

29. $\dfrac{2n^2}{10n^2} = \dfrac{1}{5}$

30. $4 \cdot 10^{13}$ km $\cdot \dfrac{3}{3.8 \cdot 10^5} \dfrac{\text{days}}{\text{km}} = \dfrac{12}{3.8} \cdot 10^{13-5}$ days $=$ $3.16 \cdot 10^8$ days

31. $k^{12-9} = k^3$

32. $y^{1+3} = y^4$

33. $v^{-2 \cdot 3} = v^{-6}$

34. $(5^4)^3 > 5^4 \cdot 5^3$

$$5^{4 \cdot 3} > 5^{4+3}$$
$$5^{12} > 5^7$$

35. **a.** $2x^5$

   b. $x \cdot x^8 = x^9$

   c. $(x^5)^2 = x^{10}$

36. **a.**

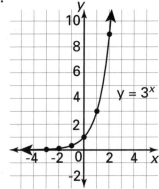

$y = 3^x$

   b. exponential growth curve

37. **a.** $6(\$1 - 2\text{¢}) = \$6 - 12\text{¢} = \$5.88$

   b. $4(\$15 + 5\text{¢}) = \$60 + 20\text{¢} = \$60.20$

   c. $.15 \cdot \$40 = \$6.00$

38. Samples:

   a. 3^4 or 9^2

   b. 16^2 or 2^8

   c. 32^3 or 2^{15}

   d. 3^{16} or 9^8

LESSON 8-9   pp. 533–538

1. **a.** $\dfrac{8}{125}$

   b. $\dfrac{1}{\left(\frac{5}{2}\right)^3} = \dfrac{1}{\frac{5}{2}} \cdot \dfrac{1}{\frac{5}{2}} \cdot \dfrac{1}{\frac{5}{2}} = \dfrac{1}{\frac{125}{8}} = \dfrac{8}{125}$

2. **a.** $\dfrac{64}{27}$

   b. $\dfrac{1}{\left(\frac{3}{4}\right)^3} = \dfrac{1}{\frac{3}{4}} \cdot \dfrac{1}{\frac{3}{4}} \cdot \dfrac{1}{\frac{3}{4}} = \dfrac{1}{\frac{27}{64}} = \dfrac{64}{27}$

3. (b); sample: Let $x = 3$. Then $\dfrac{x^6}{x^3} = \dfrac{3^6}{3^3} = \dfrac{729}{27} = 27$ and $x^3 = 3^3 = 27$.

4. (d); sample: Let $m = 3$ and $n = 2$. Then $\left(\frac{m}{n}\right)^2 = \left(\frac{3}{2}\right)^2 = \frac{9}{4}$ and $\frac{m^2}{n^2} = \frac{3^2}{2^2} = \frac{9}{4}$.

5. (c); $\left(\frac{3x}{y}\right)^{-2} = \frac{1}{\left(\frac{3x}{y}\right)^2} = \frac{1}{\frac{9x^2}{y^2}} = \frac{y^2}{9x^2}$

6. a. True
  b. True
  c. True
  d. False: $3^4 = 81$ and $4 \cdot 3^2 = 4 \cdot 9 = 36$

7. False

8. True

9. A counterexample is a special case for which a pattern is false.

10. $\left(\frac{x^8}{x^4}\right)^{-2} = \frac{x^{-16}}{x^{-8}} = x^{-16--8} = x^{-8} = \frac{1}{x^8}$

$\left(\frac{x^8}{x^4}\right)^{-2} = (x^{8--4})^{-2}) = (x^4)^{-2} = x^{-8} = \frac{1}{x^8}$

11. Sample: Let $x = 3$. Then $(2x)^3 = (2 \cdot 3)^3 = 6^3 = 216$ and $2x^3 = 2 \cdot 3^3 = 2 \cdot 27 = 54$.

12. Product of Powers Property

13. Power of a Product Property

14. Power of a Quotient Property

15. Negative Exponent Property

16. a. Yes. $\frac{1}{4} + \frac{1}{3} = \frac{3+4}{3 \cdot 4} = \frac{7}{12}$

  b. Sample: Let $z = y = 3$. Then $\frac{1}{z} + \frac{1}{y} = \frac{1}{3} + \frac{1}{3} = \frac{2}{3}$ and $\frac{y+z}{yz} = \frac{3+3}{3 \cdot 3} = \frac{6}{9} = \frac{2}{3}$.

  c. $\frac{1}{z} + \frac{1}{y} = \frac{1}{2} + \frac{1}{5} = .5 + .2 = .7$ and $\frac{y+z}{yz} = \frac{5+2}{5 \cdot 2} = \frac{7}{10} = .7$

  d. Yes

17. Sample: Let $a = 2$ and $b = 3$. Then $2^2 + 3^2 = 13$ and $(2 + 3)^2 = 5^2 = 25$. The counterexample shows that the pattern is not true.

18. Sample: Let the price be $100. A 30% discount gives $.7(100) = \$70$. Another 10% discount gives $.9(70) = \$63$. So you are paying 63% of the original price.

19. $\frac{81}{625x^4} \cdot \frac{4}{9} = \frac{36}{625x^4}$

20. $x^5 \cdot \frac{9}{x^2} = 9x^3$

21. $100 \cdot \frac{a^9}{8b^3} = \frac{25a^9}{2b^3}$

22. a. $\frac{4}{3}\pi \cdot 3^3 = 36\pi$

  b. $\frac{4}{3}\pi \cdot (3k)^3 = 36\pi k^3$

23. $\frac{6n^5}{x} = 3n$

$6n^5 = 3nx$

$\frac{6n^5}{3n} = x$

$2n^4 = x$

24. $100{,}892{,}000 \cdot \$649 \approx 6.55 \cdot 10^{10} = 65.5$ billion dollars

25. $a + 10 = 30$
$a = 20$

26. $k = -7$

27. $((2^{14})^9)^2 < (2^{14})^{92} < 2^{1492}$
$2^{14 \cdot 9 \cdot 2} < 2^{14 \cdot 92} < 2^{1492}$
$2^{252} < 2^{1288} < 2^{1492}$
2^{1492} is largest.

28. $4000(.9)^{15}(1.23)^{16} = 4000(.20589)(27.446) = 22{,}603.69$
The value of the car is about $23{,}000.

29. a.

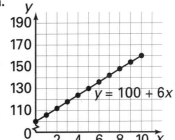

  b.

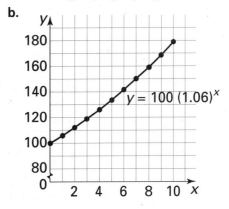

29. c. Sample: Of two accounts, each starting with $100, which has more money in it at the end of 10 years, one that earns 6% compound interest or one that has $6 deposited in it each year? Answer: the one that earns 6% compound interest.

30. a. $2x + 3y = 4$

$$3y = -2x + 4$$
$$y = -\frac{2}{3}x + \frac{4}{3}$$

b. $4x + 6y = 8$

$$6y = -4x + 8$$
$$y = -\frac{2}{3}x + \frac{4}{3}$$

c. $6x + 9y = 12$

$$9y = -6x + 12$$
$$y = -\frac{2}{3}x + \frac{4}{3}$$

d. $2ax + 3ay = 4a$

$$3ay = -2ax + 4a$$
$$y = -\frac{2}{3}x + \frac{4}{3}$$

31. (a) $5m^2$

32.

$n =$	2	3	4	5	6	7	8	9	10
$x = 2$	4	8	16	32	64	128	256	512	1024
3	9	27	81	243	729				
4	16	64	256	1024					
5	25	125	625						
6	36	216							

Samples: $2^{10} = 2^9 \cdot 2^1 = 512 \cdot 2 = 1024$;
$$4^4 = (2^2)^4 = 2^8 = 256$$

CHAPTER 8

PROGRESS SELF-TEST   p. 542

1. a. $4^{12-6} = 4^6 = 4096$
   b. $\frac{4^{12}}{4^6} = \frac{16{,}777{,}216}{4096} = 4096$

2. $\frac{5}{5} \cdot \frac{10^{20}}{10^{10}} = 1 \cdot 10^{10} = 10{,}000{,}000{,}000$

3. $8^{-5} = \frac{1}{8^5} = \frac{1}{32{,}768}$

4. $b^{7+11} = b^{18}$

5. $5^3 \cdot y^{4 \cdot 3} = 125y^{12}$

6. $\frac{3}{12} \cdot z^{6-4} = \frac{1}{4}z^2$

7. $y^{10 \cdot 4} = y^{40}$

8. $\frac{3^2}{x^2} \cdot \frac{x^4}{3^4} = \frac{x^2}{3^2} = \frac{x^2}{9}$

9. $\frac{48}{12} \cdot a^{3-4} \cdot b^{7-1} = 4a^{-1}b^6$

10. $6 \cdot 11^0 = 6 \cdot 1 = 6$

11. Sample: Does $3 \cdot 2^2 = (3 \cdot 2)^2$?
$$3 \cdot 4 = 6^2?$$
$$12 = 36?$$
No; this is a counterexample with $x = 2$.

12. Product of Powers Property

13. $6500(1.05)^5 = \$8295.83$

14. $1900(1.058)^3 \approx 2250.15$
interest: $2250.15 - 1900 = \$350.15$

15. $135{,}000(1.03)^5 = 156{,}279.375$
The population will be about 157,000.

16. $135{,}000(1.03)^{-2} = 127{,}250.4477$
The population was about 127,000.

17. a. yes; exponential decay
   b. no
   c. no
   d. yes; exponential growth

18.

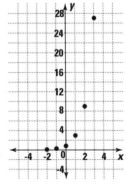

19. $(1.30)^3 = 2.197$

20. $V = \frac{4}{3}\pi \cdot (6.96 \cdot 10^6)^3$

$V \approx 1412.3 \cdot 10^{18}$

$V \approx 1.41 \cdot 10^{21}$ km^3

CHAPTER 8

REVIEW pp. 543–545

1. a. 81

b. -81

c. 81

2. $-1 \cdot 2^5 \cdot (-2)^5 = -1 \cdot 32 \cdot -32 = 1024$

3. $4 \cdot 7^0 = 4 \cdot 1 = 4$

4. $3 \cdot 2^3 - 2^2$

$= 3 \cdot 8 - 4$

$= 24 - 4$

$= 20$

5. $2^{3 \cdot 3 - 6} = 2^3 = 8$

6. $\frac{9}{3} \cdot 10^{6-8} = 3 \cdot 10^{-2} = 0.03$

7. $\frac{1}{5^3} = \frac{1}{125}$

8. $\frac{1}{2^5} = \frac{1}{32}$

9. $\frac{2^3}{7^3} = \frac{8}{243}$

10. $(-1)^4 \cdot \frac{4^4}{3^4} = 1 \cdot \frac{256}{81} = \frac{256}{81}$

11. $(3^{-1})^{-4} = 3^4 = 81$

12. $10 \cdot \left(\frac{5}{2}\right)^3 = 10 \cdot \frac{125}{8} = \frac{625}{4}$

13. $x^{4+7} = x^{11}$

14. $r^{3+8}t^{5+2} = r^{11}t^7$

15. $x^3y^{2+10} = x^3y^{12}$

16. $p^{4+1}q^2 = p^5q^2$

17. $n^{15-2} = n^{13}$

18. $a^{12-4+6} = a^{14}$

19. $\frac{3}{3} \cdot \frac{1}{a^{5-4}} \cdot c = \frac{c}{a}$

20. $\frac{15}{12} \cdot x^{2-1} \cdot \frac{1}{y^{6-5}} = \frac{5x}{4y}$

21. $3^3x^{5 \cdot 3} + x^{3 \cdot 5} = 27x^{15} + x^{15} = 28x^{15}$

22. $3^4m^{4 \cdot 4} + 9^2m^{2 \cdot 2} = 81m^{16} + 81m^4$

23. $\frac{1}{5} \cdot m^{6-2} = 5^{-1}m^4$

24. $4 \cdot \frac{1}{t^2} \cdot w^{8-1} = 4t^{-2}w^7$

25. $10^{5-2} = 10^3 = 1000$

26. $\frac{(2 \cdot 6 - 1)^{11}}{(2 \cdot 6 - 1)^4} = \frac{11^{11}}{11^4} = 19{,}487{,}171$; or $\frac{(2 \cdot 6 - 1)^{11}}{(2 \cdot 6 - 1)^4} = (2 \cdot 6 - 1)^{11-4} = 11^7 = 19{,}487{,}171$

27. $\frac{x}{y^2}$

28. $\frac{2n^4p^2}{m}$

29. $\frac{x^3}{y^3}$

30. $\frac{b^5}{a^5}$

31. $4^5x^5 = 1024x^5$

32. $5^4y^4 = 625y^4$

33. $\frac{2^5}{n^5} = \frac{32}{n^5}$

34. $\frac{t^{7 \cdot 4}}{2^4} = \frac{t^{28}}{16}$

35. $(-3)^3n^3 = -27n^3$

36. $-2^3y^3 = -8y^3$

37. $4 \cdot \frac{k^3}{3^3} = \frac{4k^3}{27}$

38. $45 \cdot \frac{t^2}{3^2} = \frac{45t^2}{9} = 5t^2$

39. $2 \cdot 4^2x^2 = 2 \cdot 16x^2 = 32x^2$

40. $11 \cdot 10^3k^3 = 11 \cdot 1000k^3 = 11{,}000k^3$

41. a. True

b. True

c. False

d. False

42. a. Yes; $(3^2)^4 = 3^{2 \cdot 4} = 3^8$

b. Yes; $(5^2)^2 = 5^{2 \cdot 2} = 5^4$

c. Yes; There is evidence that the pattern is true.

43. Sample: Does $(1 + 1)^3 = 1^3 + 1^3$?

$2^3 = 1 + 1$?

$8 = 2$?

No; this is a counterexample with $a = b = 1$.

44. Sample: Does $(2^3)^2 = 2^{(3^2)}$?

$8^2 = 2^9$?

$64 = 512$?

No; this is a counterexample with $x = 2$.

45. Power of a Product Property

46. Quotient of Powers Property

47. Zero Exponent Property

48. Product of Powers Property

49. Power of a Quotient Property

50. Zero Exponent Property and Multiplicative Identity Property

51. Negative Exponent Property

52. Negative Exponent Property and Power of a Quotient Property

53. Sample: $\left(\frac{x^3}{x}\right)^8 = (x^{3-1})^8 = (x^2)^8 = x^{16}$; or

$\left(\frac{x^3}{x}\right)^8 = \frac{x^{3 \cdot 8}}{x^{1 \cdot 8}} = \frac{x^{24}}{x^8} = x^{24-8} = x^{16}$

54. repeated multiplication, or Power of a Product Property

55. $2500(1.057)^3 = \$2952.33$

56. $3000(1.057)^4 = \$3744.74$
interest: $3744.74 - 3000 = \$744.74$

57. $1200(1.06)^2 = \$1348.32$

58. (a) $x \cdot (1.10)^2 = 1.21x$
(b) $x \cdot (1.02)^{10} \approx 1.219x$
Investment (b) yields more money.

59. $7.25(1.056)^4 = \$9.02$ per hour

60. $16.95(1.03)^8 = \$21.47$

61. a. $8000 \cdot 2^4 = 128{,}000$
b. After 4 hours there will be 128,000 bacteria.

62. a. $8000 \cdot 2^{-3} = 1000$
b. The bacteria count was 1000 three hours earlier.

63. $P = 1{,}500{,}000 \cdot (0.97)^n$

64. $P = 1{,}500{,}000 \cdot (0.97)^6 = 1{,}249{,}458$

65. $P = 1{,}500{,}000 \cdot (0.97)^0 = 1{,}500{,}000 \cdot 1 = 1{,}500{,}000$; this is the population now.

66. $436.4(0.983)^{12} \approx 355$

67. a. $436.4(0.983)^{-3} \approx 459$
b. The death rate 3 years earlier (1977) was about 459 per 100,000 people.

68. a. $\frac{3}{2} \cdot \frac{3}{2} = \frac{9}{4}$
b. $\left(\frac{3}{2}\right)^5 = \frac{3^5}{2^5} = \frac{243}{32}$

69. $\left(\frac{9}{10}\right)^x = (0.9)^x$

70. $\frac{5.6 \cdot 10^9}{1.48 \cdot 10^8} = 3.78 \cdot 10^1 \approx 38$ people per km

71. $\frac{4}{3}\pi \cdot (1.08 \cdot 10^3)^3 \approx 5.28 \cdot 10^9$; about 5 billion cubic miles

72. a. $\left(\frac{1}{6}\right)^3 = \frac{1}{216}$
b. 6^{-3}

73. $\left(\frac{1}{3}\right)^4 = \frac{1}{81}$

74. linear

75. exponential

76. exponential

77. linear

78.

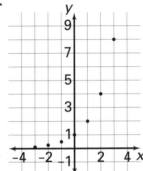

79.

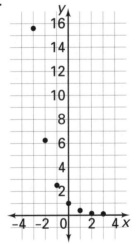

80.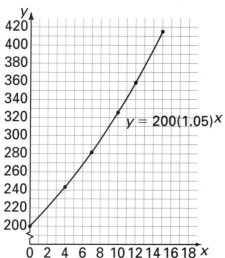

$y = 200(1.05)^x$

81. $y = 5 \cdot (1.04)^x$; if the growth factor g is greater than 1, exponential growth always overtakes constant increase.

82. **a.** (ii)
   b. (iv)
   c. (i)
   d. (iii)

QUADRATIC EQUATIONS AND SQUARE ROOTS

LESSON 9-1   pp. 548–553

1. **a.** Sample: $y = x^2$

   b. Sample: $y = 7x^2$

2. The word *quadratic* comes from the Latin word for square.

3. parabola

4. Samples: path of a basketball shot at a hoop, path of a stream of water from a fountain

5. **a.**

x	y
-4	8
-3	4.5
-2	2
-1	0.5
0	0
1	0.5
2	2
3	4.5
4	8

   b.

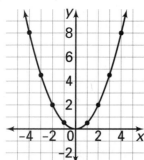

   c. The graph is a parabola which opens up, whose axis of symmetry is $x = 0$, and vertex is (0, 0).

6. **a.**

x	y
-4	-8
-3	-4.5
-2	-2
-1	-0.5
0	0
1	-0.5
2	-2
3	-4.5
4	-8

   b.

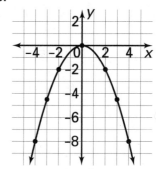

   c. The graph is a parabola which opens down and whose axis of symmetry is $x = 0$, and vertex is (0, 0).

7. The vertex of the parabola is (0, 0), the origin.

8. $x = 0$

9. **a.** up

   b. down

10. **a.** Graphs will vary.

   b.

x	y
-2	12
-1.5	6.75
-1	3
-0.5	0.75
0	0
0.5	0.75
1	3
1.5	6.75
2	12

10. c.

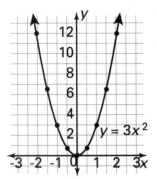

d. The vertex is a minimum.

e. $3x^2 = 12$

$x^2 = 4$

$x = 2$ or $x = -2$

f. $3x^2 = 15$

$x^2 = 5$

$x = \sqrt{5}$ or $x = -\sqrt{5}$

11. a. $(6, 10)$

b. This parabola opens up.

c. This parabola has a minimum.

12. 144 ft

13. 100 ft

14. $200 = 16t^2$

$\frac{200}{16} = t^2$

$12.5 = t^2$

$3.54 \approx t$

15. $5 - 3.54 = 1.46$ seconds

16. a.

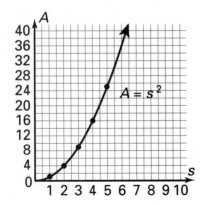

b. The right half of the graph is identical. There cannot be any negative values for the length of a side of a square, so the graph of $A = s^2$ lies entirely in the first quadrant.

17. $16 = \frac{1}{9}(x + 1)^2$

$144 = (x + 1)^2$

$12 = x + 1$ or $-12 = x + 1$

$11 = x$ or $-13 = x$

18. $\pi r^2 = 40$

$r^2 = \frac{40}{\pi}$

$r = \sqrt{\frac{40}{\pi}}$ or $r = -\sqrt{\frac{40}{\pi}}$

$r \approx 3.568$ or $r \approx -3.568$

19. $x^{4+3}y^{1+3} = x^7y^4$

20. $\frac{9}{6} \cdot a^{9-6} = \frac{3}{2}a^3$

21. $\frac{2^3 a^3}{5^3} = \frac{8a^3}{125}$

22. a. Sample: Adam bought 21 comic books for a total of $16. If each comic book has the same price, how much more will he have to pay to add 50 more comic books to his collection?

b. $16 \cdot 50 = 21n$

$800 = 21n$

$\frac{800}{21} = n$

$\$38.10 = n$

23. It is at least 5 km and at most 11 km since $8 - 3 = 5$ and $8 + 3 = 11$.

24. (c) $w < 1$

25. $7500 - 1800 - k$ or $5700 - k$

26. $d = 15 + 0.05(15)^2$

$d = 15 + 0.05(225)$

$d = 15 + 11.25$

$d = 26.25$

27. The shape of the lighted area is a parabola. The parabola becomes more narrow.

1. Sample: Stopping distance is the distance a car travels after the driver decides to stop.

2. $s = .05(40)^2 + 40$
   $s = .05(1600) + 40$
   $s = 80 + 40$
   $s = 120$ ft

3. $s = .05(55)^2 + 55$
   $s = .05(3025) + 55$
   $s = 151.25 + 55$
   $s = 206.25$ ft

4. False; the stopping distance for a car traveling 30 mph is 75 ft and the stopping distance for a car traveling 60 mph is 240 ft.

5. True; $a = 0.05$, $b = 1$, $c = 0$

6. **a.**

x	y
-3	14
-2	9
-1	6
0	5
1	6
2	9
3	14

b.

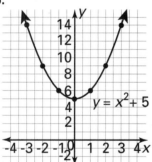

c. vertex: (0, 5); minimum
d. y-intercept: 5

7. **a.**

x	y
-3	12
-2	5
-1	0
0	-3
1	-4
2	-3
3	0

b.

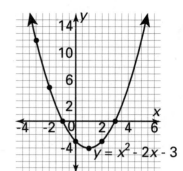

c. vertex: (1, -4); minimum
d. y-intercept; -3

8. **a.**

x	y
-3	-22
-2	-7
-1	2
0	5
1	2
2	-7
3	-22

b.

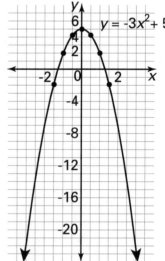

c. vertex: (0, 5); maximum
d. y-intercept: 5

9. **a.** vertex: (-3, 1)
   b. $x = -3$

10. TABLE FOR Y = X ^ 2 – 2X

X	Y
-1	3
-0.5	1.25
0	0
0.5	-0.75
1	-1
1.5	-0.75
2	0
2.5	1.25
3	3

11. $x = 1$

12. a. vertex: (-4, 35)

    b. $x = -4$

    c. 19; 5; -13

13. If $a > 0$, the parabola opens up. If $a < 0$, the parabola opens down.

14. a.

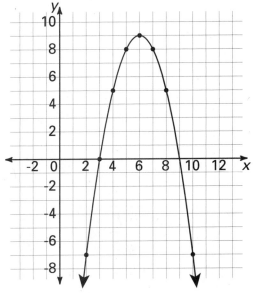

    b. vertex: (6, 9)

    c. $x = 6$

    d. (3, 0) and (9, 0)

15. (c) The graph opens up and the y-intercept is -1.

16. (d) The graph opens down and the y-intercept is -1.

17. (a) The graph opens up and the y-intercept is 0.

18. (b) The graph opens up and the y-intercept is 1.

19. (b) Sample: if $x = 1$, $y = 1 - 6 + 8 = 3$. Graph (b) contains this point.

20. a. $500 = 16t^2$

       $31.25 = t^2$

       $5.59 \approx t$

    b. Sample: How long does it take a stone to fall 500 ft from the top of a cliff?

21. He must change the y-values to their opposites and turn his graph upside-down.

22. $-3n^2 = -1200$

     $n^2 = 400$

     $n = 20$ or $n = -20$

23. $x^2 = 16 \cdot 40$

     $x^2 = 640$

     $x = \sqrt{640} \approx 25.3$ or

     $x = -\sqrt{640} \approx -25.3$

24. $\dfrac{c}{c + d + r}$

25. $\dfrac{c + d + r}{c + d + r - 3}$

26.   Sample

X	X ^ 2 – 2X – 3
-3	12
-2	5
-1	0
0	-3
1	-4
2	-3
3	0

IN-CLASS ACTIVITY   p. 561

1. a. From the outer to inner, the parabolas are as follows: $y = 0.5x^2$; $y = x^2$; $y = 2x^2$, and $y = 3x^2$.

    b. As a gets larger the parabola narrows.

    c. The graph of $y = 7x^2$ will be a graph of a parabola that is narrower than any of those in part **a**.

2. Close to the vertex, the parabolas tend to look more alike.

3. A window of $10 \leq x \leq 25$ and $-400 \leq y \leq -200$ seems to show a similar graph.

LESSON 9-3 pp. 567–566

1. As the value of a increases, the graphs of $y = ax^2$ look narrower and narrower.

2.

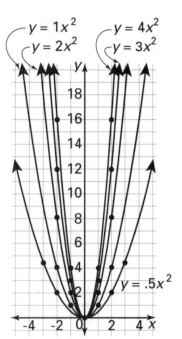

3. a.

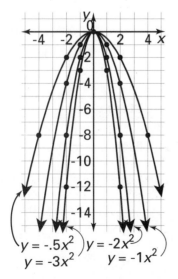

b. As a gets smaller, the graph of $y = ax^2$ looks thinner and thinner.

4. at about 45 years of age

5. at about ages 17 and 73

6. a.

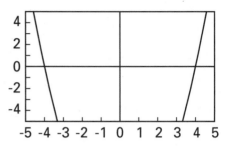

b.

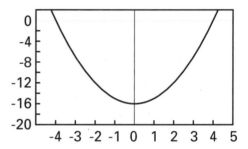

7. Sample: $-10 \leq x \leq 10$ and $-10 \leq y \leq 30$

8. Sample: $-5 \leq x \leq 10$ and $-25 \leq y \leq 10$

9. a.

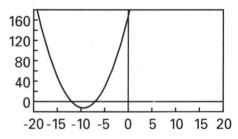

b. vertex: $(-9, -12)$

c. $x = -9$

d. x-intercepts: -7 and -12

10. a. $\frac{-1+7}{2} = 3$

b. $-(3)^2 + 6(3) + 7 = -9 + 18 + 7 = 16$

11. a.

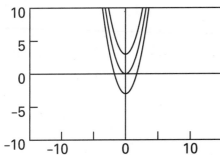

b. Sample: All the parabolas look alike in the window. They have different vertices and are translation images of each other.

c. It will be congruent to those in part **a**. It will be a translation image of them and have vertex $(0, 6)$.

d.

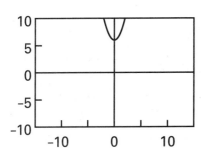

12. a. Sample: $9 \le x \le 11$; $-10 \le y \le 15$

b. Sample: $-8 \le x \le 15$; $0 \le y \le 8$

13. a.

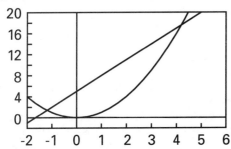

b. $(-1.25, 1.25)$; $(4, 17)$

14. a.

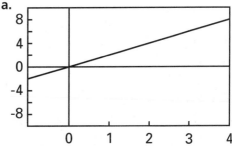

b. when $x = 0$, $y = 0$ and when $x = 1$, $y = 2$

rate of change: $\frac{2-0}{1-0} = \frac{2}{1} = 2$

15. a.

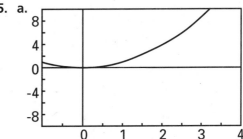

b. when $x = 0$, $y = 0$ and when $x = 1$, $y = 1$

rate of change: $\frac{1-0}{1-0} = \frac{1}{1} = 1$

16. a.

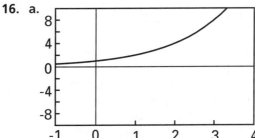

b. when $x = 0$, $y = 1$ and when $x = 1$, $y = 2$

rate of change: $\frac{2-1}{1-0} = \frac{1}{1} = 1$

17. $3x^2 + 9 = 156$

$3x^2 = 147$

$x^2 = 49$

$x = 7$ or $x = -7$

18. $7x^2 + 2x + 5 = x^2 - 10x$

$7x^2 - x^2 + 2x + 10x + 5 = 0$

$6x^2 + 12x + 5 = 0$

19. a. Belleville: $y = 1.2x + .45$
Carrolton: $y = 1x + 1.25$
$1.2x + .45 = x + 1.25$
$.2x + .45 = 1.25$
$.2x = .8$
$x = 4$
The rides cost the same for 4 miles.
b. It is cheaper to travel in Belleville for distances less than 4 miles. Try any value for x such that $x < 4$ in each of the cost equations; the fare will be cheaper in Belleville.

20. a. $20 \text{ ft} \cdot \frac{1}{3} \frac{\text{minute}}{\text{ft}} = 6\frac{2}{3}$ minutes
b. $f \text{ ft} \cdot \frac{1}{3} \frac{\text{minute}}{\text{ft}} = \frac{f}{3}$ minutes

21. a. $-4(-7)(15) = 420$
b. $6^2 - 4(-7)(15) = 36 + 420 = 456$
c. $\sqrt{6^2 - 4(-7)(15)} = \sqrt{456} \approx 21.4$

22. a.

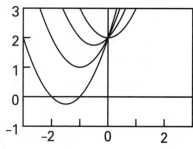

b. As the value of b increases, the graph shifts to the left and down.
c. It will have the same shape as the graphs in part **a**, but will be far off to the left with a vertex in the third quadrant.
d. The vertex will lie in the first quadrant.

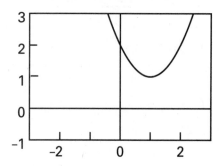

1. a parabola
2. 35 yards
3. about 7 ft or 84 inches
$$ (h = -0.025(39)^2 + 39 + 6 $$
$$ h = -0.025(1521) + 39 + 6 $$
$$ h = 6.975) $$
4. 5 feet
$$ (h = -\frac{60^2}{45} + \frac{4(60)}{3} + 5 $$
$$ h = -80 + 80 + 5 $$
$$ h = 5) $$
5. a. 55 yards
b. 11.1 feet
$$ (h = \frac{-55^2}{45} + \frac{4(55)}{3} + 5 $$
$$ h = -67.\overline{2} + 73.\overline{3} + 5 $$
$$ h \approx 11.1) $$
6. a parabola
7. 20 yards
8. 15 yards
9. about 1.5 and 2.5 seconds
10. a little more than 4 seconds
11. 2 seconds
12. 45 meters
13. 25 meters
14. after 2 and 4 seconds
15. 35 meters
$$ (y = 30 \cdot 7 - 5 \cdot 7^2 $$
$$ y = 210 - 245 $$
$$ y = -35) $$
16. a. $y = -2(1) + 1 + 10 = 9$
b. Sample: When the diver is one meter from the edge of the diving board, he is 9 meters above the surface of the water.

17. The maximum height the diver reaches is 10.125 m above the surface of the water. (Use an automatic grapher and trace key to find the y-coordinate of the vertex of the parabola.)

18. The diver will hit the water 2.5 meters in front of the platform. (Use an automatic grapher and trace key to find the x-coordinate of the parabola where it crosses the x-axis on the positive side of the y-axis.)

19. a.

x	y
-3	$\frac{9}{2}$
-2	2
-1	$\frac{1}{2}$
0	0
1	$\frac{1}{2}$
2	2
3	$\frac{9}{2}$

b.

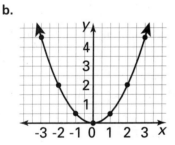

20. a.

x	y
-3	-27
-2	-16
-1	-7
0	0
1	5
2	8
3	9

b.

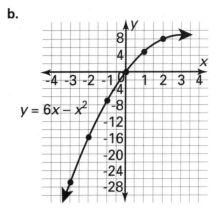

$y = 6x - x^2$

21. $A = (8, 4)$; $B = (9, 7)$

22. $x = 7$

23. (c); $(ab)^2 = a^2b^2$

24. a. $\frac{22}{11} + \frac{7}{11} = \frac{29}{11}$

b. $\frac{2y}{y} + \frac{x}{y} = \frac{2y + x}{y}$

c. $\frac{ac}{c} + \frac{b}{c} = \frac{ac + b}{c}$

25. $(-6 + 3, 0 - 5) = (-3, -5)$

26. (b)

27. $\frac{4(2 + \sqrt{2})}{4} = 2 + \sqrt{2} \approx 3.4$

28. a. $\sqrt{4^2 - 4(6)(-2)} = \sqrt{16 + 48} = \sqrt{64} = 8$

b. $\frac{-4 + \sqrt{4^2 - 4(6)(-2)}}{2(6)} = \frac{-4 + 8}{12} = \frac{4}{12} = \frac{1}{3} \approx 0.33$

c. $\frac{-4 - \sqrt{4^2 - 4(6)(-2)}}{2(6)} = \frac{-4 - 8}{12} = \frac{-12}{12} = -1$

29. Samples: spinning of the ball; air resistance; wind

LESSON 9-5   pp. 573–578

1. Quadratic Formula: If $ax^2 + bx + c = 0$ and $a \neq 0$, then $x = \frac{-b \pm \sqrt{b^2 - 4ac}}{2a}$.

2. True

3. $\frac{-10 + 4}{2} = \frac{-6}{2} = -3$ and $\frac{-10 - 4}{2} = \frac{-14}{2} = -7$

4. a. $a = -1$; $b = 2$; $c = 22$

b. $x = \frac{-2 \pm \sqrt{2^2 - 4(-1)(22)}}{2(-1)} = \frac{-2 \pm \sqrt{4 - -88}}{-2}$

$= \frac{-2 \pm \sqrt{92}}{-2}$

c. $x \approx -3.8$ or $x \approx 5.8$

d. about 5.8 meters

5. a. $a = 12$; $b = 7$; $c = 1$

b. $x = \dfrac{-7 \pm \sqrt{7^2 - 4(12)(1)}}{2(12)}$

$x = \dfrac{-7 \pm \sqrt{49 - 48}}{24}$

$x = \dfrac{-7 \pm \sqrt{1}}{24}$

$x = \dfrac{-7 \pm 1}{24}$

$x = \dfrac{-7 + 1}{24} = \dfrac{-6}{24} = -\dfrac{1}{4}$ or

$x = \dfrac{-7 - 1}{24} = \dfrac{-8}{24} = -\dfrac{1}{3}$

c. $12\left(\dfrac{-1}{4}\right)^2 + 7\left(\dfrac{-1}{4}\right) + 1 = \dfrac{3}{4} + -\dfrac{7}{4} + 1 = 0$

$12\left(\dfrac{-1}{3}\right)^2 + 7\left(\dfrac{-1}{3}\right) + 1 = \dfrac{4}{3} + -\dfrac{7}{3} + 1 = 0$

6. a. $a = 3$; $b = 1$; $c = -2$

b. $x = \dfrac{-1 \pm \sqrt{1^2 - 4(3)(-2)}}{2(3)}$

$x = \dfrac{-1 \pm \sqrt{1 - -24}}{6}$

$x = \dfrac{-1 \pm \sqrt{25}}{6}$

$x = \dfrac{-1 \pm 5}{6}$

$x = \dfrac{-1 + 5}{6} = \dfrac{4}{6} = \dfrac{2}{3}$ or

$x = \dfrac{-1 - 5}{6} = \dfrac{-6}{6} = -1$

c. $3\left(\dfrac{2}{3}\right)^2 + \left(\dfrac{2}{3}\right) - 2 = \dfrac{4}{3} + \dfrac{2}{3} - 2 = 0$

$3(-1)^2 + (-1) - 2 = 3 - 1 - 2 = 0$

7. a. $a = 1$; $b = 6$; $c = 9$

b. $x = \dfrac{-6 \pm \sqrt{6^2 - 4(1)(9)}}{2(1)}$

$x = \dfrac{-6 \pm \sqrt{36 - 36}}{2}$

$x = \dfrac{-6 \pm 0}{2}$

$x = \dfrac{-6}{2}$

$x = -3$

c. $(-3)^2 + 6(-3) + 9 = 9 - 18 + 9 = 0$

8. a. $a = -1$; $b = 0$; $c = 4$

b. $x = \dfrac{0 \pm \sqrt{0^2 - 4(-1)(4)}}{2(-1)}$

$x = \dfrac{0 \pm \sqrt{0 - -16}}{-2}$

$x = \dfrac{0 \pm \sqrt{16}}{-2}$

$x = \dfrac{0 \pm 4}{-2}$

$x = \dfrac{0 + 4}{-2} = \dfrac{4}{-2} = -2$ or

$x = \dfrac{0 - 4}{-2} = \dfrac{-4}{-2} = 2$

c. $-(-2)^2 + 4 = -4 + 4 = 0$

$-(2)^2 + 4 = -4 + 4 = 0$

9. $(5.53)^2 - 3(5.53) =$

$30.5809 - 16.59 =$

$13.9909 \approx 14$

$(-2.53)^2 - 3(-2.53) =$

$6.4009 + 7.59 =$

$13.9909 \approx 14$

This is close enough to 14 given these approximations.

10. a. $20m^2 - 6m - 2 = 0$

b. $a = 20$; $b = -6$; $c = -2$

$x = \dfrac{-(-6) \pm \sqrt{(-6)^2 - 4(20)(-2)}}{2(20)}$

$x = \dfrac{6 \pm \sqrt{36 - -160}}{40}$

$x = \dfrac{6 \pm \sqrt{196}}{40}$

$x = \dfrac{6 \pm 14}{40}$

$x = \dfrac{6 + 14}{40} = \dfrac{20}{40} = 0.50$ or

$x = \dfrac{6 - 14}{40} = \dfrac{-8}{40} = -0.2$

11. a. $3w^2 - w - 5 = 0$

b. $a = 3; b = -1; c = -5$

$$x = \frac{-(-1) \pm \sqrt{(-1)^2 - 4(3)(-5)}}{2(3)}$$

$$x = \frac{1 \pm \sqrt{1 - -60}}{6}$$

$$x = \frac{1 \pm \sqrt{61}}{6}$$

$$x \approx \frac{1 \pm 7.81}{6}$$

$$x \approx \frac{1 + 7.81}{6} \approx 1.47 \text{ or}$$

$$x \approx \frac{1 - 7.81}{6} \approx -1.14$$

12. a. $2x^2 + x - 3 = 0$

b. $a = 2; b = 1; c = -3$

$$x = \frac{-1 \pm \sqrt{(1)^2 - 4(2)(-3)}}{2(2)}$$

$$x = \frac{-1 \pm \sqrt{1 - -24}}{4}$$

$$x = \frac{-1 \pm \sqrt{25}}{4}$$

$$x = \frac{-1 \pm 5}{4}$$

$$x = \frac{-1 + 5}{4} = 1.00 \text{ or}$$

$$x = \frac{-1 - 5}{4} = -1.50$$

13. a. $3p^2 - 19p - 14 = 0$

b. $a = 3; b = -19; c = -14$

$$x = \frac{-(-19) \pm \sqrt{(-19)^2 - 4(3)(-14)}}{2(3)}$$

$$x = \frac{19 \pm \sqrt{361 - -168}}{6}$$

$$x = \frac{19 \pm \sqrt{529}}{6}$$

$$x = \frac{19 \pm 23}{6}$$

$$x = \frac{19 + 23}{6} \text{ or } x = \frac{19 - 23}{6}$$

$$x = \frac{42}{6} \quad \text{ or } x = \frac{-4}{6}$$

$$x = 7.00 \quad \text{ or } x = -0.67$$

14. a. $a = 2; b = 3; c = -2$

$$x = \frac{-3 \pm \sqrt{3^2 - 4(2)(-2)}}{2(2)}$$

$$x = \frac{-3 \pm \sqrt{9 - -16}}{4}$$

$$x = \frac{-3 \pm \sqrt{25}}{4}$$

$$x = \frac{-3 \pm 5}{4}$$

$$x = \frac{-3 + 5}{4} = \frac{1}{2} \text{ or } x = \frac{-3 - 5}{4} = -2$$

b.

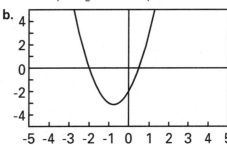

15. a. Solve $10 = -0.8t^2 + 6t$.

$0.8t^2 - 6t + 10 = 0$

$a = 0.8; b = -6; c = 10$

$$x = \frac{-(-6) \pm \sqrt{(-6)^2 - 4(.8)(10)}}{2(.8)}$$

$$x = \frac{6 \pm \sqrt{36 - 32}}{1.6}$$

$$x = \frac{6 \pm \sqrt{4}}{1.6}$$

$$x = \frac{6 \pm 2}{1.6}$$

$$x = \frac{6 + 2}{1.6} = 5.0 \text{ or } x = \frac{6 - 2}{1.6} = 2.5$$

The ball will reach a height of 10 m at 2.5 seconds and 5 seconds.

b.

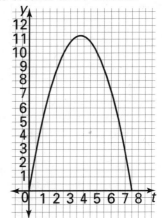

c. The parabola does reach a height of 10 m at 2.5 seconds and 5 seconds.

16. a. $\frac{3x^2 - 6x - 45}{3} = \frac{0}{3}$

$x^2 - 2x - 15 = 0$

b. $a = 1; b = -2; c = -15$

$x = \frac{-(-2) \pm \sqrt{(-2)^2 - 4(1)(-15)}}{2(1)}$

$x = \frac{2 \pm \sqrt{4 - -60}}{2}$

$x = \frac{2 \pm \sqrt{64}}{2}$

$x = \frac{2 \pm 8}{2}$

$x = \frac{2 + 8}{2} = 5$ or $x = \frac{2 - 8}{2} = -3$

17. $h = 10(1) - 4.9(1)^2 = 10 - 4.9 = 5.1$;
5.1 m above the cliff

18. $h = 10(3) - 4.9(3)^2 = 30 - 44.1 = -14.1$;
14.1 m below the cliff

19. $h = .12(3)^2 + 2(3) + 5 = -1.08 + 6 + 5 = 9.92$;
about 10 ft

20. The ball has moved forward either 5 ft or
about 11.7 ft.

21. about 13.5 feet

22. $\frac{3 + -1}{2} = 1$

23. (d); the y-intercept is -1.

24. $200 - 12w$ reams

25. $5 \cdot 12 \cdot 9 = 540$

26. $V = 15a \cdot 8b \cdot 6c = 720abc$ in^3

27. Nero had 4 hits.

LESSON 9-6   pp. 579–585

1. $28 = -x^2 + 2x + 27$ or $-x^2 + 2x - 1 = 0$

2. No; $28.5 = -x^2 + 2x + 27$ has no solutions
because its discriminant is negative.
$(b^2 - 4ac = 2^2 - 4(-1)(-1.5) = 4 - 6 = -2)$

3. Yes; when $x = 0$ and when $x = 2$

4. when $x \approx 5.24$ (Solve: $10 = -x^2 + 2x + 27$ or
$-x^2 + 2x + 17 = 0$ or check graph on automatic
grapher.)

5. The discriminant is $b^2 - 4ac$. It can
be evaluated to find the number of real
solutions of a quadratic equation.

6. a. 2
b. 0
c. 1

7. a. $(-16)^2 - 4(1)(64) = 256 - 256 = 0$
b. 1
c. $x = \frac{-(-16) \pm \sqrt{0}}{2(1)}$

$x = \frac{16}{2} = 8$

8. a. $(-3)^2 - 4(4)(8) = 9 - 128 = -119$
b. 0
c. no real solutions

9. a. $(-10)^2 - 4(25)(1) = 100 - 100 = 0$
$(a = 25; b = -10; c = 1)$
b. 1
c. $x = \frac{-(-10) \pm \sqrt{0}}{2(25)}$

$x = \frac{10}{50} = \frac{1}{5}$

10. a. $(-13)^2 - 4(5)(9) = 169 - 180 = -11$
b. 0
c. no real solutions

11. a. The diving platform is 5 m high.
$(d = -5(0)^2 + 10(0) + 5 = 0 + 0 + 5 = 5)$
b. After 0.4 and 1.6 seconds the diver is 8
meters above the water.
$(8 = -5t^2 + 10t + 5$ or $-5t^2 + 10t - 3 = 0$
$a = -5; b = 10; c = -3$

$x = \frac{-10 \pm \sqrt{10^2 - 4(-5)(-3)}}{2(-5)}$

$x = \frac{-10 \pm \sqrt{40}}{-10}$

$x = \frac{-10 + \sqrt{40}}{-10} \approx 0.4$ or $x = \frac{-10 - \sqrt{40}}{-10} \approx 1.6$)

c. The diver enters the water after about 2.4
seconds; -0.4 is not a meaningful solution.
$(-5t^2 + 10t + 5 = 0$
$a = -5; b = 10; c = 5$

$x = \frac{-10 \pm \sqrt{10^2 - 4(-5)(5)}}{2(-5)}$

$x = \frac{-10 \pm \sqrt{200}}{-10}$

$x = \frac{-10 + \sqrt{200}}{-10} \approx -0.4$ or

$x = \frac{-10 - \sqrt{200}}{-10} \approx 2.4$)

12. a. $4x^2 + 8x - 5 = 0$

$a = 4; b = 8; c = -5$

$x = \dfrac{-8 \pm \sqrt{8^2 - 4(4)(-5)}}{2(4)}$

$x = \dfrac{-8 \pm \sqrt{144}}{8}$

$x = \dfrac{-8 + 12}{8} = \dfrac{1}{2}$ or $x = \dfrac{-8 - 12}{8} = -\dfrac{5}{2}$

b. $4x^2 + 8x + 1 = 0$

$a = 4; b = 8; c = 1$

$x = \dfrac{-8 \pm \sqrt{8^2 - 4(4)(1)}}{2(4)}$

$x = \dfrac{-8 \pm \sqrt{48}}{8}$

$x = \dfrac{-8 + \sqrt{48}}{8} \approx -0.13$ or $x = \dfrac{-8 - \sqrt{48}}{8} \approx -1.86$

c. $4x^2 + 8x + 10 = 0$

$a = 4; b = 8; c = 10$

discriminant: $8^2 - 4(4)(10) = 64 - 160$

$\qquad\qquad\qquad\qquad = -96$

no real solution

13. The discriminant must be zero.

$6^2 - 4(1)(h) = 0$

$36 - 4h = 0$

$36 = 4h$

$9 = h$

14. a. $10 = -16t^2 + 28t + 6$ or

$\qquad 0 = -16t^2 + 28t - 4$

b. positive $(28^2 - 4(-16)(-4) = 784 - 256 = 528)$

c. 2

15. a. $18 = -16t^2 + 28t + 6$ or

$\qquad 0 = -16t^2 + 28t - 12$

b. positive $(28^2 - 4(-16)(-12) = 784 - 768 = 16)$

c. 2

16. $60x^2 - 120 = 0$

$60x^2 = 120$

$x^2 = 2$

$x = \pm\sqrt{2} \approx \pm1.414$

17. The ball is 12 feet high at its peak.

18. a. $50 - 2 = 48$ ft

b. $h = -.016(48)^2 + .8(48) + 2$

$h = -36.864 + 38.4 + 2$

$h = 3.536$

about 3.5 ft

19. down

20. up

21. Sample: $y = -x^2$

22. a. $x = 25$

b. $y = 21$

c. $z = 14$

23. a. $a < \dfrac{1}{3}$

b. $b > \dfrac{1}{3}$

c. $c > 0$

24. a. $\dfrac{-5}{a}$

b. $\dfrac{-b}{a}$

c. $\dfrac{-b}{a}$

d. $\dfrac{-b}{a}$

25. $\dfrac{15 \cdot 14 \cdot 13 \cdot 12 \cdot 11 \cdot 10 \cdot 9}{7 \cdot 6 \cdot 5 \cdot 4 \cdot 3 \cdot 2 \cdot 1} = 6435$

26. 16, 25, 36, 49, 64, and 81

27.

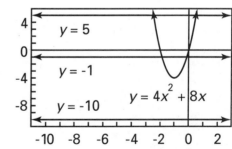

For this parabola, when $y = 5$, $x = \dfrac{1}{2}$ or $x = \dfrac{-5}{2}$; when $y = -1$, $x \approx -0.13$ or $x \approx -1.86$. There is no x-value associated with $y = -10$.

1. **a.** $(GH)^2 = 2^2 + 1^2$
   $(GH)^2 = 5$
   $GH = \sqrt{5}$
   $GI = 2\sqrt{5}$
   b. $(GI)^2 = (2 \cdot 2)^2 + (2 \cdot 1)^2$
   $(GI)^2 = 4^2 + 2^2$
   $(GI)^2 = 16 + 4$
   $(GI)^2 = 20$
   $GI = \sqrt{20}$
   c. On the calculator, $2\sqrt{5} \approx 4.472$;
   $\sqrt{20} \approx 4.472$
2. **a.** $5\sqrt{3} \approx 8.66$; $\sqrt{75} \approx 8.66$
   b. $(5\sqrt{3})^2 = 5\sqrt{3} \cdot 5\sqrt{3}$
   $= 5 \cdot 5 \cdot \sqrt{3} \cdot \sqrt{3}$
   $= 25 \cdot 3$
   $= 75$
   and, $\sqrt{75}^2 = \sqrt{75} \cdot \sqrt{75} = 75$
   c. $\sqrt{75} = \sqrt{25} \cdot \sqrt{3} = 5\sqrt{3}$
3. $\sqrt{pq}$
4. **a.** 2.65
   b. 2.24
   c. 5.92
   d. 5.92
5. greater than or equal to zero
6. **a.** 4
   b. $\sqrt{4} \cdot \sqrt{5} = 2\sqrt{5}$
7. **a.** 25
   b. $\sqrt{25} \cdot \sqrt{2} = 5\sqrt{2}$
8. **a.** 100
   b. $\sqrt{100} \cdot \sqrt{7} = 10\sqrt{7}$
9. $\sqrt{128} \approx 11.31$
   $8\sqrt{2} \approx 8 \cdot 1.41 \approx 11.31$
10. $c^2 = 10^2 + 10^2$
    $c^2 = 200$
    $c = \sqrt{200}$
    $c = \sqrt{100} \cdot \sqrt{2}$
    $c = 10\sqrt{2}$ cm

11. $\dfrac{6}{2} + \dfrac{\sqrt{18}}{2}$
    $= 3 + \dfrac{\sqrt{9} \cdot \sqrt{2}}{2}$
    $= 3 + \dfrac{3\sqrt{2}}{2}$
    $= 3 + \dfrac{3}{2}\sqrt{2}$
12. $\dfrac{12}{2} \pm \dfrac{\sqrt{12}}{2}$
    $= 6 \pm \dfrac{\sqrt{4} \cdot \sqrt{3}}{2}$
    $= 6 \pm \dfrac{2\sqrt{3}}{2}$
    $= 6 \pm \sqrt{3}$
13. $\sqrt{6} \cdot \sqrt{a} \cdot \sqrt{6} \cdot \sqrt{4} \cdot \sqrt{b}$
    $= \sqrt{6^2} \cdot \sqrt{2^2} \cdot \sqrt{ab}$
    $= 6 \cdot 2 \cdot \sqrt{ab}$
    $= 12\sqrt{ab}$
14. $\sqrt{6^2} \cdot \sqrt{a^2} \cdot \sqrt{b^2} = 6ab$
15. $6^2 - 3^2 = t^2$
    $36 - 9 = t^2$
    $27 = t^2$
    $\sqrt{27} = t$
    $\sqrt{9} \cdot \sqrt{3} = t$
    $3\sqrt{3} = t$
16. $y^2 + y^2 = 10^2$
    $2y^2 = 100$
    $y^2 = 50$
    $y = \sqrt{50}$
    $y = \sqrt{25} \cdot \sqrt{2}$
    $y = 5\sqrt{2}$
17. $\sqrt{2} \cdot (\sqrt{2} \cdot \sqrt{9})$
    $= \sqrt{2^2} \cdot \sqrt{3^2}$
    $= 2 \cdot 3 = 6$
18. $(\sqrt{4} \cdot \sqrt{5}) \cdot \sqrt{5}$
    $= \sqrt{2^2} \cdot \sqrt{5^2}$
    $= 2 \cdot 5 = 10$

19. $\sqrt{5^2} \cdot \sqrt{11^2} = 5 \cdot 11 = 55$
20. $\sqrt{10^2} \cdot \sqrt{9^2} \cdot \sqrt{6^2} = 10 \cdot 9 \cdot 6 = 540$
21. $4a^2 = 48$
$\quad a^2 = 12$
$\quad a = \pm\sqrt{12}$
$\quad a = \pm(\sqrt{4} \cdot \sqrt{3})$
$\quad a = \pm 2\sqrt{3}$
$\quad$ Check: $(2(2\sqrt{3}))^2 = (4\sqrt{3})^2 = 16 \cdot 3 = 48$
$\quad\quad (2(-2\sqrt{3}))^2 = (-4\sqrt{3})^2 =$
$\quad\quad\quad 16 \cdot 3 = 48$

22. $\quad 9 \cdot 6 = x^2$
$\quad\quad 54 = x^2$
$\quad \pm\sqrt{54} = x$
$\pm(\sqrt{9} \cdot \sqrt{6}) = x$
$\quad\quad \pm 3\sqrt{6} = x$
$\quad$ Check: $\dfrac{9}{3\sqrt{6}} = \dfrac{3}{\sqrt{6}} \approx 1.225$ and
$\quad\quad\quad \dfrac{3\sqrt{6}}{6} = \dfrac{\sqrt{6}}{2} \approx 1.225,$
$\quad\quad$ so $\dfrac{9}{3\sqrt{6}} = \dfrac{3\sqrt{6}}{6}$
$\quad\quad \dfrac{9}{-3\sqrt{6}} = \dfrac{-3}{\sqrt{6}} \approx -1.225$ and
$\quad\quad\quad \dfrac{-3\sqrt{6}}{6} = -\dfrac{\sqrt{6}}{2} \approx -1.225,$
$\quad\quad$ so $\dfrac{9}{-3\sqrt{6}} = \dfrac{-3\sqrt{6}}{6}$

23. a. $\sqrt{25} \cdot \sqrt{3} = 5\sqrt{3}$
$\quad$ **b.** $\sqrt{4} \cdot \sqrt{3} = 2\sqrt{3}$
$\quad$ **c.** $5\sqrt{3} + 2\sqrt{3} = 7\sqrt{3}$
24. a. Area $= \sqrt{18} \cdot 5\sqrt{2}$
$\quad\quad = \sqrt{9} \cdot \sqrt{2} \cdot 5 \cdot \sqrt{2}$
$\quad\quad = \sqrt{3^2} \cdot \sqrt{2^2} \cdot 5$
$\quad\quad = 3 \cdot 2 \cdot 5$
$\quad\quad = 30$ square units
$\quad$ **b.** The height is longer since
$\quad\quad \sqrt{18} = \sqrt{9} \cdot \sqrt{2} = 3\sqrt{2}.$

25. $\sqrt{20w^2} = w\sqrt{20}$ or
$\quad \sqrt{20w^2} = \sqrt{4} \cdot \sqrt{5} \cdot \sqrt{w^2} = 2w\sqrt{5}$
26. $a = 1, b = 4, c = -9$
$\quad x = \dfrac{-4 \pm \sqrt{4^2 - 4(1)(-9)}}{2(1)}$
$\quad x = \dfrac{-4 \pm \sqrt{52}}{2}$
$\quad x = \dfrac{-4 \pm 2\sqrt{13}}{2}$
$\quad x = -2 \pm \sqrt{13}$
27. The discriminant equals zero.
28. $d = 4.9(3)^2 = 4.9(9) = 44.1$ meters
29. $d = 4.9(\sqrt{10})^2 = 4.9(10) = 49$ meters
30. a. $10 = 4.9t^2$
$\quad$ **b.** $\dfrac{10}{4.9} = t^2$
$\quad\quad 1.43 \approx t$
31. 2 (discriminant: $1^2 - 4(1)(-1) = 1 + 4 = 5$)
32. 0 (discriminant: $1^2 - 4(1)1 = 1 - 4 = -3$)
33. 2 (discriminant:
$\quad (-12)^2 - 4(2)(-18) = 144 + 144 = 288$)
34. 1 (All linear equations have one solution.)
35. $0.25q + 0.10d \geq 5.20$
36. $B + 4 = 3B + 1$
$\quad\quad 4 = 2B + 1$
$\quad\quad 3 = 2B$
$\quad\quad 1.5 = B$
$\quad$ Each box weighs 1.5 kg.
37. If the lengths of the two legs of a right triangle are equal, the hypotenuse has length equal to the product of the length of a leg and $\sqrt{2}$. Suppose x is the length of each of the legs. Then (hypotenuse)$^2 = x^2 + x^2 = 2x^2$. Thus, the length of the hypotenuse is $x\sqrt{2}$.

LESSON 9-8 pp. 593–598

1. The absolute value of a number is the distance between its corresponding point and the origin.
2. 50

3. 1.3

4. 0

5. 16

6. $|4| = 4$

7. $8 + 4 = 12$

8. True

9. Samples: (6, 6), (-6, 6)

10. **a.** $|x| = 11$

    b. $x = 11$ or $x = -11$

11. $t = 25$ or $t = -25$

    Check: $|25| = 25$;

           $|-25| = 25$

12. $|x - 3| = 2$

    $x - 3 = 2$ or $x - 3 = -2$

       $x = 5$ or $x = 1$

    Check: $|5 - 3| = |2| = 2$;

            $|1 - 3| = |-2| = 2$

13. $|x - 3| = 42$

    $x - 3 = 42$ or $x - 3 = -42$

       $x = 45$ or $x = -39$

    Check: $|45 - 3| = |42| = 42$;

            $|-39 - 3| = |-42| = 42$

14. $|300 - x| = 10$

    $300 - x = $ 10 or $300 - x = -10$

        $-x = -290$ or $-x = -310$

          $x = $ 290 or $x = 310$

    Check: $|300 - 290| = |10| = 10$

            $|300 - 310| = |-10| = 10$

15. $|-28 - 11| = |-39| = 39$

16. $|-81 - -57| = |-81 + 57| = |-24| = 24$

17. $|17.5 - n|$ or $|n - 17.5|$

18. 11

19. $|n|$

20. 11

21. 8

22. 1; $n = 0$

23. 0; no real solution

24. 2; $p = \frac{1}{2}$ or $p = -\frac{1}{2}$

25. 2; $q = 31$ or $q = -31$

26. $3 - 7 = -4$; $3 + 7 = 10$

27. $-3 - 7 = -10$; $-3 + 7 = 4$

28. $a - 7$; $a + 7$

29. **a.** $x - y$

    b. $y - x$

    c. $|x - y|$ or $|y - x|$

30. **a.** $2 - 0.001 = 1.999$ cm

    b. $2 + 0.001 = 2.001$ cm

    c.

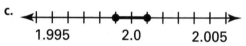

      1.995   2.0   2.005

    d. $|d - 2| \le 0.001$

31. $\frac{\sqrt{25} \cdot \sqrt{7}}{5} = \frac{5\sqrt{7}}{5} = \sqrt{7}$

32. $\frac{\sqrt{100} \cdot \sqrt{3}}{6} = \frac{10\sqrt{3}}{6} = \frac{5\sqrt{3}}{3}$

33. $\frac{16 \pm \sqrt{144} \cdot \sqrt{2}}{4} = \frac{16 \pm 12\sqrt{2}}{4} = 4 \pm 3\sqrt{2}$

34. False; $\sqrt{80} = \sqrt{16 \cdot 5} = 4\sqrt{5} \ne 8\sqrt{10}$

35. **a.** $r^2 + r^2 = 20^2$

          $2r^2 = 400$

           $r^2 = 200$

           $r = \sqrt{200}$

           $r = \sqrt{100} \cdot \sqrt{2}$

           $r = 10\sqrt{2}$ ft

    b. $10 \cdot 1.414 = 14.1$ ft

    c. $(BD)^2 = 10^2 + 20^2$

         $(BD)^2 = 500$

           $BD = \sqrt{5} \cdot \sqrt{100}$

           $BD = 10\sqrt{5}$

           $BD \approx 22.4$ ft

36. 2; discriminant: $1^2 - 4(17)(-20) = 1 + 1360 = 1361 > 0$

37. $a = 2$, $b = -16$, $c = -4$

$$x = \frac{-(-16) \pm \sqrt{(-16)^2 - 4(2)(-4)}}{2(2)}$$

$$x = \frac{16 \pm \sqrt{256 + 32}}{4}$$

$$x = \frac{16 \pm \sqrt{288}}{4}$$

$$x = \frac{16 \pm 12\sqrt{2}}{4}$$

$$x = 4 + 3\sqrt{2} \text{ or } x = 4 - 3\sqrt{2}$$

38. a. $x = 0$
  b. y-axis

39. a.

x	y
-6	9
-5	8
-4	7
-3	6
-2	5
-1	4
0	3
1	2
2	1
3	0
4	1
5	2
6	3

  b.

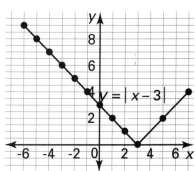

  c. The graph is an angle with vertex (3, 0).

40. a.

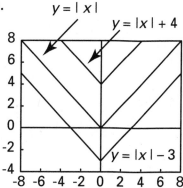

  b. The graph is a right angle with vertex at $(0, k)$.

  c. Sample: When $k = 5$, the equation is $y = |x| + 5$. The graph should be a right angle with vertex at (0, 5), which it is.

LESSON 9-9   pp. 599–604

1. a. $3 + 8 = 11$
  b. $(DE)^2 = 3^2 + 8^2$
  $(DE)^2 = 9 + 64$
  $(DE)^2 = 73$
  $DE = \sqrt{73} \approx 8.5$ blocks

2. $|60 - 18| = 42$

3. $|-3 - 11| = 14$

4. $|-1 - 6| = 7$

5. $|3 - -2| = 5$

6. $RT = \sqrt{|6 - -1|^2 + |-2 - 3|^2}$
  $RT = \sqrt{7^2 + 5^2}$
  $RT = \sqrt{74} \approx 8.6$

7. a. (-4, -5)
  b. $|3 - -5| = 8$
  c. $|-4 - 1| = 5$
  d. $DG = \sqrt{|-4 - 1|^2 + |3 - -5|^2}$
  $RT = \sqrt{8^2 + 5^2}$
  $RT = \sqrt{89} \approx 9.4$

8. $H = (10, 3)$

$FG = \sqrt{|10 - 14|^2 + |18 - 3|^2}$

$FG = \sqrt{4^2 + 15^2}$

$FG = \sqrt{241} \approx 15.5$

9. $H = (-4, 10)$

$FG = \sqrt{|-11 - -4|^2 + |10 - -3|^2}$

$FG = \sqrt{7^2 + 13^2}$

$FG = \sqrt{218} \approx 14.8$

10. $AB = \sqrt{|0 - -3|^2 + |0 - -4|^2}$

$AB = \sqrt{3^2 + 4^2}$

$AB = \sqrt{25} = 5$

11. $AB = \sqrt{|4 - 0|^2 + |11 - 7|^2}$

$AB = \sqrt{4^2 + 4^2}$

$AB = \sqrt{32} = 4\sqrt{2} \approx 5.7$

12. $DC = \sqrt{|5 - 11|^2 + |1 - -7|^2}$

$DC = \sqrt{6^2 + 8^2}$

$DC = \sqrt{100} = 10$

13. $EF = \sqrt{|-3 - -1|^2 + |5 - -8|^2}$

$EF = \sqrt{2^2 + 13^2}$

$EF = \sqrt{173} \approx 13.2$

14. $(1, 2)$

15. $6 + 1 = 7$ km

16. distance $= \sqrt{6^2 + 1^2}$

$= \sqrt{37} \approx 6.1$ km

17. distance $= \sqrt{1^2 + 2^2}$

$= \sqrt{5} \approx 2.2$ km

18. $A = (5, 8 - 6) = (5, 2)$

$B = (5 + 6, 8) = (11, 8)$

$C = (5, 8 + 6) = (5, 14)$

$D = (5 - 6, 8) = (-1, 8)$

19. $\sqrt{|0 - a|^2 + |0 - b|^2} = \sqrt{|a|^2 + |b|^2}$

20. $\sqrt{|a - c|^2 + |b - d|^2}$

21. $JK = \sqrt{|-5 - 1|^2 + |0 - 8|^2}$

$JK = \sqrt{6^2 + 8^2}$

$JK = \sqrt{100} = 10;$

$KL = \sqrt{|1 - 16|^2 + |8 - 0|^2}$

$KL = \sqrt{15^2 + 8^2}$

$KL = \sqrt{289} = 17$

$JL = |-5 - 16| = 21$

22. $5^2 = |1 - 4|^2 + |1 - y|^2$

$25 = 9 + (1 - y)^2$

$16 = (1 - y)^2$

$\pm 4 = 1 - y$

$4 = 1 - y$ or $-4 = 1 - y$

$-3 = y$ or $5 = y$

23. 29.732137

24. 1.4142136

25. $x = 3.5$ or $x = -3.5$

26. $|x + 7| = 5$

$x + 7 = 5$ or $x + 7 = -5$

$x = -2$ or $x = -12$

27. **a.** $t = \pm 3$

b. $t = 81$

c. $t = 9$ or $t = -9$

28. $\dfrac{-40}{12} \pm \dfrac{\sqrt{4} \cdot \sqrt{5}}{12} = -\dfrac{10}{3} \pm \dfrac{\sqrt{5}}{6}$

29. 2; the line $y = 10$ intersects the graph twice.

30. **a.** $3x = -4$

$x = -\dfrac{4}{3}$

b. $3x + 6 = x + 2$

$2x + 6 = 2$

$2x = -4$

$x = -2$

c. $3x + 6 = x^2 + 2$

$0 = x^2 - 3x - 4$

$x = \dfrac{-(-3) \pm \sqrt{(-3)^2 - 4(1)(-4)}}{2(1)}$

$x = \dfrac{3 \pm \sqrt{25}}{2}$

$x = \dfrac{3 \pm 5}{2}$

$x = \dfrac{3 + 5}{2}$ or $x = \dfrac{3 - 5}{2}$

$x = 4$ or $x = -1$

30. d. $3x + 6 = x^2 + 2x$

$$0 = x^2 - x - 6$$

$$x = \frac{-(-1) \pm \sqrt{(-1)^2 - 4(1)(-6)}}{2(1)}$$

$$x = \frac{1 \pm \sqrt{25}}{2}$$

$$x = \frac{1 \pm 5}{2}$$

$$x = \frac{1 + 5}{2} \text{ or } x = \frac{1 - 5}{2}$$

$$x = 3 \quad \text{ or } x = -2$$

31. a. $x^2 + 9x - 5 = 0$

$$x = \frac{-9 \pm \sqrt{9^2 - 4(1)(-5)}}{2(1)}$$

$$x = \frac{-9 \pm \sqrt{101}}{2}$$

$$x = \frac{-9 + \sqrt{101}}{2} \text{ or } x = \frac{-9 - \sqrt{101}}{2}$$

$$x \approx 0.52 \quad \text{ or } x \approx -9.52$$

b.

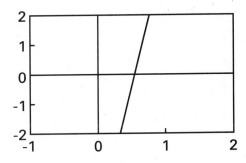

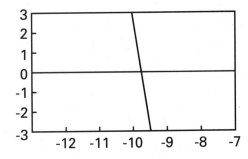

32.

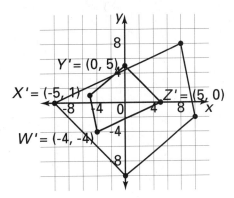

$Y' = (0, 5)$
$X' = (-5, 1)$
$Z' = (5, 0)$
$W' = (-4, -4)$

33. $15x - 10 = 180$

$$15x = 190$$

$$x = \frac{190}{15} = 12\tfrac{2}{3}$$

34. $\dfrac{\$5.00 - .25}{.70} = \dfrac{\$4.75}{.7} = 6.8$

You can buy at most 6 croissants.

35.

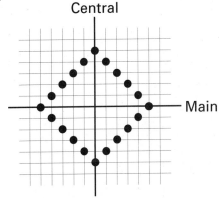

Central

Main

CHAPTER 9

PROGRESS SELF-TEST p. 609

1. $x = \dfrac{-(-9) \pm \sqrt{(-9)^2 - 4(1)(20)}}{2(1)}$

$$x = \frac{9 \pm \sqrt{1}}{2}$$

$$x = \frac{9 + 1}{2} \text{ or } x = \frac{9 - 1}{2}$$

$$x = 5 \quad \text{ or } x = 4$$

2. $x = \dfrac{-(-3) \pm \sqrt{(-3)^2 - 4(5)(-11)}}{2(5)}$

$x = \dfrac{3 \pm \sqrt{229}}{10}$

$x = \dfrac{3 + \sqrt{229}}{10}$ or $x = \dfrac{3 - \sqrt{229}}{10}$

$x \approx 1.81$ or $x \approx -1.21$

3. Discriminant: $(-7)^2 - 4(8)(11) = 49 - 352 = -303 < 0$; no real solutions

4. $x = \dfrac{-(-16) \pm \sqrt{(-16)^2 - 4(1)(64)}}{2(1)}$

$x = \dfrac{16 \pm \sqrt{0}}{2}$

$x = \dfrac{16}{2}$

$x = 8$

5. 2

6. (a)

7. a.

x	y
-3	-18
-2	-8
-1	-2
0	0
1	-2
2	-8
3	-18

b.

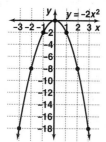

$y = -2x^2$

8. a.

x	y
-3	24
-2	15
-1	8
0	3
1	0
2	-1
3	0

b.

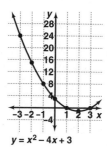

$y = x^2 - 4x + 3$

9. False; the parabola opens up since $3 > 0$.

10. (2, -2)

11. (1, 0); (3, 0)

12. $x = 2$

13. $\sqrt{100} \cdot \sqrt{5} = 10\sqrt{5}$

14. $\dfrac{\sqrt{25} \cdot \sqrt{3}}{5} = \dfrac{5\sqrt{3}}{5} = \sqrt{3}$

15. $\sqrt{5} \cdot \sqrt{x} \cdot \sqrt{9} \cdot \sqrt{5} \cdot \sqrt{y}$

$= \sqrt{5^2} \cdot \sqrt{3^2} \cdot \sqrt{xy}$

$= 5 \cdot 3 \cdot \sqrt{xy}$

$= 15\sqrt{xy}$

16. Sample:

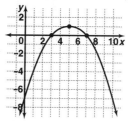

17. (7, -6)

18. True

19. $UV = \sqrt{|2 - 7|^2 + |\text{-}6 - 4|^2}$

$UV = \sqrt{5^2 + 10^2}$

$UV = \sqrt{125}$

$UV = \sqrt{25} \cdot \sqrt{5} = 5\sqrt{5}$

20. $\sqrt{|3 - x|^2 + |\text{-}2 - y|^2}$

21. $-16t^2 + 21t + 40 = 0$

$$x = \frac{-21 \pm \sqrt{(21)^2 - 4(-16)(40)}}{2(-16)}$$

$$x = \frac{-21 \pm \sqrt{3001}}{-32}$$

$$x = \frac{-21 + \sqrt{3001}}{-32} \text{ or } x = \frac{-21 - \sqrt{3001}}{-32}$$

$x \approx -1.06 \qquad$ or $x \approx 2.4$

about 2.4 seconds; disregard -1.06 because the ball could not reach the ground before it was thrown.

22. $-16t^2 + 21t + 40 = 43$

$-16t^2 + 21t - 3 = 0$

$$x = \frac{-21 \pm \sqrt{(21)^2 - 4(-16)(-3)}}{2(-16)}$$

$$x = \frac{-21 \pm \sqrt{249}}{-32}$$

$$x = \frac{-21 + \sqrt{249}}{-32} \text{ or } x = \frac{-21 - \sqrt{249}}{-32}$$

$x \approx 0.2 \qquad$ or $x \approx 1.1$

about .2 second and about 1.1 seconds

23.

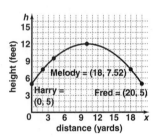

24. $h = -0.07(18)^2 + 1.4(18) + 5$

$= -22.68 + 25.2 + 5$

$= 7.52$ ft

25. $x^2 = 30$

$x \approx \pm 5.48$

26. $x = \pm 57$

27. $3 - n = 0.5$ or $3 - n = -0.5$

$-n = -2.5$ or $\quad -n = -3.5$

$n = 2.5$ or $\quad n = 3.5$

REVIEW $\hspace{3cm}$ pp. 610–613

1. $t^2 = 25$

$t = 5$ or $t = -5$

2. $36 = x^2$

$x = 6$ or $x = -6$

3. $g^2 = 49$

$g = 7$ or $g = -7$

4. $p^2 = 12$

$p = \pm\sqrt{12}$

$p = \pm\sqrt{4} \cdot \sqrt{3}$

$p = 2\sqrt{3}$ or $p = -2\sqrt{3}$

5. $a = 6$, $b = 7$, $c = -20$

$$y = \frac{-7 \pm \sqrt{7^2 - 4(6)(-20)}}{2 \cdot 6}$$

$$y = \frac{-7 \pm \sqrt{49 + 480}}{12}$$

$$y = \frac{-7 \pm 23}{12}$$

$$y = \frac{-7 + 23}{12} \text{ or } y = \frac{-7 - 23}{12}$$

$$y = \frac{16}{12} \qquad \text{or } y = \frac{-30}{12}$$

$$y = \frac{4}{3} \qquad \text{or } y = -\frac{5}{2}$$

6. $a = 1$, $b = 7$, $c = 12$

$$x = \frac{-7 \pm \sqrt{7^2 - 4(1)(12)}}{2 \cdot 1}$$

$$x = \frac{-7 \pm \sqrt{49 - 48}}{2}$$

$$x = \frac{-7 \pm 1}{2}$$

$$x = \frac{-7 + 1}{2} \text{ or } x = \frac{-7 - 1}{2}$$

$$x = \frac{-6}{2} \qquad \text{or } x = \frac{-8}{2}$$

$x = -3 \qquad$ or $x = -4$

7. $a = 1, b = -14, c = 49$

$$v = \frac{-(-14) \pm \sqrt{(-14)^2 - 4(1)(49)}}{2 \cdot 1}$$

$$v = \frac{14 \pm \sqrt{196 - 196}}{2}$$

$$v = \frac{14 \pm 0}{2}$$

$$v = \frac{14}{2}$$

$$v = 7$$

8. $a = 2, b = -14, c = 3$

$$h = \frac{-(-14) \pm \sqrt{(-14)^2 - 4(2)(3)}}{2 \cdot 2}$$

$$h = \frac{14 \pm \sqrt{196 - 24}}{4}$$

$$h = \frac{14 \pm \sqrt{172}}{4}$$

$$h = \frac{14 \pm 2\sqrt{43}}{4}$$

$$h = \frac{7 \pm \sqrt{43}}{2}$$

9. $a = 1, b = -7, c = -2$

$$k = \frac{-(-7) \pm \sqrt{(-7)^2 - 4(1)(-2)}}{2 \cdot 1}$$

$$k = \frac{7 \pm \sqrt{49 + 8}}{2}$$

$$k = \frac{7 \pm \sqrt{57}}{2}$$

$$k = \frac{7 + \sqrt{57}}{2} \text{ or } k = \frac{7 - \sqrt{57}}{2}$$

$$k = 7.27 \quad \text{ or } k = -0.27$$

10. $a = 2, b = 1, c = -3$

$$m = \frac{-1 \pm \sqrt{(1)^2 - 4(2)(-3)}}{2 \cdot 2}$$

$$m = \frac{-1 \pm \sqrt{1 + 24}}{4}$$

$$m = \frac{-1 \pm \sqrt{25}}{4}$$

$$m = \frac{-1 + 5}{4} \text{ or } m = \frac{-1 - 5}{4}$$

$$m = \frac{4}{4} \quad \text{ or } m = \frac{-6}{4}$$

$$m = 1.00 \text{ or } m = -1.50$$

11. $a = 22, b = 2, c = 3$

$$a = \frac{-2 \pm \sqrt{(2)^2 - 4(22)(3)}}{2 \cdot 22}$$

$$= \frac{-2 \pm \sqrt{4 - 264}}{44}$$

$$= \frac{-2 \pm \sqrt{-260}}{44}$$

discriminant < 0

no real solutions

12. $a = 1, b = 10, c = 25$

$$x = \frac{-10 \pm \sqrt{10^2 - 4(1)(25)}}{2 \cdot 1}$$

$$x = \frac{-10 \pm \sqrt{100 - 100}}{2}$$

$$x = \frac{-10 \pm 0}{2}$$

$$x = \frac{-10}{2}$$

$$x = -5$$

13. $10m^2 - 50m + 30 = 0$

$a = 10, b = -50, c = 30$

$$m = \frac{-(-50) \pm \sqrt{(-50)^2 - 4(10)(30)}}{2 \cdot 10}$$

$$m = \frac{50 \pm \sqrt{2500 - 1200}}{20}$$

$$m = \frac{50 \pm \sqrt{1300}}{20}$$

$$m = \frac{50 \pm 10\sqrt{13}}{20}$$

$$m = \frac{5 \pm \sqrt{13}}{2}$$

$$m = \frac{5 + \sqrt{13}}{2} \text{ or } m = \frac{5 - \sqrt{13}}{2}$$

$$m \approx 4.30 \quad \text{ or } m \approx 0.70$$

14. $a = 16, b = 8, c = 5$

$$p = \frac{-8 \pm \sqrt{8^2 - 4(16)(5)}}{2 \cdot 16}$$

$$p = \frac{-8 \pm \sqrt{64 - 320}}{32}$$

$$p = \frac{-8 \pm \sqrt{-256}}{32}$$

discriminant < 0

no real solutions

15. $\sqrt{7} \cdot \sqrt{7} \cdot \sqrt{2^2} = 7 \cdot 2 = 14$

16. $\sqrt{2^2} \cdot \sqrt{3^2} - \sqrt{3} \cdot \sqrt{3} \cdot \sqrt{4^2}$

$\quad = 2 \cdot 3 - 3 \cdot 4$

$\quad = 6 - 12 = -6$

17. $\sqrt{2(20)^2} = \sqrt{20^2} \cdot \sqrt{2} = 20\sqrt{2}$

18. $\sqrt{9} \cdot \sqrt{11} = 3\sqrt{11}$

19. $\sqrt{100} \cdot \sqrt{5} = 10\sqrt{5}$

20. $\dfrac{\sqrt{25} \cdot \sqrt{6}}{5}$

$\quad = \dfrac{5 \cdot \sqrt{6}}{5}$

$\quad = \sqrt{6}$

21. $3 \cdot \sqrt{36} \cdot \sqrt{2} = 3 \cdot 6 \cdot \sqrt{2} = 18\sqrt{2}$

22. $\dfrac{6 + \sqrt{64} \cdot \sqrt{2}}{2} = \dfrac{6 + 8\sqrt{2}}{2} = 3 + 4\sqrt{2}$

23. $\dfrac{12 \pm 6 \cdot \sqrt{4 \cdot 6}}{4}$

$\quad = \dfrac{12 \pm 6 \cdot 2 \cdot \sqrt{6}}{4}$

$\quad = \dfrac{12 \pm 12\sqrt{6}}{4}$

$\quad = 3 \pm 3\sqrt{6}$

24. $\sqrt{4} \cdot \sqrt{6x} \cdot \sqrt{6x} = 2 \cdot 6x = 12x$

25. $x\sqrt{5}$

26. $xy\sqrt{2}$

27. 17

28. $-y$

29. 43

30. -1

31. $|{-6}| = 6$

32. $\text{ABS}(-0.2) = 0.2$

33. $3 - 8 = -5$

34. $20 - 15 + 2 = 7$

35. $d = 16$ or $d = -16$

36. no solution

37. $x^2 = 49$

$\quad x = 7$ or $x = -7$

38. $n^2 = 144$

$\quad n = 12$ or $n = -12$

39. $r - 10 = 5$ or $r - 10 = -5$

$\quad\quad r = 15$ or $\quad\quad r = 5$

40. $300 - s = 23$ or $300 - s = -23$

$\quad\quad -s = -277$ or $\quad\quad -s = -323$

$\quad\quad\quad s = 277$ or $\quad\quad\quad s = 323$

41. $\dfrac{-b \pm \sqrt{b^2 - 4ac}}{2a}$

42. True

43. True

44. If the discriminant is positive, then the equation has exactly two real solutions. If the discriminant equals zero, then the equation has exactly one real solution. If the discriminant is negative, then the equation has no real solutions.

45. discriminant: $(-3)^2 - 4(2)(4) = 9 - 32 = -23$
no real solutions

46. $a^2 - 3a - 8 = 0$
discriminant: $(-3)^2 - 4(1)(-8) = 9 + 32 = 41$
two real solutions

47. $8d^2 - 9d + 40 = 0$
discriminant:
$(-9)^2 - 4(8)(40) = 81 - 1280 = -1199$
no real solutions

48. $n^2 + n + 5 = 0$
discriminant: $1^2 - 4(1)(5) = 1 - 20 = -19$
no real solutions

49. **a.** $d = \dfrac{1}{2} \cdot 32 \cdot 6^2 = 576$ ft

$\quad$ **b.** $\dfrac{1}{2} \cdot 32t^2 = 2000$

$\quad\quad\quad 16t^2 = 2000$

$\quad\quad\quad\quad t^2 = 125$

$\quad\quad\quad\quad\quad t \approx 11.2$ seconds

50. **a.** $d = \dfrac{1}{2} \cdot 5.3 \cdot 4^2 = 42.4$ ft

$\quad$ **b.** $\dfrac{1}{2} \cdot 5.3t^2 = 100$

$\quad\quad\quad 2.65t^2 = 100$

$\quad\quad\quad\quad t^2 \approx 37.7$

$\quad\quad\quad\quad\quad t \approx 6.14$ seconds

51. a.

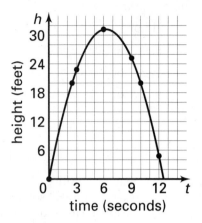

time (seconds)

b. 2.5 seconds and 10 seconds

c. $-0.8t^2 + 10t - 20 = 0$

$a = -0.8, b = 10, c = -20$

$$t = \frac{-10 \pm \sqrt{10^2 - 4(-0.8)(-20)}}{2 \cdot -0.8}$$

$$t = \frac{-10 \pm \sqrt{100 - 64}}{-1.6}$$

$$t = \frac{-10 \pm \sqrt{36}}{-1.6}$$

$$t = \frac{-10 \pm 6}{-1.6}$$

$$t = \frac{-10 + 6}{-1.6} \qquad \text{or } t = \frac{-10 - 6}{-1.6}$$

$t = 2.5$ seconds or $t = 10$ seconds

52. a. $40 - 6 = 34$

b. No, because 34 yards from the quarterback, the ball is at a height of 11.1 ft.

$(h = -0.025(34)^2 + 34 + 6$

$= -28.9 + 40 = 11.1)$

53. a. about 48 ft

b. about 0.65 seconds or 3.35 seconds

c. 4

d. Sample: What is the maximum height the ball will reach?

54. a. $0 = 20x - 5x^2$

$$x = \frac{-20 \pm \sqrt{20^2 - 4(-5)(0)}}{2(-5)}$$

$$x = \frac{-20 \pm \sqrt{20^2}}{-10}$$

$$x = \frac{-20 + 20}{-10} \text{ or } x = \frac{-20 - 20}{-10}$$

$x = 0 \qquad$ or $x = 4$

The ball will hit the ground after 4 seconds.

b. The ball reaches its vertex in half the total time; 2 seconds

$h = 20(2) - 5(2)^2 = 40 - 20 = 20$ meters

55. a. vertex: $(10, 13)$

b. $x = 10$

c. $A = (10 - 3, 4) = (7, 4)$

$B = (10 - 2, 9) = (8, 9)$

$C = (10 - 1, 12) = (9, 12)$

56. a. $x = -2$

b. vertex: $(-2, 5)$

c. 9; 14

57. False; parabolas that open down do not have a minimum.

58. True

59. $ax^2 + bx + c = 0$

60. $\frac{2 + 6}{2} = 4$

$2(4)^2 - 16(4) + 24 = 32 - 64 + 24 = -8$

vertex: $(4, -8)$

61. a.

x	y
-2	12
-1	3
0	0
1	3
2	12

b.

$y = 3x^2$

62. a.

x	y
-4	-8
-2	-2
0	0
2	-2
4	-8

b.

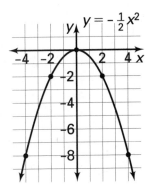

$y = -\frac{1}{2}x^2$

b.

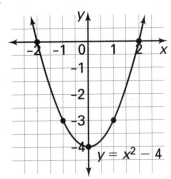

$y = x^2 - 4$

63. a.

x	y
-4	2
-3	0
-2.5	-2.5
-2	0
-1	2
0	6

b.

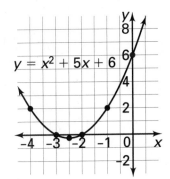

$y = x^2 + 5x + 6$

64. a.

x	y
-2	0
-1	-3
0	-4
1	-3
2	0

65. (b)

66. (a)

67. a.

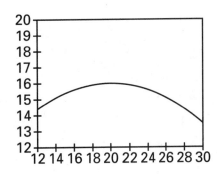

b. vertex: (20, 16)

c. maximum

68. a.

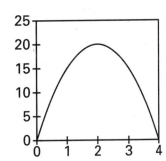

b. vertex: (2, 20)

c. maximum

69. Sample: $-5 \le x \le 15$ and $-10 \le y \le 30$

70. Sample: $-50 \le x \le 15$ and $-50 \le y \le 1$

71. $|-47 - -16| = |-31| = 31$

72. $|p - q|$ or $|q - p|$

73. $-3 + 5 = 2$; $-3 - 5 = -8$

74. a. $AB = |4 - {-7}| = |11| = 11$

    b. $AC = \sqrt{|4 - {-7}|^2 + |3 - {-5}|^2}$

        $AC = \sqrt{121 + 64}$

        $AC = \sqrt{185}$

        $AC \approx 13.6$

75. $AO = \sqrt{3^2 + 4^2} = \sqrt{25} = 5$

76. $BC = |{-5} - 3| = |{-8}| = 8$

    $BO = \sqrt{|3 - 0|^2 + |{-7} - 0|^2}$

    $BO = \sqrt{58} \approx 7.61$

    BC is longer than BO.

77. $|4 - {-5}| = 9$

78. $|20 - 2| = 18$

79. $\sqrt{50^2 + 10^2} = \sqrt{2600} = 10\sqrt{26} \approx 50.99$

80. $AB = \sqrt{|14 - {-2}|^2 + |{-20} - {-8}|^2}$

    $AB = \sqrt{256 + 144}$

    $AB = \sqrt{400}$

    $AB = 20$

81. $AB = \sqrt{|{-4} - 4|^2 + |{-3} - 12|^2}$

    $AB = \sqrt{64 + 225}$

    $AB = \sqrt{289}$

    $AB = 17$

82. $AB = \sqrt{|{-2} - {-5}|^2 + |9 - {-1}|^2}$

    $AB = \sqrt{9 + 100}$

    $AB = \sqrt{109}$

    $AB \approx 10.44$

83. a.

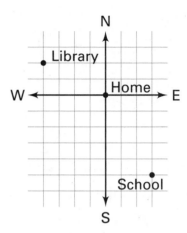

    b. $\sqrt{7^2 + 7^2} = \sqrt{2 \cdot 7^2} = 7\sqrt{2}$

84. the hypotenuse is between $(6, 2)$ and $(0, 4)$.

    hypotenuse $= \sqrt{|6 - 0|^2 + |2 - 4|^2}$

    hypotenuse $= \sqrt{36 + 4}$

    hypotenuse $= \sqrt{40}$

    hypotenuse $= 2\sqrt{10} \approx 6.3$

POLYNOMIALS

LESSON 10-1   pp. 616–620

1. (d); ($x + 4$ is the sum of two monomials.)
2. A monomial has variables with nonnegative powers. $\left(\dfrac{1}{y^2} = y^{-2}\right)$
3. **a.** Yes
   b. degree: 4
4. **a.** Yes
   b. degree: 2
5. No
6. **a.** Yes
   b. degree: 2
7. **a.** Yes
   b. degree: 9
8. **a.** No
   b. A trinomial is the sum of three monomials; xyz is the product of three monomials.
9. (a)
10. (b), (c), and (d)
11. (a), (b), and (c)
12. (d)
13. (a), (b), and (d)
14. $-8d^4 + d^3 + 16d^2$
15. $x^9 - x^7 + 2x + 4$
16. $1 \cdot 10^3 + 9 \cdot 10^2 + 3 \cdot 10 + 8$
17. $4x^2 + 6x$
18. $3x^2 + x + 2$
19.

20.

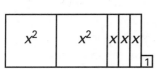

21. **a.** $4x$
    b. degree: 1
22. **a.** $3x^2$
    b. degree: 2
23. **a.** $-30n^4$
    b. degree: 4
24. **a.** $8ab$
    b. degree: 2
25. **a.** $2^6 a^6 b^6 = 64 a^6 b^6$
    b. degree: 12
26. **a.** Sample: $6x^5$
    b. Sample: $x^2 y^3$
27. **a.**

x^2	xy	xy	y^2

   b.

	x	y
x	x^2	xy
y	xy	y^2

28.

x	1	1	1
x	1	1	1
x^2	x	x	x

29. **a.** $246 = 2 \cdot 10^2 + 4 \cdot 10 + 6$
    $1032 = 1 \cdot 10^3 + 0 \cdot 10^2 + 3 \cdot 10 + 2$
    b. $1 \cdot 10^3 + 2 \cdot 10^2 + 0 \cdot 10^2$
    $\quad\quad + 4 \cdot 10 + 3 \cdot 10 + 8 = 1278$
    $246 + 1032 = 1278$
    Yes, the sums are equal.
30. **a.** $2000(1.06) = \$2120$
    b. $2000(1.06)^2 = \$2247.20$
    c. $2000(1.06)^n$

31. a.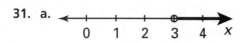

b.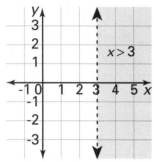

32. a. $x < 1$

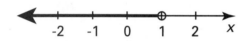

b.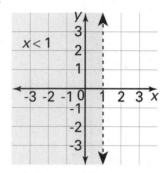

33.

34. $\frac{-4}{12} = \frac{-1}{3}$

35. a. $\frac{h}{15 \text{ feet}} = \frac{1}{3}$

$h = 5$ feet

b. $r = \sqrt{15^2 + 5^2}$

$r = \sqrt{250}$

$r = 5\sqrt{10} \approx 15.8$

The length of one rafter is about 15.8 feet.

36. Samples: monologue—a long speech by one person in a group; biped—an animal with two feet; triangle—a three-sided figure; polygraph—an instrument such as a lie detector that records several pulsations (artery, vein, heart, etc.) at the same time

---

LESSON 10-2 pp. 621–626

1. a. $500(1.05)^4 + 500(1.05)^3 + 500(1.05)^2$
$+ 500(1.05) + 500$

$= 607.753 + 578.813 + 551.25$
$+ 525 + 500$

$= \$2762.82$

b. $\$2875.37 - \$2762.82 = \$112.55$

2. a. $1200(1.07)^4 + 1200(1.07)^3 + 1200(1.07)^2$
$+ 1200(1.07) + 1200$

$= 1572.96 + 1470.05 + 1373.88$
$+ 1284 + 1200$

$= \$6900.89$

b. $1200x^4 + 1200x^3 + 1200x^2 + 1200x + 1200$

3. 90

4. a. $15x^3 + 25x^2 + 35x + 45$ dollars

b. $70x^3 + 80x^2 + 90x + 100 + 15x^3 + 25x^2$
$+ 35x + 45$

$= 85x^3 + 105x^2 + 125x + 145$

5. Joe deposited $5(1200) = \$6000$.
Nellie deposited $5(1000) = \$5000$.
Joe deposited $1000 more than Nellie.

6. Nellie will have more money than Joe.
$7996.32 - 7170.38 = \$825.94$

7. Nellie will earn more money than Joe at 7% interest.

	A	C	E
1	Year	Nellie's Balance	Joe's Balance
2		(end of year)	(end of year)
3	1	1070.00	0
4	2	2214.90	0
5	3	3439.94	0
6	4	4750.74	0
7	5	6153.29	0
8	6	6584.02	1284.00
9	7	7044.90	2657.88
10	8	7538.05	4127.93
11	9	8065.71	5700.89
12	10	8630.31	7383.95

8. a. $100 + 150(4) = \$700$

   b. $100(1.06)^4 + 150(1.06)^3 + 150(1.06)^2$
   $+ 150(1.06) + 150$

   $= 126.25 + 178.65 + 168.54 + 159 + 150$

   $= \$782.44$

   $782.44 - 700 = \$82.44$

9. $100

10. $150(1.06) + 150 = \$309$

11. $50(1.06)^2 + 400(1.06) = \$480.18$

12. a. $100

   b. $100x + 200$

   c. $100x^2 + 200x + 150$

   d. $100x^3 + 200x^2 + 150x + 300$

13. $(12+4)y^2 + (3-2)y + (-7-10) = 16y^2 + y - 17$

14. $(5+2)k^2 + (-2+-3)k + (3+-10) = 7k^2 - 5k - 7$

15. $(6-4)w^2 - w + (14-3) = 2w^2 - w + 11$

16. $(1-5)x^3 + (-4-4)x + (1--8) = -4x^3 - 8x + 9$

17. $6x^2 + 13x + 6 = 0$

   $a = 6, b = 13, c = 6$

   $x = \dfrac{-13 \pm \sqrt{13^2 - 4(6)(6)}}{2(6)}$

   $x = \dfrac{-13 \pm \sqrt{25}}{12}$

   $x = \dfrac{-13+5}{12}$ or $x = \dfrac{-13-5}{12}$

   $x = \dfrac{-8}{12} = -\dfrac{2}{3}$ or $x = \dfrac{-18}{12} = -\dfrac{3}{2}$

18. $(13-9)x^2 + (0-12)x + (6--5) = 4x^2 - 12x + 11$

19. $(2--5)y^2 + (-1--1)y + (-16-31) = 7y^2 - 47$

20. $.01(16{,}000x^3 + 22{,}000x^2 + 18{,}000x + 25{,}000)$
   $= 160x^3 + 220x^2 + 180x + 250$

21. Sample: area of a circle with radius r; degree: 2

22. Sample: volume of a cube with side x; degree: 3

23. Sample: amount of money saved if $16 was invested at some rate t two years ago, and if $48 was added to the account one year ago; degree: 2

24. a. $x^2 + 5x - 10x = x^2 - 5x$

   b. $x^2 - 5x = 0$

   $a = 1, b = -5, c = 0$

   $x = \dfrac{-(-5) \pm \sqrt{(-5)^2 - 4(1)(0)}}{2(1)}$

   $x = \dfrac{5 \pm 5}{2}$

   $x = \dfrac{5+5}{2} = 5$ or $x = \dfrac{5-5}{2} = 0$

25. 65 mph: $0.042(65)^2 + 1.1(65) = 177.45 + 71.5$
   $= 248.95$

   55 mph: $0.042(55)^2 + 1.1(55) = 127.05 + 60.5$
   $= 187.55$

   $248.95 - 187.55 = 61.4$ ft

26. $-x + \dfrac{1}{x} - \dfrac{1}{x} = -x$

27. slope $= \dfrac{0-b}{a-0} = -\dfrac{b}{a}$

28. a. $24y$

   b. $24y + 56$

   c. $24y + 56 - 32x$

29. (c)

30. $(-5 + 2 + 10)n + (1 + 1)k = 7n + 2k$

31. area of shaded region: $51x - 11x = 20$

$$40x = 20$$
$$x = \frac{1}{2}$$

dimensions: $x = .5$; $3x = 1.5$

32. a. Nellie ends up with more money than Joe when rates are not less than 3.72%. Solve by trial and error: change the rates in the formulas in columns C and E of the spreadsheet.

b. Joe ends up with more money than Nellie when rates are less than 3.72%. Solve by trial and error: change the rates in the formulas in columns C and E of the spreadsheet.

LESSON 10-3   pp. 627–632

1. $12x^2$

2. $12x^3y^4$

3. a. $3x(x + 4) = 3x^2 + 12x$

b.

4. a. $2x(x + 5) = 2x^2 + 10x$

b.

5. a. $x^2 + x^2 + x^2 + x + x^2 + x^2 + x^2 + x$
$= 6x^2 + 2x$

b. $(3x + 1)2x$

c. $(3x + 1)2x = 6x^2 + 2x$

6. a. $x^2 + x^2 + x^2 + x + x + x + x + x + x$
$= 3x^2 + 6x$

b. $3x(x + 2)$

c. $3x(x + 2) = 3x^2 + 6x$

7. $2h(L_1 + L_2 + L_3 + L_4)$; or
$2hL_1 + 2hL_2 + 2hL_3 + 2hL_4$

8. $a(b + c + d) = ab + ac + ad$

9. $x^3 + x^2 + x$

10. $5x^4 - 45x^3 + 10x^2$

11. $6p + 3p^3 + 15p^5$

12. $-12wy^2 + 6w^2y + 3wy$

13. $10,000 \cdot 46,329$

$= 10^4(4 \cdot 10^4 + 6 \cdot 10^3 + 3 \cdot 10^2 + 2 \cdot 10 + 9)$

$= 10^4 \cdot 4 \cdot 10^4 + 10^4 \cdot 6 \cdot 10^3 + 10^4 \cdot 3 \cdot 10^2$
$\quad + 10^4 \cdot 2 \cdot 10 + 10^4 \cdot 9$

$= 4 \cdot 10^8 + 6 \cdot 10^7 + 3 \cdot 10^6 + 2 \cdot 10^5 + 9 \cdot 10^4$

$= 463,290,000$

14. $w(7 + 2w) = 7w + 2w^2$

15. $w(5w - 1) = 5w^2 - w$

16. $2xy + x^2 + 2xy + 3x^2 = 4x^2 + 4xy$

17. $2x(3x + 1) + 2x \cdot x = 6x^2 + 2x + 2x^2$
$\qquad\qquad\qquad\qquad = 8x^2 + 2x$

18. $10x^2 - 12x^2 = -2x^2$

19. $6a^3b^3c^2$

20. $2x^2 + 6x - 3x^2 = -x^2 + 6x$

21. $ay^2 - 2ay + ya^2 + 2ya$
$= ay^2 + ya^2$

22. $m^5 - 3m^4 + 2m^3 - m^5 + 5m^4 + 6m^2$
$= 2m^4 + 2m^3 + 6m^2$

23. $6n^2$

24. a. $50

b. $80

c. Sample: $x = 1.065$

d. $80 + 60 + 70 + 45 + 50 = $305

e. Wanda has put her money in a noninterest-bearing account.

25. a. No

b. $2x^{-3}$ cannot be written as a product of variables with nonnegative exponents.

26. a. Yes

b. degree: $4 + 3 = 7$

27. Sample: $-4x^7 + 5x + 1$

28. $\frac{20}{2} \cdot x^{2-1} \cdot y^{1-1} = 10x$

29. $\frac{3 + 4v}{2v}$

30. slope: $\frac{16 - 8}{-1 - -5} = \frac{8}{4} = 2$

$$y - 8 = 2(x - -5)$$
$$y - 8 = 2x + 10$$
$$y = 2x + 18$$

31. $y = 3x + 5$

32. a. $\dfrac{200 \text{ miles}}{\frac{1}{2} \text{ hour}} = \dfrac{200}{\frac{1}{2}} \dfrac{\text{miles}}{\text{hour}} = 400 \dfrac{\text{miles}}{\text{hour}}$

b. Sample: jet aircraft

33. a. $\dfrac{14 \text{ meters}}{7 \text{ seconds}} = \dfrac{14}{7} \dfrac{\text{meters}}{\text{second}} = 2 \dfrac{\text{m}}{\text{sec}}$

b. Sample: snake

34. a. $\dfrac{15 \text{ inches}}{3 \text{ days}} = \dfrac{15}{3} \dfrac{\text{inches}}{\text{day}} = 5 \dfrac{\text{in.}}{\text{day}}$

b. Sample: snail

35. a. Move the decimal point six places to the left.

b. Sample:

$43{,}918.6 \div 10^6$

$43{,}918.6 \cdot 10^{-6}$

$= 10^{-6}(4 \cdot 10^4 + 3 \cdot 10^3 + 9 \cdot 10^2$
$\qquad + 1 \cdot 10 + 8 + 6 \cdot 10^{-1})$

$= 10^{-6} \cdot 4 \cdot 10^4 + 10^{-6} \cdot 3 \cdot 10^3$
$\qquad + 10^{-6} \cdot 9 \cdot 10^2 + 10^{-6} \cdot 1 \cdot 10$
$\qquad + 10^{-6} \cdot 8 + 10^{-6} \cdot 6 \cdot 10^{-1})$

$= 4 \cdot 10^{-2} + 3 \cdot 10^{-3} + 9 \cdot 10^{-4}$
$\qquad + 1 \cdot 10^{-5} + 8 \cdot 10^{-6} + 6 \cdot 10^{-7}$

$= 0.0439186$

LESSON 10-4   pp. 633–637

1. a. $(w^2 + 5w + 4)(w + 6)$

b. $w^2 \cdot w + 5w \cdot w + 4 \cdot w + w^2 \cdot 6$
$\qquad + 5w \cdot 6 + 4 \cdot 6$

$= w^3 + 5w^2 + 4w + 6w^2 + 30w + 24$

$= w^3 + 11w^2 + 34w + 24$

2. The Extended Distributive Property: To multiply two sums, multiply each term in the first sum by each term in the second sum.

3. $(5 \cdot 4 + 4 \cdot 2 + 3) \cdot (2 + 7) = 31 \cdot 9 = 279$;

and $5 \cdot 2^3 + 39 \cdot 2^2 + 31 \cdot 2 + 21$

$\qquad = 40 + 156 + 62 + 21 = 279$

4. $y^2 \cdot y + 7y \cdot y + 2 \cdot y + y^2 \cdot 6 + 7y \cdot 6 + 2 \cdot 6$

$= y^3 + 7y^2 + 2y + 6y^2 + 42y + 12$

$= y^3 + 13y^2 + 44y + 12$

5. $x \cdot 2x^2 + x \cdot 3x + x \cdot -1 + 1 \cdot 2x^2$
$\qquad + 1 \cdot 3x + 1 \cdot -1$

$= 2x^3 + 3x^2 + -x + 2x^2 + 3x + -1$

$= 2x^3 + 5x^2 + 2x - 1$

6. $m^2 \cdot 3m^2 + m^2 \cdot -4m + m^2 \cdot -2 + 10m \cdot 3m^2$
$\qquad + 10m \cdot -4m + 10m \cdot -2 + 3 \cdot 3m^2$
$\qquad + 3 \cdot -4m + 3 \cdot -2$

$= 3m^4 - 4m^3 - 2m^2 + 30m^3 - 40m^2 - 20m$
$\qquad + 9m^2 - 12m - 6$

$= 3m^4 + 26m^3 - 33m^2 - 32m - 6$

7. $x^2 \cdot x^2 + x^2 \cdot -4x + x^2 \cdot 8 + 4x \cdot x^2$
$\qquad + 4x \cdot -4x + 4x \cdot 8 + 8 \cdot x^2$
$\qquad + 8 \cdot -4x + 8 \cdot 8$

$= x^4 - 4x^3 + 8x^2 + 4x^3 - 16x^2 + 32x$
$\qquad + 8x^2 - 32x + 64$

$= x^4 + 64$

8. Does $[3(10) + 2 - 1] \cdot [10 - 5(2) + 8] =$
$3(10)^2 - 14(10)(2) + 23(10) - 5(2)^2$
$\qquad + 13(2) - 8$?

$(30 + 1)(18 - 10)$
$\qquad = 3(100) - 280 + 230 - 20 + 26 - 8$?

$248 = 248$

Yes, it checks.

9. $(x + y + 5)(x + y + 2)$

$= x^2 + xy + 2x + xy + y^2 + 2y$
$\qquad + 5x + 5y + 10$

$= x^2 + 7x + 2xy + 7y + y^2 + 10$

10. $5c \cdot c - 4d \cdot c + 1 \cdot c + 5c \cdot -7d + -4d \cdot -7d$
$+ 1 \cdot -7d$

$\quad = 5c^2 - 4cd + c - 35cd + 28d^2 - 7d$

$\quad = 5c^2 - 39cd + c + 28d^2 - 7d$

11. $(n - 3)(n + 4)(2n + 5)$

$\quad = (n^2 + 4n - 3n - 12)(2n + 5)$

$\quad = (n^2 + n - 12)(2n + 5)$

$\quad = 2n^3 + 5n^2 + 2n^2 + 5n - 24n - 60$

$\quad = 2n^3 + 7n^2 - 19n - 60$

12. volume of cube with sides $(n + 1)$:
$(n + 1)(n + 1)(n + 1)$

$\quad = (n^2 + 2n + 1)(n + 1)$

$\quad = n^3 + n^2 + 2n^2 + 2n + n + 1$

$\quad = n^3 + 3n^2 + 3n + 1$

volume of cube with sides n: n^3
$n^3 + 3n^2 + 3n + 1 - n^3 = 3n^2 + 3n + 1$

13. $x^2 + 4x + 4x + 16 - (x^2 - 16x - 16x + 256)$

$\quad = x^2 + 8x + 16 - x^2 + 32x - 256$

$\quad = 40x - 240$

14. $a \cdot a + a \cdot b + a \cdot -c + b \cdot a + b \cdot b + b \cdot -c$
$+ c \cdot a + c \cdot b + c \cdot -c$
$- (a \cdot a + a \cdot -c + c \cdot a + c \cdot -c)$

$\quad = a^2 + ab - ac + ab + b^2 - bc + ac$
$+ bc - c^2 - (a^2 - ac + ac - c^2)$

$\quad = 2ab + b^2$

15. $m^2 - 2mn - 3mp - 4mq + 2mn - 4n^2 - 6np$
$- 8nq + 3mp - 6np - 9p^2 - 12pq$
$+ 4mq - 8nq - 12pq - 16q^2$

$\quad = m^2 - 4n^2 - 9p^2 - 16q^2 - 12np$
$- 16nq - 24pq$

16. a. In a first degree polynomial, the highest exponent on a variable is 1. In a second degree polynomial, the highest exponent is 2. To find the degree of the product of these two polynomials, you add the exponents of unlike variables or take the exponent of the product of like variables. In either case, the degree will be three.

b. It must be of degree $m + n$.

17. After 10 years Plan B is worth \$40.70 more than Plan A.

1	Year	Plan A	Plan A	Plan B	Plan B
2		Deposit	End-of-Year Balance	Deposit	End-of-Year Balance
3	1	100	106.00	200	212.00
4	2	100	218.36	0	224.72
5	3	100	337.46	200	450.20
6	4	100	463.71	0	477.22
7	5	100	597.53	200	717.85
8	6	100	739.38	0	760.92
9	7	100	889.74	200	1018.57
10	8	100	1049.13	0	1079.69
11	9	100	1218.08	200	1356.47
12	10	100	1397.16	0	1437.86

18. After Clue 1: x can be 7, 6, 5, 3, or -2.
After Clue 2: x can be 7, 6, 5, or -2.
After Clue 3: x can be 7, 5, or -2.
After Clue 4: x can be 7 or -2.

19. a. Simplify: $\sqrt{100} \cdot \sqrt{2} = 10\sqrt{2}$

b. Sample: What is the length of the diagonal of a square with side 10?

20. a.–c.

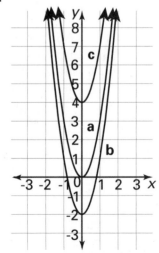

21. $\frac{14}{6} \cdot a^{3-1} \cdot \frac{1}{b^{2-1}} = \frac{7a^2}{3b}$

22. $-\frac{150}{100} \cdot \frac{1}{m^{6-5}} \cdot n^{8-3} = -\frac{3n^5}{2m}$

23. $y = 81$

24. $(2x^2 - 3x + 40) - (3x^2 + 5) = -x^2 - 3x + 35$

25. **a.** $x^2 + x - x - 1 = x^2 - 1$

    b. $x^3 + x^2 - x^2 - x + x + 1$

       $= x^3 + 1$

    c. $x^4 + x^3 - x^3 - x^2 + x^2 + x - x - 1$

       $= x^4 - 1$

    d. $x^5 + x^4 - x^4 - x^3 + x^3 + x^2 - x^2$

       $- x + x + 1$

       $= x^5 + 1$

    e. $x^9 + 1$

    f. $x^{101} + 1$; the degree of the product must be $100 + 1 = 101$ and from parts **a–e**, we know that the only terms that will not cancel will be x^{101} and a 1 that will be positive since 101 is odd.

IN-CLASS ACTIVITY

1. **a.** $(2x + 1)(3x + 4)$
    b. $6x^2 + 11x + 4$
    c. $6x^2 + 11x + 4$

2. $x^2 + 6x + 8$

	x	1	1	1	1
x	x^2	x	x	x	x
1	x	1	1	1	1
1	x	1	1	1	1

3. $x^2 + 5x + 6$

	x	1	1	1
x	x^2	x	x	x
1	x	1	1	1
1	x	1	1	1

4. $2x^2 + 11x + 5$

	x	x	1
x	x^2	x^2	x
1	x	x	1
1	x	x	1
1	x	x	1
1	x	x	1
1	x	x	1

5. $9x^2 + 18x + 5$

	x	x	x	1
x	x^2	x^2	x^2	x
x	x^2	x^2	x^2	x
x	x^2	x^2	x^2	x
1	x	x	x	1
1	x	x	x	1
1	x	x	x	1
1	x	x	x	1
1	x	x	x	1

6. Answers will vary.

7. **a.** $A = (2x + 3)^2$
    b. $4x^2 + 12x + 9$
    c. $4x^2 + 12x + 9$

8. $x^2 + 8x + 16$

	x	1	1	1	1
x	x^2	x	x	x	x
1	x	1	1	1	1
1	x	1	1	1	1
1	x	1	1	1	1
1	x	1	1	1	1

9. $9x^2 + 6x + 1$

	x	x	x	1
x	x^2	x^2	x^2	x
x	x^2	x^2	x^2	x
x	x^2	x^2	x^2	x
1	x	x	x	1

LESSON 10-5   pp. 639–645

1. a. dimensions: $(x + 3)$ by $(x + 4)$
   b. $x^2 + 4x + 3x + 12 = x^2 + 7x + 12$
2. a. $(2w + 6)(w + 7)$
   b. $2w^2 + 14w + 6w + 42 = 2w^2 + 20w + 42$
3. F: product of the FIRST terms of the binomials
   O: product of the OUTSIDE terms of the binomials
   I: product of the INSIDE terms of the binomials
   L: product of the LAST terms of the binomials

4. a. $ac + ad + bc + bd$
   b.

	a	b
c	ac	bc
d	ad	bd

5. a. $n^2 + n + 4n + 4 = n^2 + 5n + 4$
   b.

	n	4
n	n^2	$4n$
1	n	4

6. Does
$$(5 + 2 \cdot 2)(7 + 2 \cdot 2) = 35 + 24 \cdot 2 + 4 \cdot 2^2?$$
$$9 \cdot 11 = 35 + 48 + 16?$$
$$99 = 99$$
Yes, it checks.
7. $x^2 - 4x - 3x + 12 = x^2 - 7x + 12$
8. $a^2 + 7a - 10a - 70 = a^2 - 3a - 70$
9. $21m^2 - 18mn + 14mn - 12n^2$
   $= 21m^2 - 4mn - 12n^2$
10. $9k^2 + 8k + 27k + 24 = 9k^2 + 35k + 24$
11. $a^2 - 6a + 6a - 36 = a^2 - 36$
12. $4x^2 + 6xy - 6xy - 9y^2 = 4x^2 - 9y^2$
13. a. dimensions: $(40+2d)$ feet by $(20+2d)$ feet
   b. $(40 + 2d)(20 + 2d) - 40(20)$
   $= 800 + 80d + 40d + 4d^2 - 800$
   $= 120d + 4d^2$ ft^2
14. a. dimensions: $(y - 12)$ ft by $(x - 12)$ ft
   b. $(y - 12)(x - 12)$
   $= xy - 12y - 12x + 144$ ft^2
15. $(3x + 4)(3x + 4)$
   $= 9x^2 + 12x + 12x + 16$
   $= 9x^2 + 24x + 16$
16. a. $(550 + 500)(450 + 400)$
   $= 1050 \cdot 850 = 892,500$
   b. $(f + p)(j + s) = fj + fs + pj + ps$
17. $(3y + 2)^2$
   $= (3y + 2)(3y + 2)$
   $= 9y^2 + 6y + 6y + 4$
   $= 9y^2 + 12y + 4$
18. a. $x^5 + 2x^3 - x^2 - 2$
   b. Check: Does
   $$(4^2 + 2)(4^3 - 1) = 4^5 + 2 \cdot 4^3 - 4^2 - 2?$$
   $$(18)(63) = 1024 + 128 - 16 - 2?$$
   $$1134 = 1134$$
   Yes, it checks.

19. a.

x	-4	-3	-2	-1	0	1	2	3	4
y	14	6	0	-4	-6	-6	-4	0	6

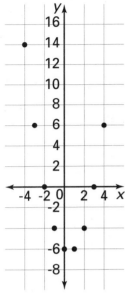

b. (same as part **a**)

c. They are the same; the equation in part **b** is the expansion of the equation in part **a**.

20. a. $\sqrt{5} \cdot \sqrt{5} + 3\sqrt{5} - 2\sqrt{5} + (-2)3$

$= 5 + 3\sqrt{5} - 2\sqrt{5} - 6$

$= \sqrt{5} - 1$

b. ≈ 1.24

c. Yes; $0.236 \cdot 5.236 \approx \sqrt{5} - 1 \approx 1.24$

21. $x(x + 1)(x + 2)$

$= x(x^2 + 2x + x + 2)$

$= x(x^2 + 3x + 2)$

$= x^3 + 3x^2 + 2x$

22. $(x + 5)(x + 7) = x^2 + 12x + 35$

23. $(y - 2)(y + 5) = y^2 + 3y - 10$

24. a. $10(6) = 60$ outfits

b. This problem can be viewed as the multiplication of the binomial $(4 + 2)$ by the trinomial $(3 + 2 + 5)$.

25. $3(a + b - c + d) + 2(a + b - c + d) = 5x$

$5(a + b - c + d) = 5x$

$a + b - c + d = x$

26. $(3 \cdot 10^5)(8 \cdot 10^3 + 9 \cdot 10^2 + 8 \cdot 10 + 1)$

$+ (6 \cdot 10^4)(8 \cdot 10^3 + 9 \cdot 10^2 + 8 \cdot 10 + 1)$

$+ (2 \cdot 10^3)(8 \cdot 10^3 + 9 \cdot 10^2 + 8 \cdot 10 + 1)$

$+ (1 \cdot 10^1)(8 \cdot 10^3 + 9 \cdot 10^2 + 8 \cdot 10 + 1)$

$+ (9)(8 \cdot 10^3 + 9 \cdot 10^2 + 8 \cdot 10 + 1)$

$= 24 \cdot 10^8 + 27 \cdot 10^7 + 24 \cdot 10^6 + 3 \cdot 10^5$

$+ 48 \cdot 10^7 + 54 \cdot 10^6 + 48 \cdot 10^5 + 6 \cdot 10^4$

$+ 16 \cdot 10^6 + 18 \cdot 10^5 + 16 \cdot 10^4 + 2 \cdot 10^3$

$+ 8 \cdot 10^4 + 9 \cdot 10^3 + 8 \cdot 10^2 + 1 \cdot 10^1$

$+ 72 \cdot 10^3 + 81 \cdot 10^2 + 72 \cdot 10 + 9$

$= 24 \cdot 10^8 + 75 \cdot 10^7 + 94 \cdot 10^6 + 69 \cdot 10^5$

$+ 30 \cdot 10^4 + 83 \cdot 10^3 + 89 \cdot 10^2$

$+ 73 \cdot 10^1 + 9$

$= 2,400,000,000 + 750,000,000 + 94,000,000$

$+ 6,900,000 + 300,000 + 83,000$

$+ 8900 + 730 + 9$

$= 3,251,292,639;$ or

$362,019 \cdot 8981 = 3,251,292,639$

27. a. $h = 6 + 96(7) - 16(7)^2$

$h = 6 + 672 - 784$

$h = -106$ ft

b. The rocket hit the ground before 7 seconds elapsed.

28. $h = 6 + 96(3) - 16(3)^2$

$h = 6 + 288 - 144$

$h = 150$ ft

29. slope: $\frac{7-4}{-3--9} = \frac{3}{6} = \frac{1}{2}$

$y - 7 = \frac{1}{2}(x - -3)$

$y - 7 = \frac{1}{2}x + \frac{3}{2}$

$y = \frac{1}{2}x + \frac{17}{2}$

30. area of large square: 100

area of shaded region: $100 - 9 = 91$

P(point in shaded area) $\frac{91}{100} = 0.91$

31. $512 - x = 0$

$\qquad 512 = x$

32. $4(0)(7) = 0$

33. Sample: $(a + b)(c + d)(e + f) =$
$ace + acf + ade + adf + bce + bcf + bde + bdf$.
Multiply the product of $(a+b)(c+d)$ by $(e+f)$
or multiply the product of $(c + d)(e + f)$ by
$(a + b)$.

LESSON 10-6   pp. 646–650

1. $x^2 + 2xy + y^2$

2. $x^2 - 2xy + y^2$

3. A perfect square trinomial is a trinomial of
the form $a^2 + 2ab + b^2$ or $a^2 - 2ab + b^2$.

4. **a.** $(n + 3)^2 = n^2 + 6n + 9$

b.

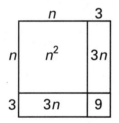

c. Check: Does $(2 + 3)^2 = 2^2 + 6 \cdot 2 + 9$?

$\qquad 25 = 4 + 12 + 9$?

$\qquad 25 = 25$

Yes, it checks.

5. **a.** $(3x + 7)^2$

b. $9x^2 + 42x + 49$

6. $m^2 - 2m(6) + 6^2 = m^2 - 12m + 36$

7. $m^2 + 2m(12) + 12^2 = m^2 + 24m + 144$

8. $(2x)^2 + 2(2x)(5) + 5^2 = 4x^2 + 20x + 25$

9. $(3y)^2 - 2(3y)(4) + 4^2 = 9y^2 - 24y + 16$

10. $(a + b)$

11. $x^2 - 13^2 = x^2 - 169$

12. $3^2 - (8p)^2 = 9 - 64p^2$

13. (b); (It is the square of a difference.)

14. $(40 + 1)^2$

$\qquad = 1600 + 2(40) + 1$

$\qquad = 1681$

15. $(30 + 7)^2$

$\qquad = 30^2 + 2(30)(7) + 7^2$

$\qquad = 900 + 420 + 49$

$\qquad = 1369$

16. $(70 - 1)(70 + 1)$

$\qquad = 70^2 - 1^2$

$\qquad = 4900 - 1$

$\qquad = 4899$

17. $(90 - 5)(90 + 5)$

$\qquad = 90^2 - 5^2$

$\qquad = 8100 - 25$

$\qquad = 8075$

18. Sample: Let $a = 3$ and $b = 5$:

Does $(3 + 5)^2 = 3^2 + 2 \cdot 3 \cdot 5 + 5^2$?

$\qquad 8^2 = 9 + 30 + 25$?

$\qquad 64 = 64$

Yes, it checks.

19. Sample: Let $a = 1$ and $b = 2$.

Does $(1 + 2)^2 = 1^2 + 2^2$?

$\qquad 3^2 = 1 + 4$?

$\qquad 9 \neq 5$

It does not check.

20. Yes, $(x - 3)^2 = (3 - x)^2$ for all values of x

since $(x - 3)^2 = x^2 - 6x + 9$ and

$\qquad (3 - x)^2 = 9 - 6x + x^2$

21. $4(9^2 + 2(9)y + y^2) = 4(81 + 18y + y^2)$

$\qquad\qquad\qquad = 324 + 72y + 4y^2$

22. $(x^2 + 2xy + y^2) - (x^2 - 2xy + y^2) = 4xy$

23. $x^2 - (\sqrt{11})^2 = x^2 - 11$

24. $\sqrt{7}^2 - \sqrt{2}^2 = 7 - 2 = 5$

25. a. $V = (s + 5)(s + 5)s$
$V = (s^2 + 10s + 25)s$
$V = s^3 + 10s^2 + 25s$

b. $V = s \cdot s \cdot (s - 2)$
$V = s^2(s - 2)$
$V = s^3 - 2s^2$

c. $V = s^3 + 10s^2 + 25s + s^3 - 2s^2$
$V = 2s^3 + 8s^2 + 25s$

d. Check: Let $s = 4$:
Does $2s^3 + 8s^2 + 25s =$
$(s + 5)(s + 5)s + s \cdot s \cdot (s - 2)$?
$2 \cdot 4^3 + 8 \cdot 4^2 + 25 \cdot 4 = 9 \cdot 9 \cdot 4 + 4 \cdot 4 \cdot 2$?
$128 + 128 + 100 = 324 + 32$?
$356 = 356$
Yes, it checks.

26. $z^2 + 8z - 11z - 88 = z^2 - 3z - 88$

27. $2c^2 + 10cd - 7cd - 35d^2 = 2c^2 + 3cd - 35d^2$

28. a. $x^2 + 3x$
b. $x^2 + 3x + 4x + 12 = x^2 + 7x + 12$
c. $x^2 + 3x + 4x + 12 - xy - 3y$
$= x^2 - xy + 7x - 3y + 12$

29. a. $0 = 2x - x$
$0 = x$

b. $0 > 2x - x$
$0 > x$
$x < 0$

30. $1.033x = 62.2$
$\dfrac{1}{1.033} \cdot 1.033x = \dfrac{1}{1.033} \cdot 62.2$
$x = \$60.2 \text{ billion}$

31. $n + n + 1 + n + 2 + n + 3 = 250$
$4n + 6 = 250$
$4n = 244$
$n = 61$
The integers are 61, 62, 63, and 64.

32. $(1 - 5)x^3 + (-4 - 4)x + (1 - -8) = -4x^3 - 8x + 9$

33. a. Sample: 3, 4, 5
$4^2 = 16; \; 3 \cdot 5 = 15$

b. Sample: 9, 10, 11
$10^2 = 100; \; 9 \cdot 11 = 99$
24, 25, 26
$25^2 = 625; \; 24 \cdot 26 = 624$
-2, -1, 0
$(-1)^2 = 1; \; -2 \cdot 0 = 0$

c. The square of the second number is one more than the product of surrounding integers.

d. Three consecutive integers can be written as $n-1$, n, and $n+1$. $n^2 = (n-1)(n+1)+1$, since $(n - 1)(n + 1) = n^2 - 1$.

LESSON 10-7

1. The chi-square statistic measures how different a set of actual observed scores is from a set of expected scores.

2. The chi-square statistic was developed in 1900 by Karl Pearson.

3. a. $\dfrac{(a_1 - e_1)^2}{e_1} = \dfrac{(22 - 20)^2}{20} = \dfrac{4}{20}$

$\dfrac{(a_2 - e_2)^2}{e_2} = \dfrac{(18 - 20)^2}{20} = \dfrac{4}{20}$

$\dfrac{(a_3 - e_3)^2}{e_3} = \dfrac{(20 - 20)^2}{20} = \dfrac{0}{20} = 0$

$\dfrac{(a_4 - e_4)^2}{e_4} = \dfrac{(17 - 20)^2}{20} = \dfrac{9}{20}$

$\dfrac{(a_5 - e_5)^2}{e_5} = \dfrac{(23 - 20)^2}{20} = \dfrac{9}{20}$

$\dfrac{4}{20} + \dfrac{4}{20} + 0 + \dfrac{9}{20} + \dfrac{9}{20} = \dfrac{26}{20} = 1.3$

b. $n = 5$, $n - 1 = 4$; $1.3 < 9.49$
No; there is no evidence to believe that the accidents are not occurring randomly.

4. a. $\dfrac{(a_1 - e_1)^2}{e_1} = \dfrac{(23-20)^2}{20} = \dfrac{9}{20}$

$\dfrac{(a_2 - e_2)^2}{e_2} = \dfrac{(22-20)^2}{20} = \dfrac{4}{20}$

$\dfrac{(a_3 - e_3)^2}{e_3} = \dfrac{(20-20)^2}{20} = \dfrac{0}{20} = 0$

$\dfrac{(a_4 - e_4)^2}{e_4} = \dfrac{(18-20)^2}{20} = \dfrac{4}{20}$

$\dfrac{(a_5 - e_5)^2}{e_5} = \dfrac{(17-20)^2}{20} = \dfrac{9}{20}$

$\dfrac{9}{20} + \dfrac{4}{20} + 0 + \dfrac{4}{20} + \dfrac{9}{20} = \dfrac{26}{20} = 1.3$

b. $n = 5,\ n - 1 = 4;\ 1.3 < 9.49$
No; there is no evidence to believe that the accidents are not occurring randomly.

5. a. $\dfrac{(a_1 - e_1)^2}{e_1} = \dfrac{(25-20)^2}{20} = \dfrac{25}{20}$

$\dfrac{(a_2 - e_2)^2}{e_2} = \dfrac{(15-20)^2}{20} = \dfrac{25}{20}$

$\dfrac{(a_3 - e_3)^2}{e_3} = \dfrac{(25-20)^2}{20} = \dfrac{25}{20}$

$\dfrac{(a_4 - e_4)^2}{e_4} = \dfrac{(30-20)^2}{20} = \dfrac{100}{20}$

$\dfrac{(a_5 - e_5)^2}{e_5} = \dfrac{(15-20)^2}{20} = \dfrac{25}{20}$

$\dfrac{25}{20} + \dfrac{25}{20} + \dfrac{25}{20} + \dfrac{100}{20} + \dfrac{25}{20} = \dfrac{200}{20} = 10$

b. $n = 5,\ n - 1 = 4;\ 10 > 9.49$
Yes; there is evidence to believe that the accidents are not occurring randomly.

6. a. $\dfrac{(a_1 - e_1)^2}{e_1} = \dfrac{(20-20)^2}{20} = 0$

$\dfrac{(a_2 - e_2)^2}{e_2} = \dfrac{(20-20)^2}{20} = 0$

$\dfrac{(a_3 - e_3)^2}{e_3} = \dfrac{(20-20)^2}{20} = 0$

$\dfrac{(a_4 - e_4)^2}{e_4} = \dfrac{(20-20)^2}{20} = 0$

$\dfrac{(a_5 - e_5)^2}{e_5} = \dfrac{(20-20)^2}{20} = 0$

$0 + 0 + 0 + 0 + 0 = 0$

b. $n = 5,\ n - 1 = 4;\ 0 < 9.49$
No; there is no evidence to believe that the accidents are not occurring randomly.

7. $\dfrac{(30-20)^2}{20} = \dfrac{100}{20} = 5$

$\dfrac{(18-20)^2}{20} = \dfrac{4}{20} = \dfrac{1}{5}$

$\dfrac{(12-20)^2}{20} = \dfrac{64}{20} = \dfrac{16}{5}$

$5 + \dfrac{1}{5} + \dfrac{16}{5} = 8.4$

$n = 3,\ n - 1 = 2;\ 8.4 > 5.99$
No; a chi-square value of 8.4 would occur less than 5% of the time. This is enough evidence to question whether students were guessing randomly.

8. The chi-square statistic should not be used for an expected frequency less than 5.

9. Autumn: $\dfrac{(13-14.75)^2}{14.75} = \dfrac{3.0625}{14.75}$

Winter: $\dfrac{(13-14.75)^2}{14.75} = \dfrac{3.0625}{14.75}$

Spring: $\dfrac{(12-14.75)^2}{14.75} = \dfrac{7.5625}{14.75}$

Summer: $\dfrac{(21-14.75)^2}{14.75} = \dfrac{39.0625}{14.75}$

$\dfrac{3.0625}{14.75} + \dfrac{3.0625}{14.75} + \dfrac{7.5625}{14.75} + \dfrac{39.0625}{14.75} = \dfrac{52.75}{14.75} \approx 3.58$

$n = 4,\ n - 1 = 3;\ 3.58 < 7.81$
The chi-square value equals 3.58. Such a value would occur over 10% of the time. There is not enough evidence to say earthquakes occur more in certain seasons.

10. Outcome 1: $\dfrac{(10-8)^2}{8} = \dfrac{4}{8} = \dfrac{1}{2}$

Outcome 2: $\dfrac{(6-8)^2}{8} = \dfrac{4}{8} = \dfrac{1}{2}$

Outcome 3: $\dfrac{(4-8)^2}{8} = \dfrac{16}{8} = 2$

Outcome 4: $\dfrac{(6-8)^2}{8} = \dfrac{4}{8} = \dfrac{1}{2}$

Outcome 5: $\dfrac{(14-8)^2}{8} = \dfrac{36}{8} = \dfrac{9}{2}$

$\dfrac{1}{2} + \dfrac{1}{2} + 2 + \dfrac{1}{2} + \dfrac{9}{2} = 8$

$n = 5,\ n - 1 = 4;\ 8 < 9.49$
The chi-square value equals 8. Such a value would occur almost 10% of the time. There is not enough evidence to call the spinner unfair.

11. beginning: $\dfrac{(59-46)^2}{46} = \dfrac{169}{46}$

middle: $\dfrac{(40-46)^2}{46} = \dfrac{36}{46}$

end: $\dfrac{(39-46)^2}{46} = \dfrac{49}{46}$

$\dfrac{169}{46} + \dfrac{36}{46} + \dfrac{49}{46} \approx 5.52$

$n = 3,\ n - 1 = 2;\ 5.52 < 5.99$

The chi-square value is about 5.52. Such a value would occur over 5% of the time. There is not enough evidence to say that more runs are scored in one part of the game.

12. a. $(70 + 1)^2$

$= 70^2 + 2(70) + 1$

$= 4900 + 140 + 1$

$= 5041$

b. $(70 - 1)^2$

$= 70^2 - 2(70) + 1$

$= 4900 - 140 + 1$

$= 4761$

13. a. $9a^2 - 2(3a)b + b^2 = 9a^2 - 6ab + b^2$
b. $9a^2 + 2(3a)b + b^2 = 9a^2 + 6ab + b^2$
c. $9a^2 + 3ab - 3ab - b^2 = 9a^2 - b^2$

14. a. $5y - 25 - y^2 + 5y = -25 + 10y - y^2$
b. $16x^4 + 32x^3y + 16x^2y^2 + 32x^3y$
$+ 64x^2y^2 + 32xy^3 + 16x^2y^2$
$+ 32xy^3 + 16y^4$

$= 16x^4 + 64x^3y + 96x^2y^2 + 64xy^3 + 16y^4$

15. a. $8p(4p + 2)$
b. $3p(p + 1)$
c. $8p(4p + 2) - 3p(p + 1)$

$= 32p^2 + 16p - (3p^2 + 3p)$

$= 29p^2 + 13p$

16. a. \$1500
b. \$1000
c. Sample: $x = 1.06$
$1000(1.06)^4 + 1100(1.06)^3 + 1200(1.06)^2$
$+ 1400(1.06) + 1500$

$= 1262.476 + 1310.117 + 1348.32$
$+ 1484 + 1500 = \$6904.91$

17. $12y^4 + (-3 + 5)y^3 + (-7 + -3)y^2$
$+ (1 + -2 + 2)y + (1 + 6)$

$= 12y^4 + 2y^3 - 10y^2 + y + 7$

18. $(1 - 3)x^2 + (-4 - -2 - 14)x + (1 - 8)$

$= -2x^2 - 16x - 7$

19. $(3 + 4)(6 + 8) = 7(14) = 98$ teams
20. Answers will vary.

CHAPTER 10

PROGRESS SELF-TEST p. 660

1. $13x^2 - 7x - 23$
2. degree: 2
3. trinomial
4. $4(3v^2 + 2v - 9) = 12v^2 + 8v - 36$
5. $-5z^3 + 35z^2 - 40z$
6. $9x^2 + 24x - 24x - 64 = 9x^2 - 64$
7. $12y^2 - 64y - 6y + 32 = 12y^2 - 70y + 32$
8. $d^2 - 2(12)d + 144 = d^2 - 24d + 144$
9. $x^3 - 6x^2 + 9x - 3x^2 + 18x - 27$

$= x^3 - 9x^2 + 27x - 27$

10. $15x^3 - 4x^2 - 9x - 1$
11. $3t^3 + 8t^2 - 7t + 1$
12. $ax + bx + 2x + ay + by + 2y + 5a + 5b + 10$
13. $(4x + 1)(3x + 2) - x(x + 10)$

$= 12x^2 + 8x + 3x + 2 - x^2 - 10x$

$= 11x^2 + x + 2$

14. $ac + bc + 2ad + 2bc$

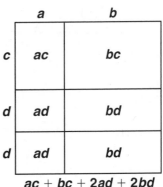

	a	**b**
c	*ac*	*bc*
d	*ad*	*bd*
d	*ad*	*bd*

ac + bc + 2ad + 2bd

15. $(30 - 1)(30 + 1)$

$\quad = 30^2 - 1$

$\quad = 900 - 1$

$\quad = 899$

16. $2 \cdot 10^4 + 6 \cdot 10^3 + 3 \cdot 10^2 + 8 \cdot 10 + 4$

17. $80x^2 + 60x + 90$ dollars

18. $80(1.04)^2 + 60(1.04) + 90$

$\quad = 86.53 + 62.4 + 90$

$\quad = \$238.93$

19. $\frac{861 + 748 + 812 + 939}{4} = 840$

20. $\frac{(861 - 840)^2}{840} = \frac{441}{840}$

$\quad \frac{(748 - 840)^2}{840} = \frac{8464}{840}$

$\quad \frac{(812 - 840)^2}{840} = \frac{784}{840}$

$\quad \frac{(939 - 840)^2}{840} = \frac{9801}{840}$

$\quad \frac{441}{840} + \frac{8464}{840} + \frac{784}{840} + \frac{9801}{840} = \frac{19,490}{840} \approx 23.2$

21. Yes; the number of events n is 4: $n - 1$ is 3. Look at the third row of the table. The chi-square statistic 23.2 is greater than the critical value 16.3 that would occur with probability .001. So it is very unlikely that the sophomores were given fewer lines by chance.

22. $2y(5y - 3)(y + 9)$

$\quad = 2y(5y^2 + 45y - 3y - 27)$

$\quad = 10y^3 + 84y^2 - 54y$

CHAPTER 10

REVIEW

pp. 661–663

1. a. $7x^2 + 4x + 1$

  b. degree: 2

2. a. $8m^4 + 10m^3 - 6m^2 - 3m$

  b. degree: 4

3. a. $3.9x^2 + 1.7x + 19$

  b. degree: 2

4. a. $(4y^5 - 6y^3 + 4y + 2) - (4y^5 - 2y^3 + 8y)$

$\quad\quad = -4y^3 - 4y + 2$

  b. degree: 3

5. $k - 4 - k^2 - 1 = -k^2 + k - 5$

6. $5p^2 - 1 - 6p^2 + p = -p^2 + p - 1$

7. $ac + ad + a + bc + bd + b + c + d + 1$

8. $x^4 + 4x^2 - x^4 + 3x = 4x^2 + 3x$

9. $(y - 1)(y^2 - 1) = y^3 - y - y^2 + 1$

10. $x^3 + 3x^2 + x^2 + 3x - x - 3 = x^3 + 4x^2 + 2x - 3$

11. $ax + bx + 3x + a + b + 3$

12. $y^3 + 2y^2 + 3y - 2y^2 - 4y - 6 = y^3 - y - 6$

13. $3k^3 + 12k^2 - 3k$

14. $5x^2y + 15xy^3$

15. $8x^2 - 2x - 8 + 12x - 28 = 8x^2 + 10x - 36$

16. $x^2 + 7x - 3x - 21 = x^2 + 4x - 21$

17. $y^2 - 13y + y - 13 = y^2 - 12y - 13$

18. $ac - ad - bc + bd$

19. $a^2 - 15a + 15a - 225 = a^2 - 225$

20. $144b^2 + 12mb - 12mb - m^2 = 144b^2 - m^2$

21. $-4z^2 - 4z - z - 1 = -4z^2 - 5z - 1$

22. $a^3 - a + 3a^2 - 3$

23. $d^2 - 2d + 1$

24. $(2t)^2 + 2(2t)(3) + 3^2 = 4t^2 + 12t + 9$

25. $3((4x)^2 + 2(4x)5 + 5^2)$

$\quad = 3(16x^2 + 40x + 25)$

$\quad = 48x^2 + 120x + 75$

26. $a_1^2 - 2a_1e_1 + e_1^2$

27. $x(x^2 + 2x + 1) = x^3 + 2x^2 + x$

28. $m^2 + 6mn + 9n^2 - (m^2 - 6mn + 9n^2) = 12mn$

29. (a)

30. (b), (c), and (d)

31. (a), (c), and (d)

32. (b)

33. Sample: x^4

34. Sample: $a^4 - 2a^2b + b^2$

35. 30,200,901

36. 12,210

214

37. $9 \cdot 10^4 + 8 \cdot 10^3 + 1 \cdot 10^2 + 3$

38. $4 \cdot 10^6 + 5 \cdot 10^3 + 6 \cdot 10^2$

39. a. $250x^4 + 250x^3 + 250x^2 + 250x + 250$

 b. $250(1.08)^2 + 250(1.08) + 250$

$$= 291.60 + 270 + 250$$

$$= \$811.60$$

40. a. $25y^6 + 50y^5 + 75y^4$ dollars

 b. $25(1.05)^3 + 50(1.05)^2 + 75(1.05)$

$$= 28.94 + 55.125 + 78.75$$

$$= \$162.82$$

41. a. 50

 b. $\dfrac{(56-50)^2}{50} = \dfrac{36}{50} = .72$

 $\dfrac{(44-50)^2}{50} = \dfrac{36}{50} = .72$

 $.72 + .72 = 1.44$

 c. $n = 2$, $n - 1 = 1$; $1.44 < 3.84$
 No; the chi-square value 1.44 is less than the critical value 3.84 that would occur with probability .05.

42. a. $\dfrac{143 + 38 + 51 + 40 + 36}{7} = 44$

 Tuesday–Friday: 44

 Monday: $3(44) = 132$

 b.
 $\dfrac{(143-132)^2}{132} = \dfrac{121}{132}$

 $\dfrac{(38-44)^2}{44} = \dfrac{36}{44}$

 $\dfrac{(51-44)^2}{44} = \dfrac{49}{44}$

 $\dfrac{(40-44)^2}{44} = \dfrac{16}{44}$

 $\dfrac{(36-44)^2}{44} = \dfrac{64}{44}$

 $\dfrac{121}{132} + \dfrac{36}{44} + \dfrac{49}{44} + \dfrac{16}{44} + \dfrac{64}{44} = \dfrac{616}{132} = 4.67$

 c. Yes. The chi-square value 4.67 is less than the critical value 9.49 that would occur with probability .05.

43. a. $65°$

 b. $\dfrac{(57-65)^2}{65} = \dfrac{64}{65}$

 $\dfrac{(58-65)^2}{65} = \dfrac{49}{65}$

 $\dfrac{(60-65)^2}{65} = \dfrac{25}{65}$

 $\dfrac{(61-65)^2}{65} = \dfrac{16}{65}$

 $\dfrac{(65-65)^2}{65} = \dfrac{0}{65}$

 $\dfrac{(69-65)^2}{65} = \dfrac{16}{65}$

 $\dfrac{(74-65)^2}{65} = \dfrac{81}{65}$

 $\dfrac{(75-65)^2}{65} = \dfrac{100}{65}$

 $\dfrac{(72-65)^2}{65} = \dfrac{49}{65}$

 $\dfrac{(68-65)^2}{65} = \dfrac{9}{65}$

 $\dfrac{(63-65)^2}{65} = \dfrac{4}{65}$

 $\dfrac{(58-65)^2}{65} = \dfrac{49}{65}$

 $\dfrac{64}{65} + \dfrac{49}{65} + \dfrac{25}{65} + \dfrac{16}{65} + \dfrac{0}{65} + \dfrac{16}{65} + \dfrac{81}{65} + \dfrac{100}{65}$

 $+ \dfrac{49}{65} + \dfrac{9}{65} + \dfrac{4}{65} + \dfrac{49}{65} = \dfrac{462}{65} \approx 7.11$

 c. Yes. The chi-square statistic 7.11 is less than the critical value 19.7 that would occur with probability .05. This is not a high enough chi-square value to support a claim that the temperatures are different throughout the year.

44. a. $4x^2 + 16x$

 b. $2x(2x + 8)$

45. a. $2x^2 + 8x + 8$

 b. $(x + 2)(2x + 4)$

46.

	a	b
c	ac	bc
d	ad	bd

$$ac + bc + ad + bd$$

47. a. $xy + 3y + 2x + 6$
  b. $(x + 3)(y + 2)$
  c. Yes

48. $(5m + 3)(4m + 1) - (3m - 1)(m + 2)$

$= (20m^2 + 5m + 12m + 3)$
$\quad - (3m^2 + 6m - m - 2)$
$= 17m^2 + 12m + 5$

49. $10x(x^3 + x^2 + x) - (x + 1)^2$

$= (10x^4 + 10x^3 + 10x^2) - (x^2 + 2x + 1)$
$= 10x^4 + 10x^3 + 9x^2 - 2x - 1$

50. $\frac{1}{2} \cdot (15)(6x) - (2x)^2 = 45x - 4x^2$

51. $3x(7x) - \pi x^2 = 21x^2 - \pi x^2$

52. $3x(8x + 1)(x + 12)$

$= 3x(8x^2 + 96x + x + 12)$
$= 24x^3 + 288x^2 + 3x^2 + 36x$
$= 24x^3 + 291x^2 + 36x$

53. $x(x + 1)(x - 1)$

$= x(x^2 - 1)$
$= x^3 - x$

CHAPTER 11
LINEAR SYSTEMS

LESSON 11-1

pp. 666–671

1. **a.** A system is a set of sentences joined by the word "and" which together describe a single situation.

   b. Sample: $\begin{cases} y = -2x + 3 \\ y = -3x + 6 \end{cases}$

2. the word "and"

3. True

4. It represents the intersection of the solution sets for each condition in the system.

5. **a.** $\begin{cases} y = 2x + 4 \\ x + 2y = 3 \end{cases}$

   b. (-1, 2)

   c. $2(-1) + 4 = -2 + 4 = 2$; and

   $-1 + 2(2) = -1 + 4 = 3$

6. **a.** $9(-1) = -9$; and

   $2(-1) - 7 = -2 - 7 = -9$

   b. Sample: $x = -1$ and $y = -9$; {(-1, -9)}

7. Yes, substitute (4, 8) in the system.

   $10(4) - 8 = 40 - 8 = 32$; and

   $8 - 4 = 4$

8. **a.** $x + y = 18$ and $x - y = 8$

   b.

   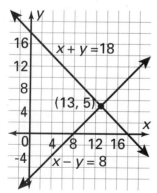

   c. 13 and 5

9. no solution

10. **a.**

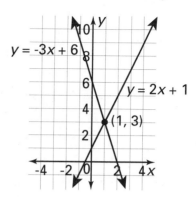

   b. Solution (1, 3)

   $2(1) + 1 = 3$; and

   $-3(1) + 6 = -3 + 6 = 3$

11. **a.**

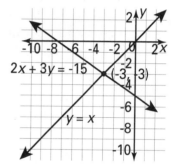

   b. Solution (-3, -3)

   $-3 = -3$; and

   $2(-3) + 3(-3) = -6 - 9 = -15$

12. **a.**

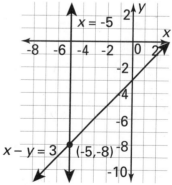

   b. (-5, -8)

13. a.

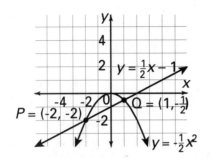

b. $(-2, -2)$ and $(1, -.5)$

14. a. Samples: $(2, 4)$; $(4, 16)$; and $(-.75, .6)$

b. Check: $2^2 = 4$ and $2^2 = 4$;

$4^2 = 16$ and $2^4 = 16$;

$(-.75)^2 \approx .6$ and $2^{-.75} \approx .6$

15. Sample: Yes; since the two lines are not parallel and the women's times are decreasing faster than the men's times, the times will be equal in 2044.

16. a. $3x + 8 = x - 12$

$2x = -20$

$x = -10$

b. $3(x + 8) = -4(x - 12)$

$3x + 24 = -4x + 48$

$7x = 24$

$x = \frac{24}{7} = 3\frac{3}{7}$

c. $3(x + 8)^2 = -3(x - 12)$

$3(x^2 + 16x + 64) = -3x + 36$

$3x^2 + 48x + 192 = -3x + 36$

$3x^2 + 51x + 156 = 0$

$x^2 + 17x + 52 = 0$

$x = \frac{-17 \pm \sqrt{17^2 - 4(1)(52)}}{2(1)}$

$x = \frac{-17 \pm 9}{2}$

$x = -4 \text{ or } x = -13$

17. a. $\frac{7 - -1}{8 - 10} = \frac{8}{-2} = -4$

b. The slope of the line through the points $(10, -1)$ and $(8, 7)$ is -4.

18. a. Sample: $\frac{325}{1} = \frac{x}{4\frac{3}{4}}$

b. $325 \cdot 4\frac{3}{4} = x$

$1543.75 \text{ miles} = x$

19. $18{,}600 \frac{\text{miles}}{\text{family}} \cdot \frac{1}{1.8} \frac{\text{family}}{\text{car}} \approx 10{,}333 \frac{\text{miles}}{\text{car}}$

20. $7\pi \cdot \frac{3}{2\pi} = \frac{21}{2}$

21. $y = 7 - 2x$

22. $8 + 3x = 2 + 6x$

$6 = 3x$

$2 = x$

23. $P + XY$

24. a.

Year	Ratio
1912	0.77
1920	0.83
1924	0.81
1928	0.83
1932	0.87
1936	0.87
1948	0.86
1952	0.86
1956	0.89
1960	0.90
1964	0.90
1968	0.87
1972	0.87
1976	0.90
1980	0.92
1984	0.89
1988	0.89
1992	0.90

24. b.

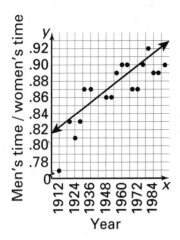

Year

c. Sample: .96; no, for the women's time to be faster than the men's time, the ratio must be greater than 1.

25. a.

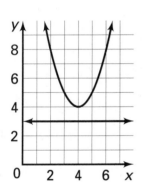

b.

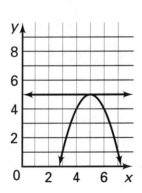

c.

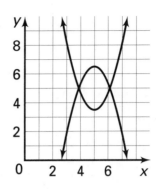

d.

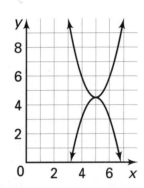

LESSON 11-2 pp. 672–675

1. False; the solutions are exact.

2. a. $x + 1 = 3x - 19$

$20 = 2x$

$x = 10$ and

$y = 10 + 1$

$y = 11$

point of intersection: (10, 11)

b. Check: $3(10) - 19 = 30 - 19 = 11$; and

$10 + 1 = 11$

3. a. $10x - 60 = 12x + 50$

$-2x = 110$

$x = -55$ and

$y = 10(-55) - 60 = -610$

point of intersection: (-55, -610)

b. Check: $12(-55) + 50 = -660 + 50 = -610$;

and $10(-55) - 60 = -550 - 60 = -610$

4. $3 \div \frac{1}{10} = 30$ tenths of a mile

$1.50 + .20(30)$

$= 1.5 + 6$

$= \$7.50$

5. $2.5 \div \frac{1}{10} = 25$ tenths of a mile

$.90 + .25(25)$

$= .90 + 6.25$

$= \$7.15$

6.

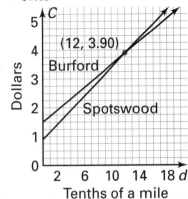

7. Taxi rides are more expensive in Burford than Spotswood for distances less than 1.2 miles (12 tenths of a mile).

8. Taxi rides in Spotswood are more expensive for distances greater than 1.2 miles (12 tenths of a mile).

9. **a.** $\$1.70 + .15d$ dollars

    b. $1.7 + .15d = 0.90 + .25d$

$0.8 = 0.1d$

$d = 8$

A ride 8 tenths of a mile, or .8 mile, long will cost the same in Manassas and Spotswood.

10. **a.** $3 + x = 21 - x$

$2x = 18$

$x = 9$ and

$y = 21 - 9$

$y = 12$

$(9, 12)$

    b. Check: $21 - 9 = 12$; and

$3 + 9 = 12$

11. **a.** $\frac{-3}{4}x + 10 = \frac{1}{2}x - 5$

$\frac{-5}{4}x = -15$

$x = 12$ and

$y = \frac{1}{2} \cdot 12 - 5$

$y = 6 - 5 = 1$

$(12, 1)$

    b. Check: $\frac{1}{2} \cdot 12 - 5 = 6 - 5 = 1$; and

$-\frac{3}{4} \cdot 12 + 10 = -9 + 10 = 1$

12. **a.** $-3x - 5 = \frac{1}{3}x + 2$

$\frac{-10}{3}x = 7$

$x = -\frac{21}{10}$; and

$y = \frac{1}{3} \cdot \frac{-21}{10} + 2$

$y = -\frac{7}{10} + 2 = \frac{13}{10}$

$\left(-\frac{21}{10}, \frac{13}{10}\right)$

    b. Check: $\frac{1}{3} \cdot \frac{-21}{10} + 2 = -\frac{7}{10} + 2 = \frac{13}{10}$; and

$-3 \cdot \frac{-21}{10} - 5 = \frac{63}{10} - 5 = \frac{13}{10}$

13. **a.** $\frac{1}{4}x^2 = x$; solve $x = \dfrac{-(-1) \pm \sqrt{(-1)^2 - 4\left(\frac{1}{4}\right)(0)}}{2\left(\frac{1}{4}\right)}$.

$x = 0$ or $x = 4$

$(0, 0)$ or $(4, 4)$

    b. Check: $0 = 0$ and $\frac{1}{4}(0)^2 = 0$; and

$\frac{1}{4}(4)^2 = \frac{1}{4}(16) = 4$

14. **a.** $290 + 5w = 200 + 8w$

$90 = 3w$

$w = 30$ weeks

    b. $290 + 5(30) = \$440$

15. Solve: $45 + 23h = 35 + 28h$

$10 = 5h$

$2 = h$

The work will cost the same for $1\frac{1}{2}$ hours of work.

16. a. Solve:
$$497{,}000 - 6000y = 983{,}000 + 20{,}000y$$
$$-26{,}000y = 486{,}000$$
$$y = -18.69$$
About 18 years, 8 months ago the cities had the same population.

b. $497{,}000 - 6000(-18.69) \approx 609{,}000.$

17.

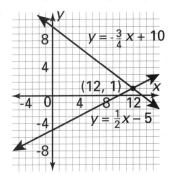

18.

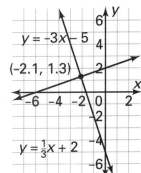

19. a. 2

b. $|x| = 5$
$x = 5$ or $x = -5$
$(5, 5)$ or $(-5, 5)$

20. a. $2x = 18$
$x = 9$

b. $2x^2 = 18$
$x^2 = 9$
$x = 3$ or $x = -3$

c. $x^2 - 9x = 0$
$$x = \frac{9 \pm \sqrt{9^2 - 4(1)(0)}}{2(1)}$$
$$x = \frac{9 \pm 9}{2}$$
$x = 0$ or $x = 9$

21. $2p^3 + 6p^2 + 2p$

22. $\frac{7}{343} \cdot m^{4-3} \cdot \frac{1}{n^{6-5}} = \frac{m}{49n}$

23.

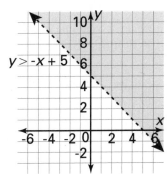

$y > -x + 5$

24. a. y-intercept: -2 (slope-intercept form)
b. y-intercept: 7 (let $x = 0$)
c. y-intercept: -7 (let $x = 0$)

25. $4x + 2y$ dollars

26. Answers will vary.

27. Sample: Ace Moving Company charges $90 per hour and a one-time fee of $45. Midway Movers charge $80 per hour and a one-time fee of $60. For how many hours of work will the cost of each company be the same? Answer: For 1.5 hours, both companies charge $180. (Solve: $90h + 45 = 80h + 60$)

LESSON 11-3   pp. 676–680

1. $3\left(\frac{8}{11}\right) + 2\left(\frac{43}{11}\right) = \frac{24}{11} + \frac{86}{11} = \frac{110}{11} = 10;$

   $4\left(\frac{8}{11}\right) + 1 = \frac{32}{11} + \frac{11}{11} = \frac{43}{11}$

Yes, it checks.

2. a. $6y + y = 14$
$7y = 14$
$y = 2$

Substitute 2 for y in one of the original equations to find x.

$x = 6(2) = 12$
$(x, y) = (12, 2)$

b. Check: Does $12 + 2 = 14$? Yes
Does $12 = 6(2)$? Yes

3. a. $12x - 5(2x - 6) = 30$

$12x - 10x + 30 = 30$

$2x = 0$

$x = 0$

Substitute 0 for x in one of the original equations to find y.

$$y = 2(0) - 6 = \text{-}6$$

$$(x, y) = (0, \text{-}6)$$

b. Check: Does $12(0) - 5(\text{-}6) = 30$?

Yes, $0 + 30 = 30$

Does $\text{-}6 = 2(0) - 6$? Yes

4. a. $\text{-}4x + 7(x - 2) = 10$

$\text{-}4x + 7x - 14 = 10$

$3x = 24$

$x = 8$

Substitute 8 for x in one of the original equations to find y.

$$y = 8 - 2 = 6$$

$$(x, y) = (8, 6)$$

b. Check: Does $6 = 8 - 2$? Yes

Does $\text{-}4(8) + 7(6) = 10$?

$\text{-}32 + 42 = 10$? Yes

5. a. $3x + 4(2x - 3) = \text{-}15$

$3x + 8x - 12 = \text{-}15$

$11x = \text{-}3$

$x = \frac{\text{-}3}{11}$

Substitute $\frac{\text{-}3}{11}$ for x in one of the original equations to find y.

$$y = 2\left(\frac{\text{-}3}{11}\right) - 3 = \frac{\text{-}6}{11} - 3 = \frac{\text{-}39}{11}$$

$$(x, y) = \left(\frac{\text{-}3}{11}, \frac{\text{-}39}{11}\right)$$

b. Check:

Does $3\left(\frac{\text{-}3}{11}\right) + 4\left(\frac{\text{-}39}{11}\right) = \text{-}15$?

$\frac{\text{-}9}{11} + \frac{\text{-}156}{11} = \frac{\text{-}165}{11} = \text{-}15$? Yes

Does $\frac{\text{-}39}{11} = 2\left(\frac{\text{-}3}{11}\right) - 3$?

$\frac{\text{-}6}{11} - \frac{33}{11} = \frac{\text{-}39}{11}$? Yes

6. $\begin{cases} B + G = 180 \\ B = 3G \end{cases}$

$3G + G = 180$

$4G = 180$

$G = 45$

Substitute 45 for G in one of the original equations to find B.

$$B = 3(45) = 135$$

The boys received \$135; the girls, \$45.

7. a. $7t - t = 30$

$6t = 30$

$t = 5$

Substitute 5 for t in one of the original equations to find B.

$$B = 7(5) = 35$$

b. Check: Does $35 = 7(5)$? Yes

Does $35 - 5 = 30$? Yes

8. $\begin{cases} x + y = 100 \\ 37x + 45y = 4220 \end{cases}$

From first equation, $x = 100 - y$.

$37(100 - y) + 45y = 4220$

$3700 - 37y + 45y = 4220$

$8y = 520$

$y = 65$

Substitute 65 for y in one of the original equations to find x.

$$x = 100 - 65 = 35$$

35 acres cost \$37 each and 65 acres cost \$45 each.

9. $1.25L = L + 200,000$

$.25L = 200,000$

$L = 800,000$

Substitute 800,000 for L in one of the original equations to find T.

$$T = 800,000 + 200,000$$

Profit for last year was \$800,000; this year, \$1,000,000.

10. a. $\begin{cases} M + J = 11{,}000 \\ \phantom{M + {}} J = 3M \end{cases}$

b. $M + 3M = 11{,}000$

$4M = 11{,}000$

$M = 2750$

Substitute 2750 for M in one of the original equations to find J.

$J = 3(2750) = 8250$

Mary will receive \$2750; John, \$8250.

11. $40K + 30K = 1400$

$70K = 1400$

$K = 20$ and

$A = 40(20) = 800$

$B = 30(20) = 600$

12. $\begin{cases} \phantom{A + {}} A = 5S \\ A + S = 16 \end{cases}$

$5S + S = 16$

$6S = 16$

$S = 2\frac{2}{3}$ fl oz

Substitute $2\frac{2}{3}$ for S in one of the original equations to find A.

$A = 5 \cdot \frac{8}{3} = \frac{40}{3} = 13\frac{1}{3}$ fl oz

13. From second equation, $y = \text{-}1 - 2x$.

$4x - 3(\text{-}1 - 2x) = 8$

$4x + 3 + 6x = 8$

$10x = 5$

$x = \frac{5}{10} = \frac{1}{2}$

Substitute $\frac{1}{2}$ for x in one of the original equations to find y.

$y = \text{-}1 - 2\left(\frac{1}{2}\right) = \text{-}1 - 1 = \text{-}2$

$(x, y) = \left(\frac{1}{2}, \text{-}2\right)$

14. From second equation, $b = 3a - 1$.

$8a - 1 = 4b$ and $3a = b + 1$

$8a - 1 = 4(3a - 1)$

$8a - 1 = 12a - 4$

$\text{-}4a = \text{-}3$

$a = \frac{3}{4}$

Substitute $\frac{3}{4}$ for a in one of the original equations to find b.

$b = 3\left(\frac{3}{4}\right) - 1 = \frac{9}{4} - 1 = \frac{5}{4}$

$(a, b) = \left(\frac{3}{4}, \frac{5}{4}\right)$

15. a. $\begin{cases} m - 70 = v \\ m + v = 1250 \end{cases}$

b. $m + m - 70 = 1250$

$2m = 1320$

$m = 660$

Substitute 660 for m in one of the original equations to find v.

$v = 660 - 70 = 590$

Noah's math score was 660; his verbal score, 590.

16. a. $\begin{cases} h = 4950 + 120m \\ h = 6950 + 75m \end{cases}$

$4950 + 120m = 6950 + 75m$

$45m = 2000$

$m = 44.\overline{4}$ minutes

b. Substitute $\frac{2000}{45}$ for m in one of the original equations to find the height.

$4950 + 120(44.\overline{4}) \approx 10{,}283$ ft

17. a.

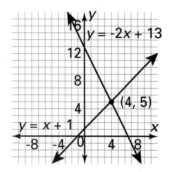

or

$x + 1 = -2x + 13$

$3x = 12$

$x = 4$

Substitute 4 for x in one of the original equations to find y.

$y = 4 + 1 = 5$

$(x, y) = (4, 5)$

b. Check: Does $4 + 1 = 5$? Yes

      Does $-2(4) + 13 = 5$?

          $-8 + 13 = 5$? Yes

18. a.

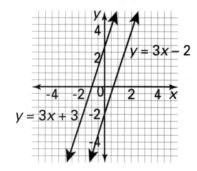

or

$3x - 2 = 3x + 3$

$-2 = 3$?

No solution

b. Check: No solution, the lines are parallel. Three times a number minus two could never give the same value as three times the same number plus 3. That is, for all real numbers x, $2x + 1 \neq 2x - 3$.

19. $3a - 2b - a - b = 2a - 3b$

20. $x^2 + (x - 1)^2 = x^2 + x^2 - 2x + 1 = 2x^2 - 2x + 1$

21.

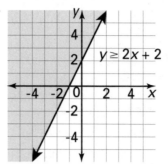

22. $9y = -5x + 7$

$y = \frac{1}{9}(-5x + 7)$

$y = \frac{-5}{9}x + \frac{7}{9}$

23. $\frac{120 \text{ miles}}{40 \text{ min}} = \frac{120}{40} \frac{\text{miles}}{\text{min}} = 3 \frac{\text{miles}}{\text{min}} \cdot \frac{60 \text{ min}}{1 \text{ hour}} = 180 \frac{\text{miles}}{\text{hour}}$

24. a. $n + d$

b. $5n + 10d$ cents

25. Elylov: \$6,750,166;

Lovely: \$3,249,834;

$$\begin{cases} L + E = \$10 \text{ million} \\ \dfrac{L}{35,729} = \dfrac{E}{74,212} \end{cases}$$

From second equation,

$74,212L = 35,729E$

$L = \frac{35,729}{74,212} E$

Substitute in equation 1.

$\frac{35,729}{74,212}E + E = 10,000,000$

$\frac{109,941}{74,212}E = 10,000,000$

$E = 6,750,166$

Substitute 6,750,166 for E in one of the original equations to find L.

$L = 10,000,000 - 6,750,166$

$= 3,249,834$

26. a. $94.3 + s$ mph

b. $94.3 - s$ mph

c. $\frac{94.3m}{60}$ miles

d. Yes, its rate of $94.3 - 25 = 69.3$ mph is faster than the speed limit.

1. **a.** Solve systems by adding equations when the coefficients of the same variable are opposites.

   b. The goal is to obtain an equation that contains only one variable.

2. Generalized Addition Property of Equality

3. **a.**
$$2x + 8y = 2$$
$$+ \ \underline{-2x - 4y = 6}$$
$$4y = 8$$
$$y = 2$$

   Substitute 2 for y in one of the original equations to find x.
$$2x + 8(2) = 2$$
$$2x + 16 = 2$$
$$2x = -14$$
$$x = -7$$
$$(x, y) = (-7, 2)$$

   b. Check: Does $2(-7) + 8(2) = -14 + 16 = 2$? Yes
   Does $-2(-7) - 4(2) = 14 - 8 = 6$? Yes

4. **a.**
$$a + b = 11$$
$$+ \ \underline{a - b = \ \ 4}$$
$$2a = 15$$
$$a = \frac{15}{2}$$

   Substitute $\frac{15}{2}$ for a in one of the original equations to find b.
$$\frac{15}{2} + b = 11$$
$$b = \frac{7}{2}$$
$$(a, b) = \left(\frac{15}{2}, \frac{7}{2}\right)$$

   b. Check: Does $\frac{15}{2} + \frac{7}{2} = \frac{22}{2} = 11$? Yes
   Does $\frac{15}{2} - \frac{7}{2} = \frac{8}{2} = 4$? Yes

5.
$$x + y = \ 90$$
$$+ \ \underline{x - y = \ 75}$$
$$2x = 165$$
$$x = \ 82.5$$

   Substitute 82.5 for x in one of the original equations to find y.
$$82.5 + y = 90$$
$$y = 7.5$$
7.5 and 82.5

6.
$$x + y = -1$$
$$+ \ \underline{x - y = \ 5}$$
$$2x = \ 4$$
$$x = \ 2$$

   Substitute 2 for x in one of the original equations to find y.
$$2 + y = -1$$
$$y = -3$$
2 and -3

7. Let A be the average speed of the airplane and W be the speed of the wind, both in miles per hour.

   to Appleton: $\dfrac{120 \text{ miles}}{\frac{5}{6} \text{ hour}} = 144$ mph

   to Washington: $\dfrac{120 \text{ miles}}{\frac{2}{3} \text{ hour}} = 180$ mph

$$A - W = 144$$
$$+ \ \underline{A + W = 180}$$
$$2A = 324$$
$$A = 162$$

   Substitute 162 for A in one of the original equations to find W.
$$162 - W = 144$$
$$W = 18$$
   The average speed of the plane was 162 miles per hour and the average wind speed was 18 miles per hour.

8. when coefficients of the same variable are equal

9.

$$-2x + 3y = -5$$
$$+ \underline{5x - 3y = 11}$$
$$3x = 6$$
$$x = 2$$

Substitute 2 for x in one of the original equations to find y.

$$2(2) - 3y = 5$$
$$-3y = 1$$
$$y = -\frac{1}{3}$$
$$(x, y) = \left(2, -\frac{1}{3}\right)$$

10.

$$-2m + -n = 5$$
$$+ \underline{2m + 3n = 7}$$
$$2n = 12$$
$$n = 6$$

Substitute 6 for n in one of the original equations to find m.

$$2m + 6 = -5$$
$$2m = -11$$
$$m = -\frac{11}{2}$$
$$(m, n) = \left(-\frac{11}{2}, 6\right)$$

11. Check: Does $3(65) + 6(11.5) = 264$?

$$195 + 69 = 264? \text{ Yes}$$

Does $3(65) + 2(11.5) = 218$?

$$195 + 23 = 218? \text{ Yes}$$

12. Plan A: $2n + m = 153$
Plan B: $2n + 4m = 195$

$$-2n + -m = -153$$
$$+ \underline{2n + 4m = 195}$$
$$3m = 42$$
$$m = 14$$

Substitute 14 for m in one of the original equations to find n.

$$2n + 14 = 153$$
$$2n = 139$$
$$n = 69.5$$

The hotel is charging $69.50 per night and $14 per meal.

13. Yes; by the Generalized Addition Property of Equality,

$$\frac{3}{4} - \frac{1}{5} = 75\% - 20\%$$
$$\frac{3}{4} + -\frac{1}{5} = 75\% + -20\%$$
$$\frac{11}{20} = 55\%$$

14.

$$2x - 3y = 17$$
$$+ \underline{x + 3y = 1}$$
$$3x = 18$$
$$x = 6$$

Substitute 6 for x in one of the original equations to find y.

$$2(6) - 3y = 17$$
$$-3y = 5$$
$$y = -\frac{5}{3}$$
$$(x, y) = \left(6, -\frac{5}{3}\right)$$

15.

$$4z - 5w = 15$$
$$+ \underline{-4z + -2w = 6}$$
$$-7w = 21$$
$$w = -3$$

Substitute -3 for w in one of the original equations to find z.

$$4z - 5(-3) = 15$$
$$4z = 0$$
$$z = 0$$
$$z = 0 \text{ and } w = -3$$

16.

$$2e + b = 2.70$$
$$+ \underline{-e + -b = -1.80}$$
$$e = 0.90$$

Substitute .90 for e in one of the original equations to find b.

$$2(.90) + b = 2.70$$
$$b = 0.90$$

Bacon alone should cost $0.90.

17.
$$5r + 8p = 17.15$$
$$+ \text{-}5r + \text{-}2p = \text{-}8.75$$
$$\overline{ 6p = 8.40}$$
$$p = 1.40$$

Substitute 1.40 for p in one of the original equations to find r.
$$5r + 8(1.4) = 17.15$$
$$5r = 17.15 - 11.2$$
$$5r = 5.95$$
$$r = 1.19$$

Regular gas costs \$1.19 per gallon; premium gas, \$1.40 per gallon.

18.
$$w - s = 67$$
$$+ \; w + s = 147$$
$$\overline{ 2w = 214}$$
$$w = 107$$

Substitute 107 for w in one of the original equations to find s.
$$107 + s = 147$$
$$s = 40$$

Wadlow was 107″ or 8′11″; Stratton, 40″ or 3′4″.

19. $9x + 6 = 2x - 1$
$$7x = \text{-}7$$
$$x = \text{-}1$$

Substitute -1 for x in one of the original equations to find y.
$$y = 2(\text{-}1) - 1$$
$$y = \text{-}3$$
$$(x, y) = (\text{-}1, \text{-}3)$$

20. $4(\text{-}5z) + 4z = 40$
$$\text{-}20z + 4z = 40$$
$$\text{-}16z = 40$$
$$z = \text{-}\tfrac{5}{2}$$

Substitute $-\tfrac{5}{2}$ for z in the original equations to find Q and R.
$$Q = 4\left(\text{-}\tfrac{5}{2}\right) = \text{-}10,$$
$$R = \text{-}5\left(\text{-}\tfrac{5}{2}\right) = \tfrac{25}{2}$$

21. a. $x = \dfrac{\text{-}5 \pm \sqrt{5^2 - 4(1)(\text{-}14)}}{2(1)}$
$$x = \dfrac{\text{-}5 \pm 9}{2}$$
$$x = 2 \text{ or } x = \text{-}7$$

b. same as part **a.**
$$x = 2 \text{ or } x = \text{-}7$$

22. $PQ = \sqrt{|\text{-}3 - 5|^2 + |\text{-}7 - \text{-}1|^2}$
$$PQ = \sqrt{8^2 + 6^2}$$
$$PQ = \sqrt{100}$$
$$PQ = 10$$

23. slope: $\dfrac{\text{-}7 - \text{-}1}{\text{-}3 - 5} = \dfrac{\text{-}6}{\text{-}8} = \dfrac{3}{4}$

24. a. Sample $P = 20, \quad H = 0;$
$$P = 14, \quad H = 5;$$
$$P = 8, \quad H = 10$$

b. $5P + 6H = 100$

25. $8x + y = \text{-}15$ or $\text{-}8x - y = 15$

26. $\dfrac{14}{24}(30) = 17.5$ grams

27. a. $100 - 80 + 4p + 2p + 10 = 30 + 6p$

b. $\dfrac{100 - 80 + 4p + 2p + 10}{p + 2} = \dfrac{30 + 6p}{p + 2}$

28. a. $4 \dfrac{\text{quarts}}{\text{gallon}} \cdot 5$ gallons $= 20$ quarts

b. $4 \dfrac{\text{quarts}}{\text{gallon}} \cdot n$ gallons $= 4n$ quarts

29. a.
$$d = .\overline{81}$$
$$100d = 81.\overline{81}$$
$$99d = 81$$
$$d = \tfrac{81}{99} = \tfrac{9}{11}$$

b.
$$d = .\overline{003}$$
$$1000d = 3.\overline{003}$$
$$999d = 3$$
$$d = \tfrac{3}{999} = \tfrac{1}{333}$$

c.
$$d = 3.89\overline{5}$$
$$1000d = 3895.\overline{5}$$
$$100d = 389.\overline{5}$$
$$900d = 3506$$
$$d = \tfrac{3506}{900} = \tfrac{1753}{450}$$

1. Multiplication Property of Equality
2. **a.** Equivalent systems are systems that have the same solutions.
   b. Sample:
   $$\begin{cases} 5x + 8y = 21 \\ 10x - 3y = \text{-}15 \end{cases} \text{ and } \begin{cases} \text{-}10x - 16y = \text{-}42 \\ 10x - 3y = \text{-}15 \end{cases}$$
3. **a.** -2
   b.
   $$\begin{array}{r} \text{-}12u + 10v = \text{-}4 \\ + \underline{12u - 8v = 5} \\ 2v = 1 \\ v = \tfrac{1}{2} \end{array}$$

   Substitute $\tfrac{1}{2}$ for v in one of the original equations to find u.
   $$12u - 8\left(\tfrac{1}{2}\right) = 5$$
   $$12u - 4 = 5$$
   $$12u = 9$$
   $$u = \tfrac{9}{12} = \tfrac{3}{4}$$

   $u = \tfrac{3}{4}$ and $v = \tfrac{1}{2}$

4. **a.** $\begin{cases} 9a + 15b = 24 \\ \text{-}10a + \text{-}15b = \text{-}23 \end{cases}$
   b.
   $$\begin{array}{r} 9a + 15b = 24 \\ + \underline{\text{-}10a + \text{-}15b = \text{-}23} \\ \text{-}a = 1 \\ a = \text{-}1 \end{array}$$

   Substitute -1 for a in one of the original equations to find b.
   $$9(\text{-}1) + 15b = 24$$
   $$\text{-}9 + 15b = 24$$
   $$15b = 33$$
   $$b = \tfrac{33}{15} = \tfrac{11}{5} = 2.2$$

   This is the same solution as in Example 2.

5. **a.**
   $$\begin{array}{r} \text{-}9a + 6b = \text{-}60 \\ + \underline{9a + 4b = 40} \\ 10b = \text{-}20 \end{array}$$

   b.
   $$\begin{array}{r} 6a - 4b = 40 \\ + \underline{9a + 4b = 40} \\ 15a = 80 \end{array}$$

   c.
   $$10b = \text{-}20$$
   $$b = \text{-}2$$

   Substitute -2 for b in one of the original equations to find a.
   $$3a - 2(\text{-}2) = 20$$
   $$3a = 16$$
   $$a = \tfrac{16}{3} = 5\tfrac{1}{3}$$

   $a = \tfrac{16}{3}$ and $b = \text{-}2$

6. **a.**
   $$\begin{array}{r} \text{-}2x + \text{-}6y = \text{-}38 \\ + \underline{2x + y = 3} \\ \text{-}5y = \text{-}35 \\ y = 7 \end{array}$$

   Substitute 7 for y in one of the original equations to find x.
   $$x + 3(7) = 19$$
   $$x = \text{-}2$$

   b.
   $$\begin{array}{r} x + 3y = 19 \\ + \underline{\text{-}6x + \text{-}3y = \text{-}9} \\ \text{-}5x = 10 \\ x = \text{-}2 \end{array}$$

   Substitute -2 for x in one of the original equations to find y.
   $$2(\text{-}2) + y = 3$$
   $$y = 7$$

7. Solve $\begin{cases} 6h + s = 100 \\ h + 4s = 42 \end{cases}$
   $$\begin{array}{r} \text{-}24h + \text{-}4s = \text{-}400 \\ + \underline{h + 4s = 42} \\ \text{-}23h = \text{-}358 \\ h = 15.57 \end{array}$$

   No; solving the system using this many people shows h and s will not be integers. The formation cannot be done without having people left over.

8. Solve $\begin{cases} 5p + 4s = 67 \\ p + 5s = 47 \end{cases}$

$\begin{array}{r} 5p + \quad 4s = \quad 67 \\ + \; \underline{-5p + -25s = -235} \\ -21s = -168 \\ s = \quad 8 \end{array}$

Substitute 8 for s in one of the original equations to find p.

$5p + 4(8) = 67$

$5p + 32 = 67$

$5p = 35$

$p = 7$

Yes, make 7 pentagons and 8 squares.

9. $\begin{array}{r} 20x + 4y = 120 \\ + \; \underline{3x - 4y = \quad 41} \\ 23x = 161 \\ x = \quad 7 \end{array}$

Substitute 7 for x in one of the original equations to find y.

$5(7) + y = 30$

$y = -5$

$(x, y) = (7, -5)$

10. $\begin{array}{r} -12a + -3b = -114 \\ + \; \underline{2a + 3b = \quad 24} \\ -10a = \quad -90 \\ a = \quad 9 \end{array}$

Substitute 9 for a in one of the original equations to find b.

$4(9) + b = 38$

$b = 2$

$(a, b) = (9, 2)$

11. $\begin{array}{r} -6m + 15n = 0 \\ + \; \underline{6m + \quad n = 0} \\ 16n = 0 \\ n = 0 \end{array}$

Substitute 0 for n in one of the original equations to find m.

$2m - 5(0) = 0$

$2m = 0$

$m = 0$

$(m, n) = (0, 0)$

12. $\begin{array}{r} 48m - 56n = \quad 48 \\ + \; \underline{-49m + 56n = -105} \\ -m = \quad -57 \\ m = \quad 57 \end{array}$

Substitute 57 for m in one of the original equations to find n.

$6(57) - 7n = 6$

$342 - 7n = 6$

$-7n = -336$

$n = 48$

$(m, n) = (57, 48)$

13. Solve $\begin{cases} 3x - 4y = 2 \\ 9x - 5y = 7 \end{cases}$

$\begin{array}{r} -9x + 12y = -6 \\ + \; \underline{9x - \quad 5y = \quad 7} \\ 7y = \quad 1 \\ y = \frac{1}{7} \end{array}$

Substitute $\frac{1}{7}$ for y in one of the original equations to find x.

$3x = 4\left(\frac{1}{7}\right) + 2$

$3x = \frac{18}{7}$

$x = \frac{6}{7}$

$(x, y) = \left(\frac{6}{7}, \frac{1}{7}\right)$

14. Solve $\begin{cases} 3a - 2b = 5 \\ a - 4b = 6 \end{cases}$

$\begin{array}{r} 3a - \quad 2b = \quad 5 \\ + \; \underline{-3a + 12b = -18} \\ 10b = -13 \\ b = \quad -1.3 \end{array}$

Substitute -1.3 for b in one of the original equations to find a.

$a - 4(-1.3) = 6$

$a + 5.2 = 6$

$a = .8$

$a = 0.8$ and $b = -1.3$

15. Solve $\begin{cases} x + y = 45 \\ 3x + 7y = 115 \end{cases}$

$$-3x + -3y = -135$$
$$+\ \underline{3x + 7y = \ 115}$$
$$4y = -20$$
$$y = \ -5$$

Substitute -5 for y in one of the original equations to find x.

$$x + -5 = 45$$
$$x = 50$$

50 and -5

16. Solve $\begin{cases} 7m + 2t = 185 \\ 4m + 4t = 200 \end{cases}$

$$7m + \ 2t = \ 185$$
$$+\ \underline{-2m + -2t = -100}$$
$$5m = \ \ 85$$
$$m = \ \ 17$$

From second equation in system,

$$m + t = 50$$
$$17 + t = 50$$
$$t = 33$$

17. 13 birds and 12 deer; sample reasoning: Let b = number of birds and d = number of deer. Since all animals have one head, $b + d = 25$. Since birds have two feet and deer have four feet, $2b + 4d = 74$. Solve the system $\begin{cases} b + \ d = 25 \\ 2b + 4d = 74 \end{cases}$.

$$b + \ \ d = \ \ 25$$
$$+\ \underline{-b + -2d = -37}$$
$$-d = -12$$
$$d = \ \ 12$$

Substitute 12 for d in one of the original equations to find b.

$$b + 12 = 25$$
$$b = 13$$

18. Solve $\begin{cases} 2x - 3y = 5 \\ -5x + 8y = -13 \end{cases}$

$$10x - 15y = \ \ 25$$
$$+\ \underline{-10x + 16y = -26}$$
$$y = \ -1$$

Substitute -1 for y in one of the original equations to find x.

$$2x - 3(-1) = 5$$
$$2x + 3 = 5$$
$$2x = 2$$
$$x = 1$$
$$(x, y) = (1, -1)$$

19.
$$10x + 5y = 32$$
$$+\ \underline{-(8x + 5y = 10)}$$
$$2x = 22$$
$$x = 11$$

Substitute 11 for x in one of the original equations to find y.

$$10(11) + 5y = 32$$
$$110 + 5y = 32$$
$$5y = -78$$
$$y = \frac{-78}{5}$$
$$(x, y) = \left(11, \frac{-78}{5}\right)$$

20. By substitution

$$\tfrac{1}{3}x - 2 = \tfrac{1}{2}x + 3$$

Multiply by 6 to clear fractions.

$$2x - 12 = 3x + 18$$
$$-12 = x + 18$$
$$-30 = x$$

Substitute -30 for x in one of the original equations to find y.

$$y = \tfrac{1}{3}(-30) - 2$$
$$y = -10 - 2$$
$$y = -12$$
$$(x, y) = (-30, -12)$$

21. a. $3x + y = 29$

b. $3x = y + 19$

c. By substitution,

$$y + 19 + y = 29$$
$$2y + 19 = 29$$
$$2y = 10$$
$$y = 5$$

Substitute 5 for y in one of the original equations to find x.

$$3x = 5 + 19$$
$$3x = 24$$
$$x = 8$$
$$(x, y) = (8, 5)$$

d. Check: Does $3(8) + 5 = 29$?

$$24 + 5 = 29? \text{ Yes}$$

Does $3(8) = 5 + 19$?

$$24 = 24? \text{ Yes}$$

22. a. $400 + 25w = 1400 - 25w$

$$400 + 50w = 1400$$
$$50w = 1000$$
$$w = 20 \text{ weeks}$$

b. $400 + 25(20) = 400 + 500 = \$900$

23. a. PYTHAGOREAN TRIPLES
ENTER M
5
ENTER N
3
A = 16
B = 30
C = 34

b. PYTHAGOREAN TRIPLES
ENTER M
7
ENTER N
1
A = 48
B = 14
C = 50

c. part a: Does $16^2 + 30^2 = 34^2$

$$256 + 900 = 1156?$$
$$1156 = 1156 \quad \text{Yes}$$

part b: Does $48^2 + 14^2 = 50^2$

$$2304 + 196 = 2500?$$
$$2500 = 2500 \quad \text{Yes}$$

24. a. True

b. True

c. True

25. $24{,}987 \text{ miles} \cdot \dfrac{1}{116} \dfrac{\text{hour}}{\text{miles}} \cdot \dfrac{1}{24} \dfrac{\text{day}}{\text{hours}} = 8.975$
about 9 days

26. Answers will vary.

27. Samples: M   M
                        P
              M   M

              M   M
                        P
         M   P   P   M
                        P
              M   M

$$\begin{cases} 6h + 4s = 80 \\ 4h + s = 30 \end{cases}$$

$$6h + 4s = 80$$
$$+\ \underline{-16h + -4s = -120}$$
$$-10h = -40$$
$$h = 4$$

Substitute 4 for h in one of the original equations to find s.

$$4(4) + s = 30$$
$$16 + s = 30$$
$$s = 14$$

The above formation can be done with 4 hexagons and 14 squares.

LESSON 11-6 pp. 694–698

1. They are equal.

2. (a) and (c)

3. a., b.

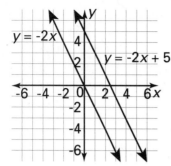

c. Sample: $y = -2x$

4. Sample: $\begin{cases} 2x + 3y = -6 \\ 4x + 6y = 24 \end{cases}$

5. Sample: $\begin{cases} 8x - 7y = 3 \\ 16x - 14y = 6 \end{cases}$

6. a. nonintersecting; divide the second equation by 4 to see that they have the same slope but are not the same line.
$\begin{cases} 2x - 3y = 12 \\ 2x - 3y = 3 \end{cases}$

b.

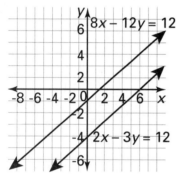

7. a. coincident; multiply the second equation by -1 to see that they are the same line, $x - y = 5$.

b.

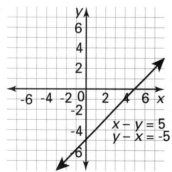

8. a. Sample: (0, -1); (1, 1); (2, 3)

b. Does $4(0) - 2(-1) = 0 + 2 = 2$? Yes
Does $4(2) - 2(3) = 8 - 6 = 2$? Yes
Does $4(1) - 2(1) = 4 - 2 = 2$? Yes

c. By substituting $y = 2x - 1$ in the equation $4x - 2y = 2$,
$4x - 2(2x - 1) = 2$
$4x - 4x + 2 = 2$
$2 = 2$
Therefore, the system has infinitely many solutions.

9. (c)

10. (a)

11. (b)

12. (a)

13. (b)

14. (c)

15. (a)

16. No; the system $\begin{cases} 39p + 21s = 396 \\ 52p + 28s = 518 \end{cases}$ represents parallel, nonintersecting lines which are equivalent to
$\begin{cases} 13p + 7s = 132 \\ 13p + 7s = 129.5 \end{cases}$

17. No, with a 10% discount, you should have paid only $9000. The full price would have been $10,000. You paid only $400 less, getting only a 4% discount.

Solve $\begin{cases} 60c + 30\ell = 1080 \\ 50c + 10\ell = 840 \end{cases}$

$\quad -2c + -\ell = -36$
$\underline{+ \; 5c + \;\ell = \;\; 84}$
$\qquad\quad 3c = \;\; 48$
$\qquad\quad\; c = \;\; 16$

Substitute 16 for c in one of the original equations to find ℓ.
$5(16) + \ell = 84$
$\qquad\quad \ell = 4$
Since the full price is $4 per square yard for linoleum and $16 per square yard for carpet, your full price would have been $500(16) + 500(4) = 8000 + 2000 = \$10,000$.

18. $\begin{cases} 5P + 3S = 94 \\ P + 2S = 28 \end{cases}$

$\qquad 5P + \quad 3S = \quad 94$
$+ \ \underline{-5P + -10S = -140}$
$\qquad\quad -7S = \ -46$
$\qquad\qquad\ S = \quad 6.57$

These are not integer values. This combination of people will not fit exactly in these formations.

19. a. $\begin{cases} t + u = 20 \\ t + 3u = 32 \end{cases}$

b. From equation 1, $t = 20 - u$.
By substitution,

$20 - u + 3u = 32$
$20 + 2u = 32$
$2u = 12$
$u = 6$

Substitute 6 for u in one of the original equations to find t.

$t + 6 = 20$
$t = 14$

c. Does $14 + 6 = 20$? Yes
Does $14 + 3(6) = 32$?
$14 + 18 = 32$? Yes

20. $\qquad 4x + 3y = \ \ 7$
$+ \ \underline{2x - 3y = 14}$
$\qquad\quad 6x = 21$
$\qquad\qquad x = \frac{21}{6} = \frac{7}{2}$

Substitute $\frac{7}{2}$ for x in one of the original equations to find y.

$2 \cdot \frac{7}{2} - 3y = 14$
$7 - 3y = 14$
$-3y = 7$
$y = \frac{7}{-3}$

$(x, y) = \left(\frac{7}{2}, \frac{7}{-3}\right)$

21. a. $1 \cdot 10^3 + 8 \cdot 10^2 + 7 \cdot 10 + 2$
b. $1.872 \cdot 10^3$

22.

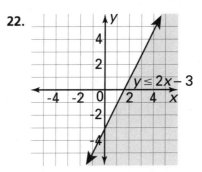

23. $1.4(15.5) = \$21.70$

24. a. $y = -12$
b. $x = 8$

25. Sample: Suppose $A_1 x + B_1 y = C_1$ and $A_2 x + B_2 y = C_2$. If $\frac{A_1}{A_2} = \frac{B_1}{B_2} = \frac{C_1}{C_2}$, the lines coincide. If $\frac{A_1}{A_2} = \frac{B_1}{B_2}$, but $\frac{A_1}{A_2} \neq \frac{C_1}{C_2}$, then the lines are parallel. If $\frac{A_1}{A_2} \neq \frac{B_1}{B_2}$, the lines intersect.

LESSON 11-7 pp. 699–703

1. a. always
b. Let y = number of years employed.
$6.2 + 1.00y > 6.0 + 1.00y$
Since $6.20 > 6.00$ is always true, y may be any real number.

2. a. $2x + 10 + -2x < 2x + 8 + -2x$
$10 < 8$
b. No solution

3. a. $-5y + 9 + 5y = 3 - 5y + 6 + 5y$
$9 = 3 + 6$
b. y may be any real number.
c. Check: Sample: Substitute any real number for y, say 3.
$-5(3) + 9 = 3 - 5(3) + 6$
$-15 + 9 = 3 + -15 + 6$
$-6 = -6$

4. $\qquad 2(2y - 5) \leq 4y + 6$
$\qquad\quad 4y - 10 \leq 4y + 6$
$4y - 10 - 4y \leq 4y + 6 - 4y$
$\qquad\qquad -10 \leq 6$

y may be any real number.

5.
$$3x + 5 = 5 + 3x$$
$$3x + 5 + \text{-}3x = 5 + 3x + \text{-}3x$$
$$5 = 5$$
x may be any real number.

6.
$$\text{-}2m = 3 - 2m$$
$$\text{-}2m + 2m = 3 - 2m + 2m$$
$$0 = 3$$
No solution

7. $2A - 10A > 4(1 - 2A)$
$$\text{-}8A > 4 - 8A$$
$$\text{-}8A + 8A > 4 - 8A + 8A$$
$$0 > 4$$
No solution

8. $\frac{1}{2}x + 6 = 3\left(\frac{1}{4}x + 2\right)$
$$\frac{1}{2}x - \frac{3}{4}x = 6 - 6$$
$$-\frac{1}{4}x = 0$$
$$x = 0$$

9. $7 + 4y > 7 - y$
$$5y > 0$$
$$y > 0$$
y may be any positive number.

10. a. $200,000 + 5000y$
b. $200,000 + 4000y$
c. $200,000 + 5000y = 200,000 + 4000y$
$$1000y = 0$$
$$y = 0$$
They are the same now.

11. a. $375m < 315m + 60m + 25$
b. $375m < 375m + 25$
$$0 < 25$$
m can be any number of months.

12. a. $375m > 315m + 60m + 25$
b. $375m > 375m + 25$
$$0 > 25$$
No solution

13. Apartment A would be cheaper.

14. Sample: $4x + 1 = 2x + 1$
15. Sample: $y - 2 = y - 1$
16. Sample: $x^2 + 2x + 1 = (x + 1)^2$
17. They are two intersecting lines because the slopes, $\frac{11}{10}$ and $\frac{12}{10}$, are not equal.

18. Multiply the second equation by $\frac{1}{2}$ to see that it is equivalent to the first equation. Since these two equations describe the same line, there are infinitely many solutions.

19. By substitution, $7 - 5x = 5x - 7$
$$\text{-}10x = \text{-}14$$
$$x = \frac{\text{-}14}{\text{-}10} = \frac{7}{5}$$
$$y = 0$$

20. Solve: $\begin{cases} 3\ell + 3s = 8.64 \\ 4\ell + 2s = 9.54 \end{cases}$
$$-6\ell - 6s = \text{-}17.28$$
$$+ \quad 12\ell + 6s = 28.62$$
$$6\ell = 11.34$$
$$\ell = 1.89$$
Substitute 1.89 for ℓ in one of the original equations to find s.
$$3(1.89) + 3s = 8.64$$
$$3s = 8.64 - 5.67$$
$$3s = 2.97$$
$$s = 0.99$$
One slice of lasagna is $1.89 and one salad is $0.99.
2 slices of lasagna and one salad would cost $2(1.89) + .99 = 3.78 + .99 = \$4.77$.

21. a.

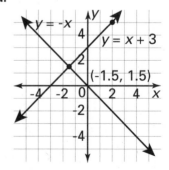

21. b. $-x = x + 3$

$-2x = 3$

$x = \dfrac{3}{-2}$

Substitute $-\dfrac{3}{2}$ for x in one of the original equations to find y.

$y = -\left(-\dfrac{3}{2}\right)$

$y = \dfrac{3}{2}$

c. $y = -x$

$\underline{+\ y =\ x + 3}$

$2y = 3$

$y = \dfrac{3}{2}$

Substitute $\dfrac{3}{2}$ for y in one of the original equations to find x.

$\dfrac{3}{2} = -x$

$-\dfrac{3}{2} = x$

d. Sample: The addition method requires the fewest steps.

22. a. $x = -1$ and $y = 1$ intersect at $(-1, 1)$.

$-1 + y = 5$

$y = 6$

$x = -1$ and $x + y = 5$ intersect at $(-1, 6)$.

$x + 1 = 5$

$x = 4$

$y = 1$ and $x + y = 5$ intersect at $(4, 1)$.

b. $4 - -1 = 5$ (a horizontal line segment)
$6 - 1 = 5$ (a vertical line segment)

$\sqrt{|4 - -1|^2 + |1 - 6|^2}$

$= \sqrt{25 + 25}$

$= \sqrt{25 \cdot 2}$

$= 5\sqrt{2}$ (a diagonal line segment)

c. Since the lines $x = -1$ and $y = 1$ form a right angle, the base and height are each 5. Area $= \dfrac{1}{2}(5)(5) = 12.5$ square units.

23. a. $\dfrac{2 \cdot 2}{3 \cdot 3} = \dfrac{4}{9}$

b. $5^2 \cdot d^{2 \cdot 2} \cdot g^2 = 25d^4g^2$

c. $\dfrac{1}{4} \cdot \dfrac{c^2}{a^2} = \dfrac{c^2}{4a^2}$

24.

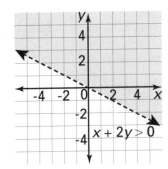

25. $\dfrac{\pi\left(\frac{d}{2}\right)^2}{2d \cdot 1.5d} = \pi\left(\dfrac{d}{2}\right)^2 \cdot \dfrac{1}{2d \cdot 1.5d} = \dfrac{\pi d^2}{12d^2} = \dfrac{\pi}{12} \approx .26$

About 26%

26. $(30 + 10 + 15 + 15)d = 2500$

$70d = 2500$

$d \approx 35.7$ m

27. $25\,\dfrac{\text{lines}}{\text{page}} \cdot w\,\dfrac{\text{words}}{\text{line}} \cdot 21\,\dfrac{\text{pages}}{\text{chapter}} = 525w\,\dfrac{\text{words}}{\text{chapter}}$

28. a. There is exactly one solution when $a \neq c$.

b. There is no solution when $a = c$ and $b \neq d$.

c. There are infinitely many solutions when $a = c$ and $b = d$.

LESSON 11-8 pp. 704–710

1. the first quadrant

2.

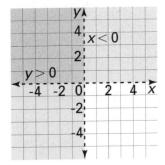

3. It is the intersection of the two half-planes described by $y \geq -3x + 2$ and $y < x - 2$.

4. half-plane

5. The "equal to" sign means that points on the boundary satisfy the conditions of the sentence.

6. No; Is $1 < 2 - 2$?
$1 < 0$? No
(2, 1) does not satisfy the second condition.

7. (0, 50); (50, 0); (25, 0); (0, 25)

8. Sample: (1, 26); (26, 1)

9. Samples: (0, 20); (1, 17); (5, 5); (6, 2)

10. There are 9 possibilities: (5, 0); (5, 1); (5, 2); (5, 3); (5, 4); (5, 5); (6, 0); (6, 1); (6, 2)

11.

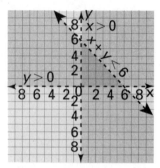

12.

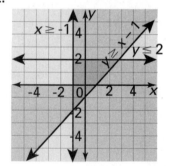

13. $\begin{cases} x \geq 0 \\ y \geq 0 \\ x + 2y \leq 10 \end{cases}$

14. $\begin{cases} x \geq 0 \\ 4x + 5y > 20 \end{cases}$

15. Sample: $\begin{cases} x \geq \text{-}1 \\ x \leq 1 \\ y \geq \text{-}2 \\ y \leq 2 \end{cases}$

16. a. $\begin{cases} 10L + 8P \leq 60 \\ L \geq 0 \\ P \geq 0 \end{cases}$

b.

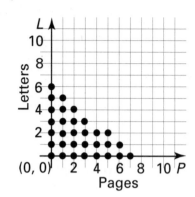

17. a.

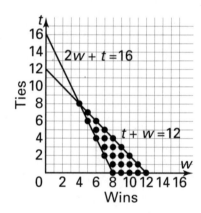

b. 25 ways

18. Let u represent number of days as understudy and p represent number of days performing the role.

$\begin{cases} 250u + 500p \geq 3000 \\ 250u + 500p \leq 5000 \\ u \geq 0 \\ p \geq 0 \end{cases}$

where u and p are integers.

a. $500p \leq 5000$, $p \leq 10$
She performed at most 10 times.

b. $250u \leq 5000$, $u \leq 20$
She understudied at most 20 times.

18. c.

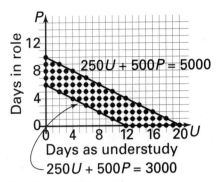

$250U + 500P = 5000$

Days in role (vertical axis): 0, 4, 8, 12

Days as understudy (horizontal axis): 0, 4, 8, 12, 16, 20 U

$250U + 500P = 3000$

19. a. $6(3 - 2x) = -12(x - 3)$
$18 - 12x = -12x + 36$
$0 = 18$
No solution

b. $6(3 - 2y) = -12\left(y - \frac{3}{2}\right)$
$18 - 12y = -12y + 18$
$0 = 0$
y may be any real number.

20. a. 3
b. $z - 3 < 0$ or $z - 3 > 0$
z can be any value except 3.

21. They are intersecting lines since they have different slopes.

22. They are parallel lines since they have the same slope and different y-intercepts; rewrite the second equation:
$-2y = -6x - 27$
$y = 3x + \frac{27}{2}$.

23. a. $\begin{cases} d + q = 27 \\ 0.10d + 0.25q = 5.10 \end{cases}$

b. Multiply the second equation by -10.
$$\begin{aligned} d + q &= 27 \\ + \underline{-1d + -2.5q} &= \underline{-51} \\ -1.5q &= -24 \\ q &= 16 \end{aligned}$$
The commuter has 11 dimes and 16 quarters.

24. a. No
b. It should be
$z - 2(-9z) = 323$
$z + 18z = 323$.

25. $(2x)^2 - 2(2x)(5) + 5^2 = 4x^2 - 20x + 25$

26. a. $x^2 = 121$
$x = \pm 11$

b. $x^2 + 21 = 121$
$x^2 = 100$
$x = \pm 10$

c. $4x^2 + 21 = 121$
$4x^2 = 100$
$x^2 = 25$
$x = \pm 5$

d. $121 = 4x^2 + 24x + 157$
$0 = 4x^2 + 24x + 36$
$0 = x^2 + 6x + 9$
By the quadratic formula,
$$x = \frac{-6 \pm \sqrt{6^2 - 4(1)(9)}}{2(1)}$$
$$x = \frac{-6 \pm 0}{2}$$
$$x = -3$$

27. $1000(1.085)^5 = 1000(1.5037) = \$1503.66$

28. a. Sample: An isosceles trapezoid is a trapezoid with base angles of equal measure.

b. Sample: $\begin{cases} y < x \\ y < 5 - x \\ y > 0 \\ y < 2 \end{cases}$

CHAPTER 11

PROGRESS SELF-TEST
p. 714

1. By substituting $3a$ for b in the first equation,
$a - 3(3a) = -8$
$a - 9a = -8$
$-8a = -8$
$a = 1$
Substitute 1 for a in one of the original equations to find b.
$b = 3(1) = 3$
$(a, b) = (1, 3)$

2. By substitution,

$$-7r - 40 = 5r + 80$$

$$-12r = 120$$

$$r = -10$$

Substitute -10 for r in one of the original equations to find p.

$$p = 5(-10) + 80$$

$$p = -50 + 80 = 30$$

$$(r, p) = (-10, 30)$$

3.
$$m - n = -1$$
$$+ \underline{-m + 2n = 4}$$
$$n = 3$$

Substitute 3 for n in one of the original equations to find m.

$$m - 3 = -1$$

$$m = 2$$

$$(m, n) = (2, 3)$$

4.
$$7x + 3y = 1$$
$$+ \underline{12x - 3y = 18}$$
$$19x = 19$$
$$x = 1$$

Substitute 1 for x in one of the original equations to find y.

$$4(1) - y = 6$$

$$-y = 2$$

$$y = -2$$

$$(x, y) = (1, -2)$$

5. By substitution,

$$x - 3 = -5x - 15$$

$$6x = -12$$

$$x = -2$$

Substitute -2 for x in one of the original equations to find y.

$$y = -5(-2) - 15$$

$$y = 10 - 15 = -5$$

The point of intersection is (-2, -5).

6. The lines coincide since their graphs are the same.

7. The lines are parallel since they have the same slope but different y-intercepts.

8.

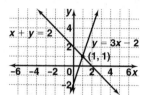

9.

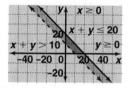

10. $\begin{cases} l = 4s \\ l + s = 95 \end{cases}$

$$4s + s = 95$$

$$5s = 95$$

$$s = 19$$

Substitute 19 for s in one of the original equations to find l.

$$l = 4(19) = 76$$

Lisa weighs 76 pounds; her baby sister, 19 pounds.

11. Solve: $\begin{cases} 3h + 4s = 21.3 \\ 5h + 2s = 22.9 \end{cases}$

$$3h + 4s = 21.3$$
$$+ \underline{-10h - 4s = -45.8}$$
$$-7h = -24.5$$
$$h = 3.5$$

Substitute 3.5 for h in one of the original equations to find s.

$$3(3.5) + 4s = 21.3$$

$$4s = 21.3 - 10.5$$

$$4s = 10.8$$

$$s = 2.7$$

The cost of a small salad is $2.70.

12. No. Let r represent the cost of a rose and d represent the cost of a daffodil.

$$\begin{cases} 10r + 15d = 35 \\ 2r + 3d = 8 \end{cases}$$

$$\begin{array}{r} 10r + 15d = 35 \\ + \; \text{-}10r + \text{-}15d = \text{-}40 \\ \hline 0 = \text{-}5 \end{array}$$

No solution; if the cost per unit were constant, the lines would be coincident and have infinitely many solutions.

13. They will never have the same population because $6{,}016{,}000 + 30{,}000y = 4{,}375{,}000 + 30{,}000y$ has no solution. The lines are parallel.

14.

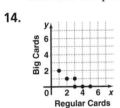

15. $12z + 8 = 12z - 3$

$8 = \text{-}3$

No solution

Check: Let $n = 12z$. By substitution, $n + 8 = n - 3$. The number on the left is always 11 greater than the number on the right.

16. $\text{-}19p < 22 - 19p$

$0 < 22$

p may be any real number.

Check: Pick any number, say -3.
Is $\text{-}19(\text{-}3) < 22 - \text{-}19(3)$?

$57 < 22 + 57?$

$57 < 79?$

Yes, the number on the left will always be 22 less than the number on the right.

1. Substitute $3a$ for b in the second equation.

$60 = a + 3a$

$60 = 4a$

$a = 15$

Substitute 15 for a in one of the original equations to find b.

$b = 3(15) = 45$

$(a, b) = (15, 45)$

2. Substitute $6y - 7$ for x in the first equation.

$6y - 7 - y = 13$

$5y = 20$

$y = 4$

Substitute 4 for y in one of the original equations to find x.

$x = 6(4) - 7$

$x = 24 - 7 = 17$

$(x, y) = (17, 4)$

3. Substitute $50 - q$ for p in the second equation.

$50 - q + 6q = 200$

$5q = 150$

$q = 30$

Substitute 30 for q in one of the original equations to find p.

$p + 30 = 50$

$p = 20$

$(p, q) = (20, 30)$

4. Multiply the first equation by $\frac{1}{10}$ to get $y = 2x + 2$, which is equivalent to $y - 2 = 2x$. Substitute $y - 2$ for $2x$ in the second equation.

$y - 2 + 4y = 29$

$5y = 31$

$y = \frac{31}{5} = 6.2$

Substitute 6.2 for y in one of the original equations to find x.

$6.2 - 2 = 2x$

$4.2 = 2x$

$2.1 = x$

$(x, y) = (2.1, 6.2)$

5. Substitute $x + 5$ for y in the second equation.

$$300 + 10x = 35(x + 5)$$
$$300 + 10x = 35x + 175$$
$$125 = 25x$$
$$x = 5$$

Substitute 5 for x in one of the original equations to find y.

$$y = 5 + 5 = 10$$
$$(x, y) = (5, 10)$$

6. Substitute $z + 8$ for q in the second equation.

$$14z + 89 = 13(z + 8)$$
$$14z + 89 = 13z + 104$$
$$z = 15$$

Substitute 15 for z in one of the original equations to find q.

$$q = 15 + 8 = 23$$
$$(q, z) = (23, 15)$$

7. Substitute $2b + 3$ for a in the second equation.

$$2b + 3 = 3b + 20$$
$$-17 = b$$

Substitute -17 for b in one of the original equations to find a.

$$a = 2(-17) + 3$$
$$a = -34 + 3 = -31$$
$$(a, b) = (-31, -17)$$

8. $16 - 2x = x + 4$
$$-3x = -12$$
$$x = 4$$

Substitute 4 for x in one of the original equations to find y.

$$y = 4 + 4 = 8$$
$$(x, y) = (4, 8)$$

9. $7x + 20 = 3x - 16$
$$4x = -36$$
$$x = -9$$
$$y = 7(-9) + 20$$
$$y = -63 + 20 = -43$$
$$(x, y) = (-9, -43)$$

10. $\frac{2}{3}x - \frac{1}{6} = \frac{1}{3}x + \frac{1}{3}$

Multiply by 6 to clear fractions.
$$4x - 1 = 2x + 2$$
$$2x = 3$$
$$x = \frac{3}{2}$$

Substitute $\frac{3}{2}$ for x in one of the original equations to find y.

$$y = \frac{2}{3} \cdot \frac{3}{2} - \frac{1}{6}$$
$$y = 1 - \frac{1}{6}$$
$$y = \frac{5}{6}$$
$$(x, y) = \left(\frac{3}{2}, \frac{5}{6}\right)$$

11.
$$\begin{array}{r} 3m + b = 11 \\ + \quad -4m - b = 11 \\ \hline -m = 22 \end{array}$$
$$m = -22$$

Substitute -22 for m in one of the original equations to find b.

$$3(-22) + b = 11$$
$$b = 11 + 66 = 77$$
$$(m, b) = (-22, 77)$$

12.
$$\begin{array}{r} 6a + 2c = 200 \\ + \quad 9a - 2c = 25 \\ \hline 15a = 225 \end{array}$$
$$a = 15$$

Substitute 15 for a in one of the original equations to find c.

$$6(15) + 2c = 200$$
$$2c = 200 - 90 = 110$$
$$c = 55$$
$$(a, c) = (15, 55)$$

13. Multiply the first equation by 10 and the second equation by -10 to clear fractions. Then add.

$$6x - 4y = 11$$
$$+ \ -2x + 4y = -23$$
$$\overline{\qquad 4x = -12}$$
$$x = -3$$

Substitute -3 for x in one of the original equations to find y.

$$6(-3) - 4y = 11$$
$$-4y = 11 + 18 = 29$$
$$y = -\frac{29}{4} = -7.25$$
$$(x, y) = (-3, -7.25)$$

14.
$$\frac{1}{2}x + 3y = -6$$
$$+ \ -\frac{1}{2}x + -y = -2$$
$$\overline{\qquad 2y = -8}$$
$$y = -4$$

Substitute -4 for y in one of the original equations to find x.

$$\frac{1}{2}x + -4 = 2$$
$$\frac{1}{2}x = 6$$
$$x = 6 \cdot 2 = 12$$
$$(x, y) = (12, -4)$$

15.
$$4f + \ g = 15$$
$$+ \ -4f + 3g = -3$$
$$\overline{\qquad 4g = 12}$$
$$g = 3$$

Substitute 3 for g in one of the original equations to find f.

$$4f + 3 = 15$$
$$4f = 12$$
$$f = 3$$
$$(f, g) = (3, 3)$$

16.
$$s + \frac{2}{3}t = \ 3$$
$$+ \ 6s + -\frac{2}{3}t = -10$$
$$\overline{\qquad 7s = \ -7}$$
$$s = \ -1$$

Substitute -1 for s in one of the original equations to find t.

$$-1 + \frac{2}{3}t = 3$$
$$\frac{2}{3}t = 4$$
$$t = 4\left(\frac{3}{2}\right) = 6$$
$$(s, t) = (-1, 6)$$

17. a. Sample: $4(5x + y) = 4(30)$

b.
$$20x + 4y = 120$$
$$+ \ 3x - 4y = \ 41$$
$$\overline{\qquad 23x = 161}$$
$$x = \ 7$$

Substitute 7 for x in one of the original equations to find y.

$$5(7) + y = 30$$
$$y = 30 - 35 = -5$$
$$(x, y) = (7, -5)$$

18. a. Sample: $-5(u - 9v) = -5(400)$

b.
$$5u + \ 6v = \ -295$$
$$+ \ -5u + 45v = -2000$$
$$\overline{\qquad 51v = -2295}$$
$$v = \ -45$$

Substitute -45 for v in one of the original equations to find u.

$$u - 9(-45) = 400$$
$$u = 400 - 405 = -5$$
$$(u, v) = (-5, -45)$$

19.
$$6y - 4z = 6$$
$$+\ \underline{-6y - 15z = -63}$$
$$-19z = -57$$
$$z = 3$$

Substitute 3 for z in one of the original equations to find y.
$$3y - 2(3) = 3$$
$$3y = 6 + 3 = 9$$
$$y = 3$$
$$(y, z) = (3, 3)$$

20.
$$-35m + 20n = 0$$
$$+\ \underline{36m - 20n = 4}$$
$$m = 4$$

Substitute 4 for m in one of the original equations to find n.
$$7(4) - 4n = 0$$
$$-4n = -28$$
$$n = 7$$
$$(m, n) = (4, 7)$$

21.
$$3a + 3b = 9$$
$$+\ \underline{-3a + 5b = -17}$$
$$8b = -8$$
$$b = -1$$

Substitute -1 for b in one of the original equations to find a.
$$a + -1 = 3$$
$$a = 4$$
$$(a, b) = (4, -1)$$

22. Multiply the second equation by $\frac{1}{-4}$.
$$46 = 2t + u$$
$$+\ \underline{\quad -5 = -2t + u}$$
$$41 = 2u$$
$$\frac{41}{2} = u$$

Substitute $\frac{41}{2}$ for u in one of the original equations to find t.
$$46 = 2t + \frac{41}{2}$$
$$46 - \frac{41}{2} = 2t$$
$$\frac{51}{2} = 2t$$
$$\frac{51}{4} = t$$
$$(t, u) = \left(\frac{51}{4}, \frac{41}{2}\right)$$

23. $2a + 4 < 2a + 3$
$$4 < 3$$
No solution

24. $12c < 18 + 12c$
$$0 < 18$$
All real numbers are solutions.

25. $7x - x = 12x$
$$6x = 12x$$
$$-6x = 0$$
$$x = 0$$
One solution

26. $-10x = 15 - 10x$
$$0 = 15$$
No solution

27. No; $2k - 2k - 7 = 2k - 2k$
$$-7 = 0 \text{ is never true; so the original sentence is never true.}$$

28. No; $100d < 100d - 100$
$$0 < -100 \text{ is never true; so the original sentence is never true.}$$

29. No solution when $b \neq c$. If the slopes are equal, but the y-intercepts are different, the lines are parallel and the system has no solution. When $b = c$, then the lines are coincident and there are infinitely many solutions.

30. When the first equation is multiplied by -3, the result is the second equation. The lines coincide and the system has infinitely many solutions.

31. When the first equation is multiplied by 5, the result is the second equation. The lines coincide and the system has infinitely many solutions.

32. These lines are parallel; they have the same slope, but different y-intercepts.

33. When the first equation is multiplied by -1, the result is the second equation. The lines coincide and the system has infinitely many solutions.

34. These lines intersect; they have different slopes.

35. (c)

36. slope

37. $\begin{cases} m + j = 210 \\ \quad\quad j = 3m \end{cases}$

$m + 3m = 210$

$4m = 210$

$m = 52.5$

Substitute 52.5 for m in one of the original equations to find j.

$j = 3(52.5) = 157.50$

Marty earned \$52.50; Joe, \$157.50.

38. $\begin{cases} 39 + .1m = c \\ 22.95 + .25m = c \end{cases}$

$39 + .1m = 22.95 + .25m$

$16.05 = .15m$

$m = 107$

At 107 miles the rental costs are equal.

39. Job (1): $7.00 + .5b$
Job (2): $7.20 + .5b$

where b represents the number of 6-month increments.

$7.20 + .5b > 7.00 + .5b$

$.2 > 0$

Job (2) always pays more than Job (1).

40. Solve: $\begin{cases} 405{,}000 + 7500y = p \\ 290{,}000 + 13{,}500y = p \end{cases}$

where p is population and y is the number of years.

$405{,}000 + 7500y = 290{,}000 + 13{,}500y$

$115{,}000 = 6000y$

$\dfrac{115}{6} = y$

$19 \approx y$

About 19 years

41. Solve: $\begin{cases} 2e + m = 1.80 \\ \quad e + m = 1.35 \end{cases}$

$\begin{aligned} 2e + \ m &= \ 1.8 \\ + \ -e + -m &= -1.35 \\ \hline e \ &= \ \ .45 \end{aligned}$

Substitute .45 for e in one of the original equations to find m.

$.45 + m = 1.35$

$m = .90$

An egg costs \$0.45; a muffin, \$0.90.

42. Solve: $\begin{cases} 3n + 2m = 315 \\ 2n + m = 205 \end{cases}$

$\begin{aligned} 3n + 2m &= \ \ 315 \\ + \ -4n - 2m &= -410 \\ \hline -n &= \ \ -95 \\ n &= \ \ \ \ 95 \end{aligned}$

The charge for a room for one night is \$95.

43. Yes. Multiply the first equation by 2 to see that $16p + 5e = 8$ is equivalent to $32p + 10e = 16$. There are infinitely many solutions.

44. Solve: $\begin{cases} 2.5s + 4a = 2395 \\ \quad\ s + a = 850 \end{cases}$

$\begin{aligned} 2.5s + 4a &= \ \ 2395 \\ + \ -4s - 4a &= -3400 \\ \hline -1.5s &= -1005 \\ s &= \ \ \ 670 \end{aligned}$

670 student tickets were sold.

45. $\begin{cases} h \geq 0 \\ c \geq 0 \\ c \leq 2 \\ 2h + 3c \leq 11 \end{cases}$

where h represents the number of batches of cookies and c represents the number of cakes

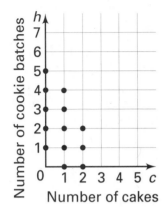

46. $\begin{cases} c \geq 0 \\ c \leq 70 \\ m \geq 0 \\ m \leq 60 \\ m + c \leq 100 \end{cases}$

where m represents the number of Montagues and c represents the number of Capulets.

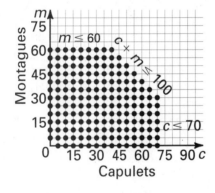

47. a. $\begin{cases} \ell \geq 8 \\ w \geq 6 \\ 2\ell + 2w \leq 50 \end{cases}$

where ℓ represents the length and w the width

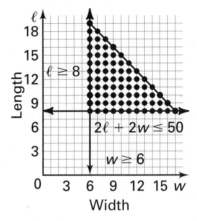

b. Let the width be the smallest possible value, or 6:

$$2\ell + 2(6) \leq 50$$
$$2\ell \leq 38$$
$$\ell \leq 19 \text{ ft}$$

48. a. $\begin{cases} 1000c + 400t \leq 5000 \\ c \geq 0 \\ t \geq 0 \\ c + t \geq 8 \end{cases}$

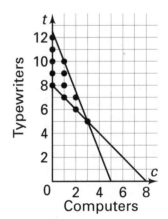

48. b. Since she must buy 8 machines, $c + t = 8$, so substitute $t = 8 - c$ in the first inequality of the system.

$$1000c + 400(8 - c) \leq 5000$$

$$1000c + 3200 - 400c \leq 5000$$

$$600c \leq 1800$$

$$c \leq 3$$

At most, Rhiann can buy 3 computers.

49.

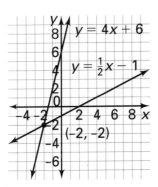

50.

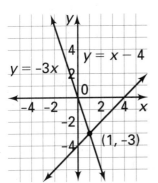

51.

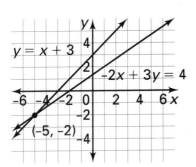

52. coincident, infinitely many solutions

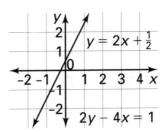

53. parallel, no solutions

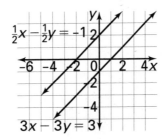

54.

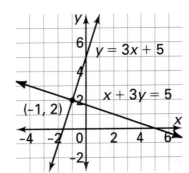

55.

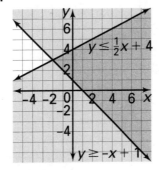

56.

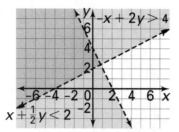

57.

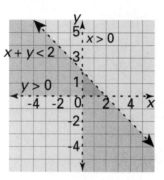

58.

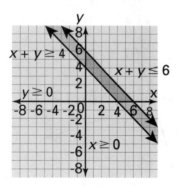

59. $\begin{cases} 40c + 70a \le 280 \\ \quad\quad c \ge 0 \\ \quad\quad a \ge 0 \end{cases}$

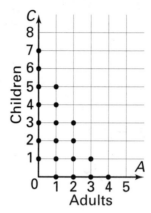

60. $\begin{cases} 5x + 15y \le 60 \\ \quad\quad x \ge 0 \\ \quad\quad y \ge 0 \end{cases}$

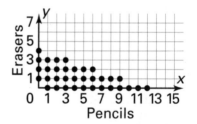

CHAPTER 12
FACTORING

1. Because $13 \cdot 17 = 221$, 13 is a *factor* of 221, and 221 is a *multiple* of 13.

2. Sample: 2; 3; 4; 5

3. 1; 5; 7; 35

4. Sample: 17; 34; 51; 68

5. Sample: 1; 2; 4; 12

6. 9 has more than two different factors: 1, 3, and 9.

7. No; because $133 = 7 \cdot 19$.

8.

9. 7 is a factor of both 7^2 and $3 \cdot 7^3$, so by the Common Factor Sum Property, it is a factor of $7^2 + 3 \cdot 7^3$.

10. $3216 = 2 \cdot 1608$

$3216 = 2 \cdot 2 \cdot 804$

$3216 = 2 \cdot 2 \cdot 2 \cdot 402$

$3216 = 2 \cdot 2 \cdot 2 \cdot 2 \cdot 201$

$3216 = 2 \cdot 2 \cdot 2 \cdot 2 \cdot 3 \cdot 67$

$3216 = 2^4 \cdot 3 \cdot 67$

11. $3^{4+1} \cdot 5^{2+1} \cdot 7^2 = 3^5 \cdot 5^3 \cdot 7^2$

12. $\dfrac{3 \cdot 5 \cdot 7^2}{3^4 \cdot 5^2} = \dfrac{7^2}{3^{4-1} \cdot 5^{2-1}} = \dfrac{49}{135}$

13. $\dfrac{3^4 \cdot 5^2}{3 \cdot 5 \cdot 7^2} = \dfrac{3^{4-1} \cdot 5^{2-1}}{7^2} = \dfrac{135}{49}$

14. encoding and decoding

15. 53, 59, 61, 67, 71, 73, 79, 83, 89, 97

16. Factors of 300: 1, 2, 3, 4, 5, 6, 10, 12, 15, 20, 25, 30, 50, 60, 75, 100, 150, 300
Factors which are multiples of 3: 3, 6, 12, 15, 30, 60, 75, 150, 300

17. 20

18. Sample: If a is a factor of b, then there is a number m with $am = b$. If a is a factor of c, then there is a number n with $an = c$. Subtracting equations: $am - an = b - c$. By the Distributive Property, $am - an = a(m - n)$. Thus, $a(m - n) = b - c$, and so a is a factor of $b - c$.

19. a. Because $2^{40} = 4 \cdot 2^{38}$ and $332 = 4 \cdot 83$, then 4 is a common factor of 2^{40} and 332. Using the Common Factor Sum Property, we know 4 is also a factor of $2^{40} + 332$.

b. No; 332 is not divisible by 8.

20.

21. Let $x = d^2$. Then, solve $x^2 - 25x + 144 = 0$. By the Quadratic Formula,

$$x = \frac{-(-25) \pm \sqrt{(-25)^2 - 4(1)(144)}}{2(1)}$$

$$x = \frac{25 \pm \sqrt{49}}{2}$$

$$x = \frac{25 \pm 7}{2}$$

$x = 16$ or $x = 9$
Since $x = d^2$,

$16 = d^2$ or $9 = d^2$

$4 = d$ or $3 = d$

$-4 = d$ or $-3 = d$

22. Venus travels

$2\pi \cdot (108 \text{ million km}) + \frac{140}{365} \cdot 2\pi \cdot (108 \text{ million km})$

$= \frac{101}{73} \cdot 2\pi \cdot (108 \text{ million km})$

$\approx 298.85\pi$ million km.

Earth travels $2\pi \cdot (150 \text{ million km})$

$= 300 \pi$ million km.

Earth travels farther.

23. $\frac{12}{19} = \frac{w}{162}$

$12 \cdot 162 = 19w$

$1994 = 19w$

$102.3 = w$

about 102 games

24. a. Highest: $\frac{75 + 80 + 90 + 100}{4} = 86.25\%$

Lowest: $\frac{75 + 80 + 90 + 0}{4} = 61.25\%$

b. Highest: $\frac{80 + 90}{2} = 85\%$

Lowest: $\frac{75 + 80}{2} = 77.5\%$

c. Highest: 90%
Lowest: 75%

25. (a); $2 \cdot 10^{128}$ is 2 followed by 128 zeros.

26. Sample:

a	p	$a^p - a$
3	3	$3^3 - 3 = 27 - 3 = 24 = 3 \cdot 8$
3	5	$3^5 - 3 = 243 - 3 = 240 = 5 \cdot 48$
4	5	$4^5 - 4 = 1024 - 4 = 1020 = 5 \cdot 204$
4	7	$4^7 - 4 = 16,380 = 7 \cdot 2340$
5	13	$5^{13} - 5 = 1,220,703,120 = 13 \cdot 93,900,240$

LESSON 12-2　　　　　　　　pp. 726–731

1. 1, 2, 7, 14, x, x^2, x^3, x^4, $2x$, $7x$, $14x$, $2x^2$, $7x^2$, $14x^2$, $2x^3$, $7x^3$, $14x^3$, $2x^4$, $7x^4$, $14x^4$

2. greatest common factor

3. $5x^2$

4. $6a$

5.

6. a. $3x(x + 2)$

b.

7. a. No; $3x^2(3x + 4)$
b. No; $3x(3x + 4)$
c. Yes
d. Yes

8. a. $(4x^3 + 2x^2)$
b. $(2x^3 + x^2)$
c. $(2x^2 + x)$
d. No

9. $(x^2 + 5)$

10. $(4p - 3)$

11. $(2a + b)$

12. $\frac{3n(4n + 5)}{3n} = 4n + 5$

13. $3xy^2$

14. $27(b^3 - c^3 + bc)$

15. $a^2(23a + 1)$

16. $4a(3 + 4a)$

17. $7p^2(2p - 3q)$

18. $\frac{100y^3}{5y} - \frac{55y^2}{5y} + \frac{30y}{5y} = 20y^2 - 11y + 6$

19. Samples:

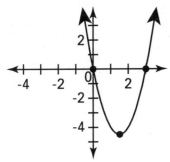

20. a.

b. $2x$

21. $\frac{3xy(-x + 2 - 3y)}{3xy} = -x + 2 - 3y$

22. $\frac{n^2(n^{12} - 3n^8 + 5n^4 - 1)}{n^2} = n^{12} - 3n^8 + 5n^4 - 1$

23. a. $(2r)^2 = 4r^2$

    b. πr^2

    c. $4r^2 - \pi r^2 = (4 - \pi)r^2$

    d. $12(4 - \pi)r^2 = (48 - 12\pi)r^2$

    e. $\frac{(48 - 12\pi)r^2}{\pi r^2} = \frac{48 - 12\pi}{\pi} \approx 3.28$

    3 drum tops

24. a. $1001 = 7 \cdot 143$

       $1001 = 7 \cdot 11 \cdot 13$

    b. $91 = 7 \cdot 13$

    c. $7 \cdot 11 \cdot 13 \cdot 7 \cdot 13 = 7^2 \cdot 11 \cdot 13^2$

    d. $\frac{7 \cdot 13}{7 \cdot 11 \cdot 13} = \frac{1}{11}$

25. a. $x^2 - 11x + 14x - 154 = x^2 + 3x - 154$

    b. By the Quadratic Formula,

$$x = \frac{-3 \pm \sqrt{3^2 - 4(1)(-154)}}{2(1)}$$

$$x = \frac{-3 \pm 25}{2}$$

$$x = 11 \text{ or } x = -14$$

26. a. $\frac{93.4 - 91.2}{3 - 10} = \frac{2.2}{-7} \approx -.31$ kg per day

    b. $\frac{2.2}{-7} \frac{\text{kg}}{\text{day}} \cdot \frac{2.2}{1} \frac{\text{lb}}{\text{kg}} \cdot 7 \frac{\text{days}}{\text{week}} = -4.84 \frac{\text{lb}}{\text{wk}}$

27. $3a^2 + 5a + 6a + 10 = 3a^2 + 11a + 10$

28. $6x^2 + 6x - 6x^2 + 12 = 18$

             $6x + 12 = 18$

                 $6x = 6$

                   $x = 1$

29. $3 + x = 12$

       $x = 9$

30. $5 + x + 1 + 4 = 12$

         $x + 10 = 12$

             $x = 2$

31. a. Line 20 shows that each value of x goes through 11 operations.

       $11 \cdot 20{,}000 \cdot .000001 = 0.22$ second

    b. 20 LET P = 50 *
(X^4 + X^3 + X^2 + X + 1)
x will now go though 8 operations.
8(20,000)(0.000001) = 0.16 second

31. c. $(0.22 - 0.16)(.25) = \$0.015$ per second

d. Sample: Each birthday from age 10 on, David has received \$50 from his uncle. He saves the money in an account that pays an annual yield of $(x - 1)\%$. How much money will he have by the time he is 14?

IN-CLASS ACTIVITY p. 732

1. a.

Dimensions: $x + 1$ by $x + 2$

Dimensions: $x + 2$ by $x + 1$

b. $(x + 2)(x + 1)$

2.
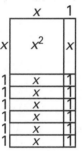

$(x + 6)(x + 1)$

3.

x | 1 1 1 1

$(x + 3)(x + 4)$

4. a.
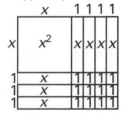

b. $(2x + 1)(x + 3)$

5.
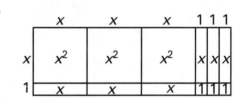

$(2x + 3)(x + 2)$

6.

$(3x + 3)(x + 1)$

7. a.
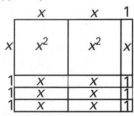

b.

Area: $4x^2 + 16x + 16$
Side: $2x + 4$

c. $2x + 4$

8. $9x^2 + 12x + 4 = (3x + 2)^2$

250

1. 1

2. a. Multiply the factors and check that you obtain the original trinomial.

  b. $(t - 3)(t - 3) = t^2 - 3t - 3t + 9 = t^2 - 6t + 9$

3. a.

Factors of 12	Sum of Factors
1, 12	13
2, 6	8
3, 4	7

  b. $x^2 + 8x + 12 = (x + 2)(x + 6)$

  c. $(x + 2)(x + 6) = x^2 + 2x + 6x + 12$
  $$= x^2 + 8x + 12$$

4. a. $pq = c$

  b. $p + q = b$

5. $2 \cdot 5 = 10;\ 2 + 5 = 7$
  $(x + 2)(x + 5)$

6. $1 \cdot 13 = 13;\ 1 + 13 = 14$
  $(p + 13)(p + 1)$

7. $5 \cdot \text{-}6 = \text{-}30;\ 5 + \text{-}6 = \text{-}1$
  $(t - 6)(t + 5)$

8. $\text{-}9 \cdot 9 = \text{-}81;\ \text{-}9 + 9 = 0$
  $(a - 9)(a + 9)$

9. $\text{-}2 \cdot \text{-}8 = 16;\ \text{-}2 + \text{-}8 = \text{-}10$
  $(q - 8)(q - 2)$

10. $\text{-}2 \cdot 6 = \text{-}12;\ \text{-}2 + 6 = 4$
  $(n - 2)(n + 6)$

11. None of the pairs of integer factors of 3 has a sum of 2.

12. a. $x(x^2 - 5x + 6)$

  b. $\text{-}2 + \text{-}3 = \text{-}5;\ \text{-}2 \cdot \text{-}3 = 6$
  $x(x - 2)(x - 3)$

13. $2(m^2 + 9m + 18) = 2(m + 3)(m + 6)$
  (since $3 \cdot 6 = 18;\ 3 + 6 = 9$)

14. $4y(y^2 - 5y - 6) = 4y(y - 6)(y + 1)$
  (since $\text{-}6 \cdot 1 = \text{-}6;\ \text{-}6 + 1 = \text{-}5$)

15. $(x + 2)(x + 3)$

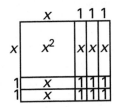

16. a. $\text{-}3 \cdot \text{-}7 = 21;\ \text{-}3 + \text{-}7 = \text{-}10$
  $y = (x - 3)(x - 7)$

  b.

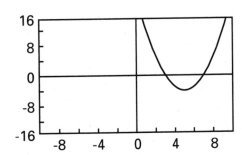

17. $7 \cdot 5 = 35;\ \text{-}7 + \text{-}5 = \text{-}12$
  $(7 - x)(5 - x)$

18. $\text{-}1 \cdot \text{-}7 = 7;\ \text{-}1 + \text{-}7 = \text{-}8$
  $(a - 7b)(a - b)$

19. $10(4 - x^2) = 10(2 - x)(2 + x)$
  (difference of two squares)

20. $5r(r^2 + 2r + 1) = 5r(r + 1)(r + 1) = 5r(r + 1)^2$
  (since $1 \cdot 1 = 1;\ 1 + 1 = 2$)

21. Let $x = 10^3$; then $10^6 + 32 \cdot 10^3 + 60$
  $= x^2 + 32x + 60 = (x + 2)(x + 30)$
  (since $2 \cdot 30 = 60;\ 2 + 30 = 32$).
  So, $10^6 + 32 \cdot 10^3 + 60$
  $= (10^3 + 2)(10^3 + 30)$
  $= 1002 \cdot 1030$
  $= 2 \cdot 501 \cdot 2 \cdot 515$
  $= 2^2 \cdot 3 \cdot 167 \cdot 5 \cdot 103$
  $= 2^2 \cdot 3 \cdot 5 \cdot 103 \cdot 167$

22. a difference of two squares:
$(28 + 22)(28 - 22) = 50(6) = 300$

23. $\frac{(a_0 - e_0)^2}{e_0} = \frac{(10 - 5)^2}{5} = \frac{25}{5} = 5$

$\frac{(a_1 - e_1)^2}{e_1} = \frac{(7 - 5)^2}{5} = \frac{4}{5}$

$\frac{(a_2 - e_2)^2}{e_2} = \frac{(2 - 5)^2}{5} = \frac{9}{5}$

$\frac{(a_3 - e_3)^2}{e_3} = \frac{(3 - 5)^2}{5} = \frac{4}{5}$

$\frac{(a_4 - e_4)^2}{e_4} = \frac{(4 - 5)^2}{5} = \frac{1}{5}$

$\frac{(a_5 - e_5)^2}{e_5} = \frac{(3 - 5)^2}{5} = \frac{4}{5}$

$\frac{(a_6 - e_6)^2}{e_6} = \frac{(5 - 5)^2}{5} = 0$

$\frac{(a_7 - e_7)^2}{e_7} = \frac{(7 - 5)^2}{5} = \frac{4}{5}$

$\frac{(a_8 - e_8)^2}{e_8} = \frac{(2 - 5)^2}{5} = \frac{9}{5}$

$\frac{(a_9 - e_9)^2}{e_9} = \frac{(7 - 5)^2}{5} = \frac{4}{5}$

$\frac{25 + 4 + 9 + 4 + 1 + 4 + 0 + 4 + 9 + 4}{5} = \frac{64}{5} = 12.8$

When $n = 10$, $n - 1 = 9$, so look in the ninth row. A chi-square value as high as 16.9 would be expected to occur 5% of the time. The chi-square value is 12.8. A chi-square value this size would be expected more than 10% of the time, so this is not an unusual distribution of digits.

24. $6x^2 - 12x + 2x - 4 = 6x^2 - 10x - 4$

25. $64a^2 + 8a - 8a - 1 = 64a^2 - 1$

26. By the Quadratic Formula,

$x = \frac{-5 \pm \sqrt{5^2 - 4(1)(4)}}{2(1)}$

$x = \frac{-5 \pm 3}{2}$

$x = -1$ or $x = -4$

27. $24(1 - 0.04(10))^2 + 45$

$= 24(1 - 0.4)^2 + 45$

$= 24(.36) + 45$

$= 8.64 + 45$

$= 53.64°F$

28. $24(1 - 0.04t)^2 + 45 = 45$

$24(1 - 0.04t)^2 = 0$

$1 - 0.04t = 0$

$-0.04t = -1$

$t = -\frac{1}{-0.04}$

$t = 25$ minutes

29. $15 \cdot \frac{3}{5} = x$

$9 = x$

30. $d^2 = 45$

$d = \pm\sqrt{45}$

$d = \pm\sqrt{9 \cdot 5}$

$d = \pm3\sqrt{5}$

31. $w + .12w = 9.25$

$1.12w = 9.25$

$w = 8.2589$

The wrench sold for $8.26.

32. a. Does $\frac{2^2 - 4 \cdot 2 + 3}{2^2 - 9} = \frac{2 - 1}{2 + 3}$?

$\frac{4 - 8 + 3}{4 - 9} = \frac{1}{5}$?

$\frac{-1}{-5} = \frac{1}{5}$?

Yes, it checks.

b. Sample: $\frac{x^2 - 1}{x^2 + 7x + 6}$ when $x \ne -1$ and $x \ne -6$

c. $\frac{(x - 1)(x + 1)}{(x + 1)(x + 6)} = \frac{x - 1}{x + 6}$

Check: Let $x = 2$.

Does $\frac{2^2 - 1}{2^2 + 7 \cdot 2 + 6} = \frac{2 - 1}{2 + 6}$?

$\frac{4 - 1}{4 + 14 + 6} = \frac{1}{8}$?

$\frac{3}{24} = \frac{1}{8}$?

Yes, it checks.

LESSON 12-4   pp. 738–743

1. Zero Product Property: If the product of two real numbers a and b is 0, then $a = 0$ or $b = 0$.

2. a. $k + 4 = 0$ or $k - 1 = 0$
$k = -4$ or $k = 1$

b. Check: $(-4 + 4)(-4 - 1) = 0(-5) = 0$
$(1 + 4)(1 - 1) = 5(0) = 0$

3. a. $64t - 16t^2 = 0$
$16t(4 - t) = 0$
$t = 0$ or $4 - t = 0$
$t = 0$ or $t = 4$
after 4 seconds

b. The x-intercepts of the graph, if any, are times when the ball is at ground level.

4. $(x + 3)(x - 1) = 0$
$x + 3 = 0$ or $x - 1 = 0$
$x = -3$ or $x = 1$

5. $(y - 5)(y + 1) = 0$
$y - 5 = 0$ or $y + 1 = 0$
$y = 5$ or $y = -1$

6. $(x - 3)(x - 9) = 0$
$x - 3 = 0$ or $x - 9 = 0$
$x = 3$ or $x = 9$

7. $(a + 9)(a + 4) = 0$
$a + 9 = 0$ or $a + 4 = 0$
$a = -9$ or $a = -4$

8. $(t - 8)(t + 8) = 0$
$t - 8 = 0$ or $t + 8 = 0$
$t = 8$ or $t = -8$

9. $(v + 7)^2 = 0$
$v + 7 = 0$
$v = -7$

10. There cannot be a negative number of players entered in a chess tournament.

11. $\frac{n^2 - n}{2} = 21$
$n^2 - n = 42$
$n^2 - n - 42 = 0$
$(n - 7)(n + 6) = 0$
$n - 7 = 0$ or $n + 6 = 0$
$n = 7$ or $n = -6$
A negative number of players does not make sense, so 7 players are entered.

12. a. factor
b. Zero Product

13. Because the product of factors is not zero.

14. $y - 15 = 0$ or $9y - 8 = 0$
$y = 15$ or $9y = 8$
$y = \frac{8}{9}$

15. $r = 0$ or $2r + 5 = 0$ or $r - 6 = 0$
$2r = -5$ or $r = 6$
$r = -\frac{5}{2}$

16. a. $a = \frac{5 \pm \sqrt{25 + 200}}{2}$
$a = \frac{5 \pm 15}{2}$
$a = 10$ or $a = -5$

b. $(a + 5)(a - 10) = 0$
$a + 5 = 0$ or $a - 10 = 0$
$a = -5$ or $a = 10$

c. Sample: Factoring; it is quicker and requires fewer calculations.

17. $y^2 - 4y - 5 = 0$
$(y - 5)(y + 1) = 0$
$y - 5 = 0$ or $y + 1 = 0$
$y = 5$ or $y = -1$

18. $b^2 + 15b + 26 = 0$
$(b + 13)(b + 2) = 0$
$b + 13 = 0$ or $b + 2 = 0$
$b = -13$ or $b = -2$

19. $7(p^2 + p - 12) = 0$
$7(p + 4)(p - 3) = 0$
$p + 4 = 0$ or $p - 3 = 0$
$p = -4$ or $p = 3$

20. $g^2 = 100$
$g = 10$ or $g = -10$

21. $2v^2 - 3v = 0$
$v(2v - 3) = 0$
$v = 0$ or $2v - 3 = 0$
$v = \frac{3}{2}$

22. $x(x^2 - 4x + 4) = 0$

$x(x - 2)^2 = 0$

$x = 0$ or $x - 2 = 0$

$x = 2$

23. a. $5^2 + 5 = 25 + 5 = 30$

$2 + 4 + 6 + 8 + 10 = 30$

b. Solve: $n^2 + n = 132$

$n^2 + n - 132 = 0$

$(n - 11)(n + 12) = 0$

$n - 11 = 0$ or $n + 12 = 0$

$n = 11$ or $n = -12$

A negative number doesn't make sense, so 11 consecutive even integers are added.

24. $ax(x - 1) = 0$

$x = 0$ or $x - 1 = 0$

$x = 1$

25. (d); since $x(ax + b) = 0$

26. $2x(x^2 - 9x + 8) = 2x(x - 8)(x - 1)$

27. $\frac{x(13x - 14)}{x} = 13x - 14$

28. $u^2 - 2uv + v^2 - u^2 + v^2 = 2v^2 - 2uv$

29. $(4e + 1)^2 = 16e^2 + 8e + 1$ square units

30. Sample:

$(3 + 4)(3 - 4) = 7 \cdot -1 = -7;$

$(\sqrt{9})^2 - (\sqrt{16})^2 = 9 - 16 = -7;$

$(3 + 4)(3 - 4) = 7(3 - 4) = 21 - 28 = -7$

31. a.

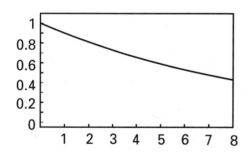

b. about 6.6 thicknesses

32. a.

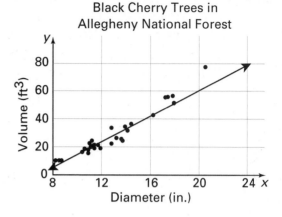

Black Cherry Trees in Allegheny National Forest

b. slope: $\frac{19.9 - 42.6}{11.2 - 16.3} = \frac{-22.7}{-5.1} = 4.45$

$19.9 = 4.45(11.2) + b$

$19.9 = 49.84 + b$

$-29.94 = b$

$y = 4.45x - 29.94$

c. $y = 4.45(15) - 29.94$

$y = 66.75 - 29.94$

$y = 36.81$

about 36.8 ft^3

33. $2x(x) = 2x^2$ square units

34. $a^2 - b^2$ square units

35. a. $(x^2)^2 - 3(x^2) - 4 = 0$

$(x^2 - 4)(x^2 + 1) = 0$

$x^2 - 4 = 0$ or $x^2 + 1 = 0$

Since $x^2 + 1$ cannot equal zero, $x^2 - 4 = 0$.

So, $x - 2 = 0$ or $x + 2 = 0$

$x = 2$ or $x = -2$

b. $(m^2)^2 - 13(m^2) + 36 = 0$

$(m^2 - 4)(m^2 - 9) = 0$

$m^2 - 4 = 0$ or $m^2 - 9 = 0$

$(m - 2)(m + 2) = 0$ or $(m - 3)(m + 3) = 0$

$m = 2$ or $m = -2$ or $m = 3$ or $m = -3$

1. a. $5x^2 + 35x + 3x + 21 = 5x^2 + 38x + 21$
b. $5x^2 + 15x + 7x + 21 = 5x^2 + 22x + 21$
c. $5x^2 + 105x + x + 21 = 5x^2 + 106x + 21$
d. $5x^2 - 105x - x + 21 = 5x^2 - 106x + 21$
e. Suppose $5x^2 + 26x + 21 = (dx + e)(fx + g)$; then $df = 5$ and $eg = 21$. Thus these multiplications are other possible ways of obtaining $df = 5$ and $eg = 21$.

2. a. a
   b. e, g

3. Substitute a number; graph

4. $(2x + 5)(x + 1)$

5. $(7x - 1)(x - 5)$

6. $(y + 9)(y + 1)$

7. $(2x + 1)(2x - 7)$

8. $(3x - 1)(x + 4)$

9. $(5k - 4)(2k - 3)$

10. Check: Does $6 \cdot \left(\frac{5}{3}\right)^2 - 7 \cdot \frac{5}{3} - 5 = 0$?

$$6 \cdot \frac{25}{9} - \frac{35}{3} - 5 = 0?$$

$$\frac{50}{3} - \frac{35}{3} - 5 = 0?$$

$$\frac{15}{3} - 5 = 0?$$

$$5 - 5 = 0?$$

Does $6 \cdot \left(-\frac{1}{2}\right)^2 - 7 \cdot -\frac{1}{2} - 5 = 0$?

$$6 \cdot \frac{1}{4} - \frac{-7}{2} - 5 = 0?$$

$$\frac{6}{4} + \frac{7}{2} - 5 = 0?$$

$$\frac{10}{2} - 5 = 0?$$

$$5 - 5 = 0?$$

Yes, they check.

11. $(2x + 7)(x + 2) = 0$
$2x + 7 = 0$ or $x + 2 = 0$
$x = -\frac{7}{2}$ or $x = -2$

12. The graphs are the same since
$(2x - 5)(x + 1) = 2x^2 - 3x - 5$.

13. $k = 5$ since $k^2 = 25$

14. a. i. $t = \frac{5 \pm \sqrt{25 + 504}}{12}$

$$t = \frac{5 \pm 23}{12}$$

$$t = \frac{7}{3} \text{ or } t = -\frac{3}{2}$$

    ii. $(3t - 7)(2t + 3) = 0$
$3t - 7 = 0$ or $2t + 3 = 0$
$t = \frac{7}{3}$ or $t = -\frac{3}{2}$

b. Sample: The Quadratic Formula, because there are many possible factors to consider.

15. a. i.

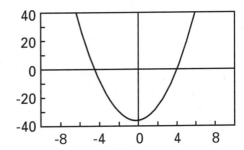

    ii. $(x - 4)(2x + 9) = 0$
$x - 4 = 0$ or $2x + 9 = 0$
$x = 4$ or $x = \frac{-9}{2}$

b. Sample: Factoring, because it is more precise.

16. a. $10x(2x^2 - 7x + 6)$
    b. $10x(2x - 3)(x - 2)$

17. $p^2(9p^2 + 12p + 4) = p^2(3p + 2)^2$

18. $(2x - 3y)(x - y)$

19. Zero Product Property: If the product of two real numbers a and b is zero, then $a = 0$ or $b = 0$.

20. $(x - 7)(x - 1) = 0$
$x - 7 = 0$ or $x - 1 = 0$
$x = 7$ or $x = 1$

21. By Quadratic Formula,

$$y = \frac{-9 \pm \sqrt{81 - 28}}{2}$$

$$y = \frac{-9 \pm \sqrt{53}}{2}$$

$$y \approx -8.14 \text{ or } y \approx -0.86$$

22. $d^2 - 8d + 16 = 0$

$(d - 4)(d - 4) = 0$

$d - 4 = 0$

$d = 4$

23. $100v^2 - 400 = 0$

$100v^2 = 400$

$v^2 = 4$

$v = \pm 2$

24. a. $(x + 7)(x + 1)$

b. $187 = 10^2 + 8(10) + 7 = (10 + 1)(10 + 7)$

$= 11(17)$

25. a. $(x^2 - 9)(x^2 + 9)$

b. $(x^2 + 9)(x + 3)(x - 3)$

26. a. cube: $4^3 = 64$ cubic units

rectangular box: $3(4)(5) = 60$ cubic units
The cube holds more than the rectangular box.

b. cube: e^3 cubic units

rectangular box: $(e - 1)(e + 1)(e) = (e^2 - 1)(e) = e^3 - e$ cubic units
The cube holds more than the box.

27. stay $= \sqrt{35^2 + 12^2}$

$= \sqrt{1225 + 144}$

$= \sqrt{1369}$

$= 37$ ft

28. $35^2 + d^2 = 50^2$

$d^2 = 2500 - 1225$

$d^2 = 1275$

$d = \sqrt{1275}$

$d \approx 35.7$ ft

29. a. $(2x + 2y)(x - y) = 2(x^2 - y^2)$

b. Yes; $(2x + 2y)(x - y)$

$= 2x^2 - 2xy + 2xy - 2y^2$

$= 2x^2 - 2y^2$

$= 2(x^2 - y^2)$

30. (c)

31. slope: $\frac{1}{2}$

y-intercept: 0

32. $8x - 5y = 1$

$-5y = -8 + 1$

$y = \frac{8}{5}x - \frac{1}{5}$

slope: $\frac{8}{5}$

y-intercept: $-\frac{1}{5}$

33. $\frac{325}{1000} = \frac{13}{40}$ or .325 of a picture

34. $abc = 6$; $a = 1$; $b = 2$; $c = 3$

LESSON 12-6   pp. 749–753

1. (d)

2. Babylonian

3. $L(100 - L) = 2475$

$L^2 - 100L + 2475 = 0$

$(L - 45)(L - 55) = 0$

$L = 45$ or $L = 55$

4. $(32 + x)(32 - x) = 903$

$32^2 - x^2 = 903$

$x^2 = 121$

$x = \pm 11$

So, the two numbers are 43 and 21.

5. Sample: 10 yards by 6 yards; 12 yards by 5 yards

6. $\begin{cases} LW = 60 \\ L + W = 17 \end{cases}$

Substitute $17 - L$ for W in the first equation.

$L(17 - L) = 60$

$17L - L^2 = 60$

$L^2 - 17L + 60 = 0$

$(L - 12)(L - 5) = 0$

$L = 12$ or $L = 5$

Substitute these values for L in one of the original equations to find W.

$12 + W = 17$ or $5 + W = 17$

$W = 5$ or $W = 12$

The dimensions are 5 yards by 12 yards.

7. The average of L and W is $\frac{17}{2}$, so let

$L = \frac{17}{2} + x$ and $W = \frac{17}{2} - x$.

$$\left(\frac{17}{2} + x\right)\left(\frac{17}{2} - x\right) = 60$$

$$\frac{289}{4} - x^2 = 60$$

$$x^2 = \frac{49}{4}$$

$$x = \frac{7}{2}$$

So $L = \frac{17}{2} + \frac{7}{2} = 12$ yards and

$W = \frac{17}{2} - \frac{7}{2} = 5$ yards.

8. $\begin{cases} x + y = 12 \\ xy = 9 \end{cases}$

Substitute $12 - x$ for y in the second equation.

$$x(12 - x) = 9$$

$$12x - x^2 = 9$$

$$x^2 - 12x + 9 = 0$$

By the Quadratic Formula,

$$x = \frac{12 \pm \sqrt{144 - 36}}{2}$$

$$x = \frac{12 \pm \sqrt{108}}{2}$$

$$x = \frac{12 \pm 6\sqrt{3}}{2}$$

$x = 6 + 3\sqrt{3}$ or $x = 6 - 3\sqrt{3}$

When either value for x is substituted in one of the original equations, it will give the other value for y.

9. His techniques for solving a quadratic equation were more general than those of the Babylonians.

10. **a.** Multiply each side by $4a$.
 b. Add b^2 to both sides.
 c. Subtract $4ac$ from both sides.
 d. Factor the left side.
 e. Take the square root of both sides.
 f. Add $-b$ to both sides.
 g. Divide both sides by $2a$.

11. None

12.

$$24(6x^2 - 5x - 1) = 24 \cdot 0$$

$$144x^2 - 120x - 24 = 0$$

$$144x^2 - 120x - 24 + 25 = 25$$

$$144x^2 - 120x + 25 = 49$$

$$(12x - 5)^2 = 49$$

$$12x - 5 = \pm\sqrt{49}$$

$$12x = 5 \pm 7$$

$$x = \frac{5 \pm 7}{12}$$

$x = 1$ or $x = -\frac{1}{6}$

13. The discriminant is negative.

$\left(\text{Solve: } \begin{cases} x + y = 15 \\ xy = 60 \end{cases}\right.$

Substitute $15 - x$ for y in the second equation.

$$x(15 - x) = 60$$

$$15x - x^2 = 60$$

$$x^2 - 15x + 60 = 0$$

discriminant: $(-15)^2 - 4(1)(60) = -15$)

14. $\begin{cases} w + 6.8 = h \\ w^2 + h^2 = 100 \end{cases}$

By substitution,

$$w^2 + (w + 6.8)^2 = 100$$

$$w^2 + w^2 + 2(6.8)w + 6.8^2 = 100$$

$$2w^2 + 13.6w + 46.24 = 100$$

$$2w^2 + 13.6w - 53.76 = 0$$

$$w^2 + 6.8w - 26.88 = 0$$

By the Quadratic Formula,

$$w = \frac{-6.8 \pm \sqrt{46.24 + 107.52}}{2}$$

$$w = \frac{-6.8 \pm \sqrt{153.76}}{2}$$

$$w = \frac{-6.8 \pm 12.4}{2}$$

$w = 2.8$ or $w = -9.6$

A width cannot be a negative number. Substitute 2.8 for w in one of the original equations.

$$2.8 + 6.8 = h$$

$$9.6 = h$$

The height is 9.6; the width, 2.8.

15. $4ab(2c - b + 3d)$

16. $(2x - 3y)(2x + 3y)$

17. $(4m - 5)(5m - 4)$

18. $x(12x^2 + 20x + 3) = 0$

$x(6x + 1)(2x + 3) = 0$

$x = 0$ or $6x + 1 = 0$ or $2x + 3 = 0$

$6x = -1$ or $2x = -3$

$x = -\frac{1}{6}$ or $x = -\frac{3}{2}$

19. $1{,}000{,}000 = 10^6 = (2 \cdot 5)^6 = 2^6 \cdot 5^6$

Each factor gives a possibility. The factors in the table are organized by the powers of 2 and then by multiplying each by a power of 5.

Years	Amount per Year
1	$1,000,000
2	500,000
4	250,000
8	125,000
16	62,500
32	31,250
64	15,625
5	200,000
25	40,000
125	8,000
625	1,600
3,125	320
15,625	64
10	100,000
50	20,000
250	4,000
1,250	800
6,250	160
31,250	32

Years	Amount per Year
20	50,000
100	10,000
500	2,000
2,500	400
12,500	80
62,500	16
40	25,000
200	5,000
1,000	1,000
5,000	200
25,000	40
125,000	8
80	12,500
400	2,500
2,000	500
10,000	100
50,000	20
250,000	4
160	6,250
800	1,250
4,000	250
20,000	50
100,000	10
500,000	2
320	3,125
1,600	625
8,000	125
40,000	25
200,000	5
1,000,000	1

20. Sample method: fitting a line to the data by eye
  a. about 19%
  b. about the year 2004
  c. about the year 2031
21. The answers may vary; Viète discovered that if x_1 and x_2 are two solutions to the quadratic equation

$$ax^2 + bx + c = 0, \text{ then } \begin{cases} x_1 + x_2 = -\dfrac{b}{a} \\ x_1 x_2 = \dfrac{c}{a} \end{cases}.$$

LESSON 12-7
pp. 754–758

1. Sample: $\frac{2}{3}$

2. Sample: $\frac{\sqrt{2}}{3}$

3. Sample: $1.\overline{3}$

4. $\frac{9944}{100} = \frac{2486}{25}$

5. Let $x = .\overline{15}$.
  $100x = 15.\overline{15}$
  $99x = 15$
  $x = \frac{15}{99} = \frac{5}{33}$

6. Let $x = 14.8\overline{3}$.
  $10x = 148.\overline{3}$
  $9x = 133.5$
  $x = \frac{133.5}{9} = \frac{1335}{90} = \frac{89}{6}$

7.

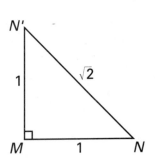

8. **a.** $AE^2 = AD^2 + DE^2$
      $= (\sqrt{3})^2 + 1^2$
      $= 3 + 1$
      $= 4$
    $AE = 2$
  b. Rational
  c. $AF^2 = AE^2 + FE^2$
      $= 2^2 + 1^2$
      $= 5$
    $AF = \sqrt{5}$
  d. Irrational
9. Sample
  a. 196
  b. $2 \cdot 2 \cdot 7 \cdot 7$
  c. 4
10. **a.** $50^2 = (2 \cdot 5^2)^2 = 2^2 \cdot 5^4$
      50^2 has six prime factors.
  b. Since 50^2 has 6 prime factors, then $13 \cdot 50^2$ has seven prime factors.
  c. There is an odd number of prime factors.
11. Irrational
12. Rational
13. Rational
14. the Greeks
15. Yes, because it equals a simple fraction.
16. Yes, for example $\sqrt{2} + -\sqrt{2} = 0$.
17. $30^2 + 30^2 = d^2$
    $2 \cdot 30^2 = d^2$
    $\sqrt{2} \cdot \sqrt{30^2} = d$
    $30\sqrt{2} = d$
  The length is irrational.
18. The circumference is 120π cm, which is an irrational number.
19. discriminant: $(-6)^2 - 4(1)(-1) = 36 + 4 = 40$
  $\sqrt{40} = 2\sqrt{10}$ is irrational, so the solutions will be irrational.

20. $\begin{cases} x + y = 562 \\ xy = 74{,}865 \end{cases}$

Substitute $562 - x$ for y in the second equation.

$$x(562 - x) = 74{,}865$$
$$562x - x^2 = 74{,}865$$
$$x^2 - 562x + 74{,}865 = 0$$

By the Quadratic Formula,

$$x = \frac{562 \pm \sqrt{315{,}844 - 299{,}460}}{2}$$

$$x = \frac{562 \pm \sqrt{16{,}384}}{2}$$

$$x = \frac{562 \pm 128}{2}$$

$x = 345$ or $x = 217$

Substituting either of these values for x in one of the original equations will give the other value.

The two numbers are 345 and 217.

21. a. $acx^2 + (ad + bc)x + bd$

$ad + bc = 7y$

b. $12x^2 + 7xy - 12y^2 = (3x + 4y)(4x - 3y)$

$a = 3;\ b = 4y;\ c = 4;\ d = \text{-}3y$ or

$12x^2 + 7xy - 12y^2 = (4x - 3y)(3x + 4y)$

$a = 4;\ b = \text{-}3y;\ c = 3;\ d = 4y$

22. $(3 + x)(3 + x) = (3 + x)^2$

23. The length of the arc is $\frac{1}{4}$ the circumference

of the circle or $\frac{1}{4}(2r)\pi = \frac{\pi r}{2}$.

The perimeter of the sector is $r + r + \frac{\pi r}{2} =$

$2r + \frac{\pi r}{2} = \left(2 + \frac{\pi}{2}\right)r$.

24. By the Quadratic Formula,

$x = \frac{\text{-}c \pm \sqrt{c^2 - 4ab}}{2b}$

25. $h = \text{-}16t^2$

$h = \text{-}16(2.4)^2$

$h = \text{-}92.16$

The well is 92.16 ft deep.

26. a. Sample:

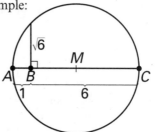

b. 2.5

c. $\sqrt{6} \approx 2.4495$; the approximate difference is about .05.

LESSON 12-8 pp. 759–764

1. Not possible; because $b^2 - 4ac = 121 - 4(7)(\text{-}4)$ $= 233$, which is not a perfect square.

2. Not possible; because $b^2 - 4ac = 0 - 4(1)(\text{-}18)$ $= 72$, which is not a perfect square.

3. $b^2 - 4ac = 144 - 4(9)(4) = 0$, which means the solutions are rational.

So, $n = \frac{12 \pm 0}{18}$

$n = \frac{2}{3}$

Factor: $\left(n - \frac{2}{3}\right)^2$ or $(3n - 2)^2$

4. Not possible; because $b^2 - 4ac = 4 - 4(1)(3) = \text{-}8$, which is not a perfect square.

5. $(4x + 1)(x + 1)$

6. $x = \frac{\text{-}b \pm \sqrt{b^2 - 4ac}}{2a}$;

if $b^2 - 4ac$ is a perfect square, then $\sqrt{b^2 - 4ac}$ is an integer. Since a and b are also integers, x must be rational.

7. Sample: $x^2 - 7$

8. Use the Quadratic Formula to solve

$16t^2 - 89t + 100 = 0$.

$t = \frac{89 \pm 39}{32}$

$t = 4$ or $t = 1.5625$

after 1.5625 seconds and 4 seconds

9. Use the Quadratic Formula to solve

$16t^2 - 88t + 100 = 0$.

$t = \frac{88 \pm \sqrt{1344}}{32}$

$t \approx \frac{88 \pm 36.66060566}{32}$

$t \approx 3.90$ or $t \approx 1.60$

after about 1.60 seconds and about 3.90 seconds

10. The discriminant is not a perfect square.

11. Sample: $k = 4$; $4x^2 + 4x - 3 = (2x - 1)(2x + 3)$

12. when the discriminant, $b^2 - 4ac$, is a perfect square

13. $30 = vt - 4.9t^2$

$4.9t^2 - vt + 30 = 0$

If $v^2 - 4(4.9)(30)$ is a perfect square, then t is rational.

$v^2 - 588$ is a perfect square when $v = 28$ meters per second.

To solve this question using a spreadsheet, you will need 17 rows and 3 columns. Cell A1 will contain the heading "V." Cells 2 through 17 in Column A will hold the numbers 25 to 40. Cell B1 will contain the heading "V * V − 588." This formula will be replicated in cells 2 through 17 in Column B. Cell C1 will contain the heading "SQRT(V * V − 588)." This formula will be replicated in cells 2 through 17 in Column C.

14. a. By the difference of two squares,

$(x + 3 + \sqrt{2})(x + 3 - \sqrt{2})$

$= (x + 3)^2 - (\sqrt{2})^2$

$= x^2 + 6x + 9 - 2$

$= x^2 + 6x + 7$

b. $b^2 - 4ac = 36 - 4(1)(7) = 36 - 28 = 8$, which is not a perfect square.

c. No, because $3 + \sqrt{2}$ and $3 - \sqrt{2}$ are not integers.

15. a. 5 is rational.

b. irrational

c. irrational

16. a. rational

b. $\frac{\sqrt{3}}{\sqrt{3} \cdot \sqrt{4}} = \frac{1}{2}$

17. Let $x = .58\overline{3}$.

$10x = 5.8\overline{3}$

$9x = 5.25$

$x = \frac{525}{900} = \frac{7}{12}$

They played 12 games and won 7 of them.

18. There are two numbers whose sum is 2.25 and whose product is 1.

Solve: $\begin{cases} x + y = \dfrac{9}{4} \\ xy = 1 \end{cases}$

Substitute $\frac{9}{4} - x$ for y in the second equation.

$x\left(\frac{9}{4} - x\right) = 1$

$\frac{9}{4}x - x^2 = 1$

$x^2 - \frac{9}{4}x + 1 = 0$

By the Quadratic Formula,

$x = \dfrac{\frac{9}{4} \pm \sqrt{\frac{81}{16} - 4}}{2}$

$x = \dfrac{\frac{9}{4} \pm \sqrt{\frac{17}{16}}}{2}$

$x = \dfrac{\frac{9}{4} \pm \frac{\sqrt{17}}{4}}{2}$

$x = \frac{9}{8} \pm \frac{\sqrt{17}}{8}$

$x \approx 1.64$ or $x \approx 0.61$

19. a. $2\pi r(r + h)$

b. $S.A. = 2\pi(5)^2 + 2\pi(5)(8)$

$= 50\pi + 80\pi = 130\pi$ cm^2 or

$S.A. = 2\pi(5)(5 + 8) = 130\pi \approx 408.4$ cm^2

The factored form is easier to use.

20. Sample: 16 has the integer factors of 1, 2, 4, 8, and 16.

21. $k = \pm 1$, $k = \pm 4$, or $k = \pm 11$; the discriminant, $k^2 + 48$, must be a perfect square. Use a spreadsheet to determine the values of k.

CHAPTER 12

PROGRESS SELF-TEST p. 768

1. $300 = 2 \cdot 150$

$300 = 2 \cdot 2 \cdot 75$

$300 = 2 \cdot 2 \cdot 3 \cdot 25$

$300 = 2 \cdot 2 \cdot 3 \cdot 5 \cdot 5$

$300 = 2^2 \cdot 3 \cdot 5^2$

2. Both 6^{1000} and 36 are divisible by 3, so by the Common Factor Sum Property, their sum is divisible by 3.

3. $5a^2b$

4. $\frac{c(8c+4)}{c} = 8c + 4$

5. $2m(6 - m^2)$

6. $50y(10x^2 + 2x + 1)$

7. $(z + 9)(z - 9)$

8. $(k - 2)(k - 7)$

9. $(3y + 1)(y - 6)$

10. $(2x - 5y)^2$

11. (a); $7^2 - 4(12) = 1$; $x^2 + 7x + 12 = (x + 3)(x + 4)$

12. If $b^2 - 4ac$ is a perfect square, it can be factored.

13.

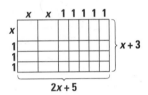

14. $q - 7 = 0$

$\qquad q = 7$

15. $\quad d^2 - d - 20 = 0$

$(d - 5)(d + 4) = 0$

$d = 5$ or $d = -4$

16. $2a - 5 = 0$ or $3a + 1 = 0$

$\quad 2a = 5$ or $\quad 3a = -1$

$\quad a = \frac{5}{2}$ or $\quad a = -\frac{1}{3}$

17. $\quad x^3 + 6x^2 - 7x = 0$

$x(x^2 + 6x - 7) = 0$

$x(x + 7)(x - 1) = 0$

$x = 0$ or $x + 7 = 0$ or $x - 1 = 0$

$\qquad\qquad x = -7$ or $\quad x = 1$

18. Because it can be written as the simple fraction $\frac{354}{100}$.

19. 4; $26^2 = (2 \cdot 13)^2 = 2^2 \cdot 13^2$

20. Sample: $\sqrt{105}$

21. $b^2 - 4ac = 324 + 360 = 684$, which is not a perfect square. Both solutions are irrational.

22. The dimensions of the artwork are $(d - 1)(d - 2)$ with area 12 ft^2.

$(d - 1)(d - 2) = 12$

$d^2 - 3d + 2 = 12$

$d^2 - 3d - 10 = 0$

$(d - 5)(d + 2) = 0$

$d - 5 = 0$ or $d + 2 = 0$

$\quad d = 5$ or $\quad d = -2$

$d = 5$ since a negative number doesn't make sense.

The frame is 5 ft by 5 ft.

23. $0 = 8t - 5t^2$

$0 = t(8 - 5t)$

$t = 0$ or $8 - 5t = 0$

$\qquad\qquad t = \frac{8}{5} = 1.6$

The ball will return in 1.6 seconds.

24. Solve: $\begin{cases} x + y = 8 \\ xy = 15.51 \end{cases}$

Substitute $8 - x$ for y in the second equation.

$x(8 - x) = 15.51$

$x^2 - 8x + 15.51 = 0$

By the Quadratic Formula,

$x = \frac{8 \pm \sqrt{64 - 62.04}}{2}$

$x = \frac{8 \pm 1.4}{2}$

$x = 4.7$ or $x = 3.3$

CHAPTER 12

REVIEW pp. 769–771

1. $175 = 5 \cdot 35$

$175 = 5 \cdot 5 \cdot 7$

$175 = 5^2 \cdot 7$

2. $8888 = 8 \cdot 1111$

$\qquad 8888 = 2^3 \cdot 11 \cdot 101$

3. $9 \cdot 49 \cdot 9 = 3^2 \cdot 7^2 \cdot 3^2 = 3^4 \cdot 7^2$

4. $2^{10} + 2^9 = 2^9(2 + 1) = 2^9 \cdot 3$

5. $7x^4 + 49x = 7x(x^3 + 7)$

6. $4a$

7. $3x^2 y$

8. $5y^3$

9. $m^2(14m^2 + 1)$

10. $3b(6b^2 - 7a + 1)$

11. $\dfrac{z(6z^2 - 1)}{z} = 6z^2 - 1$

12. $\dfrac{2x(7x + 6)}{2x} = 7x + 6$

13. $(x + 6)(x + 1)$

14. $(p + 10)(p - 1)$

15. Not factorable

16. $(x + 1)(x - 1)$

17. $4L(L^2 + 7L + 12) = 4L(L + 3)(L + 4)$

18. $(d - 10)(d + 2)$

19. (c)

20. (c)

21. $(3y - 4x)(y + 2x)$

22. $(5a - 7)(2a - 1)$

23. $3m(4m^2 + 39m + 27) = 3m(4m + 3)(m + 9)$

24. $(4k - 3)(2k + 1)$

25. $(m + 8)^2$

26. $(3a - 4b)^2$

27. $(a + 2)(a - 2)$

28. $(b + 9m)(b - 9m)$

29. $(2x + 1)(2x - 1)$

30. $25(t^2 - 1) = 25(t + 1)(t - 1)$ or

$\qquad (5t + 5)(5t - 5)$

31. $x(x - 2) = 0$

$\qquad x = 0 \ \ \text{or} \ \ x - 2 = 0$

$\qquad\qquad\qquad\qquad x = 2$

32. $z^2 + 7z + 12 = 0$

$\qquad (z + 3)(z + 4) = 0$

$\qquad z + 3 = 0 \ \ \text{or} \ \ z + 4 = 0$

$\qquad\quad z = \text{-}3 \ \ \text{or} \qquad z = \text{-}4$

33. $(y - 3)(y + 1) = 0$

$\qquad y - 3 = 0 \ \ \text{or} \ \ y + 1 = 0$

$\qquad\quad y = 3 \ \ \text{or} \qquad y = \text{-}1$

34. $2(r^2 - 5r + 6) = 0$

$\qquad 2(r - 3)(r - 2) = 0$

$\qquad r - 3 = 0 \ \ \text{or} \ \ r - 2 = 0$

$\qquad\quad r = 3 \ \ \text{or} \qquad r = 2$

35. $b^2 - 2b - 48 = 0$

$\qquad (b - 8)(b + 6) = 0$

$\qquad b - 8 = 0 \ \ \text{or} \ \ b + 6 = 0$

$\qquad\quad b = 8 \ \ \text{or} \qquad b = \text{-}6$

36. $k^2 - 9k + 14 = 0$

$\qquad (k - 7)(k - 2) = 0$

$\qquad k - 7 = 0 \ \ \text{or} \ \ k - 2 = 0$

$\qquad\quad k = 7 \ \ \text{or} \qquad k = 2$

37. $0 = (m - 4)(m + 4)$

$\qquad m - 4 = 0 \ \ \text{or} \ \ m + 4 = 0$

$\qquad\quad m = 4 \ \ \text{or} \qquad m = \text{-}4$

38. $3w(3w + 4) = 0$

$\qquad 3w = 0 \ \ \text{or} \ \ 3w + 4 = 0$

$\qquad w = 0 \ \ \text{or} \qquad 3w = \text{-}4$

$\qquad\qquad\qquad\qquad\qquad w = \text{-}\dfrac{4}{3}$

39. $(2y - 1)(3y + 2) = 0$

$\qquad 2y - 1 = 0 \ \ \text{or} \ \ 3y + 2 = 0$

$\qquad\quad 2y = 1 \ \ \text{or} \qquad 3y = \text{-}2$

$\qquad\quad y = \dfrac{1}{2} \ \ \text{or} \qquad y = \text{-}\dfrac{2}{3}$

40. $0 = (4m - 1)(4m - 1)$

$\qquad 4m - 1 = 0$

$\qquad\quad 4m = 1$

$\qquad\quad m = \dfrac{1}{4}$

41. No; $203 = 7 \cdot 29$

42. Yes; because it only has two factors—1 and 311.

43. 4 factors; $38^2 = (2 \cdot 19)^2 = 2^2 \cdot 19^2$

44. Each of the addends is divisible by 3, so the sum is divisible by 3.

45. Zero Product Property: For any two real numbers a and b, if $ab = 0$, then $a = 0$ or $b = 0$.

46. The product is not zero.

47. There is no product.

48. The product is not zero.

49. $5q = 0$ or $2q - 7 = 0$

$\quad q = 0$ or $\quad 2q = 7$

$\qquad\qquad\qquad q = \frac{7}{2}$

50. $m - 3 = 0$ or $m - 1 = 0$

$\quad m = 3$ or $\quad m = 1$

51. $2w - 3 = 0$ or $3w + 5 = 0$

$\quad 2w = 3$ or $\quad 3w = -5$

$\quad w = \frac{3}{2}$ or $\quad w = -\frac{5}{3}$

52. $y - 3 = 0$ or $2y - 1 = 0$ or $2y + 1 = 0$

$\quad y = 3$ or $\quad 2y = 1$ or $\quad 2y = -1$

$\qquad\qquad\quad y = \frac{1}{2}$ or $\quad y = -\frac{1}{2}$

53. (b); $(x - 11)(x + 11)$

54. when the discriminant, $n^2 - 4mp$, is a perfect square

55. No; $7^2 - 4(1)(-13) = 101$, which is not a perfect square

56. Yes; $7^2 - 4(1)(-60) = 289 = 17^2$

57. Yes; $2^2 - 4(3)(-21) = 256 = 16^2$

58. She was right because none of the pairs of factors of 20 has a sum of -16.

59.

Factors of 24	Sum of Factors
1, 24	25
2, 12	14
3, 8	11
4, 6	10

Since $6 + 4 = 10$, this trinomial is factorable over the integers; $(x + 6)(x + 4)$.

60. Irrational

61. Rational: $\sqrt{100} = 10$

62. Irrational

63. Irrational

64. Irrational

65. Rational

66. Rational

67. Rational

68. Let $x = 5.8\overline{7}$.

$10x = 58.\overline{7}$

$9x = 52.9$

$x = \frac{52.9}{9} = \frac{529}{90}$

69. Let $x = .\overline{428}$.

$1000x = 428.\overline{428}$

$999x = 428$

$x = \frac{428}{999}$

70. $256\pi = (r + 6)^2\pi$

$256\pi = (r^2 + 12r + 36)\pi$

$256 = r^2 + 12r + 36$

$0 = r^2 + 12r - 220$

$0 = (r - 10)(r + 22)$

$r - 10 = 0$ or $r + 22 = 0$

$\quad r = 10$ or $\quad r = -22$

A negative number doesn't make sense, so the radius of the pool is 10 ft.

71. $90 = w(w + 4)$

$90 = w^2 + 4w$

$0 = w^2 + 4w - 90$

$w = \frac{-4 \pm \sqrt{16 + 360}}{2}$

$w = \frac{-4 \pm 2\sqrt{94}}{2}$

$w = -2 \pm \sqrt{94}$

$w \approx -11.7$ or $w \approx 7.7$

A negative number doesn't make sense, so the dimensions are about 7.7 in. by 11.7 in.

72. The golf ball will hit the ground when $h = 0$.

$0 = 80t - 16t^2$

$0 = 16t(5 - t)$

$t = 0$ or $5 - t = 0$

$\qquad\qquad\quad t = 5$ seconds

73. $96 = 80t - 16t^2$

$0 = -16t^2 + 80t - 96$

$0 = -16(t^2 - 5t + 6)$

$0 = t^2 - 5t + 6$

$0 = (t - 3)(t - 2)$

$t - 3 = 0$ or $t - 2 = 0$

$t = 3$ or $t = 2$

after 2 seconds and 3 seconds

74. Solve $\begin{cases} 2\ell + 2w = 1640 \\ \ell w = 44{,}800 \end{cases}$

Substitute $820 - w$ for ℓ from the first equation, after multiplying both sides by $\frac{1}{2}$, in the second equation.

$$(820 - w)w = 44{,}800$$

$w^2 - 820w + 44{,}800 = 0$

By the Quadratic Formula,

$$w = \frac{820 \pm \sqrt{672{,}400 - 179{,}200}}{2}$$

$$w = \frac{820 \pm \sqrt{493{,}200}}{2}$$

$w \approx 761.14$ or $w \approx 58.859$

When either value for w is substituted in one of the original equations, it will give the other value for ℓ. The dimensions are about 760 ft by 59 ft.

75. Solve $\begin{cases} 2\ell + 2w = 410 \\ \ell w = 10{,}350 \end{cases}$

Substitute $205 - w$ for ℓ from the first equation, after multiplying both sides by $\frac{1}{2}$, in the second equation.

$$(205 - w)w = 10{,}350$$

$w^2 - 205w + 10{,}350 = 0$

By the Quadratic Formula,

$$w = \frac{205 \pm \sqrt{42{,}025 - 41{,}400}}{2}$$

$$w = \frac{205 \pm \sqrt{625}}{2}$$

$$w = \frac{205 \pm 25}{2}$$

$w = 115$ or $w = 90$

When either value for w is substituted in one of the original equations, it will give the other value for ℓ. The dimensions are 115 cm by 90 cm.

76. a. $4x^2 + 16x$

    b. $2x(2x + 8)$ or $4x(x + 4)$

77. a. $2x^2 + 8x + 8$

    b. $(x + 2)(2x + 4)$ or $2(x + 2)^2$

78.

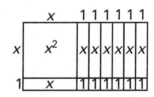

79. $9a^2 + 30ab + 25b^2 = (3a + 5b)^2$

The length of a side is $3a + 5b$.

FUNCTIONS

LESSON 13-1 pp. 774–777

1. A function can be described by a graph, by an equation, with a table, or as a set of ordered pairs.

2. Sample: A function is a correspondence between two variables in which each value of the first variable corresponds to exactly one value of the second variable.

3. Sample: Any particular positive value of x will give two different values for y.

4. **a.** $y = -(4)^2 + 2(4) + 27$
   $= -16 + 8 + 27$
   $= 19$
   b. Yes

5. **a.** Temperature equals 47° F and 50° F.
   b. No

6. Yes, $y = \frac{1}{3}x - 2$. Each value of x corresponds to one value of y.

7. Sample: $y = 100 \cdot (1.06)^x$

8. Sample: $y = x^2 + 2x + 1$

9. (c)

10. No

11. Yes

12. Yes

13. One x-value is paired with infinitely many y-values.

14. **a.** Yes, because each h-value corresponds to only one w-value.
    b. $w = 4.5h$

15. **a.** Sample: (-2, 5); (0, 3); (2, 5)
    b.
    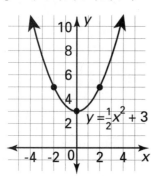

16. **a.** Sample: (400, 0); (0, -400); (200, -200)
    b.
    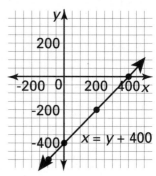

17. **a.** Let cost = y and weight in pounds = x.
    $y = .50x + 3.00$
    b. Sample: (0, 3.00); (1, 3.50); (2, 4.00)

18. **a.** Let volume = y and radius = x.
    $y = \frac{4}{3}\pi x^3$
    b. Sample: $\left(1, \frac{4}{3}\pi\right)$; $\left(2, \frac{32}{3}\pi\right)$; (3, 36$\pi$)

19. Solve: $\begin{cases} 5a + 3s = 1840 \\ a + s = 520 \end{cases}$

    $5a + 3s = 1840$
    $+ \underline{-3a + -3s = -1560}$
    $\qquad 2a = 280$
    $\qquad a = 140$

    Substitute 140 for a in one of the original equations to find
    $$s = 520 - 140 = 380.$$
    They sold 140 adult tickets and 380 student tickets.

20. $\frac{1}{8} + \frac{1}{64} = \frac{8}{64} + \frac{1}{64} = \frac{9}{64}$

21. False; the points are the same, so the slopes are the same.

22. $.03x = 24$
    $x = 800$ students

23. $100bc$ paper clips

24. $\frac{1}{n}$

25. Samples:

   a. $y = 3x - 2$

   b. $y = x^2$

   c. $y = -x^2 + 6x - 4$

LESSON 13-2   pp. 778–783

1. P of E or the probability of E

2. square root of x

3. f of x equals 100 minus x

4. $8^2 = 64$

5. $(-8)^2 = 64$

6. $\left(\frac{2}{5}\right)^2 = \frac{4}{25}$

7. ≈ 6.32

8. 2.5

9. $3 - 9 = -6$

10. $4(-2) = -8$

11. $(-2)^4 = 16$

12. $4^{-2} = \frac{1}{16}$

13. a. $c(650) = 160 + 0.15(650)$
$$= 160 + 97.5$$
$$= 257.5$$

   b. If Khalil serves meals worth \$650, his weekly wage at the Comfy Cafe will be \$257.50.

14. a. $c(1000) = 160 + 0.15(1000)$
$$= 160 + 150 = 310$$
$$d(1000) = 200 + 0.10(1000)$$
$$= 200 + 100 = 300$$
$$c(1000) > d(1000)$$

   b. If Khalil serves meals worth \$1000, his weekly wage will be greater at the Comfy Cafe.

15. a. After 24 months, the cost of owning the new car is greater than the cost of owning the used car.

   b. She would have to keep the new auto for more than 120 months or 10 years for it to be a better deal than the used one.
$$11,300 + 160t < 6,500 + 200t$$
$$4800 < 40t$$
$$120 < t$$

16. a.

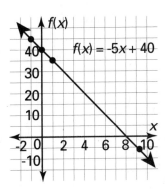

   b. x-intercept: 8

      y-intercept: 40

17. a.

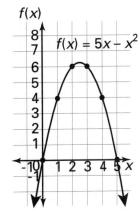

   b. x-intercepts: 0; 5

      y-intercept: 0

18. a. $c(1) = 1^3 = 1$

      $c(2) = 2^3 = 8$

      $c(3) = 3^3 = 27$

      $c(4) = 4^3 = 64$

      $c(5) = 5^3 = 125$

   b. cubing function

19. a. Answers will vary.

   b. the total number of children in p's family

20. a. $W(3) = 3200(0.75)^3$
$\quad\quad = 3200(0.421875)$
$\quad\quad = 1350$
After 3 years, the computer is worth $1350.

b.

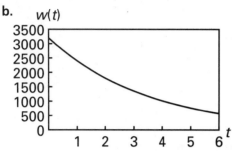

c. $t > 4$; the computer is worth less than $1000 after about 4 years.

21. a. $L(5) = 17(5) + 10 = 85 + 10 = 95$
b. $L(2) = 17(2) + 10 = 34 + 10 = 44$
c. $\frac{95-44}{3} = \frac{51}{3} = 17$
d. the slope of the graph of L

22. a.

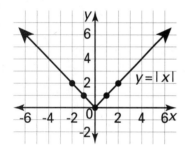

b. Yes

23. a.

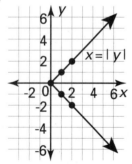

b. No

24. (d); $(16-x)(16-x) = 256 - 32x + x^2$
25. $6 \cdot \frac{1}{9} = \frac{2}{3}$
26. 7
27. $\frac{6 \pm \sqrt{4 \cdot 6}}{2} = \frac{6 \pm 2\sqrt{6}}{2} = 3 \pm \sqrt{6}$
28. a. $\frac{15}{5} + \frac{2}{5} = \frac{17}{5}$
b. $\frac{15}{5} + \frac{7}{5} = \frac{22}{5}$
c. $\frac{15}{5} + \frac{k}{5} = \frac{15+k}{5}$
29. a. $p(m) = 6^m$
b. exponential
c. 11 mailings
d. 13 mailings
30.

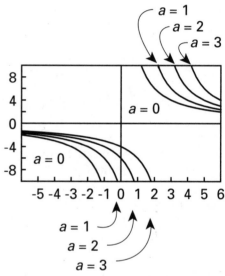

The graphs all have two branches and a value of x for which y is undefined. The undefined value occurs at $x = a$, which is different for each graph.

LESSON 13-3   pp. 784–788

1. $|-3| = 3$
2. $|2| = 2$
3. $\left|-\frac{3}{4}\right| = \frac{3}{4}$
4. $|0| = 0$
5. an angle

6. They are used in the study of error and in some situations involving distance.

7. $|60 - 90| = |-30| = 30$

8. $(60, 0)$

9. one minute

10. $d(0) = -600|0 - 2| + 1200$
$= -600(2) + 1200 = 0$
$d(1) = -600|1 - 2| + 1200$
$= -600(1) + 1200 = 600$
$d(2) = -600|2 - 2| + 1200$
$= -600(0) + 1200 = 1200$
$d(3) = -600|3 - 2| + 1200$
$= -600(1) + 1200 = 600$

11. Sample: In a test flight, a plane crosses a checkpoint going due east. It then flies 600 km/h for 2 hours and returns flying due west. $d(t)$ represents the plane's distance from the checkpoint t hours after crossing it.

12. 1.5 hours after crossing the checkpoint, the plane is 900 km east of the checkpoint.

13. 5 hours after crossing the checkpoint, the plane is 600 km west of the checkpoint.

14.

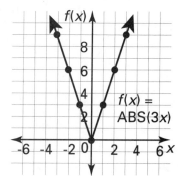

15.

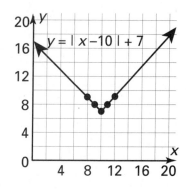

16. (d)

17.

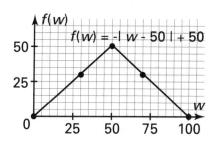

18. a. $\frac{2}{3} \cdot 120 + 5 = 80 + 5 = 85$

b. $\frac{2}{3} \cdot -120 = -80 + 5 = -75$

c. a line with slope $\frac{2}{3}$ and y-intercept 5

19. $A(\text{Moscow}) = 47°F$

20. a. $(x + 4)(x - 4)$
b. $(y - 8)(y + 2)$
c. $(a - 8b)(a + 2b)$

21. v cannot have the values 2 or 4 in the expression since the denominator cannot equal zero.

22. Solve: $\begin{cases} 10p + 7e = 423 \\ 3p + e = 95 \end{cases}$

$10p + 7e = 423$
$+ \underline{-21p + -7e = -665}$
$-11p = -242$
$p = 22$ cents

Substitute 22 cents for p in one of the original equations to find e.

$3(22) + e = 95$
$e = 95 - 66$
$e = 29$ cents

Two erasers will cost $2(0.29) = \$0.58$.

23. a. $\frac{2x}{2} + \frac{x}{2} = \frac{3x}{2}$

b. $\frac{2x}{6} + \frac{3x}{6} = \frac{5x}{6}$

c. $\frac{2x}{6} + \frac{3y}{6} = \frac{2x + 3y}{6}$

24. a. Sample: $h = -1, 0, 1, 2$

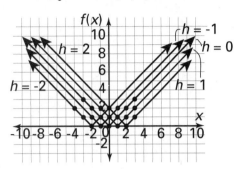

b. Sample: h is the x-intercept of the graph $f(x) = |x - h|$.

25. a. Sample: $a = -3, -1, 1, 3$

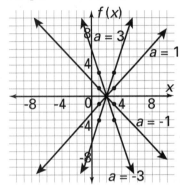

b. Samples: If $a > 0$, then the angle opens upward. If $a < 0$, then the angle opens downward. The larger $|a|$ is, the smaller the measure of the angle.

LESSON 13-4   pp. 789–793

1. The domain of a function is the set of first coordinates of the ordered pairs in the function.

2. The range of a function is the set of second coordinates of the ordered pairs in the function.

3. $184 - 51 = 133$

4. Domain: $\{1, 3, 5\}$
Range: $\{2, 4, 7\}$

5. Domain: the set of real numbers
Range: the set of real numbers

6. Domain: the set of real numbers x with $0 \le x \le 6$
Range: the set of real numbers y with $0 \le y \le 20$

7. The domain is assumed to be the largest set possible.

8. a. $t(x) = 4x$
b. $b(x) = 4x$
c. The range of t is the set of nonnegative rational numbers while the range of b is the set of whole numbers.

9. a. Domain: set of all real numbers
b. Range: set of all real numbers

10. a. Domain: set of all real numbers
b. Range: set of real numbers greater than or equal to 100

11. a. Domain: set of all real numbers
b. Range: set of real numbers greater than or equal to -3

12. a. Domain: set of real numbers greater than or equal to 0
b. Range: set of real numbers greater than or equal to -5

13. $x - 3 = 0$
$x = 3$
3 is not in the domain.

14. a.

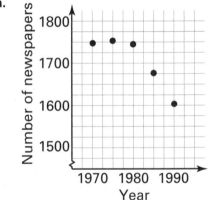

b. Since 1975, the number of newspapers has decreased.
c. 1990
d. 1756
e. Sample: the set of whole numbers with $1776 \le y \le$ current year

15. Sample:

a.

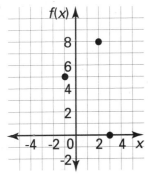

b. 6 possible functions:
{(-1, 5), (2, 8), (3, 0)};
{(-1, 5), (2, 0), (3, 8)};
{(-1, 8), (2, 5), (3, 0)};
{(-1, 8), (2, 0), (3, 5)};
{(-1, 0), (2, 5), (3, 8)};
{(-1, 0), (2, 8), (3, 5)}

16.

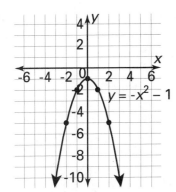

17. Domain: set of all real numbers
Range: set of all positive real numbers

18. Domain: set of all nonzero real numbers
Range: set of all nonzero real numbers

19. Domain: set of all nonnegative real numbers
Range: set of real numbers greater than or equal to 100

20. a. $f(1) = (1 - 1)(1 + 2) = 0(3) = 0$
b. $f(2) = (2 - 1)(2 + 2) = 1(4) = 4$
c. $f\left(\frac{7}{3}\right) = \left(\frac{7}{3} - 1\right)\left(\frac{7}{3} + 2\right) = \frac{4}{3} \cdot \frac{13}{3} = \frac{52}{9}$

21. Yes

22. No

23. a. $\left(1 + \frac{1}{3}\right)x = 10.00$

b. $(3 + 1)x = 30$
$4x = 30$
$x = \$7.50$

24. $1 - \frac{1}{6} = \frac{5}{6}$

25. a. Cuba

b. Compare ratios of population to square miles.

$$\frac{10,700,000}{44,218} > \frac{90,000,000}{761,604} \text{ or}$$

$$242 \frac{\text{people}}{\text{mile}^2} > 118 \frac{\text{people}}{\text{mile}^2}$$

26. $y = 2x + 6$
$y - 6 = 2x$
$(y - 6)\frac{1}{2} = x$
$\frac{1}{2}y - 3 = x$

27. a. k moves the graph vertically along the $f(x)$-axis.

b. Range: the set of real numbers greater than or equal to k

IN-CLASS ACTIVITY   p. 794

1. a. Answers may vary.
b. Answers may vary.

2. Answers may vary.

3. a. The 6 possible outcomes are 1, 2, 3, 4, 5, and 6.

b. There are 36 possible outcomes:
(1, 1), (1, 2), (1, 3), (1, 4), (1, 5), (1, 6),
(2, 1), (2, 2), (2, 3), (2, 4), (2, 5), (2, 6),
(3, 1), (3, 2), (3, 3), (3, 4), (3, 5), (3, 6),
(4, 1), (4, 2), (4, 3), (4, 4), (4, 5), (4, 6),
(5, 1), (5, 2), (5, 3), (5, 4), (5, 5), (5, 6),
(6, 1), (6, 2), (6, 3), (6, 4), (6, 5), (6, 6).

c. 1 outcome gives a sum of 2.
$P(\text{sum} = 2) = \frac{1}{36}$

d. 4 outcomes give a sum of 5.
$P(\text{sum} = 5) = \frac{4}{36}$

3. e.

sum	probability
2	$\frac{1}{36}$
3	$\frac{2}{36}$
4	$\frac{3}{36}$
5	$\frac{4}{36}$
6	$\frac{5}{36}$
7	$\frac{6}{36}$
8	$\frac{5}{36}$
9	$\frac{4}{36}$
10	$\frac{3}{36}$
11	$\frac{2}{36}$
12	$\frac{1}{36}$

4. Answers may vary.

LESSON 13-5   pp. 795–799

1. A probability function is a function whose domain is a set of outcomes for a situation, and in which each ordered pair contains an outcome and its probability.

2. $\frac{2}{36} = \frac{1}{18}$

3. 6 or 8

4. It is an angle.

5. Yes, $x = 7$.

6. a.

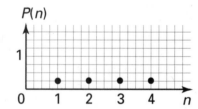

$P(n)$

     0   1   2   3   4 n

b. $P(n) = \frac{1}{4}$

c. Domain: $\{1, 2, 3, 4\}$

d. Range: $\left\{\frac{1}{4}\right\}$

7. True; $P(0) = P(3) = \frac{1}{8}$

8. Because in 3 of the 8 equally likely outcomes exactly one head comes up in the toss.

9. True

10. False

11. False

12. a. 0.2

  b. $.15 + .3 + .15 = 0.6$

  c. The range in the graph for a fair die is $\left\{\frac{1}{6}\right\}$, while the range in this graph is $\{.1, .15, .2, .3\}$.

13. Sample: Probabilities must be from 0 to 1.

14. a. $1 - \frac{3}{4} = \frac{1}{4}$

  b.

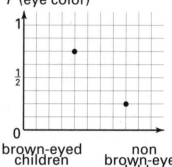

P (eye color)

Eye Color

brown-eyed children   non brown-eyed children

  c. The range of the function is $\left\{\frac{1}{4}, \frac{3}{4}\right\}$.

15. a. $1 - \left(\frac{1}{32} + \frac{1}{16} + \frac{1}{8} + \frac{1}{4} + \frac{1}{2}\right) = 1 - \frac{31}{32} = \frac{1}{32}$

  b.

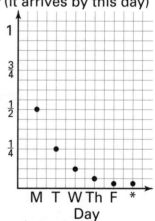

P (it arrives by this day)

M T W Th F *

Day

* = does not arrive by Friday

16. Sample: $P(E)$ = the probability that a two-headed coin toss comes up E.

17. a. 3654

b. $3654 - 3294 = 360$
360 million pounds more fish were caught in 1980 than in 1985.

c. Domain: {1960, 1965, 1970, 1975, 1980, 1985, 1990}

d. Negative

e. between 1965 and 1970

18. No, because there are infinitely many y-values for each x-value.

19. a. $(2x - 5)(x + 4)$

b. $x = 3$ since $(2(3)^2 + 3(3) - 20)$
$= 18 + 9 - 20 = 7$

20. $(1{,}000 + 5)(1{,}000 - 5)$
$= 1{,}000^2 - 5^2$
$= 1{,}000{,}000 - 25$
$= 999{,}975$

21. $2\sqrt{3} + \sqrt{3} = 3\sqrt{3}$

22. By the Pythagorean Theorem,
$AB = \sqrt{7^2 + 24^2} = 25$;
ratio of sides of triangle ABC: triangle
$DEF = \frac{24}{30} = \frac{4}{5}$

$\frac{4}{5} = \frac{7}{DF}$ $\qquad$ $\frac{4}{5} = \frac{25}{DE}$

$4DF = 35$ $\qquad$ $4DE = 125$

$DF = \frac{35}{4} = 8.75$; $\qquad$ $DE = \frac{125}{4} = 31.25$

23. $90 - 16 = 74°$

24. a.

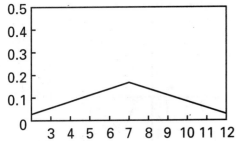

b. $-\frac{1}{36}|2 - 7| + \frac{1}{6} = -\frac{1}{36} \cdot 5 + \frac{1}{6}$

$= \frac{-5 + 6}{36} = \frac{1}{36} = 0.02\overline{7}$

c. $-\frac{1}{36}|7 - 7| + \frac{1}{6} = -\frac{1}{36} \cdot 0 + \frac{1}{6}$

$= \frac{1}{6} = 0.1\overline{6}$

d. It contains all of the points in the probability function for the outcomes from the toss of two fair dice.

LESSON 13-6
 pp. 800–805

1. 1

2. False

3. You can turn the figure 180° around some point and the figure will coincide with itself.

4.

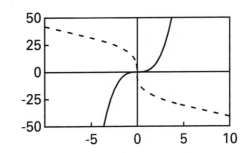

5. $y = (-1.3)^3 - (-1.3) + 1$

$= -2.197 + 1.3 + 1$

$= 0.103,$

which is close to zero.

6. $(0, 1)$

7. True

8. 1 y-intercept and no more than n x-intercepts

9. $y = 3^4 - 7(3)^3 - 9(3)^2 + 63(3)$

$= 81 - 189 - 81 + 189 = 0;$

$y = 7^4 - 7(7)^3 - 9(7)^2 + 63(7)$

$= 2401 - 2401 - 441 + 441 = 0;$

it checks.

10. No

11. a.

x	y
-2	-5
-1.5	-0.375
-1	2
-0.5	2.875
0	3
0.5	3.125
1	4
1.5	6.375
2	11

b.

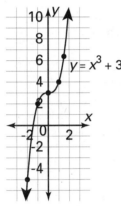

$y = x^3 + 3$

c. y-intercept: 3;
x-intercept: $\approx$ -1.4;
axis of symmetry: none;
point of rotation symmetry: (0, 3)

12. a.

x	y
-2	-16
-1.5	-6.75
-1	-2
-0.5	-0.25
0	0
0.5	0.25
1	2
1.5	6.75
2	16

b.

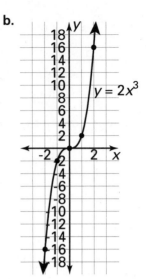

$y = 2x^3$

c. y-intercept: 0;
x-intercept: 0;
axis of symmetry: none;
point of rotation symmetry: (0, 0)

13. a.

x	y
-2	8
-1.5	3.375
-1	1
-0.5	0.125
0	0
0.5	-0.125
1	-1
1.5	-3.375
2	-8

b.

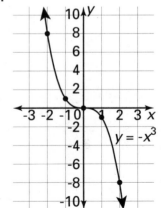

$y = -x^3$

13. **c.** y-intercept: 0;
x-intercept: 0;
axis of symmetry: none;
point of rotation symmetry: (0, 0)

14. **a.**

	A	B
1	X	VALUE
2	-6	-48
3	-5	0
4	-4	24
5	-3	30
6	-2	24
7	-1	12
8	0	0
9	1	-6
10	2	0
11	3	24
12	4	72

b.

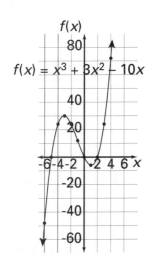

$f(x) = x^3 + 3x^2 - 10x$

c. x-intercepts: -5, 0, 2

15. **a.** Sample: the set of numbers x with
$1 \leq x \leq 2$

b.

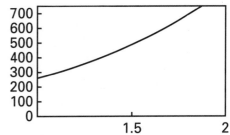

c. about $298
d. 33%

16. **a.** Domain: $\{0, 1, 2\}$
b. $\left(0, \frac{1}{4}\right), \left(1, \frac{1}{2}\right), \left(2, \frac{1}{4}\right)$

17. $S = \pi r(r + 2h)$

18. **a.** Degree: 3
b. Degree: 2

19. $\pi(4)^2(12) = 192\pi$
≈ 603.19 cm^3 $\cdot \frac{1 \text{ liter}}{1000 \text{ cm}^3} \cdot \frac{1000 \text{ milliliters}}{1 \text{ liter}} \approx 603$
milliliters

20.

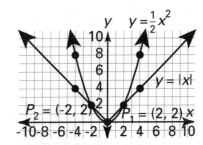

Solutions: (0, 0), (-2, 2), (2, 2)

21. $3y - 6 = 2$ or $3y - 6 = -2$
$3y = 8$ or $3y = 4$
$y = \frac{8}{3}$ or $y = \frac{4}{3}$

22. $100B^2 + 100B - 100 = 0$
$100(B^2 + B - 1) = 0$
$B^2 + B - 1 = 0$
By the Quadratic Formula,
$x = \frac{-1 \pm \sqrt{1 + 4}}{2}$
$x = \frac{-1 \pm \sqrt{5}}{2}$

23. $A^2 = 2$

$A = \pm\sqrt{2}$

24. $2y + 14 > 5y - 19$

$33 > 3y$

$11 > y$

$y < 11$

25. $14.7 = 7x + 21$

$-6.3 = 7x$

$-.9 = x$

26. $C = 160,000$

27. a. Samples:

   i. $y = x^3 - 2x$

   ii. $y = -x^4 + 2x^2$

b.

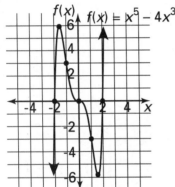

IN-CLASS ACTIVITY   p. 806

1. Sample: $m\angle A \approx 10°$;

$\dfrac{BC}{AB} = \dfrac{1.5 \text{ cm}}{8.5 \text{ cm}} \approx 0.18$

2. Sample: $m\angle D \approx 30°$;

$\dfrac{EF}{DE} = \dfrac{3.8 \text{ cm}}{6.6 \text{ cm}} \approx 0.58$

3. Sample: $m\angle G \approx 50°$;

$\dfrac{HI}{GH} = \dfrac{4.0 \text{ cm}}{3.4 \text{ cm}} \approx 1.18$

1. a. $\overline{DF}$

   b. $\overline{EF}$

   c. $\dfrac{DF}{EF}$

2. $m\angle A \approx 10°$; $\tan A \approx 0.18$

3. $m\angle D \approx 30°$; $\tan D \approx 0.58$

4. $m\angle G \approx 50°$; $\tan G \approx 1.18$

5. $\tan 57° = 1.540$

6. $\tan 3° = 0.052$

7. $\tan K = \dfrac{8}{25} = 0.5\overline{3}$

8. a. $m\angle F = 60°$

   b. $\tan F \approx 1.74$

   c. $\tan 60 \approx 1.73$

   d. The difference is $1.74 - 1.73 = 0.01$.

9. $\tan 65° \approx 2.145$

$\dfrac{h}{6} \approx 2.145$

$h \approx 6 \cdot 2.145$

$h \approx 12.9 \text{ m}$

The tree is about $12.9 + 1.7 = 14.6$ meters tall.

10. If A is the angle formed by the portion of the oblique line $y = mx + b$ above the x-axis and the positive ray of the x-axis, then $\tan A = m$.

11. a. $\dfrac{6}{5} = 1.2$

   b. approximately $50°$

12. a. $AC = \sqrt{25^2 - 7^2} = \sqrt{576} = 24$

   b. $\tan A = \dfrac{7}{24} \approx .29$

   c. $\tan B = \dfrac{24}{7} \approx 3.43$

13. $\tan(\text{angle of elevation}) = \dfrac{1}{.6} = 1.\overline{6}$

From the table on p. 808, the angle of elevation $\approx 60°$.

14. a. slope $= \tan 140° \approx -0.84$

   b. $y = -0.84x$

15. slope $= \tan(\text{angle}) = 4$; the angle is about $80°$.

16. a. $90 - 60 = 30°$

b. $P(1) = \frac{90}{360} = \frac{1}{4}$;

$P(2) = \frac{90}{360} = \frac{1}{4}$;

$P(3) = \frac{90}{360} = \frac{1}{4}$;

$P(4) = \frac{60}{360} = \frac{1}{6}$;

$P(5) = \frac{30}{360} = \frac{1}{12}$

c.

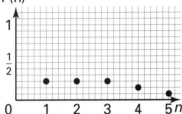

17. $2x + 4 = 0$

$2x = \text{-}4$

$x = \text{-}2$

-2 cannot be in the domain.

18. a. $3(\text{-}1 + 1)^2 - 4 = 0 - 4 = \text{-}4$

b. $3|\text{-}1 + 1| - 4 = 0 - 4 = \text{-}4$

c. $3\sqrt{\text{-}1 + 1} - 4 = 0 - 4 = \text{-}4$

19. $x = \frac{\text{-}b \pm \sqrt{b^2 - 4ac}}{2a}$

20. $a^{11 \cdot 12 + 13 - 14} = a^t$

$131 = t$

21. $m\angle E = 4m\angle F$

$m\angle F + 4m\angle F = 90$

$5m\angle F = 90$

$m\angle F = 18°$

$m\angle E = 4(18) = 72°$

22. a. $x = \frac{10\pi}{180} = \frac{\pi}{18}$

By approximation,

$\tan 10° \approx \dfrac{2\left(\frac{\pi}{18}\right)^5 + 5\left(\frac{\pi}{18}\right)^3 + 15\left(\frac{\pi}{18}\right)}{15}$

$\tan 10° \approx \dfrac{.01036494 + .02658288 + 2.61799388}{15}$

$\tan 10° \approx \dfrac{2.64490067}{15} = 0.1763267111.$

By calculator, $\tan 10° \approx 0.1763269807.$
Their difference is about .0000003.

b. $x = \frac{70\pi}{180} = \frac{7\pi}{18}$

By approximation,

$\tan 70° \approx \dfrac{2\left(\frac{7\pi}{18}\right)^5 + 5\left(\frac{7\pi}{18}\right)^3 + 15\left(\frac{7\pi}{18}\right)}{15}$

$\tan 70° \approx$

$\dfrac{5.443861066 + 9.117929435 + 18.32595714}{15}$

$\tan 70° \approx \dfrac{32.88774766}{15} = 2.192516511.$

By calculator, $\tan 70° \approx 2.747477419.$
Their difference is about .555.

23. He became a tangent. (i.e., a tan gent)

LESSON 13-8 pp. 812–816

1. $\tan 11° = 0.194$

2. $\sin 45° = 0.707$

3. $\cos 47° = 0.682$

4. $\log(10^7) = 7$

5. $(\text{-}3.489)^2 = 12.173$

6. $\sqrt{0.5} = 0.707$

7. !

8. !; $\sqrt{}$

9. $\frac{1}{x}$

10. sine

11. common logarithm

12. a. $AC^2 = 20^2 + 21^2$

$AC = 841$

$AC = 29$

b. $\sin A = \frac{20}{29} \approx 0.690$

c. $\cos A = \frac{21}{29} \approx 0.724$

d. $\tan A = \frac{20}{21} \approx 0.952$

13. a. $\sin 90° = 1$

b. $\sin 90° = 1$

14. a. $\sin 360° = 0$

b. $\sin 360° = 0$

15. **a.** sin(-70°) = -0.9

b. sin(-70°) = -0.940

16. **a.**

x	cos x
0	1
15	0.97
30	0.87
45	0.71
60	0.50
75	0.26
90	0
105	-0.26
120	-0.50
135	-0.71
150	-0.87
165	-0.97
180	-1
195	-0.97
210	-0.87
225	-0.71
240	-0.50
255	-0.26
270	0
285	0.26
300	0.50
315	0.71
330	0.87
345	0.97
360	1

b.

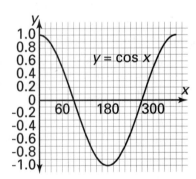

c. $y = \sin x$

17. **a.** The second column in the table below displays the common logarithmic values. The third column shows natural logarithmic values.

X	LOG X	LOG X
1	0	0
2	.030103	0.69315
3	0.47712	1.0986
4	0.60206	1.3863
5	0.69897	1.6094
6	0.77815	1.7918
7	0.84510	1.9459
8	0.90309	2.0794
9	0.95424	2.1972
10	1	2.3026

b. The first graph below displays the data from the third column. The second graph displays the data from the second column.

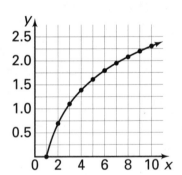

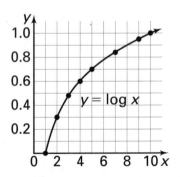

17. c. The graph of the data in the second column is the same as in the text. The graph of the data in the third column is different from that in the text. As x increases, the point $(x, \log x)$ is farther away from the x-axis than in the graph of the left-hand data.

18. a.

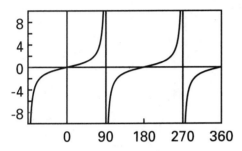

b. $\tan(-10°) \approx -0.18$

19.

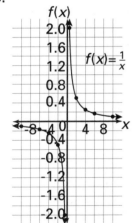

20. a parabola

21. $\tan A = \frac{2.8}{3.8} \approx 0.7$

22. $\tan 40° = \frac{h}{20}$

By calculator, $\tan 40° \approx 0.839$.

$\frac{h}{20} \approx 0.839$

$h \approx 20 \cdot 0.839$

$h \approx 16.78$

The flagpole is $16.78 + 5 = 21.78$ ft tall.

23. a. 7

b. $\frac{6}{36} = \frac{1}{6}$

24. $S(40) = 40 + \frac{40^2}{20} = 40 + 80 = 120$ ft

25. $\frac{x^2}{20} = 100$

$x^2 = 100(20)$

$x^2 = 2000$

$x \approx 44.7$ mph

26. a. $p(p + 5)(p - 1)$
$= p(p^2 - p + 5p - 5)$
$= p^3 + 4p^2 - 5p$ cubic units

b. Degree: 3

27. a.

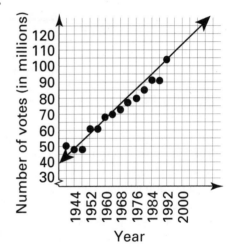

b. Sample: 115 million

28. $\frac{13 - 10}{3.5 - 2} = \frac{3}{1.5} = 2$ kph

$\frac{10}{2} = 5$

They will reach home in 5 hours, or 8:30 P.M., at this rate.

29. $\frac{17}{300} = \frac{45}{t}$

$17t = 300 \cdot 45$

$17t = 13,500$

$t \approx 794.12$ min ≈ 13 h 14 min

30. $11m = 2(m + 36)$

   $11m = 2m + 72$

   $9m = 72$

   $m = 8$

31. $3x + 9 > x$

   $2x > -9$

   $x > -\frac{9}{2}$

32. $v - 6 = 16$

   $v = 22$

33. Answers will vary.

CHAPTER 13

PROGRESS SELF-TEST   p. 820

1. $3(2) + 5 = 6 + 5 = 11$

2. Sample: A function is a set of ordered pairs for which every first coordinate is paired with exactly one second coordinate.

3. $\tan 82° \approx 7.115$

4. $\sin 30° = 0.5$

5. The tangent is the slope of the line, 4.

6. Sample: $f(x) = x^2 + 2x + 1$

7. When $x > 0$ each x-value is paired with two y-values.

8. x cannot have the values 10 or 30.

9. Yes;
   Domain: $\{0, 1, 2, 3, 4\}$
   Range: $\{1, 2\}$

10. No; (0, 1) and (0, -1) are both in the relation.

11. $P(\text{sum of } 10) = \frac{3}{36} = \frac{1}{12}$.
   (Pairs which work are (4, 6), (5, 5), and (6, 4).)

12. $P(2) = \frac{1}{10}$

13.

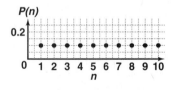

14. $b(n) = 3n$

   $h(n) = 2n$

   $3n > 2n$

   $n > 0$

The number of pieces of bread is always greater than the number of hamburgers as long as there are sandwiches to be made.

15.

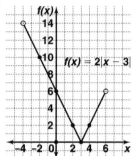

16.

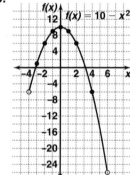

17. $f(220) = 11.75(220) + 300 = \$2885$
   $r(220) = 14.50(220) = \$3190$
   Kristin should buy her carpet at Fabulous Floor for $2885.

18.

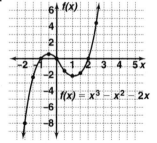

19.

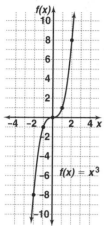

Domain: set of all real numbers
Range: set of all real numbers

C H A P T E R 13

REVIEW   pp. 821–823

1. $(2)^2 - 3(2) + 8 = 4 - 6 + 8 = 6$
2. $3^2 - 3(3) + 8 = 9 - 9 + 8 = 8$
3. $(-7)^2 - 3(-7) + 8 = 49 + 21 + 8 = 78$
4. $0^2 - 3(0) + 8 = 0 + 0 + 8 = 8$
5. $2|1 - 5| = 2|-4| = 2(4) = 8$
6. $2^3 + 2^4 = 8 + 16 = 24$
7. $-(-1.5) = 1.5$
8. $64(4) - 16(4)^2 = 256 - 256 = 0$
9. $|x + 3| = 5$

$\qquad x + 3 = 5$ or $x + 3 = -5$

$\qquad\quad x = 2$ or $\qquad x = -8$

10. $\pi r^2 = 18\pi$

$\qquad r^2 = 18$

$\qquad r = \pm\sqrt{18} = \pm 3\sqrt{2}$

11. 0.080
12. 3,628,800.000
13. 107.093
14. 1.953
15. 0.577
16. 2.550
17. 0.991

18. 0.699
19. ABS(-4) = 4.000
20. 114.589
21. Yes; (exponential)
22. Yes; (quadratic)
23. Yes; (linear)
24. Yes; (trigonometric)
25. No
26. No
27. Yes
28. No
29. Yes
30. No
31. The domain is the largest set for which the function makes sense.
32. **a.** True
    b. False: (Range: set of all real numbers)
33. (c)
34. Range: set of nonnegative real numbers
35. Domain: set of all real numbers
    Range: set of real numbers less than or equal to 1
36. Domain: set of real numbers between 0 and 18, inclusive
    Range: set of real numbers between 0 and 6, inclusive
37. 10 (The greatest possible value of $-x^2$ is 0.)
38. -9 (The smallest possible value of $5|n - 3|$ is 0.)
39. Domain: set of all real numbers except 3
40. Range: set of all nonnegative real numbers
41. $\frac{1}{4}t + 37 = 60$

$\qquad \frac{1}{4}t = 60 - 37$

$\qquad \frac{1}{4}t = 23$

$\qquad t = 23(4) = 92°$ F

42. Domain: {1850, 1900, 1950, 1960, 1970, 1980, 1990}
    Range: {1610; 102, 479; 1,970,358; 2,479,015; 2,811,801; 2,966,850; 3,485,398}

43. $G(v) = v + 250$

44. $v + 250 < 3.5v + 100$

$150 < 2.5v$

$60 < v$

$G(v) < D(v)$ for more than 60 visits.

45. **a.** Domain: Set of times of the day that the Mart is open

b. Sample: If the largest number of people MacGregor's Mart can hold is 2000, then the range is the set of whole numbers less than or equal to 2000.

46. $f(G) = |G - 437|$ or $f(G) = |437 - G|$

47. **a.** $P(1) = \frac{180°}{360°} = \frac{1}{2}$

b. $P(2) = \frac{120°}{360°} = \frac{1}{3}$

c. $P(3) = \frac{60°}{360°} = \frac{1}{6}$

48. $P(\text{sum of } 12) = \frac{1}{36}$

(The only pair of numbers which works is $(6, 6)$.)

49. $\frac{3!}{2!(3-2)!} \cdot \left(\frac{1}{4}\right)^2 \cdot \left(\frac{3}{4}\right)^{3-2} = \frac{6}{2 \cdot 1} \cdot \frac{1}{16} \cdot \frac{3}{4}$

$= \frac{18}{128} = \frac{9}{64}$

50. $1 - .75 = .25$

51. $\tan A = \frac{80}{92} = .870$

52. $\tan 70° = \frac{h}{25}$.

By calculator, $\tan 70° = 2.748$.

$\frac{h}{25} = 2.748$

$h = 25 \cdot 2.748$

$h = 68.7$ meters

The nest is $68.7 + 1.5 = 70.2$ m high.

53. Slope: $\tan 18° \approx 0.325$

54. The tangent is the slope, $\frac{4}{3}$.

$4x - 3y = 2$

$-3y = -4x + 2$

$y = \frac{4}{3}x - \frac{2}{3}$

55. Yes

56. No

57. Yes

58. Yes

59. Yes

60. No

61.

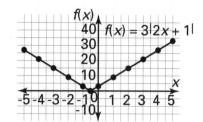

62.

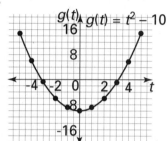

63.

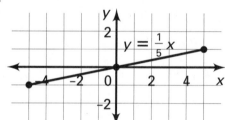

64.

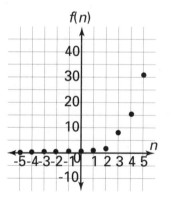

65.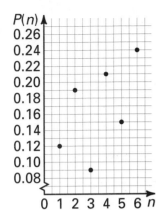

66.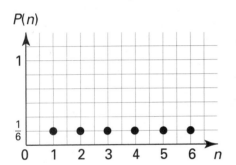

67.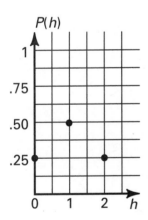

68.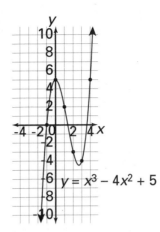

$y = x^3 - 4x^2 + 5$

69.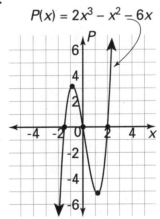

$y = x^4 - 5x^2$

70. (b)

71. a.

$P(x) = 2x^3 - x^2 - 6x$

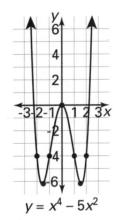

b. Since degree of $P(x)$ is 3, it has at most 3 x-intercepts.

1. pressing calculator keys
2. 28.5 $\boxed{\times}$ 32.7 $\boxed{+}$ 14.8 $\boxed{=}$
3. $13.4 - 15 \div 3$
4. **a.** $a\boxed{\times}b\boxed{-}c\boxed{=}$
   b. 72,209
5. 81.681
6. -104
7. **a.** Sample: 104 $\boxed{\pm}$ $\boxed{\div}$ 8 $\boxed{\pm}$ $\boxed{=}$
   b. 13
8. $A = \frac{1}{2}h(b_1 + b_2)$

   $A = \frac{1}{2} \cdot 6.5(4.4 + 6.7)$

   $A = \frac{1}{2} \cdot 6.5(11.1)$

   $A = 36.075$
   about 36.08 square units
9. $2(6.7)\pi \approx 42.10$ in.
10. $10 > \pi \cdot \pi$

    $10 > 9.87$
11. 5^2
12. $V = \frac{4}{3}\pi r^3$

    $V = \frac{4}{3}\pi(1.92)^3$

    $V = 29.65$ in^3
13. negative numbers
14. $2(18.5)(2) + 2(2)(9.3) + 2(18.5)(9.3)$
    $= 74 + 37.2 + 344.1$
    $= 455.3$ in^2
15. Answers may vary.
16. $\frac{5}{9}, \frac{4}{7}, \frac{3}{5}$
17. 32
18. $A = \pi r^2$

    $A = \pi(4.6)^2$

    $A = 66.5$ mi^2
19. $.05 \cdot 350 + .08 \cdot 2000$
    $= 17.5 + 160$
    $= \$177.50$
20. $\boxed{(}$ 2.08 $\boxed{+}$ 5.76 $\boxed{)}$ $\boxed{\times}$ 2.24 $\boxed{=}$

1. 10^6
2. 10^{-9}
3. 0.0001
4. 285,000,000
5. 1
6. left; exponent
7. 0.0000000246
8. 38.25 is not between one and ten.
9. **a.** Domain: set of real numbers greater than or equal to one and less than ten
   b. Domain: set of integers
10. $5.02 \cdot 10^{27}$
11. $9 \cdot 10^{-4}$
12. $7.63 \cdot 10^5$
13. $3.28 \cdot 10^{-6}$
14. $7.549876 \cdot 10^2$
15. 2.4 $\boxed{EE}$ 9 $\boxed{+/-}$
16. $6.45 \cdot 10^{11}$
17. $2.72 \cdot 10^7$
18. **a.** 10,000,000
    b. $1.0 \cdot 10^7$
19. **a.** 300,000,000
    b. $3.0 \cdot 10^8$
20. **a.** 625,000,000
    b. $6.25 \cdot 10^8$
21. **a.** 3,575,000,000
    b. $3.575 \cdot 10^9$
22. 5.480 $\boxed{EE}$ 9
23. 101
24. $2 \cdot 10^{-5}$
25. $5.69 \cdot 10^{-8}$
26. $4.00007 \cdot 10^2$
27. 392,100
28. 0.00003921
29. 0.086
30. **a.** Answers may vary.
    b. Answers may vary.
    c. Sample: 5 $\boxed{+/-}$ $\boxed{EE}$ 7 $\boxed{+/-}$